The Princeton Review®

Cracking the

PSAT®

Jeff Rubenstein and Adam Robinson

PrincetonReview.com

PENGUIN RANDOM HOUSE

The Princeton Review, Inc.
24 Prime Parkway, Suite 201
Natick, MA 01760
E-mail: editorialsupport@review.com

ISBN: 978-0-8041-2498-0
ISSN: 1549-6120

PSAT is a registered trademark of The College Board, which does not
sponsor or endorse this product.

The Princeton Review is not affiliated with Princeton University.

Editor: Kristen O'Toole
Production Editor: Jim Melloan
Production Artist: Deborah A. Silvestrini

Printed in the United States of America on partially recycled paper.

10 9 8 7 6 5 4 3 2 1

Editorial
Rob Franek, Senior VP, Publisher
Casey Cornelius, VP, Content Development
Mary Beth Garrick, Director of Production
Selena Coppock, Managing Editor
Kristen O'Toole, Editorial Director
Calvin Cato, Editor
Meave Shelton, Editor
Alyssa Wolff, Editorial Assistant

Random House Publishing Team
Tom Russell, Publisher
Alison Stoltzfus, Publishing Director
Ellen L. Reed, Production Manager
Dawn Ryan, Managing Editor
Erika Pepe, Associate Production Manager
Kristin Lindner, Production Supervisor
Andrea Lau, Designer

Contents

...So Much More Online!

More Practice...

- Free SAT online demonstration with a full-length practice SAT and interactive lessons

More Good Stuff...

- PSAT at-a-glance overview

- Articles on SAT techniques to get you ready for the next step

- Questions about test changes? We've got answers! PrincetonReview.com/SATChanges

...then College!

- Detailed profiles for hundreds of colleges help you find the school that is right for you

- Dozens of Top 10 ranking lists including Quality of Professors, Worst Campus Food, Most Beautiful Campus, Party Schools, Diverse Student Population, and tons more

- Useful information about the admissions process

- Helpful information about financial aid and scholarships

princetonreview.com

Part I
Orientation

Chapter 1
What Is the
PSAT/NMSQT?

The PSAT/NMSQT—from now on, we will just call it the PSAT—is a standardized test given primarily to high school juniors to give them a "preliminary" idea of how well they could do on SAT question types. The test is also used to determine which students are eligible for National Merit Scholar recognition. This chapter will give you a general overview of the test and how it is used, along with basic strategies to start your preparation.

When Is the PSAT Given?

The PSAT is officially administered twice each year, on one Wednesday and one Saturday in October. Your school will announce the exact dates at the beginning of the school year, or you can find out at **PrincetonReview.com**, or the College Board at **collegeboard.org**.

How Do I Sign Up for the PSAT?

You do not have to do anything to sign up for the PSAT; your school will do all the work for you. Test registration fees can vary from school to school, so be sure to check with your guidance counselor if you have questions about how much the PSAT will cost you.

What About Students with Testing Accommodations?

If you have a diagnosed learning difference, you will probably qualify for special accommodations on the PSAT. However, it is important that you get the process started early. The first step is to speak to your school counselor who handles learning differences. Only he or she can file the appropriate paperwork. You will also need to gather some information (documentation of your condition) from a licensed practitioner and some other information from your school. Then, your school counselor will file the application for you.

You will need to apply for accommodations only once; with that single application, you will qualify for accommodations on the PSAT, SAT, SAT Subject Tests, and AP tests. The one exception to this rule is that if you change schools, you will need to have a counselor at the new school re-file your paperwork.

Does the PSAT Play a Role in College Admissions?

No. The PSAT plays no role in college admissions. It really is just a standardized test that consists of SAT question types.

The one exception is for that very small group of students, about three (yes, just 3!) percent of all students nationwide, whose PSAT scores qualify them for National Merit recognition. (We will tell you more than you ever wanted to know about that in the next section.) Recognition as a commended scholar, semifinalist, or finalist for National Merit is an impressive addition to your college admissions portfolio, and is something that you should certainly pursue if you are in serious contention for it.

What Happens to the Score Report from the PSAT?

Only you, your high school, and the National Merit Scholarship Corporation (which co-sponsors the PSAT) will receive copies of your score reports. Your PSAT score reports will not be sent to colleges.

What Will Be on the PSAT?

The Math sections of the PSAT test arithmetic, algebra, and geometry. The Critical Reading sections test your vocabulary and your ability to answer questions that reference a given passage. The Writing Skills section, oddly enough, has nothing to do with writing. It tests your ability to recognize errors from a narrow range of English grammar rules and several points of style. In this book, we will cover the math, vocabulary, and grammar that you will need...and there really will not be much else to it!

So if the PSAT is a test of generally basic math, vocabulary, some reading comprehension, and a few grammar rules, how is it different from any other test you take in school? Glad you asked! The test-makers know how Mr. Jones tests you in Math, so when they want to trick you, they do the opposite. If you approach the tricky questions the "school way," you will often take much longer than you need or get totally stuck. But, if you implement sound test-taking techniques, you can be done in seconds or at least know that you are approaching the question correctly. Think about it. When you want to do well on Mr. Jones's math test, what do you do? You practice math the way you know he will want to see it done on the test. So when the PSAT folks give you this test, practice the way you know they will test it. The good news is that the test writers want to do as little work as possible. They still use most of the same old tricks they have used since the test was first given, and we have helped generations of students overcome them. In this book, we will show you how to avoid the traps and maximize your score.

Who Writes the PSAT?

The PSAT is written and administered by Educational Testing Service (ETS), under contract by the College Board. You might think that the people at ETS are educators, professors of education, or teachers. They are not. The people who work for ETS are average people who just happen to make a living writing tests. In fact, they write hundreds of tests, for all kinds of organizations. They are a group of "testers-for-hire" who will write a test for anyone who asks.

The folks at ETS are not paid to educate; they are paid to write and administer tests. Furthermore, even though you will be paying ETS to take the PSAT, you are not their customer. The actual customers ETS caters to are the colleges, who get the information they want at no cost. This means that you should take everything that ETS says with a grain of salt and realize that its testing "advice" is not always the best advice. (Getting testing advice from ETS is a bit like getting baseball advice from the opposing team.)

Every test reflects the interests of the people who write it. If you know who writes the test, you will know a lot more about what kinds of answers will be considered "correct" answers on that test.

WHAT IS THE PRINCETON REVIEW?

Shortcuts
The Princeton Review's techniques are the closest thing there is to a shortcut to the PSAT. However, there is no shortcut to learning these techniques.

The Princeton Review is the nation's leading test-preparation company. In just a few years, we became the nation's leader in SAT preparation, primarily because our techniques work. We offer courses and private tutoring for all of the major standardized tests, and we publish a series of books to help in your search for the right school. If you would like more information about how The Princeton Review can help you, go to PrincetonReview.com or call 800-2-Review.

HOW TO USE THIS BOOK

This book is divided into two main parts. The first three sections of the book (Chapters 1–11 and the subsequent Drill Answers) contain both general testing strategies and question-specific, problem-solving instruction. The back of the book contains two practice PSATs. The study guide on page 9 provides a strategic plan for using this book. However, there is no single plan that will fit everyone, so be prepared to adapt the plan and use it according to your own needs.

The first practice test will give you an idea of your strengths and weaknesses, both of which can be sources of improvement. If you are already good at something, additional practice can make you great at it. If you are not so good at something, what you should do about it depends on how important it is. If the concept is one that frequently appears on the test, you should spend a lot of time on it. However, if a concept only comes up once in a while, you should spend very little time working on it and remember that it is something you should put off until you've done easier things or skip entirely.

How do you know which concepts are important? We will tell you throughout the book when essential techniques like Plugging In come up, but you can also get an idea from the layout of the book and the structure diagrams on page 34. For example, if you are not so great at Critical Reading or Sentence Completions, you are going to need to work on these things because they represent a lot of questions. But if you find yourself struggling with functions, you can tell that these aren't as important as Plugging In or Math Basics, because they appear in the Advanced section.

A Note About Vocabulary

Vocabulary is an important part of most standardized tests and success in life itself, though standardized tests are nothing like real life. This book will give you a lot of techniques and shortcuts that you can use on both the PSAT and the SAT. However, while there are useful tools for learning vocabulary words, there are no shortcuts that will magically place words into your brain. Important vocabulary for the PSAT (The Hit Parade in this book) is the same as it is for the SAT, so if you keep studying it from now until the SAT (and beyond), the task will be far less painful, and you will be very pleasantly surprised by how much your reading score improves.

Time Management

To manage your PSAT preparation, make use of the study guide on the following pages. This guide will break down the seemingly daunting task of PSAT prep into bite-sized pieces we call sessions. We have mapped out tasks for each session to be sure you get the most out of this book. Sessions will generally take between an hour or two, unless you are taking a practice test. The tests will be the first and last sessions, so you should be sure to set aside about two and a half hours for each of these sessions. Most other sessions will last between an hour and two hours, so plan to take a short break in the middle, and if it looks like the session is going to exceed two hours feel free to stop and pick up where you left off on the next day.

When You Take a Practice Test

You will see when to take practice tests in the session outlines. Here are some guidelines for taking these tests:

- Time yourself strictly. Use a timer, watch, or stopwatch that will ring, and do not allow yourself to go over time for any section. If you try to do so at the real test, your scores will likely be canceled.
- Take a practice test in one sitting, allowing yourself breaks of no more than two minutes between sections. You need to build up your endurance for the real test, and you also need an accurate picture of how you will do.

- Always take a practice test using an answer sheet with bubbles to fill in, just as you will for the real test. For the practice tests in the book, use the attached answer sheets. You need to be comfortable transferring answers to the separate sheet because you will be skipping around a bit.
- Each bubble you choose should be filled in thoroughly, and no other marks should be made in the answer area.
- As you fill in the bubble for a question, check to be sure you are on the correct number on the answer sheet. If you fill in the wrong bubble on the answer sheet, it will not matter if you worked out the problem correctly in the test booklet. All that matters to the machine scoring the test is the No. 2 pencil mark.

Managing the Math Sections

After you have taken the practice test, you will have three scores: math, reading, and writing. There is a lot of math in this book, so you will need to use your math score to figure out which exact subjects you need the most help in and how your study time will be best spent. The guide that appears on the next page is geared toward someone whose math score is in the middle range, from about the mid 50s to the low 60s, so if your score is lower or higher than this, you will need to make some adjustments.

If your score is lower than the range mentioned above, your plan should be to spend the three math sessions working only on Chapters 7 and 8 and doing little or nothing in Chapter 9, unless you have extra time and have thoroughly mastered the two prior chapters, including additional online practice and drills.

If your score is higher than average, you should plan to spend very little time working through Chapter 7, unless you have missed some easy questions on the math sections and you do not know why. You will want to spend most of your time working on Chapters 8 and 9, so skim Chapter 7 for anything that looks unfamiliar and work through those portions, then move on to Chapter 8 and work on the math techniques. Working on additional drills on the topics covered in Chapters 8 and 9 will fill out the three sessions devoted to math.

Session-by-Session Study Guide

Session Zero   You are involved in this session right now. Finish reading the first two chapters so you know what the test is about, why it is important for you to take, and what to expect from the rest of the book. This step may not take you long, so if you have time to devote to a session and you complete these chapters, you can go on to Session One and take the first practice test.

Session One   Take Practice Test 1 (in the back of this book) and score it. You will use these scores to get an idea of how many questions you should attempt on each section and the parts of the math sections you should study.

Session Two   Work through Chapters 3 and 4 of the Orientation. Work through Chapter 5, the Sentence Completions, and Week 1 of the Hit Parade in Chapter 11. Make flashcards for the Hit Parade vocabulary words you do not know.

Session Three   Work through the Math Basics in Chapter 7 and the corresponding drills.

Session Four   Work through the Writing Skills in Chapter 10 and associated drills. Study Week 2 of the Hit Parade.

Session Five   Work through the Critical Reading section in Chapter 6 and associated drills. Study Week 3 of the Hit Parade.

Session Six   Work through Math Techniques, Chapter 8. Techniques like Plugging In are central to doing well on the math sections, so you cannot practice these enough. If you have time, start Chapter 9. Study Week 4 of the Hit Parade.

Session Seven   Work through the Advanced Math Principles in Chapter 9. Study Week 5 of the Hit Parade.

Session Eight   Take Practice Test 2. Use the techniques you have been practicing throughout the book. Score your test and go through the explanations, focusing on where you may have missed the opportunity to use a technique and your decisions about whether you should have attempted a question or not, given your pacing goals and Personal Order of Difficulty.

Some of the terminology in this study guide may be unfamiliar to you now, but do not worry, you will get to know it soon. Also, you should refer back to this guide at each session to keep yourself on track.

One important note: In this book, any sample question you see will have a question number that indicates where it would appear on the PSAT. That is why you may see a question 4 followed by a question 14—the question number indicates the PSAT question level instead of its order in the chapter. The discussion on pages 34–37 provides more information about question numbers and order of difficulty.

HOW IS THE PSAT STRUCTURED AND SCORED?

The PSAT has five sections, which are always given in the same order.

Section	Number of Questions	Time
Critical Reading	24	25 minutes
Math	20	25 minutes
Critical Reading	24	25 minutes
Math	18	25 minutes
Writing Skills	39	30 minutes

You will receive three scores for the PSAT: a Critical Reading score, a Math score, and a Writing Skills score. Each of these scores will be reported on a scale of 20 to 80, where 20 is the lowest score and 80 is the highest score. Your scores will be mailed to your high school principal. He or she will distribute them to you about six to eight weeks after you take the test. If you are homeschooled, your score report will be mailed directly to your home.

How Does the SAT Differ From the PSAT?

The SAT differs significantly from the PSAT in structure, though the question types on the two tests are similar. The SAT has 10 sections, for a total of 3 hours and 45 minutes of testing. One of those sections doesn't count toward your score; it is an Experimental section, and its only purpose is to try out questions to see whether they can be used in later tests. The PSAT has no Experimental section and also no Essay.

Here is a breakdown of how the tests differ:

	SAT	PSAT
Structure	10 sections	5 sections
Length	3 hours 45 minutes	2 hours 10 minutes
Purpose	College admissions	NMSQT (see Chapter 2)
Scoring	2400	Selection index out of 240

Here is how an SAT might look, compared to the PSAT. (Remember, though, that the sections on the SAT can appear in a different order.)

SAT		
Section	**Number of Questions**	**Time**
Writing	1 essay	25 minutes
Critical Reading	24 multiple-choice	25 minutes
Math	20 multiple-choice	25 minutes
Writing	35 multiple-choice	25 minutes
Critical Reading	24 multiple-choice	25 minutes
Math	18 total (8 multiple-choice, 10 Grid-Ins)	25 minutes
Experimental	Number of multiple-choice questions varies	25 minutes
Math	16 multiple-choice	20 minutes
Critical Reading	19 multiple-choice	20 minutes
Writing	14 multiple-choice	10 minutes

You may have noticed that the PSAT is much shorter than the SAT, and the SAT includes an essay. However, the multiple-choice question types are the same. The Experimental section can be any of the 25-minute sections from Sections 2 through 7. Your Experimental section could be a Critical Reading, Math, or Writing section.

What Does the PSAT Score Mean for My SAT Score?

Very little. Like the SAT, the PSAT gives you a Math score, a Writing Skills score, and a Critical Reading score. The PSAT uses a 20-to-80 scale that is easy to convert to the SAT's familiar 200-to-800 scale. It seems as if you should be able to just add a zero to the end of each score to find out what your future SAT scores will be: For example, a 65 on the PSAT Math section could convert to a 650 on the SAT Math. Pretty easy, right?

Maybe a little too easy. Think about it like this: World-class sprinters can complete a 100-yard dash in under 10 seconds. Going at the same speed, an athlete should be able to run a mile in under three minutes. However, has anyone ever run a mile that quickly? Not even close! No one can run at top speed for such a long distance because fatigue sets in. Now consider that the PSAT has five sections and lasts for just over two hours, while the SAT has 10 sections and nearly hits the four-hour mark. Isn't fatigue likely to be a factor there as well? Many students are disappointed to find that their SAT scores do not match up with their PSAT scores because it is much more difficult to stay sharp for four hours than it is to stay sharp for two hours. Add in the fact that the SAT has an essay and some slightly more advanced math, and you can see that the two tests are actually quite different to the test taker.

How Much Should I Prepare for the PSAT?

Study
If you were getting ready to take a biology test, you would study biology. If you were preparing for a basketball game, you would practice basketball. So, if you are preparing for the PSAT (and eventually the SAT), study the PSAT. ETS cannot test everything, so concentrate on learning what it *does* test.

If you are in that very small percentage of students who are in contention for National Merit recognition, it may be worth your while to put in a good deal of time to prepare for this test. After all, if you can raise your scores from 71 or 72 to 74 or 76 on one or more of the sections on the PSAT, this may well put you in a better position for National Merit recognition. Otherwise, you should prepare enough so that you feel more in control of the test and have a better testing experience. (Nothing feels quite as awful as taking a test feeling like you don't know what you are being tested on or what to expect.) The other reason to prepare for the PSAT is that it will give you some testing skills that will help you begin to prepare for the tests that actually count, namely the SAT and SAT Subject Tests.

The bottom line is: The best reason to prepare for the PSAT is that it will help you get an early start on your preparation for the SAT.

Chapter 2
All About National Merit Scholarships

The NMSQT part of the name PSAT/NMSQT stands for National Merit Scholarship Qualifying Test. That means that the PSAT serves as the test that will establish whether or not you are eligible for National Merit recognition. This chapter will help you figure out what that may mean for you.

How Do I Qualify for National Merit?

To qualify for any National Merit recognition, you must:

- Be a U.S. citizen or permanent resident who intends to become a U.S. citizen
- Be enrolled full-time in high school
- Take the PSAT in the third year of high school (for four-year programs; slightly different rules apply if you are in a three-year program or other course of study)
- Be fully endorsed and recommended for a Merit scholarship by your high school principal
- Have a record of strong academic performance throughout high school
- Complete the National Merit Scholarship Corporation (NMSC) Scholarship Application
- Obtain high scores on the SAT, which you will take later in the year

The Index

How does your PSAT score qualify you for National Merit? The National Merit Scholarship Corporation uses a selection index, which is the sum of your Math, Critical Reading, and Writing Skills scores. For instance, if your PSAT scores were 60 Math, 50 Critical Reading, and 60 Writing Skills, your index would be 170.

Math + Critical Reading + Writing Skills = National Merit Index

60 + 50 + 60 = 170

The Awards and the Process

In the fall of their senior year, about 50,000 students will receive one of two letters from NMSC: either a Letter of Commendation or a letter stating that they have qualified as semifinalists for National Merit.

Commended Students   Roughly two-thirds of these students (about 34,000 total students each year) will receive a Letter of Commendation by virtue of their high scores on the test. This looks great on your college application, so if you have a reasonable chance of receiving this recognition, it is definitely worth your time to prepare for the PSAT. Make no mistake, though, these letters are not easy to get. They are awarded to students who score between the 95th and the mid-99th percentiles—that means to the top three percent in the country.

If you receive this honorable mention from NMSC, you should be extremely proud of yourself. Even though you will not continue in the process for National Merit scholarships, this commendation does make you eligible for special scholarships sponsored by certain companies and organizations, which vary in their amounts and eligibility requirements.

Semifinalists   The other third of these students—those 16,000 students who score in the upper 99th percentile in their states—will be notified that they are National Merit semifinalists. If you qualify, you will receive a letter announcing your status as a semifinalist, along with information about the requirements for qualification as a finalist. These include maintaining high grades, performing well on your SAT, and getting an endorsement from your principal.

Becoming a National Merit semifinalist is quite impressive, and if you manage it, you should certainly mention it on your college applications.

What does "scoring in the upper 99th percentile in the state" mean? It means that you're essentially competing against the other people in your state for those semifinalist positions. Since some states have higher average scores than others, this means that if you're in states like New York, New Jersey, Maryland, Connecticut, or Massachusetts, you need a higher score to qualify than if you live in other states. However, the majority of the indices are in the range of 200–215. (This means approximate scores of 70 Critical Reading, 70 Math, 70 Writing Skills.)

Many students want to know exactly what score they need. Sadly, National Merit is notoriously tight-lipped about these numbers. It releases them only on rare occasions and generally does not like to announce them. However, it is not difficult to obtain some pretty reliable unofficial data on what it takes to be a semifinalist. Below you will find the most up-to-date qualifying scores for the class of 2013 National Merit semifinalists:

Alabama	209	Montana	203
Alaska	204	Nebraska	207
Arizona	212	Nevada	208
Arkansas	202	New Hampshire	211
California	220	New Jersey	221
Colorado	212	New Mexico	208
Connecticut	218	New York	215
D.C.	221	North Carolina	213
Delaware	215	North Dakota	200
Florida	211	Ohio	212
Georgia	214	Oklahoma	206
Hawaii	211	Oregon	213
Idaho	207	Pennsylvania	214
Illinois	213	Rhode Island	211
Indiana	211	South Carolina	208
Iowa	207	South Dakota	204
Kansas	212	Tennessee	210
Kentucky	208	Texas	216
Louisiana	209	Utah	205
Maine	210	Vermont	214
Maryland	219	Virginia	217
Massachusetts	221	Washington	216
Michigan	207	West Virginia	200
Minnesota	213	Wisconsin	207
Mississippi	204	Wyoming	200
Missouri	210		

Note, however, that while these numbers are probably roughly the same from year to year, they do change to a certain degree. These should be used only to give you a rough idea of the range of scores for National Merit recognition.

Finalists   The majority of semifinalists (more than 90 percent) go on to qualify as finalists. Students who meet all of the eligibility requirements will be notified in February of their senior year that they have qualified as finalists. This means that they are now eligible for scholarship money, though it does not necessarily mean that they will receive any. In fact, only about half of National Merit finalists actually win scholarships. What determines whether a student is awarded money or not? There is a final screening process, based on criteria that NMSC does not release to the public, to determine who actually receives these scholarships. This year, there will be 8,300 Merit Scholarship winners and 1,300 Special Scholarship recipients. Unlike the Merit Scholarships, which are given by the NMSC, the Special Scholarship recipients will receive awards from corporate sponsors and are selected from students who are outstanding, but not National Merit finalists.

Though the amounts of money are not huge, every little bit helps, and the award itself looks very impressive in your portfolio. So if you think you are in contention for National Merit recognition, study hard. If not, don't sweat it too much, but do prepare for the PSAT because it is good practice for the SAT.

But I am Not a Junior in High School Yet...

If you are not yet a junior, and you are interested in National Merit, you will have to take the test again your junior year in order to qualify.

A certain number of schools give the PSAT to students in their sophomore year—and sometimes even earlier. These schools hope that earlier exposure to these tests will help their students perform better in later years. If you are not yet in your junior year, the PSAT will not count for National Merit scholarship purposes, so it is really just a trial run for you. However, it is still a good idea to go into the test prepared in order to feel and perform your best.

What If I am in a Three-Year or Other Nonstandard Course of Study?

If you are going to spend only three years in secondary school, you have two options for when to take the PSAT for National Merit purposes: You can take it either in your next-to-last year or in your last year of secondary school. However, our advice is this: If you are in any program other than a usual four-year high school, be sure to talk to your guidance counselor. He or she will consult with NMSC and help ensure that you take the PSAT at the right time. This is important, because not taking the PSAT at the right time can disqualify you from National Merit recognition.

What If I Miss the PSAT Administration My Junior Year?

If you are not concerned about National Merit scholarships, there is no reason to do anything in particular—except, perhaps, to obtain a few PSAT booklets to practice on, just to see what fun you missed.

However, if you want to be eligible for National Merit recognition, then swift action on your part is required. If an emergency arises that prevents you from taking the PSAT, you should write to the National Merit Scholarship Corporation *immediately* to request alternate testing dates. If your request is received soon enough, it should be able to accommodate you. (NMSC says that this kind of request must absolutely be received by March 1 following the missed PSAT administration.) You will also need a signature from a school official.

For More Information

If you have any questions or problems, the best person to consult is your school guidance counselor, who can help make sure you are on the right track. If you need further help, contact your local Princeton Review office at 800-2-REVIEW or **PrincetonReview.com**. Or, you can contact National Merit directly:

National Merit Scholarship Corporation
1560 Sherman Avenue, Suite 200
Evanston, IL 60201-4897
(847) 866-5100
NationalMerit.org

Chapter 3
General Strategies

In this chapter, we will discuss some strategies that apply to the PSAT as a whole. Keep these in mind throughout the entire test, and you will improve your score.

PROCESS OF ELIMINATION

You do not have to know how to solve a problem in order to get the correct answer (or to, at least, be able to make a strategic guess). If you can cross off four, or three, or even just two *wrong* answers, you are a lot closer to finding the *right* one. This technique, called Process of Elimination (which we will call POE from now on), will be your new best friend. Aggressively using POE will get you points on the PSAT.

1. What is the capital of Malawi?

If you were to see this problem on the PSAT (don't worry, you won't), you would probably be stuck—not to mention a little upset. But problems on the PSAT have answer choices, like the following:

1. What is the capital of Malawi?
   - (A) Washington
   - (B) Paris
   - (C) Tokyo
   - (D) London
   - (E) Lilongwe

Not so bad anymore, is it? By knowing which choices must be wrong, you can often figure out what the answer is—even without knowing *why* it is the correct answer.

Since four of the five choices on any given question are wrong, it is much easier to identify at least some of these and get rid of them. Sometimes, you can even get all the way to the right answer just by using POE, so use POE whenever you can.

---

5. Although the piranha, <u>a species of carnivorous fish</u>, is
                 A

   <u>native to</u> the waters of the Amazon, <u>they</u> can be seen in
     B   C

   aquariums <u>throughout</u> the world. <u>No error</u>
          D   E

How to Crack It

Here is a sample Writing Skills question in which your task is to see if you can find a grammar mistake. Often the correct answer on a Writing Skills question will jump out at you as you read the question; in some cases, however, it will not. This means we should use POE. Look at each part in turn. "A species of" is okay, so (A) cannot be the answer. "Native to" is the correct idiom, so (B) can also be crossed off. We might have a question about (C): Should the word here be "they" or "it"? If we are unsure, we can leave (C) alone for the moment. How about (D)? "Through-out the world" is okay, so (D) can be eliminated. So now we are down to either (C) or (E). The answer is (C) because "the piranha" is singular and "they" is plural.

What is most important is the technique you used, not whether you got the right answer above. You had a one-in-two shot on this problem. Those are fantastic odds, and you should take a guess. In cases where you are not sure of the answer (and this may happen often), immediately think POE. Better guesses mean more points on the PSAT!

Try to answer this question using POE before reading the explanation below.

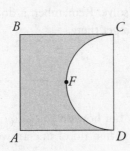

18. If *ABCD* is a square with sides 8, and arc *CFD* is a semicircle, what is the area of the shaded region?

(A) $16 - 8\pi$
(B) $16 - 16\pi$
(C) $64 - 8\pi$
(D) $64 - 16\pi$
(E) 64

How to Crack It

Even before we try to solve this problem, we can use POE. We know that the value of π is a little more than 3. If we replace π with 3 in the answers above, what do you notice? Choices (A) and (B) are negative numbers. They cannot be right. What else do we know about the figure? We know that the length of the side is 8, so the area is 64, which rules out choice (E), because the shaded area is obviously smaller than the whole square. We are already down to two answer choices! Now look at the shaded area. Is it more than or less than half? It is more than half, which is 32. Applying the same trick as we did with choices (A) and (B), we get that choice (C) is about 64 minus 24, or 40, so that works, and choice (D) is around 64 minus 48, which is 12, so that choice is out, leaving only (C).

Of course, we cannot get all the way to the right answer using just POE all of the time. But the question above was a hard question, so if we had run out of other questions that we knew we could get right and this was what we had left, it would certainly be worth attempting with POE on our side.

We know this is not how you are taught to solve problems and take tests in school. In fact, your geometry teacher would probably have a fit if you were to do most of your work in class like this. That is because in school, what matters is *how* you get a problem right. But this is not school. This is the PSAT. The only thing that matters on the PSAT is whether you have the correct bubble filled in. Therefore, do not treat the PSAT like a test in school; that is, use strategies suited to getting the best score that you can get on this test.

POE is a technique that can be used on every multiple-choice problem on the PSAT. By getting rid of answers that you know are wrong, you can improve your chances of guessing correctly and may be able to find the right answer to a question you do not know how to solve. Remember, it does not matter how you get to the right answer, as long as you get there.

POE and Guessing

So we have talked about POE, but how do you know when to apply it on the test? Should you guess if you have gotten rid of one answer? Two? Three? Well, if you can only get rid of one choice on a particular question, is that really the question you should be working on at that moment? Maybe, but only if you have nothing left to attempt that you could work all the way through and get right.

In the next chapter we will discuss pacing, which is the number of questions you should attempt to reach your target score. Most students should not attempt all of them. If you find that there are enough questions you can answer to reach your pacing goal without guessing, then go ahead and do those and keep working on questions you can answer until the time is up. If you run out of questions you can do before you reach your magic number, then you will need to use POE to strategically approach the remaining questions you must answer in order to hit your pacing goal.

HOW THE PSAT IS SCORED

To generate your final score, ETS first computes your raw score. You receive one raw score point for every correct answer and lose one-quarter of a raw score point for every wrong answer on your bubble sheet. Blanks are not counted at all. This raw score is then converted to a scaled score on the 20–80 scale. You can find sample score-conversion tables in the back of this book.

	Raw Points
Correct answer:	+1
Blank:	0
Incorrect answer:	$-\dfrac{1}{4}$

So, when should you guess? Well, let's look at the scoring system and see how it applies to guessing. The PSAT is a five-option multiple-choice test. If you guess completely randomly on five questions you should—by random chance—get one of these five correct and four of them wrong. Since you will earn one point for the one correct answer and lose one-quarter of a point for each of the four wrong answers, your net raw score will be zero. Thus, random guessing does not help you.

So do not waste your time on random guessing. However, if you are working on a problem that you need to answer to meet your pacing goals and you can eliminate even one answer with POE, you can make a strategic guess. Of course, the more answer choices you can eliminate, the better your odds for guessing correctly will be.

We have talked a little about POE already, but we will be talking throughout the book about the kinds of wrong answers you should be on the lookout for in different parts of the test, so keep an eye out for them.

Write Now

Feel free to write all over this book. You need to get in the habit of making the PSAT booklet your own.

USING YOUR BOOK

At school, you generally are not allowed to write in your textbooks. (In some cases, they will even charge you for the book if you do.) But on the PSAT, the booklet is yours—so use it. Even though you will use your calculator for figuring, you should be working extensively in your test booklet, e.g., setting up your calculations, drawing and redrawing figures, and most important, physically crossing off answers—which helps you avoid getting lost as you work through POE.

MAKING THE MATH WORK EASIER

Ballparking

Here is one of those POE tools we promised you. Ballparking means *estimating and eliminating*; that is, using the conditions in the question to get an idea of what the answer should be and then eliminating answers that are too big or too small. If you are stuck or running out of time, you will need a way to get rid of answer choices quickly so you can choose one and move on. Ballparking is a great tool for quickly rejecting answers on math questions.

Have a look at the following.

5. If 12 cans of food can feed 8 dogs for one week, how many cans of food would be needed to feed 6 dogs for 2 weeks?

    (A) 9
    (B) 12
    (C) 18
    (D) 24
    (E) 48

How to Crack It

Before you start to calculate, estimate. If 12 cans will feed eight dogs for one week, and we want to know how many cans we would need for *two* weeks, the answer is probably larger than 12. So eliminate (A) and (B). But we are only feeding *six* dogs for two weeks, so the answer must be less than 24. Eliminate (D) and (E). Now the only answer left is (C).

If you are wondering whether it is realistic to expect to be able to Ballpark down to one answer on the test, the answer is: It depends. It is fairly common on easier problems, but in those cases you can often just solve it. So we can try it where it will be useful, on a hard question.

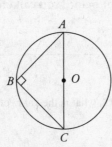

16. If the circle with center O has a radius of 3, and $AB = BC$, what is the area of triangle ABC ?

(A)   9
(B)   18
(C) 9π
(D) 18π
(E) 27π

How to Crack It

Since we know that the radius of the circle is 3, we are just a small step away from figuring out the area. The formula for the area of a circle is $A = \pi r^2$, so the area of the circle is 9π, or about 27. We can estimate that the area of the triangle is less than half the area of the circle, so (A) is the only possibility.

Look Carefully at What the Questions Are Asking For

The test writers know that students are rushed when taking the PSAT. The writers use that to their advantage when designing questions. One of the biggest mistakes students make on the PSAT is working too quickly and making careless mistakes. A common careless mistake is answering the wrong question. You need to know what they are asking for before you can choose the correct answer. Here is an example.

---

4. If $6(3p - 2q) = 18$, what is the value of $3p - 2q$?

    (A) 2
    (B) 3
    (C) 4
    (D) 6
    (E) 18

How to Crack It

You might be tempted to multiply out $6(3p - 2q)$ on this problem, which gives you $18p - 12q$. That seems like a logical first step, right? Unfortunately, if you do this, you will be doing this problem the hard way. Why? Look carefully at what the problem is asking you to solve for. The question does not ask for the value of p or q alone; it asks for the value of $3p - 2q$. What is the easiest way to figure that out? Simply divide both sides of the equation by 6, and you get $(3p - 2q) = 3$.

The moral: Always look for what the question is asking. In math class, you are almost always asked to solve for x or y, but on the PSAT you may be asked to solve for $3x - y$, or $3p - 2q$, or some other strange expression. In these cases, there is usually an easier way to solve the problem than the way you might solve it in math class.

Taking Bite-Sized Pieces

Another common way that the question writers make problems more difficult is throwing a lot of information at you at once to try to confuse you. When this happens, stay calm and take the information in bite-sized pieces. By breaking up a wordy problem, you can transform a long, difficult problem into a few shorter, easier ones. Sound good? Let's look at one together.

---

12. Lauren and Abbey are performing science experiments in which they each start off with a collection of 6 fruit flies. If Lauren's species of fruit flies triples its population every 4 days and Abbey's species of fruit flies doubles its population every 3 days, how many fruit flies will they have if they combine their collections at the end of 12 days?

   (A) 96
   (B) 162
   (C) 192
   (D) 258
   (E) 324

How to Crack It

Sure, this problem looks like it is going to be a pain, but you will see how difficult it really is when we work through it just a little bit at a time.

Lauren's species of fruit flies triples its population every 4 days.
She starts with 6.
After 4 days, she has 18.
After 8 days, she has 54.
After 12 days, she has 162.
So Lauren ends up with 162 fruit flies.

Now we will do the same with Abbey.
Abbey's species of fruit flies doubles its population every 3 days.
After 3 days, she has 12.
After 6 days, she has 24.
After 9 days, she has 48.
After 12 days, she has 96.
Abbey ends up with 96 fruit flies.

Now all we have to do is add Lauren's fruit flies to Abbey's fruit flies. 162 + 96 = 258, so the correct answer is (D). Watch out for the partial answers; 96 and 162 both appear in the list!

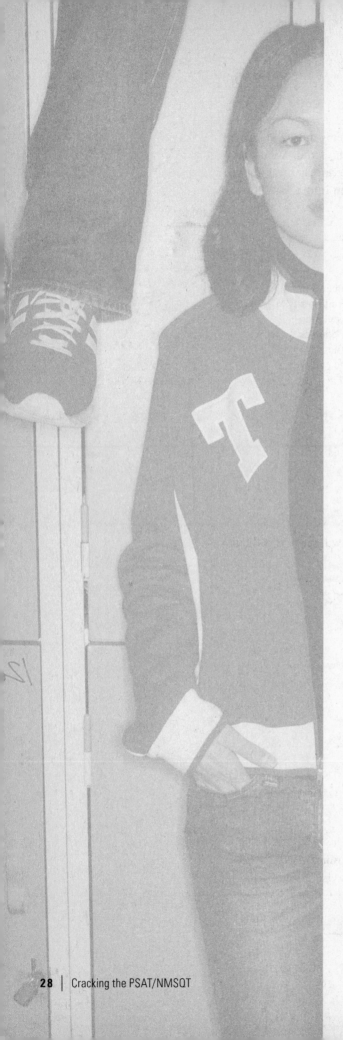

Summary

○ POE—Process of Elimination—is your best friend on most of the problems on the test. It will help you stay focused on eliminating trap (wrong) answers to help you find the best answer, and it will help you guess strategically to maximize your score.

○ Even though you are going to use your calculator during Math sections, good test-taking performances are dependent upon voraciously marking up your test booklet to keep track of steps, to reinforce important information in problems, and, of course, to use POE!

○ If you are stuck on a math question or running out of time, use Ballparking to eliminate one or more answers quickly, so you can choose an answer and move on.

○ Read the questions carefully to make sure you answer the right question, and take bite-sized pieces to work through each problem step by step. Both will help you avoid choosing traps and partial answers.

Chapter 4
Advanced Strategies

In this chapter, we will discuss an overall PSAT game plan: figuring out how many problems you should do, which problems you should do, and how to avoid the answers that ETS plants to trap the average student, whom we will call Joe Bloggs.

WHO IS JOE BLOGGS?

Joe Bloggs is the average test taker. He thinks what works in school will work just as well on the PSAT, so he goes for the most convenient answers and uses a typical high-school approach regardless of the difficulty of the question. The problem with this approach is that ETS knows how concepts are taught and tested in school, so it can choose to trick Joe wherever it likes, and it writes the hard questions to do just that. If you have ever taken a standardized test, you have probably noticed that some questions are harder than others. In fact, most sections start out easy and get harder as you go along, as we will see on the next page.

When Joe is faced with an easy question, he does fine. When he is faced with a medium question, he does all right about half of the time and gets into trouble the other half of the time. When he is confronted with a hard question, he does the same things he would do if he were working on an easy question—but, with a hard question, there are tricks and traps all over the place; consequently, he gets nearly every hard question wrong.

So how can Joe help you perform better on the PSAT? If you were walking on a path in the woods behind a friend and your friend tripped on a root, would you trip over it too? Probably not! Watch for the things that trip Joe up and avoid tripping over them yourself.

PACING

Most students think that you need to do every problem on the PSAT to get a good score. The fact is that most students actually *hurt* their score because they try to do *too many* problems.

Here is what Joe Bloggs does: Joe thinks that he has to finish every problem on the PSAT. In an attempt to do just this, he works as quickly as he can. This means that he rushes through the easy problems—the ones that he should get right—and makes some careless errors, which cost him valuable points. Then he gets to the medium problems. These take more time, are more convoluted, and have a few trap choices in them. Joe gets about half of these right. Then Joe gets to the hard questions. These are designed so Joe will get almost all of them wrong, yet Joe insists on spending lots of time on these problems—for no points at all. What kind of score does Joe get? He gets the average score of about 51.

As you can see, this probably is not the best strategy. There are two reasons it does not make sense to try every problem on the test. First, it is very difficult to finish every question while maintaining a high level of accuracy. During timed tests, people naturally rush—and then they make careless errors and unnecessarily lose points. Almost everyone is better off *slowing down*, using the time allotted to work on *fewer* problems, and answering more of those problems correctly. You will earn a higher score if you do only 75 percent of the problems on this test (while leaving the rest blank) and answer them correctly than if you do all of the problems and answer about half correctly.

Second, not every question is of the same level of difficulty. In fact, most of the problems on this test are arranged in increasing order of difficulty: The earlier questions are easier, and they get gradually harder as the section progresses. Hard questions are worth no more than easy questions, so why spend potentially more time working on them? Most testers are much better off skipping many of the hard questions and applying all their time to the easy and medium-level questions to maximize accuracy and, ultimately, raise scores.

How Many Questions Should I Answer?

Only do the number of problems you need to achieve your target score. You are *much* better off doing fewer problems and increasing your accuracy than doing too many problems and getting only a few of them right.

So what should your target score be? Well, your target score should be higher than the score you got on your practice test (now would be a good time to take Practice Test 1 if you have not already), but should still be reasonable and attainable. If you are currently scoring 50, trying to score a 65 right away will only hurt you, because you would have to rush to finish all the problems you need to do. Try to work your way up in reasonable stages. Pick a score range approximately five points higher than the range in which you are currently scoring. If you are currently scoring 50, aim for a 55; when you have reached 55, then you can aim for 60.

The Right Number of Questions for Your Target Score

The pacing charts on the next couple of pages show you how many problems you need to answer in order to get a certain score. You should use all of the time you are given to attempt only the number of problems indicated by the charts, and answer them as accurately as possible. (The numbers in the charts allow for a small margin of error.) Of course, if you find you have more time after having done this, go ahead and try a few more.

On the Math section, for instance, if you are aiming for a 55, you should just do 14 of the problems in Section 2. Which 14 problems? The 14 that *you* like the best. (More on this to come.) Many of the problems you should focus on will probably be among the first 15; but if you do not like problem number 11, skip it and do number 16 instead.

Math Target Score	Raw Points Needed	Questions to Attempt on Section 2	Questions to Attempt on Section 4
35	6	6	5
40	11	8	7
45	16	10	9
50	21	12	12
55	26	14	14
60	30	16	16
65	33	18	17
70	34	all	all
75	36	all	all
80	38	all	all

Below is the pacing chart for Critical Reading. If you are aiming for a 55, you want to answer 17 questions on each section (for a total of 34 problems). Which 17? The ones that you like best. There are plenty of Critical Reading question types to choose from; maybe you like the shorter, paragraph-length passages better than the longer passages. Do you like simple line reference questions or the more general author tone questions?

Critical Reading Target Score	Raw Points Needed	Questions to Attempt on Section 1	Questions to Attempt on Section 3
35	7	6	6
40	11	8	8
45	16	11	11
50	21	13	13
55	27	17	17
60	32	19	19
65	38	22	22
70	42	all	all
75	45	all	all
80	47	all	all

Finally, here is the pacing chart for the Writing Skills section:

Writing Skills Target Score	Raw Points Needed	Questions to Attempt on Section 5
35	5	10
40	9	15
45	13	19
50	17	23
55	21	27
60	25	31
65	28	34
70	32	all
75	35	all
80	38	all

WHICH PROBLEMS SHOULD I ANSWER?

As we mentioned on the previous page, you should focus on whichever problems are the easiest and quickest for *you*.

The Order of Difficulty

Most of the questions on the PSAT are arranged in increasing order of difficulty, as you can see on the charts below. The rest have no order of difficulty (OOD), which means it is up to you to choose the questions that are easiest for you to attempt.

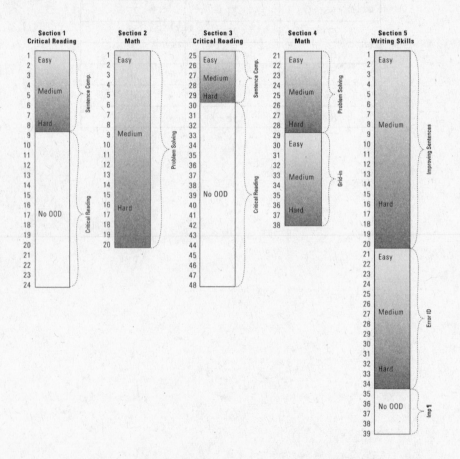

Note that the chart shows that, for sections that have an order of difficulty, approximately the first third of each section is easy, the next third is medium, and the last third is difficult. So you should always pay attention to the question number you are working on in these sections, because it will give you important information about how to approach the question. If it is an easy question, go ahead and use the techniques to answer it and do not second-guess yourself. If it is a medium question, be careful, use POE and the techniques, and watch for the occasional trick. If it is a difficult question, keep in mind that there is a reason that this question was given a higher number. Perhaps there is a Joe Bloggs answer or two, or maybe the question is worded in a tricky way or presents a great deal of information that will be easy to get tripped up in. On hard questions you need to be sure whether you should be working on that question at all, a subject that goes beyond order of difficulty and into the next topic, Personal Order of Difficulty.

Your Personal Order of Difficulty

The chart on the previous page shows questions that are considered "easy," "medium," and "hard" by the average test taker. The average number of people who get a question right determines whether that question is easy, medium, or hard by ETS standards.

But for any one test taker, who—for example—might like algebra better than geometry, a question that is usually considered "medium" might be easy. Or vice versa.

This means that you should always answer the questions on the PSAT according to your Personal Order of Difficulty, or POOD—that is, answer the ones that are easiest for you. If you are going to work on 14 math questions on a section, you want to find the easiest 14. While it is a good bet that most of the first 14 math questions will be the easiest for you, if you find one or two questions in that group that you do not like, *skip them*. Then find a few other questions elsewhere in the section that look easier for you.

Joe Bloggs Answers

This brings us to another way Joe Bloggs can help us on the PSAT. Suppose for a moment that you could look at the page of the tester next to you (obviously you cannot). Also, suppose that you know for a fact that every one of your neighbor's answers on the test is wrong. If on problem 20, he marked (C) as his answer, what would you do? Eliminate choice (C), right?

Even though you cannot look at your neighbor's page, you can use this principle to get points on the test by looking for Joe Bloggs answers. When the folks at ETS write the PSAT, they write it in a very particular way. They write it so that Joe will get most of the easy problems correct, some of the medium problems correct, and none of the hard ones correct.

How do they do this? The test writers, who have been writing questions for over 40 years, are very good at knowing what kinds of answer choices are attractive to the average person.

Joe Bloggs, the average tester, always picks the answer that first attracts him. Choices that first attract him on math problems have nice round numbers that can be easily derived from other numbers in the problem. Choices that attract him on verbal problems have familiar words that remind him of words in the question or passage.

Joe's Hunches

Should you always just eliminate any answer that seems to be correct? No! Remember what we said about Joe Bloggs:
1. His hunches are correct on easy questions.
2. His hunches are sometimes correct and sometimes incorrect on medium questions.
3. His hunches are always wrong on difficult questions.

On easy multiple-choice questions, pick the choice that Joe Bloggs would. On hard questions, be sure to eliminate the choices that Joe Bloggs would pick.

Question Type	Joe Bloggs Selects	How Joe Does
Easy	What seems right	Mostly right
Medium	What seems right	Half right
Hard	What seems right	All wrong

What does this mean for you? When you are working on easy problems, pick the choice that seems right to you. When you are working on medium problems, be careful. If you got the answer too quickly, check your work. Medium problems should take more work than easy problems. If you are working on a hard problem, eliminate the choices that first seem attractive; they are almost always traps.

Remember, Joe Bloggs gets the easy problems right. *Only cross off Joe Bloggs answers in the hard problems.* How do you know how hard a question is? By its *question number.*

Take a look at the following example.

20. Michelle rode her bicycle from her house to school at an average speed of 8 miles per hour. Later that day, she rode from school back home along the same route at an average speed of 12 miles per hour. If the round trip took her 1 hour, how many miles long is the round trip?

(A)   8

(B) $9\frac{3}{5}$

(C)   10

(D) $11\frac{1}{5}$

(E)   12

How to Crack It

Which choice do you think seems attractive at first to Joe? When he sees the numbers 8 and 12 and the word "average," he will probably average 8 and 12 to get 10. Therefore, Joe will pick (C).

But now you know better. This problem is number 20, the hardest problem on the section. You know that Joe will get it wrong. So cross off choice (C).

If Joe does not pick (C), what else might he pick? He will pick either (A) 8, or (E) 12, because those are the numbers that appear in the problem. Cross them off as well. Then strategically guess from either (B) or (D). (The answer is (B), but we are not going to spend time on why right now.) If you can quickly cross off a few choices on a hard problem and make an educated guess, you will be in great shape.

Figuring out the right number of problems to do, how to pace yourself, and how to avoid the Joe Bloggs traps are keys to a good PSAT strategy. You are probably eager to get to the rest of the book, but make sure you have taken the time to understand this chapter before moving on. A solid overall approach is crucial to getting your best score on this test.

Summary

o   Remember to memorize your pacing goals so that you know exactly how many problems to attempt—you do not have to answer every problem to hit your target score.

o   The questions on most sections are arranged in Order of Difficulty from easier to harder, which may make it easier to find the problems that are easier for you to do.

o   Use your Joe Bloggs instincts on easy and hard problems (according to the test writers' OOD). For easy problems, Joe Bloggs answers tend to be right, while on hard problems, they are almost always wrong.

Part II
Cracking the PSAT/NMSQT

Chapter 5
Sentence
Completions

A Sentence Completion question will consist of a
sample sentence in which one or two words have been
replaced by blanks. Below the sentence, you will find
five answer choices, each of which consists of a word
or words. This chapter will give you the techniques you
need to approach Sentence Completions for maximum
accuracy and minimum wasted time and stress.

Solving Sentence Completions relies on two things: first, your ability to figure out what kind of word should go in the blank, and second, your vocabulary. We will focus mostly on technique in this chapter. To work on vocabulary, turn to Chapter 11 for the Hit Parade—The Princeton Review's list of vocabulary words that show up most often on the PSAT.

THE INSTRUCTIONS

Of course, you will not want to waste valuable time during the test to read the directions, so it is wise to learn them now. Here are the instructions for Sentence Completions as you will see them on the PSAT and SAT:

Each sentence below has one or two blanks, each blank indicating that something has been omitted. Beneath the sentence are five words or sets of words labeled A through E. Choose the word or set of words that, when inserted in the sentence, best fits the meaning of the sentence as a whole.

Example:

Medieval kingdoms did not become constitutional republics overnight; on the contrary, the change was -------.

(A) unpopular (B) unexpected (C) advantageous
(D) sufficient (E) gradual   Ⓐ Ⓑ Ⓒ Ⓓ ●

ETS's answer to this sample question is (E).

ORDER OF DIFFICULTY

Sentence Completion questions will appear on both Critical Reading sections of the PSAT. They will be questions 1–8 in Section 1 and questions 25–29 in Section 3. Their order of difficulty looks like this:

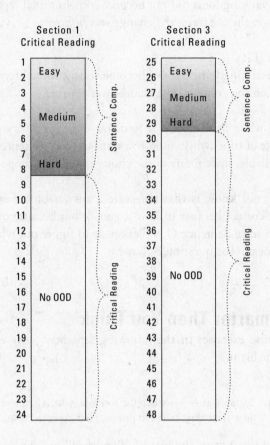

WHAT WOULD JOE DO?

Before we talk about the best way to solve Sentence Completions, we should first discuss how *not* to solve them. How does Joe Bloggs, the average student, approach Sentence Completions? The natural way, which seems most intuitive to Joe, is to do the following: He tries to solve these questions by rereading the sentence five times, trying a different word in the blank each time, and hoping to find the one that "sounds right." That is, he does the following:

Joe tries choice (A):

> Medieval kingdoms did not become constitutional republics over-night; on the contrary, the change was *unpopular*.

Joe tries choice (B):

> Medieval kingdoms did not become constitutional republics over-night; on the contrary, the change was *unexpected*.

A Reminder
On easy questions, the answers that seem right to Joe really are right; on hard questions, the answers that seem right to Joe are wrong. In both cases, though, he spends way too much time on them.

Joe tries choice (C):

> Medieval kingdoms did not become constitutional republics overnight; on the contrary, the change was *advantageous*.

Joe tries choice (D):

> Medieval kingdoms did not become constitutional republics overnight; on the contrary, the change was *sufficient*.

Joe tries choice (E):

> Medieval kingdoms did not become constitutional republics overnight; on the contrary, the change was *gradual*.

Unfortunately, while this method is intuitive, it is not a very good strategy. Not only is it a waste of time (why would you want to read the sentence *five times*?), but it is often unreliable, since many of the choices sound pretty good.

What Joe does not know is that the correct answer on a Sentence Completion question is not correct because of how it *sounds*, but because of what it *means*. So the best way to solve Sentence Completions is to figure out what the word in the blank should mean. The question is, how?

You Are Smarter Than You Think

Try the following exercise: In the following sentence, what word do you think should go in the blank?

1. Susan was ------- when the formula, which had worked just yesterday, failed to produce the expected result.

What word did you put in the blank? "Perplexed" or "confused"? Something of this sort has to be the word in the blank.

How about this one:

2. Although she was never considered pretty as a child, Margaret grew up to be a ------- adult.

What word did you put in the blank? "Beautiful" or "pretty" or "lovely"? You can figure out what the word in the blank has to mean without looking at the answer choices.

Try it once more:

> **3.** Once a cheerful person, the years of fruitless struggle
> against government waste made him a very ------- man.

Even if you could not figure out the exact word that went in the blank, you probably figured out that it had to be a word meaning "unhappy" or "bitter." That will be good enough to get the right answer, or at least to make a very good guess at the right answer.

You see, you are smarter than you think. This is why you should always approach Sentence Completion questions by *speaking for yourself*. Do not look down at the answer choices; if you do, you will be tempted to use the Joe Bloggs method of trying each word, one at a time, and hoping that one of them sounds right. In fact, you should always approach Sentence Completions the same way we just did: Read the sentence, and put your own word into the blank.

THE METHOD

As you have seen, it is entirely possible to figure out what kind of word goes in the blank just by reading the sentence carefully, and it is much faster than trying every answer choice. To make sure that you speak for yourself, you should actually place your hand over the answer choices so you are not tempted to read them until you have picked your own word for the blank.

Sentence Completion Rule #1
Cover the answer choices until you know what the answer should be.

So here is our method for solving Sentence Completions:

1. **Cover the answer choices with your hand.** This will ensure that you do not do what Joe does, which is read the sentence five times, trying one of the answer choices each time.
2. **Speak for yourself.** Read the sentence carefully, and then write your own word in the blank.
3. **Use POE.** Only after you have written your own word in the blank should you uncover the answer choices and select the word that comes closest to the word that you came up with.

But how do you know what word to put in the blank? You never have to guess randomly; in fact, ETS always puts clues into the sentences to tell you what sort of word goes in the blank. By learning how to look for these clues, you can reliably figure out what sort of word has to go in the blank, every time.

Help Yourself

Identifying clues in a sentence will help you more easily come up with a good word when you *speak for yourself*.

Speak for Yourself, Part I: Clues and Triggers

To help you speak for yourself, learn to look for the *clue* and *trigger words*.

The Clue

We just saw that you could figure out the meaning of the word in the blank without looking at the answer choices. How did you think you were able to know what word went in the blank? Without realizing it, you were using clues in the sentence. There are *always* clues in the sentence that tell you what the word in the blank is supposed to mean.

We can look back at the first sample problem and see what kind of clues we find in it.

> 1. Susan was ------- when the formula, which had worked
>   just yesterday, failed to produce the expected result.

How did you know that the word had to be something like "perplexed"? Because this sentence contains a clue: *the formula, which had worked just yesterday, failed to produce the expected result.* This clue tells us how Susan must feel: namely, that she felt "perplexed" or "puzzled." We are going to underline clues, so go ahead and underline the phrase from question 1, italicized above. Remember, this is your book, so write in it and write in your test booklet on test day.

How about in this sentence?

> 2. The park was so ------- that children could play in it for
>   hours without getting bored.

What kind of word would you put in this blank, and why? You probably chose a word like "interesting" or "varied." You probably knew this because the park is described as a place where *children could play for hours without getting bored.* This is the clue that tells us that the park must be a terribly interesting place to be.

The meaning of the word that goes in the blank is not random. Typically, you will find evidence somewhere in the sentence that tells you what the word in the blank should mean. This evidence is called the clue. *Most sentences have some clue in them. Look for the clue, underline it, and it will help you determine the word that goes in the blank.*

Why Every Sentence Needs a Clue

Every sentence on the PSAT must have some sort of clue in it, or else the question would not have just one correct answer. In that case, the question would not be a good one anymore, and ETS could not use it on the PSAT. Let's see why. Take a look at this problem:

1. John made some ------- comments about Marcus's artwork.

    (A) intelligent
    (B) critical
    (C) interesting
    (D) dry
    (E) appreciative

Can you see why this problem would never appear on the PSAT? Because any of the answers might work. There is not enough information in the sentence to make one choice better than any other. Without a clue, the question simply will not work. Look at this example:

1. John made some ------- comments about Marcus's artwork, which John thought was fantastic.

    (A) intelligent
    (B) critical
    (C) interesting
    (D) dry
    (E) appreciative

In this case, the word that would best fit would be (E), because of the clue *which John thought was fantastic*. Note that if the clue changes, so does the meaning of the word in the blank. Although Choice C may be tempting to select as the correct answer, you must follow the positive connotation of *fantastic*.

1. John made some ------- comments about Marcus's artwork, which John thought was the worst he had ever seen.

    (A) intelligent
    (B) critical
    (C) interesting
    (D) dry
    (E) appreciative

In this case, the answer would be (B). By changing the clue, we changed the meaning of the word that should go in the blank.

Suppose you are having trouble identifying the clue, though. There are two questions you can ask yourself to help you find it.

- Who or what is the blank talking about?
- What does the sentence say about that person or thing?

We can look at number 1 on page 46 again. Who or what is the sentence talking about? Susan. What does it say about her? *That her formula failed to produce the expected result,* so that is the clue.

It will work for number 2 as well. Who or what was that sentence talking about? The park. What does it say about the park? *That the children could play in it for hours without getting bored,* so that is the clue. Remember to underline it.

Trigger Words

One more important tool for figuring out the meaning of the word in the blank is *trigger words.* These are words in the sentence that tell you how the word in the blank relates to the clue. When you see a trigger word, circle it.

Trigger words are words we use every day. For instance, look at the following sentences:

I really like you, *and* _____
I really like you, *but* _____

You already know more or less how these sentences would end, don't you? The first sentence would continue with something positive that goes along with liking someone, such as:

I really like you, (and) I'd like to get to know you better.

In contrast, the second sentence would change direction and end with something not quite so nice, such as:

I really like you, (but) you're really not my type.

Now we will see how trigger words work in a sample sentence. Recall the second example:

2. (Although) she was never considered pretty as a child, Margaret grew up to be a ------- adult.

Same or Opposite?

The most common same-direction trigger words are *and, because, so, therefore, since, in fact,* and *also.*

The most common opposite-direction trigger words are *but, however, yet, although, though, in contrast, rather,* and *despite.* When you see these words, the word in the blank will usually mean the opposite of the clue.

Same-Direction Triggers	Opposite-Direction Triggers
and	but
because	however
so	yet
therefore	although/though
since	in contrast
in fact	rather
also	despite

How did you know that the word in the blank had to be a word like "beautiful"? Because the word *although* told you that there was a change in direction or contrast in the sentence: She was *not pretty as a child*, but she *was* a pretty *adult*.

There are also trigger words that indicate that the word in the blank has the same meaning as the clue. For instance:

> **4.** (Because) Susan could not stand Jim's boorish manners,
> she ------- to be near him at parties.

In this case, what sort of word goes in the blank? The trigger word *because* tells you that the word in the blank will have a similar meaning to the clue *could not stand Jim's boorish manners*. The word in the blank must therefore be something like "hated" or "despised."

Punctuation Triggers

In addition to the words in the table on the previous page, there are a couple of punctuation triggers. Both colons (:) and semicolons (;) act as same-direction triggers and show us that what follows the colon or semicolon will be an explanation or further description of something that came before. Take a look at this sentence:

> **2.** John's friend was rather -------(:) he never spoke unless he
> was forced to.

In this case, we know that the word in the blank should be a word that means "unwilling to speak"—a word like "quiet" or "taciturn" would do nicely.

Time Triggers

One other, more subtle, kind of trigger, which acts as an opposite-direction trigger, is the time trigger. A time trigger draws a contrast between what used to be true and what is true today. Here is an example:

A Reminder
Circle the triggers!

> **3.** (Once) a cheerful person, the years of futile struggle
> against government waste made him a very ------- man.

In this case, we know that the word in the blank needs to be a word opposite to "cheerful"—perhaps a word like "gloomy" or "cynical." Why? We know that at one point in the past, this person was cheerful; however, since that time, something has changed. Therefore, the word in the blank should be something that contrasts with "cheerful."

When trying to find the right word for the blank, always look for the clue and trigger words. They will tell you what sort of word you need.

Speak for Yourself—Part II

Here are a few Sentence Completion problems from which we have removed the answer choices. (The complete problems with answer choices follow.) Read the sentence, underline any clues, circle any triggers, then write your own word in the blank using the clues and triggers to guide you. Then use POE to eliminate choices that do not match yours.

1. Many feature films are criticized for their ------- content, even though television news is more often the medium that depicts violent events in excessive detail.

4. In a scathing message to his troops, General Patton insisted that he would ------- no further insubordination, no matter how brutal the ensuing engagements might become.

Now that you have identified the clues and triggers, we can crack these problems.

---

1. Many feature films are criticized for their ------- content, even though television news is more often the medium that depicts violent events in excessive detail.

   (A) discretionary
   (B) graphic
   (C) dramatic
   (D) artistic
   (E) honest

How to Crack It

The clue in this sentence is *depicts violent events in excessive detail*. The word in the blank should mean something like "violent" or "violence in detail." You can often "recycle" the clue—that is, the word or words you fill in the blank do not have to be fancy; they just need to complete the meaning of the sentence. So feel free to recycle the word violent and use it as your own word.

Now we can use POE to get the answer. Does discretionary mean violent? No. Cross it off. (Wait, what if we do not know what discretionary means? Then we should keep it for the time being. If it becomes the only answer left then we will choose it, but if we find a better match we will choose that instead.) Does graphic mean violent? Seems pretty close, so keep it for now. Does dramatic mean violent? No. Cross it off. Does artistic mean violent? Definitely not. Finally, does honest mean violent? No. So, we are left with (B), which is the answer.

Okay, ready for the next one?

4. In a scathing message to his troops, General Patton insisted that he would ------- no further insubordination, no matter how brutal the ensuing engagements might become.

   (A) impede
   (B) brief
   (C) denote
   (D) brook
   (E) expose

How to Crack It

The clues here are *insisted* and *no further insubordination, no matter how....* Did you pick a word like "tolerate" or "stand for" in this case? That is exactly the meaning of the correct answer. The words in the answer choices are hard, but eliminate what you can, keep the words you do not know, and take a good guess. The answer is (D).

Two Blanks: Twice as Easy

Some of the Sentence Completion questions will have two blanks rather than just one. To solve these questions, tackle them one blank at a time. Choose one blank or the other, whichever seems easier to you, and figure out what word should go in the blank. (Hint: Often, but not always, the second blank is easier to figure out.) Then cross off all of the choices that do not work for that blank.

If more than one answer choice remains, then write in a word for the other blank, and see which of the remaining answer choices works best.

Have a look at these examples.

2. The scientific community was ------- when a living specimen of the coelacanth, which ichthyologists had feared was -------, was discovered by deep-sea fishermen.

   (A) perplexed . . common
   (B) overjoyed . . dangerous
   (C) unconcerned . . exterminated
   (D) astounded . . extinct
   (E) dismayed . . alive

Shoe Store
If you were shopping for shoes and one shoe did not fit, would you bother trying on the other? Half wrong is all wrong. If one answer does not fit, cross out the whole choice.

How to Crack It

The clue for the second blank is that a *living specimen* was found, which the scientists *feared was*.... So the second blank must mean something like "dead." Only choices (C) and (D) are possible, so we can eliminate the others. Now look at the first blank. How did the scientists feel about the discovery? They were probably happy about it. Of (C) and (D), which choice works with the first blank? Choice (D).

Here is another.

5. Chang realized that she had been ------- in her duties; had she been more -------, the disaster may well have been avoided.

    (A) unparalleled . . careful
    (B) irreproachable . . aware
    (C) derelict . . vigilant
    (D) arbitrary . . interested
    (E) neglectful . . insensible

How to Crack It

The clue for the second blank is that the *disaster may well have been avoided*, so the second blank must be a word like "careful." This will allow us to eliminate (D) and (E). The word in the first blank must be a word like "neglectful," since Chang failed to do her duty. The only remaining choice that works for the first blank is (C).

Here is one more.

5. Although Jane's professors reproached her as a ------- during her first year in college, she became attentive and ------- once she found a major that interested her.

    (A) neophyte . . assiduous
    (B) sycophant . . critical
    (C) malingerer . . focused
    (D) beginner . . average
    (E) candidate . . distracted

How to Crack It

Remember to cover the answers before reading the sentence! Although we know that the first blank is probably a bad thing (because Jane's professors *reproached* her), we do not have great clues. So we should move on to the second blank. The clue for the second blank is *attentive*, so we can recycle it and use attentive as our own word. Then we can eliminate (B), (D), and (E), because they don't mean anything close to *attentive*.

Now we have a better idea of what goes in the first blank. Because of the trigger *although,* the first blank means a person who is the opposite of *attentive*. Perhaps we would write down *slacker*. Our two remaining answer choices are (A) and (C). If you don't know what *neophyte* means, remember to leave it there—it could be correct. (C) does mean *slacker* though, so that is our best answer.

Relationship Between the Blanks

Remember we said that most questions have clues? Well, in some tricky questions the clues may be unclear or missing altogether because one blank is the clue for the other blank. In this case we will have to do things a little bit differently, namely, use the relationship between the blanks to eliminate answers that do not have that same relationship. For example, take a look at the question that follows:

> 5. Because their new album is more ------- than previous ones, the band may alienate their fans who like ------- music.

If you tried to fill in the blanks with your own words, you might come up with something like *traditional* for the first blank and *experimental* for the second. But you could just as easily switch those words in the blanks and the sentence would still make sense, so we cannot do this one blank at a time. The word that goes in the first blank is dependent on the word in the second blank, and vice versa. So the key is to focus on the relationship between the blanks—whether the words are the same or different.

In this sentence, we are clearly looking for words that are different. So we would eliminate any answer choices with words that are the same or that do not have any relationship at all.

Here is another one. Keep in mind that triggers can really help you because they tell you about the relationship between clues and blanks.

4. The author is reliably -------; every book he writes is more ------- than the one before.

    (A) dull . . inspired
    (B) exceptional . . hackneyed
    (C) artistic . . informed
    (D) imaginative . . creative
    (E) original . . lackluster

How to Crack It

The sentence does not have clues for the individual blanks, so we must look for triggers that will tell us whether the relationship between the blanks is the same or different. First, there is a semicolon, which tells us the two parts of the sentence go in the same direction. Also, the words *reliably* and *every book he writes* are clearly describing a relationship of similarity between the blanks. So we would note that the words should be the same, and go through our answer choices. (A), (B), and (E) are clearly opposites, and the words in (C) do not really have a relationship, so we are left with (D) as our best answer.

FINAL WORDS

As the questions become more difficult, you will probably find harder words in the answer choices. Although you will have a word of your own to compare to the answers and use POE, you might find many or most of the answer choices are words you do not know. When this happens, get rid of whatever you can quickly and strategically guess if you need to answer another question or two to hit your pacing goal. If you cannot come up with your own word using the method we discussed earlier, then you should skip that question altogether. For example, some harder questions might also use a tough vocabulary word in the clue. If you do not know what the clue means, you will not be able to fill in the blank with your own word and you are most likely going to get that question wrong. If it is a two-blank question and you can fill in one of the blanks, you might try to eliminate a few and guess, but only if you have worked through the whole section and have run out of questions you can do with certainty. Remember that your pacing goal should guide your process.

Summary

- The first step on Sentence Completion questions is to cover the answer choices with your hand.

- Next, speak for yourself: Read the sentence, and put your own word in the blank.

- To help you figure out the meaning of the word that goes in the blank, find the clues in the sentence. Also, pay close attention to trigger words.

- Only after you have come up with your own word for the blank should you look down at the answer choices. Pick the word that comes closest to the word that you created. Be sure to use POE and evaluate every answer choice.

- On two-blank questions, just do one blank at a time.

Chapter 6
Critical Reading

This chapter deals only with passage-based reading questions. You will see a passage followed by questions about the content of the passage. These questions are supposed to measure how well you understand what you read, but in reality they mostly measure how efficiently you can locate specific pieces of information. There are two types of passages—short ones and long ones—and we are going to examine both.

AN OPEN-BOOK TEST

Answering passage-based reading questions is like taking an open-book test; all of the information that you could be asked about is right in front of you, so you never have to worry about any history, chemistry, or literature that you may (or may not!) have learned in school. Although you will have to use the passage to answer the questions, there is not enough time to read the passage thoroughly, master all its details, and then painstakingly select the one choice that answers the question perfectly. What you need is a way to get in and out of this section with as little stress and as many points as possible.

If someone were to give you a 10-volume encyclopedia and ask you in what year Louis Pasteur invented pasteurization, would you begin reading at the A's and work all the way through to the P's? No! You would go right to the entry on Pasteur and read only the few lines that you needed to. That is how to approach passage-based reading questions on the PSAT.

THE METHOD

1. Read the blurb
2. Work the passage
3. Choose a question and paraphrase it
4. Read what you need to answer the question
5. Answer the question
6. POE

Step 1: Read the Blurb

Long passages usually begin with a short introduction in italics that will give you a little background about the passage. If you see one, read it! It will give you some good context before you start reading the passage. If there is no blurb (most short passages do not have one) then move on to step 2.

Step 2: Work the Passage

For some passages you can go right to the questions. This is especially true for many nonfiction passages. For fiction passages—and for all passages if you feel you need to read the passage first—get through the passage *quickly*.

When reading the passage, remember that there is no way you can be asked about every single detail, nor is it possible to master every detail in the time provided. When you are asked about specific details, you can *and should* go back to the passage. So, in your first read-through, you should just get through the passage quickly to get a sense of what it is generally about.

Once again, though, do not get wrapped up in the details of the passage. If something is confusing, leave it for now and stay focused on the big picture. Re-reading a confusing portion of the passage will cost invaluable time. There may not be any questions about that part of the passage anyway, and even if there are questions about it, they are probably going to be good questions to skip or save for last.

Passage Types

Critical Reading passages come from four broad subject areas:

1. Science: Discoveries, controversies, or other topics in physics, chemistry, astronomy, biology, medicine, botany, zoology, and the other sciences.
2. Humanities: Excerpts from essays about art, literature, music, philosophy, or folklore; discussions of artists, novelists, or historical figures.
3. Social sciences: Topics in politics, economics, sociology, or history.
4. Narrative: Usually excerpts from novels, short stories, or humorous essays. (We have yet to see a poem on the PSAT)

ETS usually includes a passage involving a historically overlooked community or social group. This passage is usually either a social science or humanities passage.

Step 3: Choose a Question and Paraphrase It

All points are created equal, but not all questions are. The math sections and the sentence completions have an order of difficulty to help you make POOD decisions before you even read a question, but the reading passages do not give you this hint. You are going to have to use your judgment as you go along, taking into consideration such things as how long or complicated the question stem is and whether or not the things it asks about in the passage are hard to understand.

If the question is easy to understand, then it may be a good question to attack right away. Questions that you have to spend time just trying to interpret should be put off until later. If you attack such a question, make sure you can articulate what it is asking. If the part of the passage that you need to read in order to answer the question is particularly difficult, then you should probably put off that question until later or skip it altogether. But if the reading is a breeze (or at least pretty straightforward), you probably want to do it now.

The question can still be tough if there are tricks in the answer choices, but we will talk about what to watch out for when we get to POE.

Once we have chosen a question it is time to paraphrase it. We do this so that we know what we are looking for when we go to the passage. We must know this because we want to read actively, which means we are going to be actively searching for the information we need and thinking about it, not just passively staring at words on a page.

Take a look at the following question:

> The author mentions the Israeli-Palestinian conflict in the
> last paragraph (lines 92-97) in order to

This question is asking us for the *purpose* of something, in other words, why did the author talk about something? What's the something? The Israeli-Palestinian conflict. When we read we will want to know what the author says about this and why, so the question is *Why does the author talk about the Israeli-Palestinian conflict?*

Take a minute to read the questions below and think about what they are asking you to find out, then paraphrase them.

42. According to the passage, the parrot became uncooperative because

43. The author's use of irony in line 55 suggests that

44. The primary purpose of the passage is

45. The argument about crows in the third paragraph would be most strengthened if which of the following were true?

Explanations

42. The question is asking why the parrot became uncooperative, so we can paraphrase it as, *Why did the parrot become uncooperative?* Just make it into a question by starting with one of the "W" words. This question looks pretty simple, as it is not asking us to think about anything beyond what the passage says, so this is a question we would certainly want to try on our first pass through the questions.

43. *What does the author's use of irony in line 55 tell us?* Questions that ask about what is *suggested* or *implied* can sometimes be pretty tough, because we do not always know what the question is after; it could be a number of things. Paraphrasing the question as above will at least get us focused on looking for whatever information is given on the topic in the passage, but we may have to focus on the answers and use POE carefully here. This would be a good question to hold off until later.

44. *What is the primary purpose of the passage?* Another way to think about this question is, *Why did the author write this passage?* The author is trying to get a point across or convince us of something, so we should focus on trying to figure out what that is. We should also hold off on general questions like this until we have worked more specific questions and therefore have more background.

45. This question asks us to go outside the information given in the passage. The answer must still be something we can derive from the passage, but it is probably going to be pretty tough. The answer choices are going to present new information. Notice that the question stem says *if which of the following were true.* This is definitely a question to do last and only if we are attempting every question. To paraphrase it, we will actually want to try to break it down into a few questions, rather than just one, as follows: *What is the third paragraph trying to convince us of about crows?* and *What kind of information would make this more likely?*

If you have to do this question, be sure to use bite-sized pieces to figure out what steps you must take to answer the question. In fact, any time there is more than one question hidden in the question, see if you can break it down into a couple of questions.

Step 4: Read What You Need to Answer the Question

The PSAT is a standardized test. That means that the answers cannot be a matter of opinion. If the folks at ETS are going to put a question on the test and say that the answer is (D), they need to be able to prove that (D) actually *is* the best answer and that no one who truly understood the question and the passage could disagree. They need to be able to point to a line in the passage and say, "See that sentence there? That means the answer *has* to be (D)." Because the test is designed this way, you absolutely cannot leave out step 4. If you are about to select an answer choice and you cannot point to a line or lines in the passage that prove that answer is correct, then you haven't picked the right answer. Do not simply choose based on your memory or on your gut. You cannot depend on things you have learned in school, and under no circumstances should you make things up. ("Yeah, I guess the War of 1812 could've been fought against the Australians…") Also, if a question gives you a line reference, be sure to read at least five lines above and below that reference. *Find* the answer in the passage. It is in there!

Step 5: Answer the Question

Remember how we covered our answers and jotted down our own words for Sentence Completions, so we would not be distracted by ETS's answer choices? The same goes for passage-based reading questions. It does you no good to know that the answer is in line 39 if you have no idea what line 39 means! You must make sure you know the answer to the question before you go to the choices. This often means taking a long-winded paragraph and condensing it down to a handful of words. (ETS often uses exact words from the passage to trick you into picking wrong answers, which is another good reason to substitute your own wording.) As you read the following paragraphs, consider what the key ideas are and how you might boil them down into a sentence or two.

1. We are told that the trouble with Modern Man is that he has been trying to detach himself from nature. He sits in the topmost tiers of polymer, glass, and steel, dangling his pulsing legs, surveying at a distance the writhing life of the planet. In this scenario, Man comes on as a stupendous lethal force, and the Earth is pictured as something delicate, like rising bubbles at the surface of a country pond, or flights of fragile birds.

2. When in the course of human events it becomes necessary for one people to dissolve the political bands which have connected them with another, and to assume among the powers of the earth the separate and equal station to which the Laws of Nature and of Nature's God entitle them, a decent respect to the opinions of mankind requires that they should declare the causes which impel them to the separation.

Answers

1. *Some say that the Earth is delicate and that Modern Man's detachment from it can really mess it up.*

2. *When people declare independence, they had better tell the world why.*

Note that these answers are short! If you found yourself copying phrases such as "surveying at a distance" or "the course of human events," you are missing the point. Copying long phrases means that you do not understand them. You cannot go to the choices and expect to get the right answer unless you comprehend what you have read.

Step 6: POE

Process of Elimination is the single most important step. After all, what good is understanding the passage and finding the correct answer if you do not fill in the correct little bubble? None, according to ETS; there is no partial credit on the PSAT. So you need to know what makes a good answer and what makes a bad answer in ETS-land. Some things to keep in mind:

POE Done Right

- **Evaluate every answer choice.** The directions tell you to pick the "best" answer, and you can only do that if you have read through each one. Remember, ETS knows how to write answers that sound great but are actually wrong, and you are much more likely to avoid those traps if you work through each question completely.
- **Be aggressive.** There will be lots of things wrong in the answer choices, and if part of an answer choice is wrong, the whole thing is wrong. The "best" answer does not have to sound good or make you happy—it just has to be free of error, which means it is supported by the passage and answers the question, but may not be particularly impressive.
- **Stick to the passage.** If you know more about the War of 1812 than the author of the passage does, that is great, but it is not necessarily going to help you on the PSAT. Any answer choice that requires you to know outside information is wrong—everything you need is in the passage.

POE Tips

- **Beware exact phrasing.** ETS often uses exact words from the passage in the wrong answers because they sound familiar and, therefore, test takers are likely to pick them. Who would likely pick these types of answers? Joe Bloggs! Correct answers to specific questions are usually *paraphrases* of information in the passage.
- **For General questions, pay attention to scope.** For example, if a passage gives a brief overview of the effects of the Industrial Revolution on city growth in England and you are asked for the primary purpose, you might find incorrect answers such as "detail the Bessemer process of steel manufacturing" (too specific) or "chart the spread of the Industrial Revolution throughout Europe" (too broad). Often, answers that are too specific are just mentioned once or twice in the passage, and answers that are too broad simply cannot be accomplished in 100 lines or fewer.
- **Avoid extremes and give no offense.** Last but certainly not least, ETS rarely makes extreme or offensive answer choices correct on its tests. If you see an answer choice that is extreme or potentially offensive to a certain group of people, eliminate it. The reason for this is simple: The

Buzzwords
Beware answer choices that contain the following words:
must
always
impossible
never
cannot
each
every
totally
all
solely
only

more extreme an answer choice is, the easier it is to prove that answer choice wrong. The more offensive a passage is, the more likely it is that ETS will get sued. ETS does not like to be proven wrong or get sued, so "best" answers are wishy-washy and offend no one.

Here are some examples of extreme or offensive answer choices:

> Everyone believes that Shakespeare was the greatest writer in history.
>
> Nineteenth-century scientists were foolish and ignorant to believe in the existence of ether.
>
> The judges deliberately undermined the constitution in the landmark case.

In the first example, the passage would have to state that every single person in the world believes Shakespeare is the greatest—but if the author wrote that in the passage this question would be pretty easy to answer, right? Besides, how could the author know that? Can he read your mind? So it comes down to what can be supported by the passage once again.

In the second and third examples, an observation is made about some group that they (or their grandchildren) would probably be offended by. PSAT passages are very reasonable and wishy-washy, so offensive answers would not be consistent with the passage.

Likewise, PSAT passages are usually not extreme in tone, so you can eliminate answer choices in questions that ask about the author's tone using extreme words like *condemnation, ridicule, adulation,* and *cynicism.*

CRACKING READING QUESTIONS

The Long Reading passages on the PSAT seem daunting to many students. However, the PSAT does not test you on how you read the passages; what really matters is how well you answer the questions. The same major question types appear for Short and Long Reading passages. Once you know how to answer the questions, dealing with passages will be easy, whether they are short or long.

Unlike Sentence Completions, passage-based reading questions are not arranged in a set order of difficulty, so it will be up to you to identify which questions will be easiest for you to do. Do not worry; we will show you what to expect and how to pick the best questions for your skills.

Major Question Types

There are six major question types that turn up on Short and Long passages:

Vocabulary in Context
Detail
Infer/Imply/Suggest
Purpose
Tone
Primary Purpose

SHORT PASSAGES—WHAT TO EXPECT

For Critical Reading short passages, questions will be based on short, paragraph-long passages. The questions will be numbered 9–12 on Section 1 and 30–33 in Section 3. They generally will not have a blurb or any introductory material, and they will usually be followed by only one or two questions per passage. The object: Answer the questions correctly, using as little time and effort as possible. On the next few pages we will use Short Reading passages to look at the most common question types you will encounter on the PSAT.

Use the Method

1. **Read the blurb.** There is usually no blurb on Short Reading.
2. **Work the passage.** This might even mean going right to the questions.
3. **Choose a question and paraphrase it.** Figure out what the question is asking.
4. **Go back to the passage and find the answer.** Critical Reading on the PSAT is like an open-book test. Do not rely on your memory!
5. **Answer the question.** Before you pick an answer, answer the question yourself.
6. **POE.** Use your pencil to cross out answers that do not fit with the answer you came up with.

Vocabulary-in-Context

Some vocabulary questions, which we will call "Vocab-in-Context" questions, ask you for the meaning of a word in the passage. Here is an example:

In line 12, "domestic" most nearly means

Vocab-in-Context questions come in two flavors: Either they will ask about difficult words (so you do not already know the meaning) or about secondary definitions of simple words (so you will be tempted to pick a meaning that you are already familiar with). You should treat Vocab-in-Context questions like Sentence Completions questions—pretend the word is a blank and think about how to fill it based on the context of the sentence. So while it looks like these questions test your vocabulary, you are much better off depending on the context surrounding the word—again, it is an open-book test.

These questions are more common in Long Reading, but they occasionally pop up in Short Reading as well. Work these questions like Sentence Completions: Come up with your own word to replace the word in the question.

There is a kernel of truth in the saying, "It's no use carrying an umbrella if your shoes are leaking." Wet is wet. But too many people give in to fatalism of the worst kind
Line when the going gets tough. While almost nothing is worse
5 than cold, wet feet, there's no reason to also have a sopping head. Why add insult to injury when there is a way to make a situation even slightly better?

11. In line 1, "kernel" most nearly means

(A) essential element
(B) secret meaning
(C) crucial nourishment
(D) unintended dishonesty
(E) firm logic

How to Crack It

Following the method, we can begin with step 2 and see that the passage states that although there is some truth to a saying, the author does not fully agree with it. Step 3 reveals that this question wants the meaning of a particular word in the passage: It is a Vocab-In-Context question, so treat it like a Sentence Completion. Go back to the passage and cross out the word *kernel* to create a blank that you can fill in with your own word or phrase. Use the sentence in which *kernel* appears to find evidence to come up with a word that fits the context of the sentence. Use POE to get rid of any answers that do not match the word you came up with. If you are not down to one single answer, determine which one of the remaining choices fits best in the sentence.

When we go back to the passage and cross out *kernel*, it seems that the sentence is saying that there is "some" *truth* or a "small part" of *truth in the saying*. This is supported by the following sentence (*Wet is wet*) that goes along with the idea that an umbrella will not help. There is no reason to get rid of (A); while *essential* might seem a little strong, an *element* could be a "small part," so hold on to it for now. There is no evidence in the passage to support *secret* as seen in (B), so cross it out. If the kernel mentioned in the passage were a seed, *crucial nourishment* might make sense, but this is clearly not an actual seed. Cross off (C). Choice (D) might be tempting because at the end of the passage, the author seems to disagree with the saying, but at the beginning of the passage, she is definitely stating that there *is* truth to the statement. Choice (E) is also tempting, because *firm logic* seems to support the idea that there is truth in the statement. However, *firm logic* is a little strong for our phrase "a small part," and something supported by *firm logic* would not so easily be dismissed in a passage as short as this one. This leaves choice (A) as the correct answer.

Detail

Detail questions are relatively straightforward. They essentially ask: "What does the passage say?" Detail questions often use phrases such as

> The author indicates that . . .

> According to the passage . . .

> Lines 24-28 refer to a . . .

Here is a detail question.

If you think of a linguist's job at all, you may
envision someone compiling a lexicon while surrounded
by dusty stacks of books and dictionaries rather than an
adventurer such as Alexandra Aikhenvald. Worldwide,   *Line*
linguistic diversity has dropped 60 to 70 percent over   *5*
the past century. The situation is even direr in parts of
South America: The Atlantic coast of Brazil has lost 99
percent of the languages spoken by various groups there.
Aikhenvald's goal is to record Amazonian languages before
it is too late. She's traveled through the remotest jungles   *10*
and navigated rivers inhabited by giant anaconda snakes to
reach villages accessible only by canoe. In her explorations,
Aikhenvald discovered previously undocumented
languages and heard languages spoken that researchers had
believed extinct.   *15*

30. The author indicates that Aikhenvald regards
     "Amazonian languages" (line 9) as

   (A) extinct and without hope of being resurrected
   (B) widely spoken in areas readily accessible to
        researchers
   (C) severely at risk and under time constraints
   (D) spoken by more young than elderly inhabitants
        of the Amazon
   (E) unworthy of in-depth study

How to Crack It

The passage as a whole is about a language researcher who goes to extremes to document endangered languages. The question is asking what Aikhenvald thinks about *Amazonian languages*. This is a Detail question, so use the line reference and go to the passage and see what the passage says. It is important to read a couple of lines before and after the reference when answering a question, as the information will rarely be in the line you are asked to view. The passage states that *Aikhenvald's*

Stick To the Passage
Do not make things up.
Your answer must be
supported by the passage.

Critical Reading | **67**

goal is to record Amazonian languages before it is too late, so we need an answer that mentions that Aikhenvald has to do her work before she runs out of time. Choice (A) has nothing to do with time, and is closer to what *researchers* mentioned in the last sentence might believe, not Aikhenvald. Choice (B) is contradicted by information in the passage: The languages are disappearing, not *widely spoken,* and are in areas that are difficult to get to, not *readily accessible.* Choice (C) looks pretty good— *severely* is not extreme because it is supported by the passage—so hold onto it. The passage does not mention any age division of the speakers she found in the Amazon, so get rid of (D). Eliminate (E); there is no way Aikhenvald would face giant snakes for something she thought was *unworthy of in-depth study*! The correct answer is (C).

Infer/Imply/Suggest

Certain questions will use phrases such as

The author suggests that . . .

The passage implies that . . .

It can be inferred from the passage that . . .

When ETS uses these words, it is trying to trick you into thinking that you need to "read between the lines" or discover some "hidden meaning." But in reality, these questions are very similar to Detail questions! The right answer will always be supported by something stated in the passage.

Parkinson's disease is an incurable, progressive, degenerative brain disease that affects the way nerves control muscles. Since the disease has no cure, it becomes
Line more severe over time and causes the gradual deterioration
5   of cells in the brain. Generally, Parkinson's disease is thought to be caused by a combination of unknown environmental and genetic factors. However, recent studies have linked some cases of early-onset Parkinson's (a rarer form of the disease that strikes patients under the age of
10 fifty) to specific genes shared by sufferers. No such link has been found in patients over fifty.

9. It can be reasonably inferred from the discussion of the causes of Parkinson's disease that

(A) the factors that cause Parkinson's disease in patients over fifty are only environmental
(B) the word "degenerative" refers to a disease that becomes less severe over time
(C) early-onset Parkinson's patients are exposed to the same environmental factors as patients over fifty
(D) the cure for Parkinson's disease will eventually be found through genetic research
(E) research has been done on the causes of early-onset Parkinson's

How to Crack It

We have an Inference question here, so check to see if each answer choice is stated in the passage. Remember, POE is your best friend! It tells you that it is safe to get rid of (A), because the phrase *only environmental* is too extreme to be a correct answer for this passage. Choice (D) predicts the future, which is never a good idea—who says that a cure *will* be found? What if the planet gets hit by a comet first? Choice (B) is contradicted by the passage, which says that Parkinson's "becomes more severe over time," and (C) is not supported by the passage. But (E), on the other hand, must be true if recent studies have made discoveries about early-onset Parkinson's, as the passage indicates, and *must be true* is what we want on Inference questions. Choice (E) it is!

Purpose

So far, we have looked at questions that ask what the passage says. Purpose questions are different: They ask why the author or passage does something. These questions often use phrases such as

> The author mentions _____ in order to . . .

> The reference to _____ primarily serves to . . .

> The primary purpose of the passage is to . . .

When you see Purpose questions, ask: Why did the author write this?

Parkinson's disease is an incurable, progressive, degenerative brain disease that affects the way nerves control muscles. Since the disease has no cure, it becomes more severe over time and causes the gradual deterioration of cells in the brain. Generally, Parkinson's disease is thought to be caused by a combination of unknown environmental and genetic factors. However, recent studies have linked some cases of early-onset Parkinson's (a rarer form of the disease that strikes patients under the age of fifty) to specific genes shared by sufferers. No such link has been found in patients over fifty.

Line
5

10

10. The author mentions "recent studies" in line 7 in order to

 (A) explain a possible difference of one form of a disease
 (B) suggest that environmental factors are irrelevant
 (C) highlight an error in common scientific wisdom
 (D) connect two divergent theories on what factors cause a disease
 (E) strengthen a controversial argument

How to Crack It

This passage tells us that some ideas about Parkinson's may not apply to a particular form of the disease. As we read about ten lines around line 7, we will need to find out why the author discussed "recent studies." We will not guess, though—we will let the author tell us. Thankfully, we have a pretty good tool for finding the right part of the text. Remember when we talked about trigger words in the Sentence Completions section? Well, they are equally useful in the passage reading sections. Notice the trigger word *however* in the beginning of the phrase *however, recent studies have linked...*. That is just the thing we are interested in and it is telling us that there is a change in direction, so the new studies must tell us about an exception or a difference. We can get rid of (B), (C), and (E) on this basis. Now compare choices (A) and (D): What is different? Choice (D) mentions connecting the different things, while (A) does not. Was there any mention of a connection between the two? No. So, (D) is out and the answer is (A).

Notice also that the use of the word *irrelevant* in choice (B) is too strong and the word *common* in choice (C) is not supported by the passage. Even if you cannot figure out the magic bullet to answer the question every time, stay on the lookout for ways to get rid of answers. POE is king in the Critical Reading section.

Do not POE if You Do not Know
Never eliminate a word you do not know. It is better to keep a word that you cannot define than it is to get rid of an answer that just might be correct!

Tone

Tone questions typically ask the following:

> In the passage as a whole, the author's tone is best described as . . .

> The author's attitude in the first paragraph is best characterized as . . .

Before you look at the answer choices, decide if the tone is positive, negative, or neutral. When going through the answers, stay away from extremes.

Adopting a completely computerized voting system is unfeasible. If ballots are recorded only in a machine's memory with no physical proof, a recount becomes
Line impossible. Vigilant election officials may ensure integrity
5 and security at the polls, yet errors accidental or malicious could be introduced into software long before Election Day. If a voter chooses "X" but the machine records "Y," there is no way to recover the intended vote. If computers are used in voting, there should also be a paper ballot that permits
10 voters to verify their choices. Advances in technology are beneficial and should be integrated into the voting process to improve accessibility and ease of ballot casting, but we should not reject paper ballots entirely.

33. The author's tone in lines 1-4 ("Adopting . . . impossible") is best described as

(A) malevolent
(B) resolute
(C) objective
(D) euphoric
(E) optimistic

How to Crack It

The gist of the passage is that voting should not be done solely using a computerized method. This is a Tone question that asks about a specific part of the passage. Going back and reading the lines referred to in the question shows that the author is taking a very firm position, stating that a *computerized voting system is unfeasible* and a recount is *impossible*. We have already discussed extreme language, so you can see that the author's use of *impossible* shows a very strong position indeed. Speaking of extreme, check out (A)! The author has a strong opinion, but there is definitely no evidence that the author is "wishing evil or harm to others," which is what *malevolent* means. Hold on to (B); *resolute* means "firmly resolved; set in purpose or opinion," which matches "very firm position." Get rid of (C); while the last sentence of the passage is somewhat objective, the part of the passage the question asks about does not show two sides of the issue. (D) and (E) are both pretty positive, and there is definitely no support for that tone in the passage. (D) in particular goes too far. The correct answer is (B).

POE Extreme Emotions
PSAT authors usually avoid extremes. They may have strong opinions, but they rarely go off the deep end.

Primary Purpose

Primary Purpose questions, and their less common cousins, Main Point questions, typically look like this.

The author of the passage primarily argues that . . .

The main idea of the passage is . . .

With these questions, do not get caught up in the details of the passage. Focus on the overall message.

I adore artichokes. I'll eat them steamed, boiled, or
fried and be in gustatory heaven. My sister, however,
becomes nauseated at the very smell of artichokes.

Line Obviously, two people can have divergent responses to the
5   same food, and the same is true of people's responses to
pain. In a scientific study, a hot object was applied to the
skin of two volunteers. At the exact same temperature, the
volunteers not only gave vastly different ratings for the
pain, but an MRI* showed differing responses within the
10 brain of each person. It may be scientifically correct when
someone says your pain is all in your mind, but it doesn't
make it hurt any less.

* Magnetic Resonance Imaging. A medical technique used to visualize internal
parts of the body.

12.   The author's primary purpose in writing the passage
is to demonstate that

(A) volunteers in scientific studies sometimes
exaggerate responses to an experimental
stimulus

(B) many of the people in the author's family have
intense feelings about particular foods

(C) men have a very different reaction than women
do to the exact same stimulus

(D) brain imagery shows that a particular stimulus
does not affect all people in the same way

(E) people feel pain to a greater degree when it is
measured by medical or scientific devices

The Devil is in the Details

On Primary Purpose
questions, answers that
deal with only one part
of the passage are
usually wrong.

How to Crack It

On a Primary Purpose question, when you read the passage, ask yourself: Why is
the author writing this? This passage generally is about how two people can respond
differently to the same thing (such as food or pain), and that the difference can be
measured scientifically. Choice (A) is incorrect. There is no evidence that the
volunteers *sometimes exaggerate responses*. The passage seems to support the opposite, that what is not very painful to one person really is more painful to another.
Get rid of (A). Choice (B) is about a very specific part of the passage used to set
up the idea of different responses to the same thing. There is no evidence for *many
of the people in the author's family*. We are given only the examples of the author
and the author's sister. Also, the passage is about more than just food. Where is
the pain? Cross off (B). Choice (C) can be tempting. The purpose of the passage
is certainly to show that people have different reactions to the same thing, but (C)
goes beyond what the passage is saying by stating that men and women specifically
respond differently based on gender. There is no evidence in the passage for this,
so eliminate (C). Be careful! Choice (D) may seem extreme because of the phrase
all people in the same way, but the answer says *not all*. Also, the answer fairly states
the author's purpose. Hold on to (D) and check out (E). Choice (E) is not supported. Nothing in the passage states that the pain was increased because of the
measurements collected. The passage stated that one person felt more pain from
the exact same thing than another person did. The correct answer is (D).

LONG PASSAGES—WHAT TO EXPECT

Critical Reading long passages are generally from forty to 100 lines, with six to twelve questions for each passage. The questions will be numbered 13–24 on Section 1 and 34–48 in Section 3. Remember, passage-based reading questions are not arranged in a set order of difficulty, so it will be up to you to identify which questions will be easiest for you to do. Answering Long Reading questions is very similar to answering Short Reading questions. Still, dealing with the passage presents its own complications.

Here are some concepts that can help you.

The Blurb

The blurb is short and often provides helpful context. Do not skip it!

Working the Passage

If you read the passage, try to get through it in two minutes or less. Do not get stuck on details. You just want to get the general idea and a mental map of where things are. The goal is to get to the questions as soon as you can.

Line References and the Window

Line reference questions direct you to a specific place in the passage.

> **15.** The author refers to the "journey of the soul" (line 35) in order to

Read roughly five lines before and five lines after the line reference, so that you understand the general context. Most questions can be answered within this "window."

Chronology and Lead Words

Not all questions have line references.

> **16.** The discussion of the hedgehog's reincarnation indicates that

Where will you look to find the answer? What should you look for?

On the PSAT the questions follow the chronology of the passage. From the questions above, you know that the answer to question 16 will come after line 35 of the passage. If question 17 has a line reference too—for example, line 52—then you know that the answer to question 16 will fall between line 35 and 52.

A lead word is an easily spotted phrase from the question, such as *hedgehog's reincarnation*. To find the answer to question 16, just scan the passage around lines 35–52 to find out what you need to know about the hedgehog's reincarnation.

Remember the Method

1. **Read the blurb.**
2. **Work the passage.** Do not get stuck on details; just get the general idea or skip it!
3. **Choose a question and paraphrase it.** Use your own words for what the question is asking.
4. **Go back to the passage and find the answer.** Like an open-book test, the answer is there for you. Go find it!
5. **Answer the question.** Before you select an answer, answer the question yourself.
6. **POE.** Use your pencil to cross out answers that do not fit with the answer you came up with.

Personal Order of Difficulty

Long Reading questions have no set order of difficulty, so you have to make your own order. In general, you should

- mostly answer questions in order.
- skip hard or confusing questions initially—you can come back to them if you have time.
- save Primary Purpose questions for last.

TRY IT YOURSELF

Now that you know the steps for Critical Reading passages, it is time to try them out. Remember to look back to The Method if you need a reminder of how to do something!

Questions 39-48 are based on the following passage.

The following passage comes from a nineteenth-century British novel, The Picture of Dorian Gray, *about the influence of one member of the idle rich upon another. In the opening paragraph, Dorian Gray is speaking to Lord Henry Wotton about a portrait that's recently been painted of himself by another friend, Basil Hallward.*

"Dear Basil! I have not laid eyes on him for a week. It is rather horrid of me, as he has sent me my portrait in the most wonderful frame, specially designed by himself, and, though
Line
5 I am a little jealous of the picture for being a whole month younger than I am, I must admit that I delight in it. Perhaps you had better write to him. I don't want to see him alone. He says things that annoy me. He gives me good advice."

Lord Henry smiled. "People are very fond of giving away what they need most themselves. It is what I call the depth of
10 generosity."

"Oh, Basil is the best of fellows, but he seems to me to be just a bit of a Philistine. Since I have known you, Harry, I have discovered that."

"Basil, my dear boy, puts everything that is charming in
15 him into his work. The consequence is that he has nothing left for life but his prejudices, his principles, and his common sense. The only artists I have ever known who are personally delightful are bad artists. Good artists exist simply in what they make, and consequently are perfectly uninteresting
20 in what they are. A great poet, a really great poet, is the most unpoetical of all creatures. But inferior poets are absolutely fascinating. The worse their rhymes are, the more

picturesque they look. The mere fact of having published a
book of second-rate sonnets makes a man quite irresistible.
He lives the poetry that he cannot write. The others write the
poetry that they dare not realize."

"I wonder is that really so, Harry?" said Dorian Gray,
putting some perfume on his handkerchief out of a large,
gold-topped bottle that stood on the table. "It must be, if you
say it. And now I am off. Imogen is waiting for me. Don't
forget about tomorrow. Good-bye."

As he left the room, Lord Henry's heavy eyelids drooped,
and he began to think. Certainly few people had ever
interested him so much as Dorian Gray, and yet the lad's mad
adoration of some one else caused him not the slightest pang
of annoyance or jealousy. He was pleased by it. It made him a
more interesting study. He had been always enthralled by the
methods of natural science, but the ordinary subject-matter
of that science had seemed to him trivial and of no import.
And so he had begun by vivisecting himself, as he had ended
by vivisecting others. Human life—that appeared to him
the one thing worth investigating. Compared to it there was
nothing else of any value. It was true that as one watched life
in its curious crucible of pain and pleasure, one could not
wear over one's face a mask of glass, nor keep the sulphurous
fumes from troubling the brain and making the imagination
turbid with monstrous fancies and misshapen dreams. There
were poisons so subtle that to know their properties one
had to sicken of them. There were maladies so strange that
one had to pass through them if one sought to understand
their nature. And, yet, what a great reward one received!
How wonderful the whole world became to one! To note the
curious hard logic of passion, and the emotional coloured life
of the intellect—to observe where they met, and where they
separated, at what point they were in unison, and at what
point they were at discord—there was a delight in that! What
matter what the cost was? One could never pay too high a
price for any sensation.

39. Dorian's statement about Basil in lines 6-7 ("I don't . . .
advice.") implies that Dorian

(A) wishes to avoid Basil
(B) believes that Basil's advice does not apply to
      him
(C) is jealous of Basil's skill as a painter
(D) would prefer not to be reminded of his faults
(E) does not wish to be without Sir Harry

How to Crack It

This looks like a pretty straightforward Inference question. First, we will paraphrase it: What is it asking? What does Dorian's statement tell us about him? This is kind of open-ended; we do not know exactly what we are looking for, so we will go to the passage and, as we read, pay attention to the things we know for sure about Dorian based on what he has said and what he may be responding to in the context.

Remember, we want to read about five lines above and below the indicated lines, so we should start at the beginning of the passage and continue through the next couple of exchanges of dialogue. In fact, the statement in quotation marks can pretty much stand alone in this case. In the dialogue after the quote, Lord Henry does not address Dorian's statement in a way that tells us anything about Dorian, so there is not much to be found there. In the statements themselves, Dorian says something a little surprising, though. Basil says things *that annoy him,* but what sort of things are these? Not advice of just any kind, but *good advice.* So Dorian is annoyed by good advice.

Now we can take a look at the answer choices. On our first pass through the answers, remember, we want to get rid of the answers that are clearly wrong. Then we will slow down and be a bit more careful once we are down to two. Also, because this is an Inference the key part of the process is the one we are engaged in now— we need to use POE to eliminate answers that are not supported by the passage. To think of it another way, we need to cross out answers that do not have to be true. (A) says Dorian wishes to avoid Basil. Does this have to be true? Not really. In fact, this answer is a bit deceptive: Dorian says he *doesn't want to see him alone.* (B) also does not have any support in the passage. (C) is another deceptive answer; Dorian says he is jealous of the painting, not of Basil. (D) looks pretty good, right? We decided that Dorian did not like good advice. (E) has nothing to do with anything we read. So the answer is (D). There was no close second, so we did not need to slow down and agonize over the choice on this question.

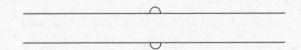

40. The statement in lines 8-10 ("People are . . . generosity.") implies that Sir Henry believes

(A) that Basil is uncommonly generous
(B) that Dorian should take Basil's advice
(C) that Basil would benefit from some good advice
(D) that giving advice is a foolish endeavor
(E) one is not constrained from giving advice to others even if one needs it oneself

How to Crack It

Here we must figure out what Lord Henry believes about something. This is another Inference question, so we want to pay attention to the evidence the passage gives us and try to decide for ourselves ahead of time, if we can. Although we read this part of the passage when we did number 39, we should read about five lines above and below again because now we are trying to answer a different question and we need to look specifically for that answer. If you lost a sock and a favorite pen somewhere in your house and you searched for and found the sock in a corner of the living room, you might have to search that same area again when you started looking for the pen, because the pen is different than what you were searching for before.

As we read, we can ask ourselves things about what we are reading, such as: Who or what is Lord Henry talking about? He is talking about Basil. In fact, the whole subject of discussion here is Basil, so it is a good bet that this will be what the belief is about. What does he *say or imply* about Basil? In response to Dorian's observation about advice, Lord Henry says that *people are very fond of giving away what they are most in need of.* What people? He must mean Basil. This implies that Basil could use some of what he is giving away, which is *good advice.*

Now take a look at the answers. Choice (A) is deceptive; the reference to generosity is there to tempt us. (B) is out because Lord Henry's belief appears to be about Basil, not Dorian. (C) looks pretty close to what we said. (D) is not supported, but might look tempting because Lord Henry's tone implies skepticism toward something, though we do not really know what he thinks of advice. Choice (E) seems like it could be relevant because it is talking about giving advice, but it does not specify Basil giving the advice. So the answer is (C).

---

41. Sir Henry's observation in lines 20-26 ("A great . . . realize.") depends most on the distinction between

    (A) the temporary and the permanent
    (B) subjective reflections and observations of others
    (C) great poetry and the poet's writing ability
    (D) one's social persona and the character of one's work
    (E) relevant and irrelevant considerations

**Remember to Read
What You Need
to Answer the Question**
This is usually about five
lines above and below
the lines they send you
to, but if it still does not
seem like you have much
information relevant to
answering the question,
then you probably have
not read enough.

How to Crack It

This question should strike you as being a bit harder than some of the others we have seen. The question of what distinction something depends on is pretty abstract. We will have to paraphrase this using smaller bites rather than just one big gulp. First of all, what observation did Sir Henry make? We must characterize or describe what the main idea of this part of the passage is. Then we will need to think about what sorts of things he is comparing. As you can see, reading just the lines in question is definitely not going to be enough context.

To get at what Lord Henry is really talking about we are probably going to need to read the whole paragraph or so. As we read we should keep in mind what we are looking for, which, as we decided above, is the distinction Lord Henry draws. This sort of information is often stated directly somewhere in the vicinity of the lines we are interested in, just not necessarily in the lines the question directs us to. This is why reading enough context is so important at this point.

What is Lord Henry trying to convince us of in this paragraph? The information is in the first few sentences of the paragraph, and it says that Basil puts all that is good about himself into his work, so there is nothing left for his personality. Then Sir Henry goes further by saying this is true of poets in general, that *the great ones are unpoetical,* whatever that means, while *the inferior ones are fascinating.* So the distinction is between work and personality.

Now we can take a look at the answers. Choice (A) is totally irrelevant. Choice (B) seems to mean something, but we might not be sure what, so keep it for now. Choice (C) looks like it might be on target, as it is talking about poetry and poetic abilities. Choice (D) talks about personality and work, which was what we decided was relevant to the answer in our analysis above. Choice (E) is not related to anything we read in the passage, though it might look tempting, because how could relevant things not be relevant to some distinction?

We have not managed to get all the way to the answer, so now we are going to need to slow down and try to eliminate some of the answer choices we have left. Choice (B) looks pretty confusing, so let's leave it for now. When an answer is weird or unintelligible or uses garbled language, leave it alone for the time being. If there is nothing else left, we will have to choose it; otherwise, we will try to find a better answer. We are going to take a close look at choices (C) and (D). If possible, we want to compare them and only pay attention to the parts that are different. The two have hardly anything in common, so we will have to focus instead on trying to find something wrong with each of the two remaining answers. We already said choice (C) was relevant, so we should take it apart and see if we can find a flaw. The question is about making a distinction, so every answer has two main parts; we will look at one side at a time. The first part says *great poetry.* That was definitely something that was being compared to something else, so it is probably okay. The right side says *the poet's writing ability.* Was that something that was under comparison in this paragraph? Take a look back at the paragraph. There are things that are kind of like that in there, but not about how ability is different from poetry, so (C) is out. Notice, also, that this means that choice (C) does not answer the question. Choice (D) matched our expectation of what we were looking for, so we will give it a quick check just because we still have that weird answer choice (B) lingering in the background. The first part of the answer talks about *one's social persona,* which means someone's outward personality in society, so that looks pretty good. The second part says *the character of one's work,* which seems to mean what kind of work someone does, and that is what Lord Henry contrasts with personality, so this answer is both supported by the text and answers the question. We will ignore the confusing answer (B) and pick choice (D).

This was a tough one. Take a closer look at what made it tough and remind yourself of what to look for when you see questions like these on the test. We would definitely want to leave this question for later and only do it if our pacing goals required us to attempt nearly all of the questions in the section. Notice also that we did not abandon POE when we were down to two and just pick something on a hunch. If we were really stuck we would have, but the possibility of getting stuck on a hard question and having to guess is part of the reason we would save this one for last or choose to skip it altogether.

---

42. Dorian Gray's attitude toward Lord Henry can best be described as one of

    (A) concealed distrust
    (B) ironic irreverence
    (C) sincere respect
    (D) morbid fearfulness
    (E) paralyzing awe

How to Crack It

Questions about tone often have an extreme answer choice or two, and this one is no exception. There are a couple of answers we could get rid of almost without reading the passage. We are not going to do that if we can attempt the question, of course—and this question does not look too bad—but if we were short on time and had run out of easier questions, we could get rid of (D) and (E) because they are simply over the top. They use language like *morbid,* which means dying, and *paralyzing,* which would mean that Dorian is frozen like a deer caught in headlights. We would need some real evidence in the passage to justify something that extreme, but we are not going to find it.

To approach the question we need to look for something Dorian says or does that shows us how he feels about Lord Henry. In line 12 he suggests that Basil is a *Philistine* compared to Lord Henry. Maybe we do not know what this means exactly, but it sounds bad, and in the surrounding lines Lord Henry and Dorian were criticizing Basil. In lines 29–30, Dorian acknowledges that *if you say something it must be true,* so it looks like he obviously has a positive view of Lord Henry. We can get rid of choices (A) and (B) because they do not match, and we are left with (C), so we should choose it.

POE Tone Questions
Before you look at the answer choices, decide if the tone is positive, negative, or neutral. When going through the answers, stay away from extremes unless the text is extreme.

---

43. The fact that Lord Henry's "eyelids drooped" (line 32) indicates that

(A) he has grown tired due to the extensive conversation
(B) his attitude has become thoughtful
(C) he would like to join Dorian at the theater
(D) he is irritated that Dorian has become involved with an actress
(E) he is interested in what will occur when he and Dorian meet with Basil again

How to Crack It

Why did Lord Henry's *eyelids droop*; what is the author trying to tell us about Lord Henry by telling us about this gesture? (Remember: Everything in the passage is there for a reason.) It is right there in the same sentence, *he began to think*. Checking out some more context we find Lord Henry doing a lot more thinking. Now we can look at the answers. (A) suggests he has grown tired, but we really have no evidence for this; this answer is there to trap people who do not go back and read the appropriate part of the passage. (B) looks like a match. There is no support for answers (C), (D), or (E), so get rid of them. (B) is the only answer left, so we can select it and move on.

Here is a more complex question.

44. Lord Henry's reaction to Dorian's "mad adoration" (lines 34-35) implies that he views his relationship to Dorian as most akin to that of

(A) an audience member to an actor in a play
(B) a scientist to a laboratory animal
(C) a detective to a criminal at large
(D) an attorney to his client
(E) a storyteller to the romantic hero

Read What You Need
Usually five lines before and after a line reference is enough to answer the question. If not, read more! This is especially true of fiction passages.

How to Crack It

This question should set off some alarm bells. It is asking us to compare something in the passage to some new information that might seem to have very little to do with the subject matter of the passage. A glance at the answer choices shows that we are being asked about some kind of analogy. We do not want to focus on the answers, but a glance can give us some useful information when we are confronted with a weird question or one in which we are unsure of what the question is asking. The first thing we want to know here is, what *is* Lord

Henry's reaction to Dorian's "mad adoration"? Then we will need to characterize it in the abstract, that is, what *sort* of reaction is it? This way we can match it to the abstractness of the answers. In the passage we find that Lord Henry is untroubled by Dorian's fling, and for some reason likes that he does not mind. Then he goes on to talk about science and psychology and why people are interesting to study and a bunch of other tough language that has something to do with science. Henry's thoughts on science and studying things are key. What things? *Human life.* Choices (C) and (D) have nothing to do with this, so we can get rid of them. (A) is also unsupported, but if you happen to have read the book *The Picture of Dorian Gray*, by Oscar Wilde, you might remember that his crush is an actress. Outside information is not necessary, and besides, Lord Henry is not a passive observer, as choice (A) implies. Choice (E) might look tempting because of the deceptive reference to Dorian's adoration of someone else, but that is a trick. Choice (B) matches what we have been looking for, so choose it.

---

45. To Lord Henry, "the mask of glass" and the "sulphurous fumes" most nearly represent

    (A) a window to look through and a veil that obscures
    (B) a defense and a danger
    (C) objects to be studied
    (D) tools of the scientific trade
    (E) things that trouble the mind

How to Crack It

This question might be on the complicated side because it asks us what something *represents*, not merely what it *means*, as in a Vocab-in-Context question. We probably do not want to do this one on the first pass through the questions, but we might need to pick it up on the second pass, depending on how many questions we must answer to reach our pacing goals. As we read, we should consider what sort of things the objects mentioned are and what they are intended for. Once we have figured this out, we may have enough information to answer the question. The part of the passage that talks about this is pretty tough, as it turns out. There is some kind of extended metaphor being used and these objects are part of it. If this part of the passage is totally bewildering, we might want to bail at this point, especially if there are other easier questions to do. If we decide to attempt this one we can cross out (A), (D), and (E), because they are all too literal for a question about a part of the passage that is intensively figurative. (C) is deceptive, because we are not interested here in the things to be studied, but rather the reaction of the person doing the studying. (B) is supported because the mask of glass refers to something to protect someone's face and the sulphurous fumes, since they trouble the mind, are a danger, so the answer is (B).

Chronology and Lead Words
Remember, on the PSAT the questions follow the chronology of the passage. If there is no line reference for a question, look at the questions before and after it to find a "window" in which you can scan for lead words from the question.

---

46. The quote in lines 47-49 ("There were poisons . . . them.") most likely indicates an attempt to convey which of the following beliefs held by Lord Henry?

(A) the study of life can be sickening and therefore not worth it

(B) there are things about man that are disturbing to consider and these qualities make him repellent

(C) the understanding of some complex subjects may require one's immersion in the subject

(D) some toxic chemicals have been found to be useful for study in the natural sciences

(E) there are dangers in the study of any subject, but those that occur in the natural sciences are not worth the risk

How to Crack It

Here, we need to figure out what Lord Henry believes, based on something stated in the passage, so we will need to think about what we know from the passage and be sure to read enough context. The line in question refers to certain poisons as being subtle, but the passage is not really about poisons, so there is a metaphor in use here. (In fact, the language is pretty tough in this part of the passage, so this is another question we should be saving for later, during our second pass through the questions.) How did this come up in the first place? In the lines before, Lord Henry is thinking about the fact that people are the only interesting things to study when he says, in lines 41–42, *human life—that appeared to him the one thing worth investigating.* In fact, this is the main point of the paragraph, and we have come back to it a few times to answer our questions about what Lord Henry is thinking or why he brings up something else in the paragraph. But how is this related to the idea of poison and getting sick? This is not necessarily easy to figure out, but notice in the sentence before that he says that *as one watched life…one could not wear over one's face a mask of glass.* What would a mask do? It would protect. In the line we are asked about, he says that *to know the poisons… one had to sicken of them.* So in general he seems to be saying that we cannot be protected and we have to take the poison. He is talking about studying people, after all, so he must be saying that if you are going to study people, you are going to have to get involved and it might hurt. Whew! That was rough.

Let's check out the answers. Choice (A) looks pretty poor, since Lord Henry clearly says at the end of the paragraph that any price is worth paying. Choice (B) is not supported, as he does not make any judgments about people in this section of the text. Choice (C) looks like it might be relevant, but it is not clear how, so keep it for now. Choice (D) is far too literal for something this figurative. Choice (E) might look tempting if you had not read carefully, but this part of the passage was not about the natural sciences; it was about the study of man, so get rid of this deceptive answer and pick (C). Fortunately, we did not have to figure out exactly what it meant, but if we had, we would see that it is saying just what Lord Henry was getting at, that sometimes you cannot stay apart from what you study.

47. The "great reward" referred to in line 51 is most likely

(A) good sensations

(B) a curious logic of the passions

(C) the knowledge of man's troubled nature

(D) a life of the imagination untroubled by monstrous dreams

(E) the keen understanding of human nature

How to Crack It

The question is asking us *What is the great reward?* In reading that part of the passage we find a good deal of evidence in subsequent sentences like *to note* the curious hard logic of passion and *to observe* where they met and that *one can never pay too high a price for any sensation.* So the reward has something to do with *noting* and *observing* and *sensation.* Watch out for choice (A); it is a bit obvious and it does not provide the full picture. Choice (B) should look suspicious because it just repeats an exact phrase from the passage; this is deceptive and almost certain to be wrong. (C) looks all right, as it refers to knowledge, which is kind of what we are looking for. (D) is another deceptive answer that quotes the text, so we can eliminate that. (E) also looks like what we were looking for, so we should keep that as well. The two answers we have left, (C) and (E), are pretty similar, so we can compare them. How are they different? (C) refers to man's nature as *troubled*, but is otherwise nearly the same as (E), while (E) says a *keen understanding.* Does Lord Henry think of man's nature as troubled? He might. He does refer to poisons, maladies, and high prices to be paid, but is this the whole story? Let's leave it for the moment and take a look at choice (E). Certainly an understanding of human nature is supported and the same as the majority of choice (C), but what about a *keen* understanding? Going back to the portion of the passage that we read to get an answer of our own, we find that it spends several sentences describing the nature of the understanding that would be gained, as in *to observe where they met, and where they separated, at what point they were in unison, and at what point they were in discord,* so the keen understanding seems to be pretty well supported. It might look like we are stuck now, but we have one more tool to try. Remember, the answer choice has to answer the question being asked. Does choice (C) do that? Not really, because the knowledge of man's troubles would only be half of the reward of understanding, whereas some of the paragraph clearly indicates that his reward would be an understanding of good *and* bad things, as, for example, *the emotional coloured life of the intellect.* Of course, the passage also mentions that when one has the reward, *how wonderful the whole world became,* which does not match the tone of choice (C) either. Therefore, our best answer is choice (E).

48. In line 53, "curious" most nearly means

    (A) paradoxical
    (B) interesting
    (C) thoughtful
    (D) excessive
    (E) overly emotional

How to Crack It

This is a Vocab-in-Context question, and we will approach it the same way as a Sentence Completion. We will go to the passage, cross out the word "curious," and use the evidence in that sentence (and the surrounding sentences, if necessary) to fill in a word of our own. Then we will use POE to get rid of answers that do not match our word and, hopefully, pick the one remaining answer. Remember, when the word is an "easy" word, like curious, watch out for answers that are too obvious. What is too obvious? A lot of the time, Joe Bloggs does not bother to go back to the passage for his answers, so what would he pick if he just wanted something that means curious? Choices (B) and (C) look pretty suspicious now, right? We are not going to cross them out until we attempt the question, though.

When we go back to the passage and cross out *curious*, we find it followed by the phrase *the hard logic of passion*. What do logic and passion have to do with each other? Isn't this a bit of a contradiction? So maybe we should use a word like *contradictory* or *paradoxical*. Look! Paradoxical is one of our answer choices. Check the other answers quickly, and if nothing else works, we will choose (A). We had already decided to be wary of options (B) and (C), but *interesting* and *thoughtful* do not mean *contradictory*, so they are out. Neither *excessive* nor *overly emotional* means *contradictory* either, so we can get rid of them too. So (A) is the answer.

Notice, if we did not know what paradoxical meant, we could still get the answer because we can POE our way there. Remember, if you do not know a word or understand an answer choice, you should keep it for the time being; it might be the right answer.

BEYOND THE BASICS

In addition to the techniques we have discussed thus far, we have a few final points to round out our repertoire.

Literary Terms

There may be one or two questions on the test that ask about the literary devices the author uses to make a point. These are not anything to be afraid of; they are usually relatively simple once you know the terminology, but they can be skipped if you are very uncomfortable with this question type. ETS tends to stick to the basics, so we will do some review:

- A **simile** is a comparison using "like" or "as." *The smoke curled out of the chimney like a snake being charmed out of its basket.*
- A **metaphor** is a figure of speech that is technically false but that suggests a likeness or analogy. When Romeo says that *Juliet is the sun*, he doesn't mean that she is literally a big ball of hydrogen gas 93 million miles away; he means that she *resembles* the sun in that she is radiant and makes him feel warm all over.
- An **extended metaphor** occurs when a metaphor is, you guessed it, extended to cover several comparisons. *From the top of the building, the people below were ants, scurrying to and fro with their parcels, stopping briefly to touch antennae in greeting, and disappearing back into their tunnels to continue their work.*
- **Personification** is the treatment of something inanimate as if it were alive. *The sun smiles down upon the trees and flowers.*
- **Hyperbole** is deliberate exaggeration. *I beat your PSAT score by about a trillion points.*
- **Verbal irony** occurs when there is a discrepancy between what someone says and what the situation indicates the speaker meant. *You dropped your car keys into the sewer? Smooth move!* Sarcasm is probably the most common type of verbal irony: It is verbal irony used to hurt someone's feelings.
- **Situational irony** occurs when people plan for events to turn out one way, but they turn out another. Contrary to the old Alanis Morissette song, rain on your wedding day is not ironic. It is a downer, but there is no reason not to expect it. On the other hand, moving your wedding from Seattle to Phoenix to avoid the chance of rain, and then having a downpour in Phoenix on your wedding day while it is clear and sunny in Seattle—*that is* ironic.
- A **paradox** is a statement that looks like a contradiction, yet is actually true in a sense. *Less is more.*

Dual Passages

You will probably see two dual passages, which are passages that relate to each other somehow with questions that cover both of them. Dual passages can be short or long passages (usually one set of each), and there will typically be some differences in how the authors view the topic. Dual passages can have questions that ask about only one passage in addition to questions that ask about both passages; the questions that ask about both passages are usually more difficult, so the best strategy is:

1. Work Passage 1 and the questions that ask about only Passage 1.
2. Work Passage 2 and the questions that ask about only Passage 2.
3. Work the questions that ask about both passages.

It is especially important in dealing with step 3 to arrive at your own answers and write them down; just like two-blank Sentence Completions, these can be tricky if you try to deal with too much information at once. Below is an example of a typical dual passage and some questions that you might see on the PSAT.

Questions 9-12 are based on the following passages.

Passage 1

Dreams of sending a manned mission to Mars are unlikely to come to fruition without the implementation of what NASA terms In Situ Resource Utilization (ISRU)
Line strategies: the use of Martian resources to support the
5   expedition. Scientists believe that the Martian landscape could yield the rocket fuel, energy, water, and oxygen necessary for a sustained human presence on the Red Planet. Without the use of ISRUs, the cost of transporting fuel, materials, and vital supplies from Earth would be prohibitive,
10 not to mention potentially dangerous. Despite the eagerness of scientists to explore Mars, no one would advocate sending explorers some forty million miles from Earth with no viable way of returning.

Passage 2

While sending a person to Mars would certainly represent
15 a triumph of human ingenuity and courage, the current state of technology makes such a mission unlikely in the near future. Some optimists argue that we can simply apply the lessons learned in sending people to the Moon to this more formidable situation. But there are forty million miles
20 separating Mars from Earth, a vast distance. As one scientist stated, "A distress message from the Moon would reach Earth in 1.8 seconds. But that same message would take almost 10 minutes to reach us from Mars. The time lag could be fatal." With so many pressing scientific issues here on Earth,
25 time and money should not be spent on a mission that would contribute more to human vanity than to scientific progress.

We will begin with question 9.

─────────────────○─────────────────

9. The author of Passage 1 argues that ISRUs

   (A) are prohibitively expensive
   (B) reduce dangers of spaceflight
   (C) can generate food and water
   (D) will solve certain problems
   (E) have not yet been built

How to Crack It

The author of Passage 1 explains that ISRUs would allow humans on Mars to generate a variety of resources that would be too expensive to bring to Mars. Choice (A) is wrong because the author does not say that ISRUs are too expensive; *transporting needed resources* would be too expensive. Choice (B) does not quite work because the author does not say that ISRUs reduce the dangers of spaceflight. Choice (C) is half right, which means all wrong—we are not told that ISRUs can generate food. There is no discussion of whether ISRUs have been built yet, so choice (E) is wrong. Choice (D) is the best answer.

─────────────────○─────────────────

Now we can try some questions about both passages.

─────────────────○─────────────────

10. The authors of both passages would most likely agree that

   (A) an unmanned mission to Mars should be undertaken
   (B) ISRUs are essential to certain manned space voyages
   (C) scientific issues on Earth require immediate attention
   (D) distress signals from the moon travel to Earth too slowly
   (E) the distance between Mars and Earth poses challenges

How to Crack It

For question 10, it is a good idea to deal with each author separately. We will start with the author of Passage 1. Author 1 did not discuss unmanned missions, so we can eliminate choice (A). Author 1 believes that ISRUs are necessary to a mission to Mars, so hold on to choice (B). Author 1 does not discuss scientific issues on Earth, so we can eliminate choice (C). Author 1 also does not discuss distress signals, so eliminate choice (D). Author 1 certainly agrees with choice (E): ISRUs are meant to address those challenges. So we have narrowed our answers down to choices (B) and (E). Now we will examine whether the author of Passage 2 would agree with either of those. Author 2 does not address ISRUs, so eliminate choice (B). Author 2 opposes manned travel to Mars because of certain challenges. Choice (E) is the best answer.

11. Compared to the author of Passage 1, the author of Passage 2 is more

   (A) foreboding
   (B) judgmental
   (C) ambivalent
   (D) optimistic
   (E) sympathetic

How to Crack It

Question 11, with its one-word answers, asks you to compare the attitudes of the two authors. The author of Passage 1 supports manned space travel to Mars with ISRUs. The author of Passage 2 opposes manned missions to Mars because of potentially fatal dangers. Choice (A), *foreboding*, is a good description of Author 2's attitude and is correct. It would be difficult to call Author 2 judgmental, as opposed to worried, so choice (B) does not work. Certainly the more positive choices in (D) and (E) don't work. Authors are rarely ambivalent in PSAT passages, and Author 2 is no exception.

POE is even more critical when down to two answer choices. Refer to page 90: Down to Two for further details.

12. The author of Passage 2 would most likely respond to the author of Passage 1's proposal to use ISRUs by

(A) agreeing that ISRUs could make a manned trip to Mars possible

(B) questioning whether ISRUs are sufficiently developed at this time

(C) arguing that ISRUs do not address key risks of a manned Mars mission

(D) insisting that manned space travel should never be attempted

(E) claiming that scientific issues on the Moon should be resolved first

How to Crack It

When asked what the author of one passage would say about the other passage, as in question 12, consider what the author *did* say on the topic referenced in the question. Here, although Author 2 does not explicitly discuss ISRUs, there is no question that the author is against manned space travel to Mars because of potentially fatal risks. So choice (A) is easy to eliminate as Author 2 does not support the use of ISRUs. Likewise, we do not know whether Author 2 believes ISRUs are developed enough or not, so eliminate choice (B). Choice (D) is too extreme; Author 2 opposes manned space travel to Mars, but not necessarily *all* manned space travel ever. Choice (E) is wrong because of the reference to the Moon—Author 2 is interested in scientific issues on *Earth*. Choice (C) is the best choice: Author 2 specifically mentions the travel time of distress signals as a key risk; ISRUs can do nothing to address that risk.

Down to Two

Last but certainly not least, one final word about POE: Just about all test takers get to a point, particularly on passage-based reading questions, at which they are going back and forth between two answers, trying to decide which is better. At this point, stop yourself from arguing FOR each answer choice ("I like this one because…") and start actively searching for a reason to eliminate one or the other ("This one doesn't sound right because…"). You can use the following steps in any order, together or separately, to help you get down to one answer choice.

- **Find the fatal flaw.** Four out of five answer choices have *something* in them that makes them wrong, whether it is a word that is too extreme, a small phrase that is not supported by the passage, or something that is outside the scope of the passage. Usually, you are tempted to pick that answer choice anyway because the rest of it is exactly what you think the correct answer looks like. But would you buy a pair of shoes in which one fits really well and the other doesn't fit at all? No! The same logic applies to Critical Reading answer choices—find the fatal flaw, and you can eliminate the whole answer choice.
- **Find the difference.** ETS will not put two identical answer choices on the PSAT. Either the answers will say different things, or they will say nearly the same thing in different ways; for example, one is phrased in a more extreme way than the other. Focus on the differences between the answers and you will have an easier time figuring out which one is better supported by the passage and which one has the flaw. Do not be afraid to go back to the passage and look for flaws: Is the information really there? Does it answer the question?

POE Criteria

Here is what to look for:

- Extreme wording
- Goes too far
- Recycles words from the passage
- Half right = all wrong
- Extreme or uncaring attitude

Drill 1

Answers can be found in Part III.

Questions 1-6 are based on the following passages.

Passage 1 is adapted from a 2008 essay. Passage 2, adapted from an 1857 novel, is about a self-proclaimed "herb doctor," who is actually a salesman of a sham medicine. The herb doctor has just sold his medicine to an old man, and is now trying to sell it to a hunter from Missouri.

Passage 1

A couple years ago, I was diagnosed with a minor joint inflammation in my right knee. It was nothing serious, although I wasn't able to hike for a while, but soon friends and family were telling me about all sorts of treatments. Some were variations on what my doctor had told me: bed rest, ice, wearing a knee brace. But many of the other treatments were so bizarre that I wondered how my friends could honestly believe them: standing on my head, putting magnets in my shoes, eating 20 figs a day. Anything that started with the words "this will definitely work" I ignored immediately, assuming it was definitely ridiculous.

Medicine is a science of uncertainties. We try things, and see if they tend to work. If they don't, we try something else. Even the treatments we are "sure" about don't work all the time. Aspirin helps headaches most of the time, but sometimes there's nothing we can do. That's why the cure-all is so tempting. It is hard to admit that, with all we are capable of, there are still things that mankind cannot fix or heal. Phony treatments fill that need; a bogus cure is a security blanket. In the nineteenth century, when the confidence man* roamed the US, there was no patent tonic too patently ridiculous to find a buyer. The best the patient of such medicines could hope for is to feel no worse. For most, however, the medicines were essentially poisons, and could cause damage far worse than the original ailment. What is most remarkable is that many of those duped and damaged by one potion would then seek to cure these new symptoms with the next cure-all that came along.

Passage 2

"Sir," the herb doctor said with unimpaired affability, producing one of his boxes, which was small, tin, and filled with whatever bits of grass and dirt had happened to be close by, "though your manner is refined your voice is rough; in short, you seem to have a sore throat. In the name of Nature, I present you with this box; my venerable friend here has a similar one; but to you, a free gift, sir."

"I tell you I want none of your boxes," said the hunter, snapping his rifle.

"Oh, take it! Do take it," chimed in the old man; "I wish he would give me one for nothing."

"You find it lonely, eh," said the hunter, turning around; "tricked yourself, you would have a companion."

"How can he find it lonely," returned the herb doctor, "or
desire a companion, when here I stand by him; I, even I, in
whom he has trust. As for the tricking, tell me, is it humane
to talk so to this poor old man? Granting that his dependence
on my medicine is vain, is it kind to deprive him of what, in
mere imagination, if nothing more, may help him last out his
disease? For you, if you have no faith, and, thanks to your
native health, can get along without it, fine; yet, how cruel
an argument to use, with this afflicted one here. Is it not for
all the world as if some brawny boxer, aglow in December,
should rush in and put out a hospital-fire, because, since he
feels no need of artificial heat, the shivering patients shall
have none? Put it to your conscience, sir, and you will admit,
that, whatever be the nature of this afflicted one's trust, you,
in opposing it, show either a confused head or a heart amiss.
Are you so pitiless?

* A conman, particularly common in the United States in the nineteenth-century,
who often traveled from town to town and sold fake medicines.

19. The reference to "a security blanket" (line 20) can be
best understood to mean that the "bogus cure"

(A) can be used to cover up symptoms
(B) is harmful to the person who takes it, but harmless
to others
(C) can be comforting even if it is not effective
(D) is used by doctors only when other methods have
failed
(E) can help children and adults alike

20. The "confidence man" (line 21) is closest to which of the
following in Passage 2?

(A) the old man
(B) the hunter
(C) the herb doctor
(D) the brawny boxer
(E) shivering patients

21. What do the "patent tonic" (line 21) and the "box"
(line 34) have in common?

(A) Both were actually toxic in small quantities.
(B) Both were advertised to cure an ailment.
(C) Both were based on earlier folk remedies.
(D) Both were given away for free to attract
customers.
(E) Both were rejected by the medical
establishment.

22. The herb doctor refers to the "brawny boxer" (line 52) in order to point out that

   (A) the hunter should buy the box of medicine
   (B) the medicine is useful to patients who are
        experiencing chills
   (C) athletes generally do not need medicine
   (D) the herb doctor knows that the medicine will not
        work
   (E) the hunter should not disparage the old man's
        belief in the medicine

23. The author's observations in Passage 1 compared with the herb doctor's observations in Passage 2 are

   (A) less joyous
   (B) less humorous
   (C) more deceptive
   (D) more realistic
   (E) more perplexed

24. Which of the following is an observation offered by the author of Passage 1 that is NOT exhibited by a character in Passage 2?

   (A) A medicine, even if it does not physically heal,
        can bring mental relief.
   (B) Medicines are sometimes based on plants found in
        nature.
   (C) Some people were willing to purchase medicines
        with no medical support.
   (D) Buyers, after purchasing a medicine, often feel
        they have been swindled.
   (E) Medicine is generally based on trial and error.

Summary

o Long Passages
  • Read the blurb
  • Work the passage
  • Choose a question and paraphrase it
  • Read what you need to answer the question
  • Answer the question
  • POE

o Short Passages
  • Read the passage for the general idea
  • Paraphrase the question
  • Read what you need to answer the question
  • Answer the question
  • POE

o Dual Passages
  • First, tackle questions about Passage 1 only
  • Next, do questions about Passage 2 only
  • Last, attempt questions about both passages

o Down to Two
  • Eliminate based on a careful reading of each answer to try to find the fatal flaw
  • Eliminate based on the differences between the remaining answers

o Literary Terms
  • Remember to study them, even if it is just to be familiar enough to skip them!

Chapter 7
Math Basics

One of the more peculiar aspects of the PSAT (and the same applies to its big brother, the SAT) is that ETS claims that the Math section tests only seventh- to ninth-grade math. While this may be technically true—you will see no trigonometry or calculus, only concepts that you have learned in algebra and geometry—what they do not tell you is that they will use these concepts in very sneaky ways. This chapter will help you lay the foundation to avoid the test writers' traps.

HOW TO CONQUER PSAT MATH

So what do you need to do? There are three important steps:

1. **Know the basic content.** Obviously you do need to know the basics of arithmetic, algebra, and geometry. We will cover what you need to know in this chapter.
2. **Learn some PSAT-specific problem-solving skills.** Since these basic concepts appear in ways you are probably not used to from math class, you need to prepare yourself with a set of test-specific problem-solving skills designed to help you solve PSAT Math problems. We will cover the most important ones in the next chapter.
3. **Have a sound overall testing strategy.** This means knowing the order of difficulty of questions, and having a plan to pace yourself to get the maximum number of points in the time allotted. Be sure to read carefully the material in Chapter 4, to make sure you are using the strategy that will get you the greatest number of points in the time you have.

ORDER OF DIFFICULTY

The Math sections on the PSAT are Sections 2 and 4. Section 2 contains twenty multiple-choice questions. Section 4 is divided into multiple-choice and grid-in question types. Note that the order of difficulty goes from easy to hard within each of these types. For instance, on Section 4, number 28, the last multiple-choice question will be hard, but number 29, the first grid-in question, will be easy. This means that if you are going to skip some problems in Section 4, it is likely that you will want to skip some of the questions numbered 27–28 and 36–38.

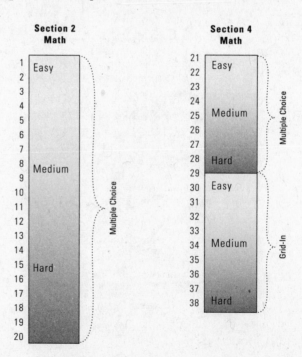

USING YOUR CALCULATOR

You are allowed to use a calculator on the PSAT, and you should definitely do so. You can use any graphing, scientific, or plain old four-function calculator, **provided that it does not have a keyboard**.

There are a few simple rules to remember when dealing with your calculator:

1. Use the calculator you are most comfortable with. You definitely do not want to be searching for the right button on test day. Ideally, you should be practicing with the same calculator you will use on test day.

2. Change your batteries the week before the test. If they run out during the test, there is nothing you can do about it.

3. Be sure to hit the "clear" or "on/off" button after each calculation to reset the calculator after an operation. A common mistake to make when using your calculator is to forget to clear your last result.

4. Your calculator is very good at calculating, but watch out for mis-keying information. (If you type the wrong numbers in, you will get the wrong result.) Check each number on the display as you key it in.

5. Remember that, while it is nice to have all those funky scientific functions (like sine, cosine, etc.), you will never need them on the PSAT. The most you will need is the basic operations of addition, subtraction, multiplication, and division; the ability to convert fractions to decimals and vice versa; and the ability to do square roots and exponents.

6. Finally, there is one really big, important rule for using your calculator:

> A calculator cannot think; it can only calculate.

What does this mean? It means that a calculator cannot think through a problem for you. You have to do the work of understanding and setting up the problem correctly to make sure you know what the right calculation will be to get the answer. Only then can you use the calculator to calculate the answer. A calculator cannot replace good problem-solving skills. It can only help make sure that you do basic calculations correctly.

Also, your calculator cannot help you set up a problem in the way pencil and paper can. You should always be sure to set up the problem in your test booklet—writing it down is still the best method—which will help you catch any errors you might make and allow you to pick up where you left off if you lose focus.

That does not mean you will not use your calculator, though—far from it. Once you have set up a math problem, move quickly to your calculator to chug your way through the arithmetic, and be careful to enter each number and operator correctly. Remember, using your calculator is already saving you time—don't rush and lose the advantage that it gives you.

Drill 1

DEFINITIONS

One of the reasons that good math students often do not get the credit they deserve on the PSAT is that they have forgotten one or more of these definitions—or they read too fast and skip over these "little" words. Be sure you know them cold and watch out for them!

Match the words with their definitions, and then come up with some examples. Answers can be found in Part III.

1. integers

2. positive numbers

3. negative numbers

4. even numbers

5. odd numbers

6. factors

7. multiples

8. prime numbers

9. distinct

a. numbers that a certain number can be divided by, leaving no remainder
Examples: _____

b. integers that cannot be divided evenly by 2
Examples: _____

c. numbers that have no fractional or decimal parts
Examples: _____

d. numbers that are greater than zero
Examples: _____

e. having a different value
Examples: _____

f. integers that can be divided by 2 evenly (with no remainder)
Examples: _____

g. numbers that are less than zero
Examples: _____

h. numbers that have exactly two distinct factors: themselves and 1
Examples: _____

i. numbers that can be divided by a certain number with no remainder
Examples: _____

10. digit

11. consecutive numbers

12. divisible

13. remainder

14. sum

15. product

16. difference

17. quotient

18. absolute value

j. a figure from 0 through 9 that is used as a placeholder
Examples: _____

k. the result of addition
Examples: _____

l. a whole number left over after division
Examples: _____

m. the result of subtraction
Examples: _____

n. can be divided with no remainder
Examples: _____

o. a number's distance from zero; always a positive value
Examples: _____

p. numbers in a row
Examples: _____

q. the result of division
Examples: _____

r. the result of multiplication
Examples: _____

Finding Factors

The easiest way to find the complete list of the factors of a number is to begin trying all the integers beginning with 1, and see which of the integers go into that number without remainders. For instance, we will find the factors of 36.

Negative Land

Think of integers as steps on a staircase leading up from the cellar (the negatives), through a doorway (zero), and above the ground (the positives). Five steps down (−5) is farther below ground than four steps down (−4) because you are one step farther away from the cellar door (0). Integers are like stairs because when climbing stairs, you cannot use a fraction of a step.

Factor List:
Does 1 go into 36? Yes, 1 times 36.
Does 2 go into 36? Yes, 2 times 18.
Does 3 go into 36? Yes, 3 times 12.
Does 4 go into 36? Yes, 4 times 9.
Does 5 go into 36? No.
Does 6 go into 36? Yes, 6 times 6.

Once you get to an integer that you have already seen in the factor list (in this case, 6) you know you are finished. So the factors of 36 are 1, 2, 3, 4, 6, 9, 12, 18, and 36.

We will try this once more. What are all the factors of 40?

Does 1 go into 40? Yes, 1 times 40.
Does 2 go into 40? Yes, 2 times 20.
Does 3 go into 40? No.
Does 4 go into 40? Yes, 4 times 10.
Does 5 go into 40? Yes, 5 times 8.
Does 6 go into 40? No.
Does 7 go into 40? No.

Remember

Every positive integer is its own greatest factor and least multiple.

We don't have to try 8, since the number 8 has already appeared in our list of factors. So the factors of 40 are 1, 2, 4, 5, 8, 10, 20, and 40.

Having trouble remembering the difference between *factors* and *multiples*? Try this mnemonic:

Factors are Few, Multiples are Many.

Twelve is a number that has a relatively large number of *factors*, but it still has only six of them. The *multiples* of 12, on the other hand, go on forever. Every number has an infinite number of multiples.

Prime Factors

When you need to find the **prime factors** of a number, you can make a prime factor tree. Let's say you need to find the prime factors of 60.

Start by writing down the number you are going to factor.

Then factor out the primes one at a time. The first prime number is 2, so that is where we will start. 60 divided by 2 is 30, so we can draw branches for the 2 and 30.

Now let's move on to 30. 30 is also divisible by 2 (30 ÷ 2 = 15), so we can draw branches for 2 and 15.

Fifteen is not divisible by 2, so we move on to the next prime number: 3. Fifteen divided by 3 is 5, so we can draw branches for 3 and 5.

Five is prime, so we are done! The prime factors of 60 are 2, 2, 3, and 5. Remember, though, if a problem asked for the *distinct* prime factors of 60, your answer would be 2, 3, and 5.

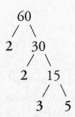

Managing Multiples

One type of question you will see frequently on the PSAT involves finding common multiples. The easiest way to find a common multiple is to start listing the multiples of the numbers you are given until you find which ones they have in common.

Here are some examples.

4. If a number p is a positive multiple of both 3 and 8, p must also be a multiple of

    (A) 5
    (B) 11
    (C) 12
    (D) 14
    (E) 18

How to Crack It

We will start by listing the multiples of 3: 3, 6, 9, 12, 15, 18, 21, 24, 27.... Now we will list the multiples of 8: 8, 16, 24, 32, 40....

Which numbers belong to both groups? 24 does. So the numbers that are multiples of both 3 and 8 must be multiples of 24. Of course, 24 itself isn't listed as an answer (that would be too easy.) But 24 (and every multiple of 24) will have a factor of 12 in it, so the answer is (C).

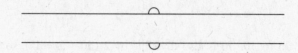

5. How many integers between 1 and 100 are multiples of both 4 and 6 ?

   (A)   8
   (B)   12
   (C)   18
   (D)   22
   (E)   24

How to Crack It

We will start by listing the multiples of 4: 4, 8, 12, 16, 20, 24, 28.... Now the multiples of 6: 6, 12, 18, 24, 30....

After just a few multiples, you should be able to see the pattern. The numbers 12 and 24 (and likewise, every multiple of 12: the numbers 36, 48, etc., will also work) are the common multiples of both 4 and 6. So the real question is, how many multiples of 12 are there between 1 and 100? That's not too difficult to figure out. We can list them with the help of a calculator: 12, 24, 36, 48, 60, 72, 84, 96. So there are a total of 8, and that is answer choice (A).

Drill 2

Answers can be found in Part III.

    a. What are 3 consecutive odd integers whose sum is 15?
_____ _____ _____

    b. What are the factors of 10? _____ _____ _____ _____

    c. What are the prime factors of 10? _____ _____

    d. What are the factors of 48? _____ _____ _____ _____ _____ _____
_____ _____ _____ _____

    e. What are the prime factors of 48? _____ _____

    f. What are the first 7 positive multiples of 6? _____ _____ _____
_____ _____ _____ _____

    g. What are the first 7 positive multiples of 4? _____ _____ _____
_____ _____ _____ _____

    h. Numbers that are multiples of both 6 and 7 are also multiples of
_____.

    i. The product of two positive integers x and y is 30 and their sum is 11.
What are x and y? _____ and _____

    j. The product of two positive integers x and y is 30 and their difference
is 13. What are x and y? _____ and _____

1. Which of the following does NOT have a remainder of 1 ?

    (A) $\dfrac{151}{75}$

    (B) $\dfrac{17}{8}$

    (C) $\dfrac{51}{3}$

    (D) $\dfrac{61}{4}$

    (E) $\dfrac{81}{10}$

2. Which of the following numbers has the digit 4 in the
thousandths place?

    (A)   4000.0
    (B)   40.0
    (C)   0.4
    (D)   0.04
    (E)   0.004

3. Which of the following numbers is NOT prime?

   (A) 11
   (B) 23
   (C) 27
   (D) 29
   (E) 31

4. Which of the following is the least of 3 consecutive integers if their sum is 21 ?

   (A) 4
   (B) 5
   (C) 6
   (D) 7
   (E) 8

5. If a, b, c, d, and e are consecutive even integers, and $a < b < c < d < e$, then $d + e$ is how much greater than $a + b$?

   (A) 10
   (B) 12
   (C) 14
   (D) 16
   (E) 18

6. All numbers divisible by both 3 and 14 are also divisible by which of the following?

   (A) 6
   (B) 9
   (C) 16
   (D) 28
   (E) 32

Exponents and Square Roots

Exponents are just a shorthand for multiplication. Instead of writing $3 \times 3 \times 3 \times 3$, you can write 3^4. Thus, you can handle exponents by expanding them out if necessary.

$$y^2 \times y^3 = y \times y \times y \times y \times y = y^5$$

$$\frac{y^4}{y^2} = \frac{y \times y \times y \times y}{y \times y} = y \times y = y^2$$

However, you can also multiply and divide exponents that have the same base using a shortcut called MADSPM. MADSPM also helps you remember how to deal with raising exponents to another power. Here is the breakdown:

- **MA** means when you see a MULTIPLICATION sign, ADD the exponents. So $y^2 \times y^3 = y^{2+3} = y^5$.
- **DS** means when you see a DIVISION sign (or fraction), SUBTRACT the exponents. So $\frac{y^5}{y^2} = y^{5-2} = y^3$.

- **PM** means when you see an exponent raised to a POWER, MULTIPLY the exponents. So $(y^2)^3 = y^{2 \times 3} = y^6$. (This is really easy to confuse with multiplication, so watch out!)

Be careful, because the rules of MADSPM don't work for addition and subtraction. For example, $3^2 + 3^5$ does NOT equal 3^7.

Here are some additional rules to remember about exponents:

- Anything to the zero power equals 1: $3^0 = 1$. Mathematicians argue about whether 0^0 is 1 or is undefined, but that will not come up on the PSAT.
- Anything to the first power equals itself: $3^1 = 3$.
- 1 to any power equals 1: $1^{3876} = 1$.
- A negative exponent means to take the reciprocal of what would be the result as if the negative were not there: $2^{-2} = \frac{1}{2^2} = \frac{1}{4}$.
- A fractional exponent has two parts (like any other fraction), the numerator, which is the power the base is raised to, and the denominator, which is the root of the base. For example, $8^{2/3} = \sqrt[3]{8^2} = \sqrt[3]{64} = 4$.

Remember that in calculating the value of a root, you are looking for what number multiplied by itself results in the number under the radical. In the above example, $\sqrt[3]{64} = 4$ because $4 \times 4 \times 4 = 64$.

When you see the square root sign, that means to take the positive root only. So, $\sqrt{9} = 3$, but not -3.

Square roots work just like exponents: You can *always* multiply and divide roots, but you can only add and subtract with the *same* root.

Multiplication and Division:

$$\sqrt{8} \times \sqrt{2} = \sqrt{8 \times 2} = \sqrt{16} = 4$$

$$\sqrt{\frac{1}{4}} = \frac{\sqrt{1}}{\sqrt{4}} = \frac{1}{2}$$

$$\sqrt{300} = \sqrt{100 \times 3} = \sqrt{100} \times \sqrt{3} = 10\sqrt{3}$$

Addition and Subtraction:

$$2\sqrt{2} + 3\sqrt{2} = 5\sqrt{2}$$

$$4\sqrt{3} - \sqrt{3} = 3\sqrt{3}$$

$2\sqrt{3} + 3\sqrt{2}$ *Cannot be added without a calculator since the terms do not have the same root.*

Drill 3

Answers can be found in Part III.

a. $3^3 \times 3^2 =$ _____

b. $\dfrac{3^3}{3^2} =$ _____

c. $\left(3^3\right)^2 =$ _____

d. $x^6 \times x^2 =$ _____

e. $\dfrac{x^6}{x^2} =$ _____

f. $\left(x^6\right)^2 =$ _____

3. If $3^4 = 9^x$, then $x =$

(A) 2
(B) 3
(C) 4
(D) 5
(E) 6

5. If $\left(3^x\right)^3 = 3^{15}$, what is the value of x ?

(A) 3
(B) 5
(C) 7
(D) 9
(E) 12

11. If $x^y x^6 = x^{54}$ and $\left(x^3\right)^z = x^9$, then $y + z =$

(A) 10
(B) 11
(C) 12
(D) 48
(E) 51

Equations and Inequalities

An **equation** is a statement that contains an equal sign, such as $3x + 5 = 17$.

To solve an equation, you want to get the variable x alone on one side of the equal sign and everything else on the other side.

The first step is to put all of the variables on one side of the equation and all of the numbers on the other side, using addition and subtraction. As long as you perform the same operation on both sides of the equal sign, you are not changing the value of the variable.

Then you can divide both sides of the equation by the *coefficient,* which is the number in front of the variable. If that number is a fraction, you can multiply everything by its reciprocal.

For example: $3x + 5 = 17$

$$
\begin{array}{rcl}
3x + 5 &=& 17 \\
-5 & & -5 \\
\hline
3x &=& 12 \\
\div 3 & & \div 3 \\
\hline
x &=& 4
\end{array}
$$

Subtract 5 from each side.

Divide each side by 3.

Always remember the rule of equations:

Whatever you do to one side of the equation, you must also do to the other side.

An **inequality** is any statement with one of these signs:

<	(less than)
>	(greater than)
≤	(less than or equal to)
≥	(greater than or equal to)

You can solve inequalities in the same way you solve equations, with one exception: Whenever you multiply or divide an inequality by a negative value, you must change the direction of the sign: < becomes >, and ≤ becomes ≥.

For example: $3x + 5 > 17$

$$
\begin{array}{rcl}
3x + 5 & > & 17 \\
-5 & & -5 \qquad \text{Subtract 5 from each side.} \\
\hline
3x & > & 12 \\
\div 3 & & \div 3 \qquad \text{Divide each side by 3.} \\
\hline
x & > & 4
\end{array}
$$

In this case, we did not multiply or divide by a negative value, so the direction of the sign did not change. However, if we were to divide by a negative value, we would need to change the direction of the sign.

$$
\begin{array}{rcl}
-4x + 3 & > & 15 \\
-3 & & -3 \qquad \text{Subtract 3 from each side.} \\
\hline
-4x & > & 12 \\
\div -4 & & \div -4 \qquad \text{Divide each side by } -4. \\
\hline
x & < & -3
\end{array}
$$

Simultaneous Equations

Simultaneous equations occur when a question presents you with two equations at the same time. They are easier to deal with than they appear. All you have to do is stack the equations, and then add or subtract them.

12. If $x - 2y = 10$ and $3x + 4y = 5$, then $4x + 2y =$

   (A) 5
   (B) 9
   (C) 15
   (D) 24
   (E) 30

How to Crack It

Simply stack the equations, making sure that all the x variables are lined up, all the y variables are lined up, and all the numbers are lined up.

$$
\begin{array}{r}
x - 2y = 10 \\
3x + 4y = 5 \\
\hline
\end{array}
$$

Now you need to decide whether to add the two equations together or subtract one from the other. The question is asking for $4x + 2y$ in this case, so that tells you to add, since $x + 3x = 4x$ and $-2y + 4y = 2y$.

$$\begin{array}{r} x - 2y = 10 \\ + \ 3x + 4y = \ 5 \\ \hline 4x + 2y = 15 \end{array}$$

That is your answer: 15. The question does not ask for the values of each variable, so you do not need to worry about figuring out anything else.

———————◯———————

Here is one more.

———————◯———————

9. If $3x + 2y = 7$ and $2x + 2y = 9$, what is the value of x ?

(A) -2
(B) 2
(C) 7
(D) 9
(E) 16

How to Crack It
Again, stack your equations.

$$\begin{array}{r} 3x + 2y = 7 \\ 2x + 2y = 9 \end{array}$$

This time the question asks for the value of x. Would adding the equations or subtracting them give you x alone? Subtracting the second equation from the first one would, because the coefficients for y are the same.

$$\begin{array}{r} 3x + 2y = \ 7 \\ - \ 2x + 2y = \ 9 \\ \hline x \qquad = -2 \end{array}$$

The y variables cancel out, and you get -2 for your answer.

———————◯———————

GEOMETRY DEFINITIONS

Lines and Angles

Common sense might tell you what a line is, but for this test you are going to have to learn the particulars of a line, a ray, and a line segment.

A **line** continues on in each direction forever. You need only two points to form a line, but that line does not end at those points. A straight line has 180 degrees on each side.

A **ray** is a line with one distinct endpoint. Again, you need only two points to designate a ray, but one of those points is where it stops—it continues on forever in the other direction. A ray has 180 degrees as well.

A **line segment** is a line with two distinct endpoints. It requires two points, and it is the length from one point to the other. A line segment has 180 degrees.

Whenever you have angles on one side of a line, remember *the rule of 180*: The angles on any line must add up to 180. These angles are called *supplementary angles*. In the figure below, what is the value of x? We know that $2x + x$ must add up to 180, so we know that $3x = 180$. This makes $x = 60$.

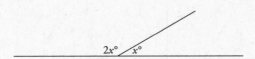

If two lines cross each other, they make *vertical angles*. These angles will always have the same measure. In the figure below, we know that z must equal 50, since $130 + z$ must equal 180. We know that y is 130, since it is across from the angle 130. We also know that x is 50, since it is across from z.

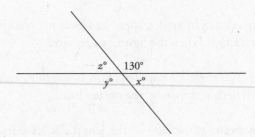

Any time you have two parallel lines and a line that crosses them, you have two kinds of angles: big angles and small angles. All of the big angles have the same measure, and all of the small angles have the same measure. In the following figure, angles a, d, e, and h all have the same measure; angles b, c, f, and g also all have the same measure. The sum of the measure of any big angle plus any small angle equals 180 degrees.

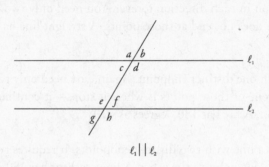

Four-Sided Figures

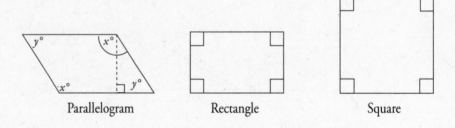

| Parallelogram | Rectangle | Square |

A figure with two sets of parallel sides is a **parallelogram**. In a parallelogram, the opposite angles are equal, and any adjacent angles add up to 180 degrees. (In the figure above, $x + y = 180$ degrees.) Opposite sides are also equal. All of the angles of a parallelogram equal 360 degrees.

If all of the angles are also right angles, then the figure is a **rectangle**. And if all of the sides are the same length, then the figure is a **square**.

The *area* of a square, rectangle, or parallelogram is *length × width*. (In the parallelogram above, the length is shown by the dotted line.)

The *perimeter* of any figure is the sum of the lengths of its sides. A triangle with sides 3, 4, and 5 has a perimeter of 12.

Thinking Inside the Box
Here is a progression of quadrilaterals from least specific to most specific:
quadrilateral = 4-sided figure
↓
parallelogram = a quadrilateral in which opposite sides are parallel
↓
rectangle = a parallelogram in which all angles equal 90°
↓
square = a rectangle in which all angles and all sides are equal

Triangles

The sum of the angles inside a triangle must equal 180 degrees. This means that if you know two of the angles in a triangle, you can always solve for the third. Since we know that two of the angles in the following figure are 90 and 60 degrees, we can solve for the third angle, which must be 30 degrees.

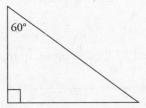

An **isosceles triangle** is a triangle that has two sides that are equal. Angles that are opposite equal sides must be equal. In the figure below, we have an isosceles triangle. Since $AB = BC$, we know that angles x and y are equal. And since their sum must be 150 degrees (to make a total of 180 degrees when we add the last angle), they each must be 75 degrees.

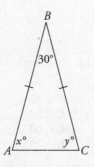

The **area** of a triangle is $\frac{1}{2}$ *base* $\times$ *height*. Note that the height is always perpendicular to the base.

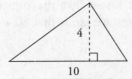

$$\text{Area} = \frac{1}{2} \times 10 \times 4 = 20 \qquad \text{Area} = \frac{1}{2} \times 6 \times 4 = 12$$

An **equilateral triangle** has three equal sides and all of its angles equal to 60 degrees.

Here is a typical example of a PSAT question on triangles.

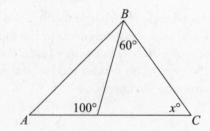

Being Aggressive on Geometry Problems

The most important problem-solving technique for tackling PSAT geometry is to learn to be aggressive. This means, whenever you have a diagram, ask yourself: *What else do I know?* Write everything you can think of on your booklet. You may not see right away why it is important, but write it down anyway. Chances are good that you will be making progress toward the answer, without even knowing it.

ETS is also fond of disguising familiar figures within more complex shapes by extending lines, overlapping figures, or combining several basic shapes. So be on the lookout for the basic figures hidden in complicated shapes.

13. In triangle *ABC* above, *x* =

(A) 30
(B) 40
(C) 50
(D) 60
(E) 70

How to Crack It

We know that the angle adjacent to the 100-degree angle must equal 80 degrees since we know that a straight line is 180 degrees. Fill it in on your diagram.

Now, since we know that the sum of the angles contained in a triangle must equal 180 degrees, we know that 80 + 60 + x = 180, so x = 40. That is answer (B).

Third Side Rule

Suppose you do not know anything about a triangle except the lengths of two of its sides. You can also then figure out that the third side must be between certain values—that is, the length of the third side must be less than the sum of the other two sides and greater than their difference.

> *The third side of a triangle is always less than the sum of the other two sides and greater than the difference between them.*

Why? Consider a triangle that looks like this:

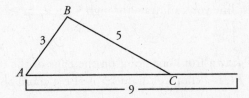

The shortest distance between two points is a straight line, right? And yet in this figure, the straight-line distance from A to C is 9, yet the scenic route from A to B to C is...8? That cannot be right! And it is not. The crooked path must be longer than the straight path, and thus any two sides of a triangle added together must be longer than the third side. In this example, $2 < AC < 8$.

14. Which of the following is a possible perimeter of a triangle with sides 5 and 8 ?

    (A) 15
    (B) 16
    (C) 17
    (D) 26
    (E) 30

No Figures?
Draw one before you do anything else. Also, remember to not draw a right triangle if the problem doesn't specify that the shape is a right triangle.

How to Crack It

To find the perimeter of a triangle, you just need to add up the sides of the triangle, so we will see what we know about the sides. We know that the two given sides add up to 13, so the perimeter will be 13 + the third side. The third side will be between the sum and difference of those other two sides. 8 + 5 = 13 and 8 − 5 = 3, so the third side will be greater than 3 and less than 13. Add these to the sum of the sides we already know (13), and the perimeter must be between 16 (13 + 3) and 26 (13 + 13). The only answer choice that fits the bill is (C).

Circles

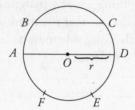

The **radius** of a circle is the distance from the center to the edge of the circle. In the figure above, *OD* is a radius. So is *OA*.

The **diameter** is the distance from one edge, through the center, to the other edge of the circle. The diameter will always be twice the measure of the radius and will always be the longest line you can draw through a circle. In the figure above, *AD* is the diameter.

A **chord** is any line drawn from one point on the edge of the circle to the other. In the figure above, *BC* is a chord. A diameter is also a chord and also the longest chord in a circle.

An **arc** is any section of the circumference (the edge) of the circle. *EF* is an arc in the figure above.

The **circumference** is the distance around the outside edge of the circle. The circumference of a circle with radius *r* is $2\pi r$. A circle with radius of 5 has a circumference of 10π.

The **area** of a circle with radius *r* is πr^2. A circle with a radius of 5 has an area of 25π.

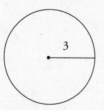

Area = 9π

Circumference = 6π

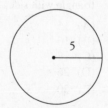

Area = 25π

Circumference = 10π

THE COORDINATE PLANE

You will probably see one or two questions on the PSAT that involve the coordinate plane. The biggest mistake that people make on these questions is getting the *x*- and *y*-axes reversed. So we will just review:

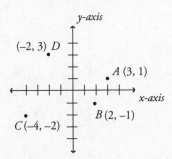

The *x*-axis is the horizontal axis, and the *y*-axis is the vertical axis. Points are given on the coordinate plane with the *x*-coordinate first. Positive *x*-values go to the right, and negative ones go to the left; positive *y*-values go up, and negative ones go down. So point *A* (3, 1) is 3 points to the right on the *x*-axis and 1 point up from there. Point *B* (2, –1) is two points to the right on the *x*-axis and 1 point down from there.

Slope is a measure of the steepness of a line on the coordinate plane. On most slope problems you need to recognize only whether the slope is positive, negative, or zero. A line that goes up and to the right has positive slope; a line that goes down and to the right has negative slope, and a flat line has zero slope. In the figure below, line 1 has positive slope, line 2 has zero slope, and line 3 has negative slope.

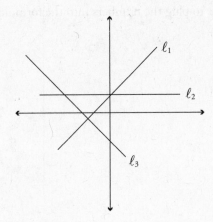

If you do need to calculate the slope, and the graph is drawn for you, here is how: slope $= \dfrac{y_2 - y_1}{x_2 - x_1}$. The *slope* of a line is equal to $\dfrac{rise}{run}$. To find the slope, take any two points on the line and count off the distance you need to get from one of these points to the other.

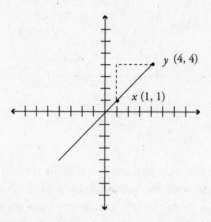

In the graph above, to get from point *x* to point *y*, we count up (rise) 3 units, and count over (run) 3 units. Therefore, the slope is $\dfrac{rise}{run} = \dfrac{3}{3} = 1$. Always remember to check whether the slope is positive or negative when you use $= \dfrac{rise}{run}$.

If you are not given a figure and you cannot draw one easily using the points given, you can find the slope by plugging the coordinates you know into the slope formula. Just remember to plug the numbers into the formula carefully!

Drill 4

Answers can be found in Part III.

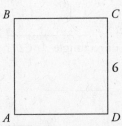

a. What is the area of square *ABCD* above? _____

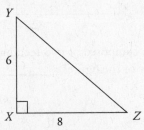

b. What is the area of triangle *XYZ* above? _____

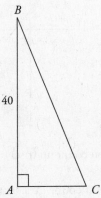

c. If the area of the triangle above is 400, what is the length of *AC*? _____

d. What is the area of the circle above with center *O*? _____

e. What is its circumference? _____

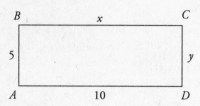

f. If *ABCD* is a rectangle, $x =$ _____ $y =$ _____
g. What is the perimeter of rectangle *ABCD* ? _____

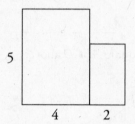

h. If the above figure is composed of two rectangles, what is the perimeter of the figure?_____

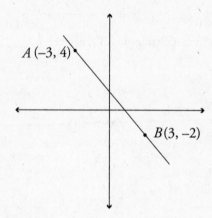

i. How many units must you count up (rise) to get from point *B* to point *A* ? _____
j. How many units must you count over (run) to get from point *A* to point *B* ? _____
k. What is the slope of the line above? _____
    (Remember, the line is going down to the right so it must have a negative slope.)

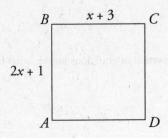

17. If *ABCD* is a square, what is the area of the square?

(A) 2
(B) 4
(C) 20
(D) 25
(E) 36

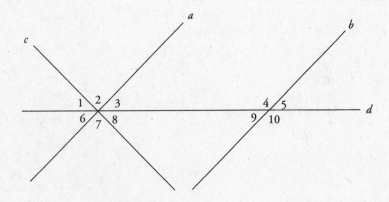

10. In the figure above, lines *a* and *b* are parallel. Which of the following pairs of angles must have equal degree measures?

     I. 1 and 5
     II. 2 and 7
     III. 3 and 9

(A) None
(B) I only
(C) II only
(D) III only
(E) II and III only

$$x + 2y = 12$$
$$2x + y = 9$$

19. Given the system of equations above, what is the value of $x + y$?

(A) 3

(B) 7

(C) $\dfrac{21}{2}$

(D) 21

(E) It cannot be determined from the information given.

10. If $x^{\frac{5}{2}} = 8x$, then x could equal

(A) 2
(B) 4
(C) 6
(D) 8
(E) 12

PROBABILITY AND COUNTING

Probability refers to the chance that an event will happen, and it is always given as a fractional value between 0 and 1, inclusive. A probability of 0 means that the event will never happen; a probability of 1 means that it is certain to happen.

$$\text{Probability} = \frac{\text{number of outcomes you want}}{\text{number of possible outcomes}}$$

For instance, if you have a die with faces numbered 1 to 6, what is the chance of rolling a 2? There is one face with the number 2 on it, out of 6 total faces. Therefore, the probability of rolling a 2 is $\frac{1}{6}$.

What is the chance of rolling an even number on one roll of this die? There are 3 faces of the die with an even number (the sides numbered 2, 4, and 6) out of a total of 6 faces. Therefore, the probability of rolling an even number is $\frac{3}{6}$, or $\frac{1}{2}$.

Here is a typical probability question:

—————————○—————————

7. In a jar there are 3 green gumballs, 5 red gumballs, 8 white gumballs, and 1 blue gumball. If one gumball is chosen at random, what is the probability that it will be red?

(A) $\dfrac{5}{17}$

(B) $\dfrac{5}{16}$

(C) $\dfrac{1}{17}$

(D) $\dfrac{1}{12}$

(E) $\dfrac{1}{10}$

How to Crack It

To solve this problem, we take the number of things we want (the 5 red gumballs) and place it over the number of possible things we have to choose from (all 17 gumballs in the jar). This gives us choice (A).

—————————○—————————

—————————○—————————

13. Sue sells $\dfrac{1}{4}$ of the tickets for the school lottery to Andrew. Sue then sells $\dfrac{2}{3}$ of the remaining tickets to Bob. Of the tickets Sue has left, Cathy buys $\dfrac{3}{5}$. Sue then purchases all of the remaining unsold tickets herself. What is the probability that Cathy will win the school lottery?

(A) $\dfrac{1}{10}$

(B) $\dfrac{3}{20}$

(C) $\dfrac{1}{4}$

(D) $\dfrac{1}{2}$

(E) $\dfrac{2}{3}$

How to Crack It

Because this problem has a series of fractions that represent multiple reductions, we begin to solve this problem by plugging in our own number! If we plug in that Sue has 100 tickets, she then gives $\frac{1}{4}$ of them (or 25 tickets) to Andrew. Sue then has 75 tickets left. The problem then states that Sue gives $\frac{2}{3}$ of those remaining tickets to Bob, which means that she has given 50 tickets to Bob. Therefore, Sue now has 25 tickets left. Of these 25 tickets, Cathy buys $\frac{3}{5}$ of them, or 15 tickets. Thus, Sue has 10 tickets left. Paying very close attention to what the question asks, we must find the probability that CATHY will win the school lottery. Therefore, when we consider "part/whole", we have 15 tickets/100 tickets for Cathy, which is 15%. Thus, choice (B) is correct.

1, 2, 3, … , 1000

Some questions may ask you how many ways something can happen. The trick here is to draw an underlined space representing each of the spots you need to fill, then for each spot write in the number of things that could fill that spot. When you are done with all the spots, multiply them.

Here is an example:

---

14. Ms. Grady will choose one boy and one girl from her class to be the class representatives. If there are 3 boys and 7 girls in her class, how many different pairs of class representatives could she pick?

   (A) 10
   (B) 13
   (C) 21
   (D) 23
   (E) 25

How to Crack It

How many spots do we need to fill? Ms. Grady wants a pair of representatives, so we need to fill two spots.

$$\underline{\phantom{\text{boys}}} \quad \times \quad \underline{\phantom{\text{girls}}}$$
$$\text{boys} \qquad\qquad \text{girls}$$

One will be a boy and the other a girl, so we need to fill one spot with the number of boys that we have to choose from and the other with the number of girls we have to choose from, then multiply them—so we have $3 \times 7 = 21$, which is choice (C).

We can try another.

12. Sandra has 6 trophies, but only has room for 3 of them on her mantle. How many possible ways can she arrange 3 of the 6 trophies on her mantle?

    (A) 18
    (B) 54
    (C) 80
    (D) 120
    (E) 216

How to Crack It

How many places does Sandra have on her mantle in which she can put trophies? She has three, so draw that many underlines. How many choices does she have for what to place in the first spot? She has six, so fill a six into the first underline. Then she has five left to choose from for the second spot and four left to choose from for the last spot; we will fill in the spots and multiply, $6 \times 5 \times 4 = 120$, so the answer is (D).

GRID-INS: THE BASICS

You will see 10 questions on the PSAT that ask you to bubble in a numerical answer on a grid, rather than answer a multiple-choice question. These questions are arranged in order of difficulty and can be solved according to the methods outlined for the multiple-choice problems on the test. Do not be concerned because there are no answer choices—your approach is the same.

Keep Left
No matter how many digits in your answer, always start gridding in the leftmost column. That way, you will avoid omitting digits and losing points.

The only difficulty with grid-ins is getting used to the way in which you are asked to answer the question. For each question, you will have a grid like the following:

We recommend that you write the answer on top of the grid to help you bubble, but it is important to know that the scoring machine only reads the bubbles. *If you bubble incorrectly, the computer will consider the answer to be incorrect.*

Here are the basic rules of gridding:

1.   If your answer uses fewer than four boxes, you can grid it anywhere you like.
     To avoid confusion, we suggest that you start at the leftmost box. For example:

2. You can grid your answer as either a fraction or a decimal, *if* the fraction will fit.

You can grid an answer of .5 as either .5 or $\frac{1}{2}$.

or

3. You do not need to reduce your fractions, *if* the fraction will fit.

If your answer is $\frac{2}{4}$, you can grid it as $\frac{2}{4}$, $\frac{1}{2}$, or .5.

or   or

4. If you have a decimal that will not fit in the spaces provided, you *must grid as many places as will fit.*

    If your answer is $\dfrac{2}{3}$, you can grid it as $\dfrac{2}{3}$, .666, or .667, but .66 is *not* acceptable.

    You do *not* need to round your numbers, so we suggest that you do not. There is no reason to give yourself a chance to make a mistake if you do not have to.

or

or

5. You cannot grid mixed numbers. Convert all mixed numbers to ordinary fractions.

    If your answer is $2\dfrac{1}{2}$, you must convert it to $\dfrac{5}{2}$ or 2.5, otherwise the computer will read your 2 1/2 as 21/2.

or

Do not Mix

Never grid in a mixed number. Change it into an improper fraction or decimal. To convert mixed fractions into improper fractions, all you have to do is multiply the denominator with the whole number in front of the fraction, then add that product to the numerator, and finally put that number over the denominator you started with.

6. You cannot grid π, square roots, variables, or negative numbers, so if you arrive at an answer with one of those terms, you have made a mistake. Check your work.

Drill 5

Answers can be found in Part III.

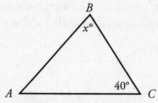

Note: Figure not drawn to scale.

33.   In triangle *ABC* above, if *AB* = *BC*, then *x* =
       (Disregard the degree symbol when gridding your answer.)

34.   The sum of 5 consecutive integers, arranged in order from least to
       greatest, is 100. What is the sum of the next 4 consecutive integers?

35.   If $5x^2 = 125$, what could be the value of $5x^3$?

36.   What is the sum of the distinct prime factors of 140 ?

Summary

○ The Math sections are arranged in Order of Difficulty, which can make it easier to spot the less difficult problems. However, remember that the test writers' idea of "easier" problems is not necessarily the same as your idea. Let your Personal Order of Difficulty be your guide.

○ Write in your test booklet to set up problems, and then use your calculator to figure out solutions. Remember to type carefully—your calculator will not check for mistakes.

○ Review basic math vocabulary before the test to make sure you do not get stuck on the "little words."

○ To tell the difference between factors and multiples, remember that Factors are Few and Multiples are Many.

○ When you have to manipulate exponents, remember your MADSPM rules.

○ Inequalities can be worked just like equations, until you have to multiply or divide by a negative. Then you need to flip the inequality sign.

○ Working with several equations at once? Just follow the guidelines of Simultaneous Equations: Stack the equations and then add or subtract to get what you are looking for.

○ Be sure to review your basic geometry rules before the test; often, problems hinge on knowing that vertical angles are equal or that a quadrilateral has 360 degrees.

○ On all geometry problems, draw figures out and aggressively fill in everything you know.

○ The third side rule says that any side of a triangle must be between the sum and the difference of the other two sides.

- Probability is always a fractional value between 0 and 1 (inclusive), and it is equal to the number of outcomes the question is asking for divided by the total number of possible outcomes.

- When doing Grid-Ins, be sure to keep to the left, and do not bother reducing fractions if they fit in the allotted spaces.

Chapter 8
Math Techniques

In the previous chapter, we mentioned that one of the keys to doing well on the PSAT is to have a set of test-specific problem-solving skills. This chapter discusses some powerful strategies, which—though you may not use them in school—are specifically designed to get you points on the PSAT. Learn them well!

PLUGGING IN

One of the most powerful problem-solving skills on the PSAT is a technique we call Plugging In. Plugging In will turn nasty algebra problems into simple arithmetic and help you through the particularly twisted problems that you will often see on the PSAT. There are several varieties of Plugging In, each suited to a different kind of question.

Plugging In Your Own Numbers

The problem with doing algebra is that it is just too easy to make a mistake.

> Whenever you see a problem with variables in the answer choices, PLUG IN.

Start by picking a number for the variable in the problem (or for more than one variable, if necessary), solve the problem using your number, and then see which answer choice gives you the correct answer.

Take a look at the following problem:

When to Plug In
- Phrases like "in terms of k" in the question
- Variables in the questions or answers

2. If x is a positive integer, then 20% of $5x$ equals

   (A) x
   (B) $2x$
   (C) $5x$
   (D) $15x$
   (E) $20x$

How to Crack It

We begin by picking a number for x. We will plug in a nice round number such as 10. When we plug in 10 for x, we change every x in the whole problem into a 10. Now the problem reads:

2. If 10 is a positive integer, then 20% of 5(10) equals

   (A)   10
   (B)   2(10)
   (C)   5(10)
   (D) 15(10)
   (E) 20(10)

Look how easy the problem becomes! Now we can solve: 20 percent of 50 is 10. Which answer says 10? (A) does.

That was a number 2, which means it was an easy problem. Now we can try it again on a harder question.

8. If $-1 < x < 0$, then which of the following has the greatest value?

    (A) x

    (B) x^2

    (C) x^3

    (D) $\dfrac{1}{x}$

    (E) $2x$

How to Crack It

This time when we pick a number for x, we have to make sure that it is between -1 and 0, because that is what the problem states. So we can try $-\dfrac{1}{2}$. If we make every x in the problem equal to $-\dfrac{1}{2}$, the problem now reads:

8. If $-1 < -\dfrac{1}{2} < 0$, then which of the following has the greatest value?

    (A) $-\dfrac{1}{2}$

    (B) $\left(-\dfrac{1}{2}\right)^2$

    (C) $\left(-\dfrac{1}{2}\right)^3$

    (D) $\dfrac{1}{-\dfrac{1}{2}}$

    (E) $2\left(-\dfrac{1}{2}\right)$

Plugging In Quick Reference

- When you see *in terms of* and variables in the answer choices, you can plug in.
- Pick your own number for an unknown in the problem.
- Do the necessary math to find the answer you are aiming for—we call this the target value. Circle the target value.
- Use POE to eliminate every answer that does not equal the target value—and be sure to check every answer choice!

Now we can solve the problem. Which has the greatest value? Choice (A) is $-\dfrac{1}{2}$, choice (B) equals $\dfrac{1}{4}$, choice (C) equals $-\dfrac{1}{8}$, choice (D) equals -2, and choice (E) equals -1. So choice (B) is the greatest.

Plugging In is such a great technique because it turns hard algebra problems into medium and sometimes even easy arithmetic questions. Remember this when you are thinking of your POOD and looking for questions to do among the hard ones; if you see variables in the answer choices, you can Plug In.

Do not worry too much about what numbers you choose to plug in; just plug in easy numbers (small numbers like 2, 5, or 10 or numbers that make the arithmetic easy, like 100 if you are looking for a percent). Of course, be sure your numbers fit the conditions of the questions (if a question states that $x > 11$, do not plug in 12).

What If There is No Variable?

Sometimes you will encounter a problem that does not contain an x, y, or z, but which contains a hidden variable. If your answers are percents or fractional parts of some unknown quantity (total number of marbles in a jar, total miles to travel in a trip), try using Plugging In.

Take a look at this problem:

8. In a certain high school, the number of seniors is twice the number of juniors. If 60% of the senior class and 40% of the junior class attend the last football game of the season, approximately what percent of the combined junior and senior class attends the game?

 (A) 60%
 (B) 53%
 (C) 50%
 (D) 47%
 (E) 40%

How to Crack It

What number, if we knew it, would make the math work on this problem incredibly easy? The number of students. So we will plug in a number and work the problem. Suppose that the number of seniors is 200 and the number of juniors is 100.

If 60% of the 200 seniors and 40% of the 100 juniors go to the game, that makes

120 seniors and 40 juniors, or 160 students. What fraction of the combined class

went to the game? $\dfrac{160}{300}$, or about 53%. So the answer is (B).

Try another one.

---

10. Paolo sells cars at a certain dealership. On Monday, Paolo sells one-third of the cars on the lot. On Tuesday, Paolo sells one-fourth of the remaining cars. If Paolo sells half of the cars left on the lot on Wednesday, and no new cars were added to or taken from the lot, what percent of the original cars did Paolo sell?

(A) 4.2%
(B) 65%
(C) 75%
(D) 85%
(E) 95.8%

How to Crack It

Clearly Paolo is selling his fair share of cars, but notice that you are missing a very important piece of information in the problem: How many cars are on the lot? That is your hidden variable!

In a problem that deals with fractions, you can find a good number to plug in by multiplying the denominators in the problem. Since we are taking $\frac{1}{3}$ of the number, then $\frac{1}{4}$ of it, and then $\frac{1}{2}$ of it, we want something that will divide evenly by 3, 4, and 2. Whatever we get when we multiply 3 by 4 by 2 will certainly fit the bill! This turns out to be 24. This quick technique can save you a lot of headaches once you get to the math.

Now we can work through the problem, using 24 for the number of cars on the lot:

First, Paolo sells one-third of the cars on the lot. If we start with 24 cars, that is 8 cars Paolo sold and 16 cars left on the lot. On Tuesday, Paolo moves one-fourth of what is left, or 4 cars; that raises Paolo's tally to 12 cars sold and leaves 12 on the lot. Finally, Paolo sells half of the remaining cars. That equals 6 cars and brings Paolo up to 18 cars sold for the week. To figure out the percentage, divide the cars Paolo sold (18) by the total number of cars on the lot (24). Thus, 18 ÷ 24 is .75, or 75%, which is answer choice (C).

Drill 1

4. On Tuesday, Martha does $\frac{1}{2}$ of her weekly homework.

On Wednesday, she does $\frac{1}{3}$ of the remaining homework.

After Wednesday, what fractional part of her homework

remains to be done?

(A) $\frac{1}{6}$

(B) $\frac{1}{5}$

(C) $\frac{1}{4}$

(D) $\frac{1}{3}$

(E) $\frac{1}{2}$

14. If $a = \frac{b}{c^2}$ and $c \neq 0$, then $\frac{1}{b^2} =$

(A) ac^2

(B) a^2c^4

(C) $\frac{1}{ac^2}$

(D) $\frac{1}{a^2c^4}$

(E) $\frac{a^2}{c^4}$

12. If $p \neq 0$, then $\dfrac{\frac{1}{8}}{2p} =$

(A) $\dfrac{1}{16p}$

(B) $\dfrac{p}{4}$

(C) $\dfrac{4}{p}$

(D) $\dfrac{4p}{3}$

(E) $4p$

18. Jodi has x dollars in her bank account. She withdraws $\dfrac{1}{6}$ of the money in her account to pay her rent and another $\dfrac{1}{6}$ of the money in her account to make her car payment. Jodi then deposits her paycheck of y dollars into her account. A week later, she withdraws $\dfrac{1}{2}$ of the money in her account to spend on a new set of knives. In terms of x, how many dollars are left in Jodi's account?

(A) $\dfrac{(4x - 3y)}{6}$

(B) $\dfrac{(3x - 5y)}{6}$

(C) $\dfrac{(2x + 2y - 3)}{6}$

(D) $\dfrac{(3x - y)}{6}$

(E) $\dfrac{(2x + 3y)}{6}$

Plugging In The Answers

You can also plug in when the answers to a problem are actual values, such as 2, 4, 10, or 20. Why would you want to do a lot of complicated algebra to solve a problem when the answer is right there on the page? All you have to do is figure out *which* choice it is.

How can you tell which is the correct answer? Try every choice *until you find the one that works*. Even if this means you have to try all five choices, Plugging In The Answers (PITA) is still a fast and reliable means of getting the right answer.

However, if you use your head, you almost never have to try all five choices. When you plug in the answer choices, begin with choice (C), the middle number. If choice (C) works, you are done. If choice (C) does not work because it is too small, try one of the larger numbers. If choice (C) does not work because it is too big, try one of the smaller numbers. You can almost always find the answer in two or three tries.

We can try PITA on the following problem.

PITA = Plugging In The Answers
Do not try to solve problems like this by writing equations and solving for *x* or *y*. Plugging In The Answers lets you use arithmetic (and your calculator!) instead of algebra, so you are less likely to make errors.

4. If the average (arithmetic mean) of 8 and x is equal to the average of 5, 9, and x, what is the value of x ?

    (A)   1
    (B)   2
    (C)   4
    (D)   8
    (E)   10

How to Crack It

Start with choice (C) and plug in 4 for x. The problem now reads:

4. If the average (arithmetic mean) of 8 and 4 is equal to the average of 5, 9, and 4 . . .

Does this work? The average of 8 and 4 is 6, and the average of 5, 9, and 4 is also 6. Therefore, (C) is the answer.

Of course, (C) will not always be the right answer. Let's try one more.

---○---

10. If $(x - 2)^2 = 2x - 1$, which of the following is a possible value of x ?

 (A) 1
 (B) 2
 (C) 3
 (D) 6
 (E) 7

How to Crack It

If we try plugging in (C), 3, for x, the equation becomes 1 = 5, which is false. So (C) cannot be right. If you are not sure which way to go next, just pick a direction. It will not take long to figure out the correct answer. If we try plugging in (B), 2, for x, the equation becomes 0 = 3, which is false. If we try plugging in (A), 1, for x, the equation becomes 1 = 1, which is true. Unlike Plugging In your own number, there is no need to check the other answer choices, because they do not contain variables; only one answer choice can work. So the answer is (A).

---○---

Plugging In More Than Once

Some Problem Solving questions will require you to plug in more than once. They look like regular Plugging In problems, usually with variables in the answer choices, but they also have the word *must, always,* or *could* in the question. You can treat these problems like normal Plugging In problems, but you will probably have to plug in more than one number before you can get down to the correct answer choice.

What you should do first is plug in an easy number and eliminate any answer choices that contradict what the question is looking for. Plugging in easy numbers will usually rule out two or three answer choices, but to get down to the just one, you will probably have to resort to something less obvious, like the weird numbers in the box.

Here is an example:

When Numbers Get Weird

Weird numbers include the following:

- Zero
- One
- Negatives
- Extreme numbers (such as 1,000,000)
- Fractions

(The acronym ZONEF can help you remember the kinds of numbers to use.)

7. If $f < g < h$, which of the following must be true?

(A) $fg < h$
(B) $f < gh$
(C) $fgh > 0$
(D) $h - g > 0$
(E) $fg < gh$

How to Crack It

There are variables in the answers and the word *must* in the question means *always*, so be prepared to plug in more than once!

For the first pass, we will use easy, small numbers: $f = 2$, $g = 3$, and $h = 4$. Now we will plug those values into each choice. (A) gives us $(2)(3) < 4$, which is false. Eliminate (A). (There is no point in trying it again with different numbers, because we already know it does not *always* work.) (B) works out to $2 < (3)(4)$, which is true, so we will keep that for now. (C) says that $(2)(3)(4) > 0$, which is also true, so (C) cannot be eliminated. (D) correctly states that $4 - 3 > 0$, so (D) stays. (E) states that $(2)(3) < (3)(4)$, which is true. (E) also makes it to the second round.

Thus far, we have only been able to eliminate one answer choice. That means it is time to plug in some weird numbers. How about if we make $f = -5$, $g = 0$, and $h = 1$? Now we will take a second pass at the answer choices. (A) is already gone, so we go straight to (B): $-5 < (0)(1)$. That is still true, so (B) remains an option. But (C) now says that $(-5)(0)(1) > 0$, which is false. Eliminate (C). (D) now works out to $1 - 0 > 0$, which is true, so (D) also remains, but (E) says that $(-5)(0) < (0)(1)$, which is false: They are equal. Eliminate (E).

At this point you might be tempted to just guess between (B) and (D). But we have not tried all of our weird numbers. Nothing in the problem says these numbers have to be integers! What if we tried $f = 0.5$, $g = 0.6$, and $h = 0.7$? Now (B) works out to $0.5 < (0.6)(0.7)$, which is false, because $(0.6)(0.7)$ is only 0.42! Eliminate (B), and that just leaves (D), which still works: $0.7 - 0.6$ is greater than 0. Select (D) and move on.

Plugging In on Geometry

You can also plug in on geometry questions, just as you can for algebra. Any time that you have variables in the answer choices, or hidden variables, plug in! As long as you follow all the rules of geometry while you solve, you will arrive at the correct answer.

Take a look at this problem.

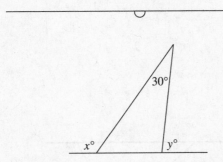

8. In the figure above, what is the value of $x + y$?

    (A) 120
    (B) 140
    (C) 180
    (D) 190
    (E) 210

How to Crack It

We could solve this problem using algebra, but why? We can plug in whatever numbers we want for the other angles inside the triangle—as long as we make sure that all the angles in the triangle add up to 180 degrees. So we plug in 60 and 90 for the other angles inside that triangle. Now we can solve for x and y: If the angle next to x is 60 degrees, then x will be equal to 120. If the angle next to y is equal to 90 degrees, then y will be equal to 90. This makes the sum $x + y$ equal to 120 + 90, or 210. No matter what numbers we choose for the angles inside the triangle, we will always get the same answer, (E).

Drill 2

8. If $3^{x+2} = 243$, what is the value of x ?

(A) 1
(B) 2
(C) 3
(D) 4
(E) 5

14. If $\dfrac{24x}{4} + \dfrac{1}{x} = 5$, then $x =$

(A) $-\dfrac{1}{6}$

(B) $\dfrac{1}{6}$

(C) $\dfrac{1}{4}$

(D) $\dfrac{1}{2}$

(E) 2

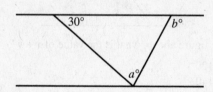

15. In the figure above, what is the value of b in terms of a ?

(A) $30 - a$
(B) $30 + a$
(C) $60 + a$
(D) $80 - a$
(E) $90 + a$

THE AVERAGE PIE

You probably remember the average formula from math class, which states:

Average (arithmetic mean) = $\dfrac{\text{total}}{\text{\# of things}}$. However, the PSAT rarely will ask you

to take a simple average. Of the three parts of an average problem—the average, the total, and the number of things—you are usually given two of these parts, but often in tricky combinations.

Therefore, the most reliable way to solve average problems is always to use the average pie:

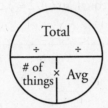

What the pie shows you is that if you know any two of these parts, you can always solve for the third. Once you fill in two of the elements, the pie shows you how to solve for the third part. If you know the total and the number of things, you can solve for the average (total divided by number); if you know the total and the average, you can solve for the number of things (total divided by average); if you know the number of things and average, you can solve for the total (number times average).

We will try this example.

─────────○─────────

9. The average (arithmetic mean) of 3 numbers is 22 and the smallest of these numbers is 2. If the remaining two numbers are equal, what are their values?

(A) 22
(B) 32
(C) 40
(D) 64
(E) 66

Total
When calculating averages, always find the total. It is the one piece of information that ETS loves to withhold.

How to Crack It

We begin by filling in our average pie. We know that 3 numbers have an average of 22. So we can fill in our pie, and the pie shows us that the sum total of these numbers must be 22 × 3, or 66.

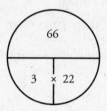

We know that one of the numbers is 2, so we can subtract it from the total we have just found, which leaves 64. What else do we know from the question? That the remaining two numbers are equal, so 64/2 = 32. So the answer is (B).

Try one more.

8. Caroline scored 85, 88, and 89 on three of her four history tests. If her average (arithmetic mean) score for all four tests was 90, what did she score on her fourth test?

(A) 90
(B) 93
(C) 96
(D) 98
(E) 99

How to Crack It

We begin with what we know: We know that the average of all four of her tests was 90. So we can fill in an average pie with this information:

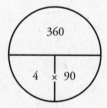

Now the pie tells us that the sum total of the scores on these four tests will be 4 × 90, or 360. Since three of these tests have a sum of 85 + 88 + 89, or 262, we know that the score on the fourth test must be equal to 360 − 262, or 98. This makes the answer (D).

MEDIAN AND MODE

There are two more terms you should know: median and mode. You will see at most one question on the PSAT that tests these ideas, but you might as well get it right.

The **median** of a group of numbers is the number in the middle, just as the "median" is the large divider in the middle of a road. To find the median, here is what you do:

- First, put the elements in the group in numerical order from lowest to highest.
- If the number of elements in your group is *odd*, find the number in the middle. That is the median.
- If you have an *even* number of elements in the group, find the two numbers in the middle and calculate their average (arithmetic mean).

Try this on the following problem:

11. If the 5 students in Ms. Jaffray's math class scored 91, 83, 84, 90, and 85 on their final exams, what is the median score for her class on the final exam?

   (A) 84
   (B) 85
   (C) 86
   (D) 88
   (E) 90

How to Crack It

First, we must place these numbers in order from lowest to highest: 83, 84, 85, 90, 91. The number in the middle is 85, so the median of this group is 85 and the answer is (B).

The **mode** of a group of numbers is the number that appears the most. (Remember: *Mode* sounds like *most*.) To find the mode of a group of numbers, simply see which element appears the greatest number of times.

33. If the 7 students in Ms. Holoway's math class scored 91, 83, 92, 83, 91, 85, and 91 on their final exams, what is the mode of her students' scores?

How to Crack It

Since the number 91 is the one that appears most often in the list, the mode of these numbers is 91. Pretty simple!

PERCENTS

Percent just means "divided by 100." So 20 percent = $\frac{20}{100} = \frac{1}{5}$ or .2.

Likewise, 400 percent = $\frac{400}{100} = \frac{4}{1} = 4$.

Any percent question can be translated into an equation—just use the following rules:

Percent	÷ 100
Of	×
What	x (or any variable)
Is, Are, Equals	=

Take a look at some examples of phrases you might have to translate on the PSAT:

8 percent of 10		$.08 \times 10 = .8$
10 percent of 80		$.1 \times 80 = 8$
5 is what percent of 80?	becomes	$5 = \dfrac{x}{100} \times 80$
5 is 80 percent of what number?		$5 = \dfrac{80}{100} x$
What percent of 5 is 80?		$\dfrac{x}{100} \times 5 = 80$

Percent Increase or Decrease

Percent Increase or *Percent Decrease* $= \dfrac{change}{original\ amount} \times 100$

For example: If an $80 item is reduced to $60 during a sale, the percent decrease is the change in price ($80 - $60 = $20) divided by the original amount ($80), which gives us .25. Multiply by 100 to get 25 percent.

RATIOS AND PROPORTIONS

Ratios

Ratios are about relationships between numbers. Whereas a fraction is a relationship between a part and whole, a ratio is about the relationship between parts. So, for example, if there were 3 boys and 7 girls in a room, the fraction of boys in the room would be $\dfrac{3}{10}$. But the ratio of boys to girls would be 3 : 7. Notice that if you add up the parts, you get the whole. 7 + 3 = 10. That is important for PSAT ratio problems, and you will see why in a moment.

Ratios vs. Fractions

$\text{Fraction} = \dfrac{\text{part}}{\text{whole}}$

$\text{Ratio} = \dfrac{\text{part}}{\text{part}}$

Ratio problems usually are not difficult to identify: The problem will tell you that there is a "ratio" of one thing to another, such as a 2 : 3 ratio of boys to girls in a club. When you see a ratio problem, drawing a ratio box will help you organize the information in the problem and figure out the correct answer.

For instance, suppose a problem tells you that there is a ratio of 2 boys to 3 girls in the physics club, which has 40 members total. Here's how you would put that information in a ratio box so that you can answer the question being asked:

Boys		Girls		Whole	
2	+	3	=		← Ratio
×		×		×	
	=		=		← Multiplier
=		=			
	=		=	40	← Actual #s

The first line of a ratio box is where you put the *ratio* from the problem. These are parts of the whole; they are not actual numbers of people, animals, books, or anything else. By themselves, they do not tell you *how many* of anything you have.

The second line of a ratio box is for the **multiplier**. The multiplier tells you how much you have to multiply the ratio by to get an actual number of something. The multiplier is the same all the way across; it does not change from column to column. Typically, the multiplier is not in the problem; you have to figure it out yourself.

The third line is for *actual numbers*, so when the problem gives you a number of people (or animals, books, etc.), that information goes in the third line.

One more thing to notice: There is a "whole" column. This is where you add up the numbers in the ratio row and actual numbers row. Do not forget to draw a column for the whole—it is usually key in figuring out the problem.

Now that you know some information from the problem and you know how the ratio box works, you can fill in the rest of the box.

Boys		Girls		Whole	
2	+	3	=	5	← Ratio
×		×		×	
8	=	8	=	8	← Multiplier
=		=		=	
16	+	24	=	40	← Actual #s

The first step is adding the ratio columns to find the whole, which is 5. Then you can find the multiplier by figuring out what you need to multiply 5 by to get 40. Once you fill in 8 for the multiplier all the way across the middle row, finding the actual number of boys and girls in the club is simple.

Now you can answer all kinds of questions about the membership of the physics club. There are 16 boys and 24 girls. Take the $\frac{part}{whole}$ from the ratio row to figure out that $\frac{3}{5}$ of the members are girls. That means $\frac{2}{5}$, or 40 percent, of the members are boys.

Try this one.

Gridding In
A ratio is usually expressed as 2 : 3 or 2 to 3, but if you need to grid a ratio, grid it as 2/3.

3. If a certain kind of lemonade is made by mixing water and lemon juice in a ratio of $3\frac{1}{2}$ cups of water for every $\frac{1}{2}$ cup of lemon juice, how many cups of lemon juice will there be in 24 cups of lemonade?

    (A) 3
    (B) 8
    (C) 16
    (D) $16\frac{1}{2}$
    (E) 21

How to Crack It

Water		Lemon	Whole
$3\frac{1}{2}$	+	$\frac{1}{2}$	4
×		×	×
6		6	6
=		=	=
21		3	24

We can set up our ratio box. We have $3\frac{1}{2}$ cups of water and $\frac{1}{2}$ cup of lemon juice, which makes a total of 4 cups of lemonade; that is our "whole." Now we need to figure out how much lemon juice is in 24 cups of lemonade, so if we put 24 into the box, we can see that we need to multiply each part by 6. This means that there will be a total of 3 cups of lemon juice in 24 cups of lemonade. This makes (A) the correct answer.

———————————○———————————

Direct Proportion/Variation

Direct Proportion problems generally ask you to make a conversion (such as from ounces to pounds) or to compare two sets of information and find a missing piece. For example, a proportion problem may ask you to figure out the amount of time it will take to travel 300 miles at a rate of 50 miles per hour.

> To solve proportion problems, just set up two equal fractions. One will have all the information you know, and the other will have a missing piece that you are trying to figure out.

$$\frac{50\ miles}{1\ hour} = \frac{300\ miles}{X\ hours}$$

Be sure to label the parts of your proportion so you know you have the right information in the right place; the same units should be in the numerator on both sides of the equal sign and the same units should be in the denominator on both sides of the equal sign. Notice how using a setup like this helps us keep track of the information we have and find the information we are looking for, so we can use bite-sized pieces to work through the question.

Now we can cross-multiply and then solve for x: $50x = 300$, so $x = 6$ hours.

Try the following problem.

———————————○———————————

2. John receives $2.50 for every 4 pounds of berries he picks. How much money will he receive if he picks 90 pounds of berries?

   (A) $27.00
   (B) $36.00
   (C) $42.25
   (D) $48.50
   (E) $56.25

How to Crack It

To solve this, set up a proportion.

$$\frac{\$2.50}{4 \; pounds} = \frac{x}{90 \; pounds}$$

Now we can cross-multiply. $4x = 2.50 \times 90$, so $4x = 225$, and $x = 56.25$. The answer is (E).

Occasionally, you may see a problem that tells you there are two equal ratios. For example, if a problem says that the ratio of 24 to 0.6 is equal to the ratio of 12 to y, you can solve for y by setting up a proportion. A proportion, after all, is really just two ratios set equal to each other.

$$\frac{24}{0.6} = \frac{12}{y}$$

Then you can cross-multiply and solve to get 0.3 for your answer.

Indirect Proportion/Variation

Indirect Proportion is simply the opposite of a direct, or ordinary, proportion. In a direct proportion when one variable increases, so does the other; however, in an indirect variation or proportion, when one variable *increases*, the other variable *decreases*, or vice versa. These types of problems are generally clearly labeled and all you have to do is apply the indirect variation formula:

$$x_1 y_1 = x_2 y_2$$

Once you memorize the formula, applying it will become second nature to you.

Other Names
Indirect Proportion is sometimes called Inverse Proportion or Inverse Variation.

Now try this one.

○
---

18. On a particular survey, the percentage of people answering a question with the same response is inversely proportional to the number of the question. If 80% of the people surveyed answered the same response to the eighth question, then, approximately, what percentage of the people surveyed answered the same answer to the 30th question?

(A) 3%
(B) 13%
(C) 18%
(D) 21%
(E) 36%

How to Crack It

The problem tells us that the numbers are inversely proportional, so we need to figure out what to put into the formula. The first piece of information is that 80 percent of the people answered the eighth question correctly; we need to know the percent of people who answered the 30th question correctly. We will make x the percent and y the question number. Your equation should look like this:

$$(80)(8) = (x_2)(30)$$

When you solve the equation, you should end up with $\dfrac{640}{30}$ or $21\dfrac{1}{3}$, which is answer choice (D) (remember, when a problem says "approximately," you will probably have to round up or down).

○

Sets

Sets are basically lists of distinct numbers. The numbers in a set are called **elements** or **members**.

For example, if a problem asks for the set of even integers greater than 0 but less than 12, the set would be {2, 4, 6, 8, 10}.

We can try one.

---

4. If set $X = \{2, 3, 5, 7\}$ and set $Y = \{3, 6, 8\}$, then which of the following represents the union of X and Y?

   (A) {3}
   (B) {2, 3}
   (C) {2, 3, 5, 7}
   (D) {3, 6 , 7, 8}
   (E) {2, 3, 5, 6, 7, 8}

How to Crack It

The question asks for the union of the two sets, so you need to combine the elements into one big set, as in (E). Watch out for (A), which is the tricky answer; it is the intersection, not the union.

Key Terms
A union is the list of each distinct number if you combine the sets. An intersection is a set of distinct numbers that appear in two different sets.

Drill 3

a. If a student scores 70, 90, 95, and 105, what is the average (arithmetic mean) for these tests? _____

b. If a student has an average (arithmetic mean) score of 80 on 4 tests, what is the total of the scores received on those tests? _____

c. If a student has an average of 60 on tests, with a total of 360, how many tests has the student taken? _____

d. If the average of 2, 8, and x is 6, what is the value of x? _____

e. What percent of 5 is 6? _____

f. 60 percent of 90 is the same as 50 percent of what number? _____

g. Jenny's salary increased from $30,000 to $33,000. By what percent did her salary increase? _____

h. In 1980, factory X produced 18,600 pieces. In 1981, factory X only produced 16,000 pieces. By approximately what percent did production decrease from 1980 to 1981? _____

i. In a certain bag of marbles, the ratio of red marbles to green marbles is 7 : 5. If the bag contains 96 marbles, how many green marbles are in the bag? _____

4. The average (arithmetic mean) of 4 numbers is 80. If two of the numbers are 50 and 60, what is the sum of the other two numbers?

11. 60% of 80 is equivalent to 40% of what number?

(A) 100
(B) 105
(C) 110
(D) 120
(E) 140

14. A group of 30 adults and 20 children went to the beach. If 50% of the adults and 80% of the children went swimming, what percent of the group went swimming?

(A) 30%
(B) 46%
(C) 50%
(D) 62%
(E) 65%

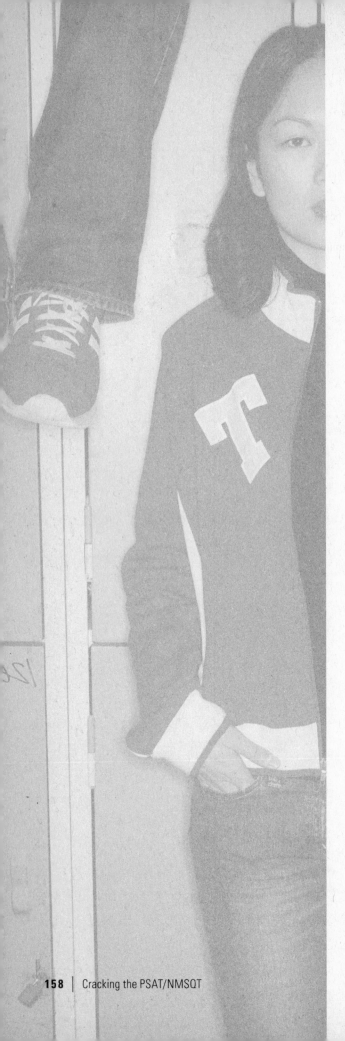

Summary

o The test is full of opportunities to use arithmetic instead of algebra—just look for your chances to use Plugging In and Plugging In The Answers (PITA).

o If a question has *in terms of* or variables in the answer choices, it is a Plugging In problem. Plug in your own number, do the math, find the target value, and use POE to get down to one correct answer.

o If a question does not have variables but asks for a fraction or a percent of an unknown number, you can also plug in there. Just substitute your own number for the unknown and take the rest of the problem step by step.

o If a question has an unknown and asks for a specific amount, making you feel like you have to write an equation, try PITA instead.

o When plugging in with geometry problems, remember to use your knowledge of basic geometry rules; e.g., there are still 180 degrees in a triangle when you are using Plugging In.

o The Average Pie can help you tackle any question about the average (arithmetic mean)—just fill what you know from the problem into the correct spots for *Total*, *Number of Things*, and *Average*.

o Use the ratio box on questions that ask about a ratio. Fill in the ratio box with information from the problem, calculate the missing piece, then solve for whatever the problem is asking for.

o Remember that there is a difference between direct and indirect (inverse) proportions. First, figure out which one you are dealing with, and then set up the correct formula and fill in the information the problem gives you.

o Sets are groups of distinct numbers.

Chapter 9
Advanced Math
Principles

Thus far we have covered basic knowledge and some PSAT-specific problem-solving skills. Now we will look at some of the more advanced skills tested on the PSAT.

FUNCTIONS

The first of our topics takes us back to school. While much of this test is not based on the math you have seen in high school recently, this is one topic that you will most likely recognize from math class. The functions on the PSAT mostly look like this:

$$f(x) = x^2 + 6x + 24$$

Most questions of this type will give you a specific value to plug in for x and then ask you to find the value of the function for that x. Each function is just a set of instructions that tells you what to do to x—or the number you plug in for x—in order to find the corresponding value for $f(x)$ (a fancy name for y). Just plug your information into that equation and follow the instructions.

We will try an easy one.

○

5. If $f(x) = x^2 + 3x - 3$, then $f(7)$ equals

    (A) 14
    (B) 20
    (C) 32
    (D) 67
    (E) 83

How to Crack It

Function questions are just testing whether you can follow the directions, so follow them! The instructions, in this case, are in the equation. So plug 7 into the equation and it should look like this: $f(7) = 7^2 + 3(7) - 3$. Do the math and $f(7) = 67$. Therefore, the answer is (D).

○

Functions with Weird Symbols

If you ever see a strange symbol on the PSAT—& or @, for example—do not worry. There are no special symbols you should have learned in school that the PSAT requires you to know. What you are looking at is another type of function problem.

> A function problem is just ETS's way of testing whether you can follow directions. The key is always to plug in numbers.

For instance, you might see a question like this one:

If @x = $2x$ + 2, what is the value of @3 ?

What ETS is asking you to do is to plug in the number that follows the @ symbol everywhere you see the variable x. So to solve for @3, you plug in 3 for x in the expression $2x$ + 2, and get 2(3) + 2, or 8.

To figure out the value of a function, all you have to do is plug in a value for x and solve.

Try the following:

---

5. If x # y = $4x$ − y, what is the value of 3 # 4 ?

   (A) 6
   (B) 8
   (C) 10
   (D) 12
   (E) 14

How to Crack It

In this case, we need to plug in whatever is to the left of the # for x, and whatever is to the right of the # for y. This means that we plug in 3 for x and 4 for y. So 3 # 4 will be equal to 4(3) − 4, or 8. This makes (B) the answer.

EXPANDING, FACTORING, AND SOLVING QUADRATIC EQUATIONS

You probably also recall studying quadratic equations in school. On the PSAT, you will likely see at least one problem that requires you to perform a complex algebraic manipulation called factoring. It may have been a little while since you have done this, so we will review.

Expanding

Most often you will be asked to expand an expression simply by multiplying it out. When working with an expression of the form $(x + 3)(x + 4)$, multiply it out using the following rule:

FOIL = First Outer Inner Last

Start with the *first* figure in each set of parentheses: $x \times x = x^2$

Now do the two *outer* figures: $x \times 4 = 4x$

Next, the two *inner* figures: $3 \times x = 3x$

Finally, the *last* figure in each set of parentheses: $3 \times 4 = 12$

Add them all together, and we get $x^2 + 4x + 3x + 12$, or $x^2 + 7x + 12$

Factoring

If you ever see an expression of the form $x^2 + 7x + 12$ on a PSAT question, there is a good chance that factoring will lead you to the answer.

The key to factoring is figuring out what pair of numbers will multiply to give you the constant term (12, in this case) and add up to the coefficient of the x term (7, in this question). (It could be more complicated if the x^2 term had a coefficient, but that rarely happens on the PSAT.)

We will try an example:

Step 1: Draw two sets of parentheses next to each other and fill an x into the left side of each. That is what gives us our x^2 term.

Step 2: 12 can be factored a number of ways: 1×12, 2×6, or 3×4. Which of these adds up to 7? 3 and 4, so place a 3 on the right side of one parenthesis and a 4 in the other.

Step 3: Now we need to figure out what the correct signs should be. They should both be positive in this case, because that will sum to 7 and multiply to 12, so fill plus signs into each parenthesis.

$$x^2 + 7x + 12$$

$$(x \quad)(x \quad)$$

$$(x \quad 3)(x \quad 4)$$

$$(x + 3)(x + 4)$$

If you want to double check your work, try expanding out $(x + 3)(x + 4)$ using FOIL and you will get the original expression.

Now try the following problem.

13. If $\dfrac{x^2 + 5x - 6}{x - 1} = 2$, then what is the value of x ?

(A) 4
(B) 1
(C) 5
(D) 6
(E) 8

How to Crack It

Since we know we can factor $x^2 + 5x - 6$, we should do so. When we factor it, we get $\dfrac{(x-1)(x+6)}{(x-1)} = 2$. Now we can cancel the $(x - 1)$ and we're left with $x + 6 = 2$. If we solve for x, we find $x = -4$ and our answer is (A).

Remember that we can also solve this problem by Plugging In The Answers!

Binomial Factoring
When a question provides a denominator like $(x-1)$ and you need to factor the numerator, $(x-1)$ will more than likely be one of the binomial's factors. Recognize this, and polynomial problems will be much easier!

Solving Quadratic Equations

Sometimes you will need to factor to solve an equation. In this case, there will be two possible values for x, called the roots of the equation. To solve for x, use the following steps:

Step 1: Make sure that the equation is set equal to zero.
Step 2: Factor the equation.
Step 3: Set each parenthetical expression equal to zero. So if you have $(x + 2)(x - 7) = 0$, you get $(x + 2) = 0$ and $(x - 7) = 0$. When you solve for each, you get $x = -2$ and $x = 7$. Therefore, -2 and 7 are the solutions or roots of the equation.

Try the following problem.

———————————————○———————————————

14. If $x^2 + 2x - 15 = 0$, then the possible values of x are

    (A)   2 and 4
    (B)   –13 and –4
    (C)   5 and –4
    (D)   –5 and 3
    (E)   6 and 3

How to Crack It

Work the steps:

Step 1: The equation is already set equal to zero.
Step 2: We can now factor the left side of the equation, to get $(x + 5)(x - 3) = 0$.
Step 3: When we set each parenthetical expression equal to zero, we get $x = -5$ and $x = 3$. Therefore, the answer is (D).

———————————————○———————————————

Drill 1

Answers can be found in Part III.

5. If a function f is defined by $f(x) = \dfrac{5x + 9}{x - 1}$ where $x \neq 1$, what is the value of $f(3)$?

(A) 8
(B) 12
(C) 14
(D) 20
(E) 24

10. For all values of a and b, $a \blacklozenge b = \dfrac{a}{2} + 3b - 7$. What is the value of $6 \blacklozenge 8$?

(A) 14
(B) 20
(C) 27
(D) 33
(E) 37

12. If -3 is one of the solutions of the quadratic equation $x^2 + 8x + k = 0$, what is the other value of x ?

(A) -15
(B) -5
(C)   3
(D)   5
(E)   15

15. If $\dfrac{x^2 + 2x - 8}{x^2 - 7x + 10} = 4$, what is the value of x ?

(A) -4
(B)   0
(C)   2
(D)   5
(E)   8

19. For all values of x, a function f is defined by $f(x) = x^2 + 7x + 12$. If $f(a) = 2$, what could be a value of a ?

(A) -5
(B) -3
(C)   2
(D)   5
(E)   30

THE PYTHAGOREAN THEOREM

Whenever you have a right triangle, you can use the Pythagorean theorem. The theorem says that the sum of the squares of the legs of the triangle (the sides next to the right angle) will equal the square of the hypotenuse (the side opposite the right angle).

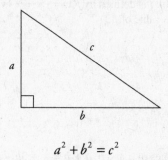

$$a^2 + b^2 = c^2$$

Two of the most common ratios of sides that fit the Pythagorean theorem are $3 : 4 : 5$ and $5 : 12 : 13$. Since these are ratios, any multiples of these numbers will also work, such as $6 : 8 : 10$, and $30 : 40 : 50$.

Try the following example.

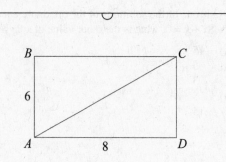

33. If *ABCD* is a rectangle, what is the perimeter of triangle *ABC* ?

How to Crack It

We can use the Pythagorean theorem to figure out the length of the diagonal of the rectangle—since it has sides 6 and 8, its diagonal must be 10. (If you remembered that this is one of those well-known Pythagorean ratios, you did not actually have to do the calculations.) Therefore, the perimeter of the triangle is 6 + 8 + 10, or 24.

Let's try another one.

13. Gerald and Frank work in the same office. To drive home, Gerald drives 12 miles north, then 5 miles east. Frank drives 16 miles west, then 12 miles south. What is the distance from Gerald's to Frank's house?

(A) 17
(B) 24
(C) 33
(D) 45
(E) 60

How to Crack It:

The easiest way to solve this is to draw the directions and the distances that both Gerald and Frank travel. If we place a point that represents their office, we should draw Gerald's route directly up 12 miles and to the right for 5. Frank travels from the same point of origin directly to the left for 16 miles and then down for 12. A drawing of this should look like the following:

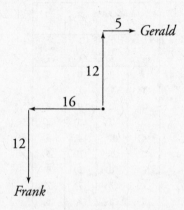

We can then see that we have two right triangles formed. Using the common ratios, we can fill in the hypotenuse of the triangle with sides 5 and 12 with 13 and the hypotenuse of the triangle with sides 12 and 16 with 20. We then have a continuous line between the two hypotenuses. We can add 20 and 13 to get 33 in choice (C).

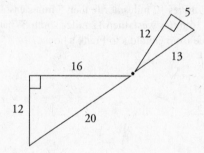

SPECIAL RIGHT TRIANGLES

There are two specific right triangles, the properties of which may play a role in some harder PSAT math problems. They are the right triangles with angles 45-45-90 and 30-60-90. These triangles appear at the front of each Math section, so you do not have to memorize them.

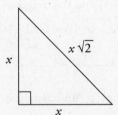

An isosceles right triangle has angles that measure 45, 45, and 90 degrees. Whenever you have a 45-45-90 triangle with sides of x, the hypotenuse will always be $x\sqrt{2}$. This means that if one of the legs of the triangle measures 3, then the hypotenuse will be $3\sqrt{2}$.

This right triangle is important because it is half of a square. Understanding the 45-45-90 triangle will allow you to easily find the diagonal of a square from its side, or find the side of a square from its diagonal.

Here is an example.

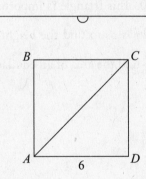

13. In square *ABCD* above, what is the perimeter of triangle *ABC* ?

(A) $6\sqrt{2}$

(B) 8

(C) $12 + \sqrt{2}$

(D) $12 + 6\sqrt{2}$

(E) 18

How to Crack It

This question looks like a question about a square, and it certainly is in part, but it is really more about the two triangles formed by the diagonal.

In this square, we know that each of the triangles formed by the diagonal AC is a 45-45-90 right triangle. Since the square has a side of 6, using the 45-45-90 right triangle rule, each of the sides is 6 and the diagonal is $6\sqrt{2}$. Therefore, the perimeter of the triangle is $6 + 6 + 6\sqrt{2}$, or $12 + 6\sqrt{2}$ —the answer is (D).

The other important right triangle to understand is the 30-60-90 right triangle.

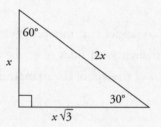

A 30-60-90 triangle with a short side of x will have a hypotenuse of $2x$ and a middle side of $x\sqrt{3}$. If the smallest side (the x side) of the triangle is 5, then the sides measure 5, $5\sqrt{3}$, and 10. This triangle is important because it is half of an equilateral triangle, and it allows us to find the height of an equilateral triangle, which is what we will need to find the area of an equilateral triangle.

Try the following.

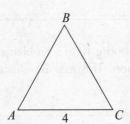

13. Triangle *ABC* above is equilateral, with sides of length 4. What is its area?

(A) 3
(B) $4\sqrt{2}$
(C) $4\sqrt{3}$
(D) 8
(E) $8\sqrt{3}$

Triangle Tip
An easy way to figure out the height of an equilateral triangle is take half of its side and multiply it by the square root of 3.

How to Crack It

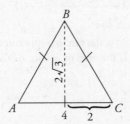

To find the area of the triangle, we need to know the base and the height. The question tells you that the base (line segment *AC*) is 4; now we need to find the height, which is *perpendicular* to the base. You can create the height by drawing a line from angle *B* straight down to the base, as you can see in the drawing above. Now you have two 30-60-90 triangles, and you can use the rules of 30-60-90 triangles to figure out the height. Half of the base would be 2, and that is the side across from the 30 degree angle, so you would multiply it by $\sqrt{3}$ to get the height.

Now we know that the base is 4 and the height is $2\sqrt{3}$, so plugging those numbers into the formula for area of a triangle, we get $A = \dfrac{1}{2} \times 4 \times 2\sqrt{3}$, which equals $4\sqrt{3}$. Thus, (C) is the correct answer.

OVERLAPPING FIGURES

Very often on a difficult geometry problem you will see two figures that overlap: a triangle and a square, a triangle and a circle, or a square and a circle.

> The key to solving overlapping figure problems is figuring out what the two figures have in common. This may be something you have to draw in yourself.

Take a look at the following problem.

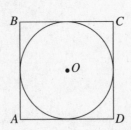

16. In the figure above, the circle with center O is drawn in square $ABCD$. If the area of square $ABCD$ is 36, what is the area of circle O ?

(A) 18
(B) 24
(C) 9π
(D) 12π
(E) 36π

How to Crack It

Go ahead and draw the diameter in the figure through point O and parallel to the base. We mentioned earlier that we want to write down things we know about the figure, so we should write the formulas for both of the figures we have been given. The question mentions the area of the square and the area of the circle, so write $A = s^2$ for the square and $A = \pi r^2$ for the circle.

Now we can take the information we have been given and take bite-sized pieces to crack the question. Since we know that the area of the square is 36, we can solve the first equation to get $s = 6$, so $d = 6$ as well. Now we will take that information to the other formula, that of the circle, the area of which we are being asked to find. The radius is half of the diameter, so $A = \pi 3^2 = 9\pi$, and our answer is choice (C).

Here is another one.

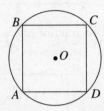

19. In the figure above, *ABCD* is a square drawn in the circle with center *O*. If the area of the circle is 16π, what is the area of square *ABCD* ?

(A) 4
(B) 16
(C) $16\sqrt{2}$
(D) 32
(E) $32\sqrt{2}$

How to Crack It

What do the square and the circle have in common? A diagonal of the square is a diameter of the circle. Go ahead and draw that on the figure now. Once again, we have two formulas we might need here, $A = s^2$ for the square and $A = \pi r^2$ for the circle. We know something about the circle, so we will use that information to take the next bite: Subbing in 16π for the area, we can solve and get $r = 4$. This tells us that the diameter is 8 and so is the diagonal of the square. What now? We could use the Pythagorean theorem to solve for the sides, but if you understand your special right triangles, you will know that when you draw a diagonal in a square it divides it into two 45-45-90 triangles. Since we multiply the length of the side by $\sqrt{2}$ in these special right triangles to find the diagonal, we can just divide by $\sqrt{2}$ to find the side, which gives us $8/\sqrt{2}$ as the length of a side of the square. We won't bother getting the decimal equivalent or rationalizing because if we put this right into the area formula we get $\left(\dfrac{8}{\sqrt{2}}\right)^2 = \dfrac{64}{2} = 32$, which is answer choice (D).

Quick Review
- An interior angle is an angle formed by two radii.
- A sector is the portion of the circle between the two radii.

PROPORTIONALITY IN A CIRCLE

Here is one more rule that plays a role in more advanced circle problems.

> Arc measure is proportional to interior angle measure, which is proportional to sector area.

This means that whatever fraction of the total degree measure is made up by the interior angle, the arc described by that angle is the same fraction of the circumference, and the pie piece created has the same fraction of the area.

Take a look at the figure below:

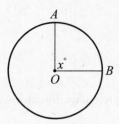

If angle *x* is equal to 90 degrees, which is one-quarter of 360 degrees, then the arc *AB* is equal to one-quarter of the circumference of the circle and the area of the sector of the circle enclosed by radii *OA* and *OB* is equal to one-quarter of the area of the circle.

To see how this works in a question, try number 18.

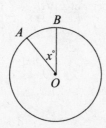

18. The circle above with center O has a radius of 4. If $x = 30$, what is the length of arc AB ?

(A) $\dfrac{\pi}{6}$

(B) $\dfrac{2\pi}{3}$

(C) 3

(D) $\dfrac{3\pi}{2}$

(E) 3π

How to Crack It

Since the interior angle x is equal to 30 degrees, which is $\dfrac{1}{12}$ of 360 degrees, we know that the arc AB will be equal to $\dfrac{1}{12}$ of the circumference of the circle. Since the circle has radius 4, its circumference will be 8π. Therefore, arc AB will measure $\dfrac{1}{12} \times 8\pi$, or $\dfrac{2\pi}{3}$, choice (B).

11. Points A and B lie on a circle with center O such that the measure of $\angle OAB$ is 45 . If the area of the circle is 64π, what is the perimeter of $\triangle AOB$?

(A) $8 + 8\sqrt{2}$
(B) $16 + 8\sqrt{2}$
(C) $16 + 16\sqrt{2}$
(D) $32 + 16\sqrt{2}$
(E) $64 + 16\sqrt{2}$

How to Crack It

This time a diagram is not provided for you, so drawing the circle should be your first step. Since points A and B lie on the circle, $\overline{OA}$ and $\overline{OB}$ are both radii, and equal in length, making $\triangle AOB$ isosceles. The problem indicates that $\angle OAB$ is 45 degrees, which means that $\angle OBA$ is also 45 degrees, which makes $\triangle AOB$ a 45-45-90 triangle (remember those special right triangles?).

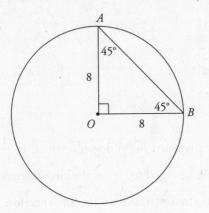

Given the circle's area of 64π, the radii of the circle (which are the legs of the isosceles right triangle) are 8, and the hypotenuse is $8\sqrt{2}$, making the perimeter $8 + 8 + 8\sqrt{2}$, or $16 + 8\sqrt{2}$, which is answer choice (B).

TANGENTS TO A CIRCLE

A tangent is a line that intersects the edge of a circle at exactly one point. A radius drawn to the point of tangency forms a 90 degree angle with the tangent line. This comes up occasionally on hard problems, so take a look at the example below. As you work through this question, if you are thinking that you would never know how to do it yourself, there is still a valuable lesson here: perhaps this question is not in your POOD! If so, you should look instead for a plug in question or math you are more familiar with, even if it is a number 19 or 20.

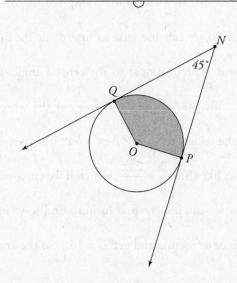

18. In the figure above, $\overline{NP}$ and $\overline{NQ}$ are tangent to the circle with center O at points P and Q, respectively. If the area of the shaded region is 24π, what is the circumference of the circle?

(A)   8π
(B)   12π
(C)   16π
(D)   40π
(E)   64π

How to Crack It

The key is remembering that any line or line segment drawn tangent to a circle is perpendicular to a radius drawn from the center of the circle to that tangent point; this means both ∠OQN and ∠OPN equal 90 degrees. With ∠QNP given as 45 degrees, that leaves the central ∠QOP of quadrilateral QNPO. Since all quadrilaterals contain 360 degrees and since 45 of the remaining 180 degrees are accounted for, that remaining angle must be 135 degrees. As all circles contain 360 degrees of arc, this means the shaded area represents $\dfrac{135}{360}$ or $\dfrac{3}{8}$ of the area of the entire circle.

Remember, we want to write down the formulas for quantities the question talks about, so those are $A = \pi r^2$ and $C = 2\pi r$. Thus far we do not have anything we can put directly into a formula, so what do we know? We are told that the area of the shaded sector is 24π, so we can use that to figure out the area of the whole circle, because we know it is proportional to the central angle. In fact, we have already figured out that this part of the circle is $\dfrac{3}{8}$ of the whole, so the whole area must be $\dfrac{8}{3}$ times the sector, so $\left(\dfrac{8}{3}\right) \times 24\pi = 64\pi$ (this is a shortcut to using a proportion, which looks like this: $\dfrac{3}{8} = \dfrac{24\pi}{x}$, which if we cross-multiply and solve for x gives us 64π). Now we can use the first formula and solve for $r = 8$. We can put this right into the second formula and get $C = 16\pi$, so the answer is (C).

Drill 2

Answers can be found in Part III.

13. If two sides of a triangle are 3 and 7, which of the following could be the perimeter of the triangle?

(A)   4
(B)   10
(C)   15
(D)   20
(E)   21

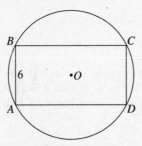

8. In the figure above, rectangle *ABCD* is inscribed in circle *O*. If the length of side *AB* is 6 and the area of the rectangle is 48, what is the area of circle *O* ?

(A)   10
(B)   10π
(C)   25π
(D)   50π
(E)   100π

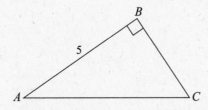

Note: Figure not drawn to scale.

14. In the figure above, if triangle *ABC* is isosceles, what is the perimeter of the triangle?

(A)   12.5

(B) $10\sqrt{2}$

(C) $10 + 5\sqrt{2}$

(D) $15\sqrt{2}$

(E)   25

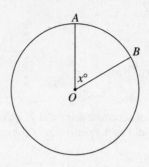

16. The circle shown above has its center at O. If $x = 60$ and the length of arc AB is 2π, what is the area of circle O?

(A) 4
(B) 6
(C) 6π
(D) 12π
(E) 36π

18. A circle with center O has diameter $\overline{AB}$. Segment $\overline{AC}$ is tangent to the circle at point A and has a length of 5. If the area of the circle is 36π, what is the perimeter of triangle ABC?

(A) 13
(B) 15
(C) 25
(D) 30
(E) 60

Summary

o   On Functions questions, simply use the formula they provide and plug in the numbers they give you—whether the problem contains $f(x)$ or weird symbols.

o   Quadratics generally require that you *expand* or *factor*—the general rule is, if you see a quadratic in one form, switch it to the other.

o   There is no trigonometry on the PSAT—the Pythagorean theorem, common right triangles (such as 3 : 4 : 5 and 5 : 12 : 13), and special right triangles (45-45-90 and 30-60-90) are the only tools you need to figure out angles and lengths in a right triangle.

o   When you see overlapping figures, figure out which measurement the two figures have in common.

o   Circles that show an interior angle (an angle that extends from the center of the circle) have proportionality. The interior angle over the whole degree measure (360 degrees) equals the same fraction as the arc enclosed by that angle over the circumference. Likewise, both of these fractions are equal to the area of the segment over the entire area of the circle.

o   When you see a line that is "tangent to" a circle, remember two things:
   •   The line intersects the circle at exactly one point.
   •   The radius of the circle that intersects the tangent line is perpendicular (90 degrees) to that tangent line.

Chapter 10
Writing Skills

For some of you, taking a test of your writing skills would be a good thing; for others, it is not as appealing. But do not worry—there is no essay on the PSAT. What the Writing Skills section really tests is a few grammar rules and your skill at correcting sentences using those rules. Even if you have not had many grammar lessons in school, this chapter will teach you what you need to know and help you approach the Writing Skills section like a pro.

WHAT TO EXPECT

The Writing Skills section contains 39 questions, including 14 Error Identification questions, 20 Improving Sentences questions, and five Improving Paragraphs questions. If these questions do not sound like any writing you have studied in school, you are not mistaken. The Writing Skills section is much more about test-taking skills than it is about actual writing skills. It will be the last section of the PSAT, and you will be allotted 30 minutes to complete it.

PSAT Grammar

The grammar ETS chooses to test on the PSAT is basic. Even if you have not done much grammar in school, you can perform well on this section; learning just a few rules will take you a long way. While we cannot cover every single scenario that you might see on test day, ETS is actually quite predictable and likes to test the same few rules over and over. We will cover those rules in this chapter, and if you need more in-depth work in any of the areas covered here, you may refer to The Princeton Review's *Grammar Smart*.

How to Do Well
- Review/learn PSAT grammar
- Know how to attack each question type
- Know which questions to answer and which ones to skip

Question Strategy

Every question type on the PSAT can be cracked, and the Writing Skills questions are no exception. While reviewing the basic grammar you need, you will also learn how to crack Error ID and Improving Sentences questions. After you solidify your approach to these question types, you will learn how to crack Improving Paragraphs questions by employing the grammar and skills you have already mastered.

To Do or Not To Do

Most of the Writing Skills questions (specifically, the Improving Sentences questions and Error ID questions) are arranged in a rough order of difficulty, with the exception of the Improving Paragraphs questions, which are the last five questions of the section. As usual, this means that the early questions will have fairly obvious answers that you should not second guess, the middle third will be fairly straightforward but will contain some tricks, and the last third should be approached with caution. The Writing Skills section is a little different than the other two sections, though, because it is more about knowing the rules that are tested and less about having to think hard about how to solve something or what the passage means.

If you spot the mistake in a sentence immediately, you are already close to getting the answer. Stay focused on what kind of error ETS is testing in that question, and use POE. If you do not initially spot an error, you will have to proceed more carefully. Do not trust your ear, especially on the later (hard) questions.

SNEAK PREVIEW

Before we review some basic grammar rules, we will look at the two main question types that appear in the Writing Skills section.

Improving Sentences

15. This is an example of an Improving Sentences question <u>that does not contain</u> an error.

    (A) that does not contain
    (B) that has not been containing
    (C) which has not been contain
    (D) which is not being with
    (E) about which there is nothing to indicate it being with

Improving Sentences questions give you a sentence, part or all of which is underlined. The underlined part may or may not contain a grammatical error. There are some important things you need to know about Improving Sentences questions:

- Answer choice (A) always repeats the underlined portion exactly as it appears in the initial sentence. Thus, you never need to read answer choice (A)—you already did when you first read the sentence.
- Approximately 20 percent of the sentences will be correct as written, so do not be afraid to choose answer choice (A) if you have eliminated the other choices.
- The non-underlined portion of the sentence is always correct. Make sure to read it carefully. Many students focus only on the underlined part since that is where the error must be (if there is one); however, often you can find the underlined error only by focusing carefully on the sentence as a whole.
- Do not try to revise the sentence in your head; you never know how ETS is going to fix it, and your perfect revision may not be listed. Work with the answer choices they give you and look for the *best* answer.

Error IDs

21. This is an example of an Error ID question that has no
    A   B   C D
    error. No error
         E

An Error ID question gives you a sentence that has four words or phrases underlined, each with a corresponding letter underneath. At the end of each sentence will be "No error"—choice (E). There are some important things you need to know about Error IDs:

- There is never more than one error per sentence.
- If there is an error, it is always underlined.
- Approximately 20 percent of all Error ID questions are correct as written, so do not be afraid to choose choice (E).
- As you work through the sentence, you should search for what MUST be wrong instead of what COULD be wrong.

THE METHOD

There are many similarities in the way we approach Error IDs and Improving Sentences. Here are some things to keep in mind for both question types:

- **Do not make decisions based on sound.** One of the biggest ways the test writers try to trip you up is to use an error that sounds correct to you because you hear it so often in everyday life. For example, the sentence "Everyone should bring their own lunch" sounds perfectly normal, yet it contains a grammatical error (pronoun agreement, which you will hear more about later). Alternatively, ETS can put in words that sound odd because you are not used to hearing them, but are, in fact, perfectly correct. The important thing is to move beyond "It sounds bad" or "It sounds okay" as the sole reason you eliminate or choose an answer choice. Learn the basic grammar rules ETS tests, and look for them.
- **Use POE aggressively.** Focus on eliminating everything you can, based on the rules of grammar, not on picking something that stands out as a "good" sentence.
- **Trim the fat.** One technique that will help you decide if an answer choice contains an error is "trimming the fat." This means taking a sentence and getting rid of the extraneous words and phrases that are just there for distraction. For example, take the following sentence: "Japan, since the early part of the 1980s when Japanese products became popular with consumers, have been able to export the high-quality technology demanded by foreign markets." There is a long, distracting phrase separating *Japan* and *have* so that it is easy to forget that these two words have to agree in number to be correct—and they do not. It should be *Japan...has,* because Japan is *one* country. So when you see prepositional phrases or phrases offset by commas, ignore them while you figure out if the surrounding words are correct. You can even cross them out, but do not make it impossible to read; you may need to see those words later.

Improving Sentences

When you first read an Improving Sentences question, either you will spot an error in the sentence or you will not. What you *do not* want to do, above all, is read the sentence five or six times, replacing the underlined portion with each of the answer choices. This is a huge waste of time and will end in your picking an answer based on your ear, not on your knowledge of grammar rules. Remember, ETS knows how to trick your memory and your ear.

Plan A: If You Spot an Error Immediately

1. Try to articulate what the error is, so that you avoid picking an answer solely by ear. For instance, say to yourself, "There is a subject-verb agreement error, because *Japan* is singular and *have* is plural." If you are confident it is an error, then eliminate (A) and any answer choices that contain the same error.
2. Compare the remaining answer choices and note how they differ. Eliminate any answer choices that contain new errors or change the intended meaning of the original sentence. If you get down to two answers that both seem grammatically correct, pick the more concise (usually shorter) answer.
3. Repeat step 2 until you are down to one answer choice.

Plan B: If You Do Not Spot an Error Immediately

1. Compare the answer choices and note how they differ. Eliminate any answer choices that contain errors.
2. Repeat step 1 until you have one answer choice left.

Error IDs

Again, when you first read an Error ID, one of two things will happen: Either you will spot an error immediately, or you will not. It does not really matter if you do or not; there are ways to get the correct answer regardless.

Plan A: If You Spot an Error Immediately

1. Again, try to articulate to yourself what the error is, so that you avoid picking an answer solely by using your ear.
2. Check the other answers just to be safe.
3. Select your original answer if you are confident it truly is an error.

Plan B: If You Do Not Spot an Error Immediately

1. Check each underlined portion individually, thinking about the grammar rules that might apply to it. For example, if the word *everyone* is underlined, say to yourself, "*Everyone* is a pronoun, so I need to check for agreement, ambiguity, and case."
2. Eliminate answers that you know are grammatically correct.
3. Select the answer that violates a rule or (E) if there is no error.

Now that we have discussed how to tackle each question type, we are going to move on to reviewing the grammar. We will do problems as we go along to practice the techniques.

GRAMMAR RULES

To do well on the Writing Skills section, you need to remember some basic grammar rules. Fortunately, PSAT grammar is not difficult, nor is it extensive. In fact, the PSAT really tests only five basic grammatical concepts:

1. verbs
2. nouns
3. pronouns
4. prepositions
5. other little things

> **No Error?**
> As we have mentioned, about 20 percent of Error ID questions and Improving Sentences questions contain no error. If you have used your checklist and cannot find a mistake, chances are there is no mistake. Do not be afraid to pick *No error*—choice (E) on Error ID or choice (A) on Improving Sentences questions.

These are the five areas in which a sentence can go wrong. They will function as a checklist for you—every time you read a sentence, you will look at these five areas to find the error. If you do not find one after checking these five things, then there probably is no error.

Verbs

A **verb** is an action word. It tells what the subject of the sentence is doing. There are three types of errors you can see with verbs:

- agreement
- parallelism
- tense

Agreement

> Verbs must always *agree* in number with the subjects with which they are paired: singular with singular, plural with plural.

Subject-verb agreement is heavily tested on the PSAT, so whenever you see a verb in the underlined portion of a sentence make sure it agrees in number with the subject it refers to. That is, plural with plural and singular with singular. Remember, the subject is the thing the sentence is talking about. If you are given a singular subject (*Jake, the car, she, Europe*), it must be paired with a singular verb (*is, was, plays, rocks*). Singular verbs generally have an *s* on the end, like plural nouns.

Let's look at a question.

---

1. The statistics released by the State Department <u>makes the economic situation look bleaker than it really is</u>.

   (A) makes the economic situation look bleaker than it really is
   (B) makes the economic situation look bleaker than they really are
   (C) make the economic situations look bleaker than it really is
   (D) make the economic situation look bleaker than it really is
   (E) make the economic situation look more bleak than they really are

How to Crack It

The verb *makes* appears in the underlined portion of the sentence, so we need to check the subject. This sentence is about *the statistics*, so the subject is plural. Do not be confused by all of the other words that appear after it, *released by the State Department,* they are just there to distract us. We are only interested in the simple subject, which is plural. The verb *makes* is singular, though, so there is a problem with the sentence as it is written. We can go ahead and cross out choice (A) now. Remember, we do not need to read it because it repeats the underlined portion of the sentence exactly. We can also cross out (B) right away because it repeats the same error.

Answer choices (C) and (D) are identical except for the words *situation* and *situations*. Which is correct? The verb it is paired up with *is,* which is singular, so the singular *situation* is correct. We can eliminate (C). Comparing (D) and (E) we find that (E) uses *they...are,* which is plural, so we can get rid of that and choose (D).

Sometimes, though, you will have to do more work to figure out if the subject of the sentence is plural or singular. Here are some things to watch out for:

Collective Nouns

These can be a little tricky, but they have one thing in common: They are all *groups* of people, places, or things. A group is singular and takes a singular verb.

> The *family* is
> The *jury* is
> The *group* is
> The *audience* is
> The *company* is
> The *government* is
> The *United States* (or any other country) is

Compound Subjects

Just One!
Words that end with "one", "thing", or "body" are always singular.

Subjects joined by *and* are plural: Bill and Pat *were* going to the show. However, subjects joined by *or* can be either singular or plural (the same is true for *nor*). If the last noun given is singular, then the sentence takes a singular verb; if the last noun given is plural, it takes a plural verb.

The following pronouns also take singular verbs:

> Either *is*
> Neither *is*
> None *is*
> Each *is*
> Anyone *is*
> No one *is*
> Everyone *is*

Let's try a question.

Just the Answer, Please
Remember, when solving Error ID questions, all you have to do is identify the error. Do not worry if you are not sure how to fix an error—ETS only cares if you can identify it.

27. Pam Cruise and Jim Braswell, <u>neither</u> of <u>whom takes</u> the
                            A   B

    bus to work, <u>is secretly plotting</u> <u>to take</u> over the world.
         C   D

    <u>No error</u>
     E

How to Crack It

If you do not immediately spot the error, go through each answer choice and eliminate anything that contains no error. Answer choice (C) gives us the singular verb *is*. When we Trim the Fat to get rid of the phrase between the subject and the verb, we see that *is* has been paired up with a plural subject here: *Pam Cruise and Jim Braswell.* Therefore, the correct answer is (C).

Parallelism

> The next thing you need to check when you see a verb is whether it is *parallel* to the other verbs in the sentence.

In other words, do the verbs use the same form? For example, *to run, to walk,* and *to sing* are in the same form, whereas *to walk* and *singing* are not. Be particularly careful to watch for parallelism when you see lists of verbs.

Here is a question that tests our skills.

---

8. As a competitor in the Iron Man competition, Paula was required to swim 2.4 miles, bike 112 miles, and <u>running the last 26 miles</u>.

   (A) running the last 26 miles
   (B) to run the last 26 miles
   (C) run the last 26 miles
   (D) ran the last 26 miles
   (E) she had to run the last 26 miles

How to Crack It

We can tell from comparing the answer choices that it all boils down to which form the verb *run* should be in, so we should look at the sentence for clues. The first verb in the list is *to swim,* and the second one is *bike.* When a list starts with *to,* the rest of the verbs can start with *to,* or the rest of the verbs can leave off the *to,* like *bike* does in this sentence. *Running, to run, ran,* and *she had to run* are not parallel to *swim* and *bike,* so (A), (B), (D), and (E) can be eliminated. (C) is our best answer.

Tense

> Finally, verbs need to be in the proper *tense,* such as past, present, or future. Verb tenses should generally be consistent in a sentence unless the meaning requires different tenses.

Look at this example:

Throughout the Middle Ages, women work
<u>A</u>   <u>B</u>

beside men, knowing that the effort of men and
<u>C</u>

women alike was <u>essential</u> to survival. <u>No error</u>
              D   E

How to Crack It

The verb *work* refers to something that happened *throughout the Middle Ages,* according to the sentence, and the Middle Ages definitely happened in the past. *Work,* though, is in the present tense, so it is erroneous, and (B) is the correct answer.

Just Perfect

If you see the verbs *have, has,* or *had* paired up with other verbs on the PSAT, you are probably looking at verbs in a *perfect* form, such as the past perfect or present perfect. Here is how and when you should use those forms:

Past perfect verbs describe something in the past that took place *before another event in the past*. It uses the word *had,* then the verb. For example:

I *had sung* all night until my neighbor called the police.
Leigh *had skied* every day before she broke her leg.

Present perfect usually tells you about an event that started in the past and is continuing through the present. It can also refer to an event that happened at an unspecified time in the past. Present perfect uses the words *have* or *has,* depending on whether a singular or plural verb is needed, and then the verb. For example:

> The dogs *have sung* along with me before.
> My neighbor *has glared* at me ever since.

Verbs in the perfect form have to be constructed properly when used (*have sung* instead of *have sang*), and they should be used only if needed for the above situations; it is not correct to substitute them for simple past, present, and future verbs.

NOUNS

Nouns are words that indicate a person, place, thing, or idea. Anything you can touch, talk about, discuss, or think about is a noun in that context. PSAT sometimes tests noun agreement. When two or more nouns in a sentence refer to each other, they need to agree in number: singular with singular and plural with plural.

Give this question a try:

———————————————————◯———————————————————

26. If your friends are not good students now they will
    ————   ——————————— ——— ————
     A   B   C

probably not be a good student in college. No error.
    ———————————————————   ————————
            D   E

How to Crack It

Did you see an error? In the first part of the sentence it says *students*, while in the later part of the sentence it says *student.* Are we to believe that your friends will morph into one person when they go to college? The answer is (D).

———————————————————◯———————————————————

PRONOUNS

Pronouns are words that take the place of nouns. As with verbs, there are three types of errors that pronouns can have:

- agreement
- ambiguity
- case

Agreement

> **Pronouns** must agree in number with the nouns they replace. Singular pronouns replace singular nouns; plural pronouns replace plural nouns.

After all we have learned about verb agreement this may seem obvious, but there are some additional tricks that ETS especially likes to pull with pronouns. To learn how to get around them, first we are going to look at some pronouns that are *always* singular.

Either *is*
Neither *is*
Each *is*
Anybody *is*
No one *is*
Everyone *is*
Everything *is*

Pronouns starting with *any* and *every* can be tricky because the words *any* and *every* seem to imply that there are several people or things, but just remember: If you see *one, body,* or *thing* at the end of the word, it is singular. Also, the word *none* can be singular or plural, but ETS prefers to treat it as singular, so you should too.

ETS also likes to write questions with the word *their* used as a singular pronoun, like many people do in everyday speech: *Everyone should clean up their stuff.* However, in ETS-land, *their* is still always considered plural. If it is being used to replace a singular pronoun (like *everyone*), it is wrong. (This is another way the test writers will try to trick you if you are using your ear, but it is easy to spot once you know about it!) Do not worry about whether *their* should be replaced with *his, his or her,* or some other option—you will not have to choose on the PSAT. You just need to know that *their* is plural and should replace only plural subjects, such as *the students, Al and Susan,* or *voters.*

Try this question.

---○---

Everyone <u>on the softball</u> team <u>who came up</u> to bat
      A   B

<u>squinted at the pitcher</u> in order to keep the sun's glaring
            C

<u>rays out of their eyes</u>. <u>No error</u>
          D   E

How to Crack It

Is there an underlined pronoun late in this sentence? There sure is: *their eyes*. Whose eyes are being referred to? Let's Trim the Fat to check this sentence:

> "*Everyone*...squinted...to keep the sun's...rays...out of *their* eyes."

> *Everyone* is singular, but *their* is plural, so it cannot replace *everyone*.

The answer is (D).

---○---

Ambiguity

> When you see a pronoun in a sentence on the PSAT, you should make sure it is perfectly clear what the pronoun replaces.

For example:

> *After looking over the color samples, Mary agreed with Martha that her porch should be painted green.*

Whose porch is being painted green? Mary's or Martha's? This sentence has a problem with pronoun *ambiguity,* which means you cannot tell which noun the pronoun is supposed to replace.

Whenever you spot a pronoun, especially late in a sentence, look to see what the pronoun is referring to. If there is more than one possibility, the pronoun has an ambiguity error. If it is perfectly clear what noun (or pronoun) the pronoun replaces, move on and check for agreement and case. Let's try one:

The director <u>told</u> the star of the production that <u>he</u> was
        A   B
making far too much money <u>to tolerate</u> such nasty
                              C
<u>treatment from</u> the producer. <u>No error</u>
        D   E

How to Crack It

When you identify answer choice (B) as a pronoun, you should immediately try to figure out which noun (or pronoun) it is referring to. Here, who is making too much money—the director or the star? From the sentence there is no way to tell, so (B) has a pronoun ambiguity error and is the correct answer. You might think the sentence would make more sense if the word *he* referred to the director—or the star. However, the sentence itself does not give you any clues pointing to either one, so the pronoun is ambiguous.

Subject Pronouns

Singular	Plural
I	we
you	you
he	they
she	they
it	they
who	who

Object Pronouns

Singular	Plural
me	us
you	you
him	them
her	them
it	them
whom	whom

Case

Pronouns come in two "flavors," or cases: **subjective** and **objective**. The subject is the person or thing performing the action in the sentence. The object is the person or thing *receiving* the action. Think of it this way: An object just sits there. It doesn't *do* anything—things are done to it. The subject, however, *does* something.

Subjects and objects are represented by different pronouns. For example, *I* is a subject pronoun, as in the sentence "I did it," while *me* is an object pronoun, as in "It happened to me." See how the subject does something, and the object has something done to it?

Look at the following example:

———————————◯———————————

The leading roles in the <u>widely acclaimed</u> play, a modern
                              A

<u>version</u> of an Irish folktale, were <u>performed by</u> Jessica
    B   C

<u>and him</u>. <u>No error</u>
    D   E

How to Crack It

Look at the pronoun that comes at the end of the sentence. *Him* is in the object case, so we need to know if that is correct. In this case, *performed by...him* is correct. You would need the subject case if you were going to say *he performed*, but as it stands, the pronoun is correct. The rest of the underlined portions of the sentence also check out, so the answer is (E).

———————————◯———————————

The I/Me Rule

Are you always getting corrected on your use (or misuse) of *I* or *me*? When in doubt about whether a pronoun needs a subject or object case, Trim the Fat to figure out whether it is performing the action or being acted upon. Which of the following sentences is correct?

> *The book belongs to Jerry and I.*
> *The book belongs to Jerry and me.*

We can trim the fat and take out *Jerry and*. Now we are left with *The book belongs to _____*. What goes in the blank, *I* or *me*? *Me* is correct, because *to* is a preposition (more on those in a moment) and we need an *object* pronoun to come after the preposition. Here is a trickier one:

> *Clare is more creative than I.*
> *Clare is more creative than me.*

Be careful. This may look as if the pronoun is an object, but actually the sentence is incomplete. What the sentence really says is, "Clare is more creative than I am." The *am* is understood. When in doubt, say the sentence to yourself, adding *am*, *is*, or *are*. If any form of *to be* makes sense, the sentence requires a subject pronoun.

PREPOSITIONS

Prepositions add information about a noun, generally to give one noun's relationship to something else, either in time or space. (For example: *over, under, around, along, by, to, beside, near, with, beyond, before, after, at, in, on,* etc.)

Prepositions are *always* followed by a noun or pronoun, which is called the *object* of the preposition. In the sentence "I threw the ball to him," *to* is the preposition and *him* is the object. (Notice that *him* is an *object* pronoun.) Together they create the prepositional phrase *to him*. It is important to recognize prepositional phrases because they often appear as distractions on the PSAT, and you will want to get rid of them when you trim the fat.

DRILL 1

Identify the prepositions and their objects in the following sentences: Answers can be found in Part III.

1. Lina walked over the bridge.
2. The ball went beyond the green.
3. Please shelve the dictionary with the other reference books.
4. I want to return the movie to her.

DRILL 2

Another reason prepositions are important is that some words have to be paired with certain prepositions. These word pairs are called *idioms,* and unlike subject-verb agreement and pronoun ambiguity, you will not have certain rules to fall back on to solve an idiom problem on the test; you will just have to memorize them. Here are some questions involving idioms that are commonly tested on the PSAT; fill in the blanks, check your answers, and make flash cards to memorize any that you don't know. Answers can be found in Part III.

1. I am *indebted* _____ you.
2. I am *resentful* _____ you.
3. I am *delighted* _____ you.
4. I am *jealous* _____ you.
5. I am *worried* _____ you.
6. I am *astounded* _____ you.
7. The women had a *dispute* _____ politics.
8. You have a *responsibility* _____ take care of your pet.
9. My friends are not so *different* _____ your friends.
10. Scott is *considered* _____ the best composer at the conservatory.

Try an Error ID example:

---

28. Despite the poor weather, my sister and I were planning
        A   B   C
on attending the festival. No error
        D   E

How to Crack It
Though we may hear similar sentences every day and not realize there is a grammar mistake, the word *planning* is part of an idiom: *planning to*. A correct use would read *planning to attend*, so (D) has an error and is the correct answer.

OTHER LITTLE THINGS
The final area of grammar we are going to cover is Other Little Things—some areas that are tested on the PSAT but do not fall into our other categories. The areas are:

- faulty comparisons
- misplaced modifiers
- adjectives/adverbs
- voice
- active/passive

Faulty Comparisons
Whenever you see a PSAT question that makes a comparison, check for these types of errors.

Apples to Apples
One type of error is comparing things that cannot actually be compared. A correct comparison compares apples to apples, not apples to banana pudding. For example, look at the following sentence:

> *Larry goes shopping at Foodtown because the prices are better than Shop Rite.*

Even though it is pretty common to hear sentences like this in everyday speech, it is actually wrong and you will probably see something like this in a couple of test questions. This one can be tricky to spot for the very reason we stated above, that lots of people talk this way and we know what they mean, so we give them the benefit of the doubt and assume they are speaking correctly. But we cannot do that on the PSAT. Remember, do not trust your ear; when you see comparison words such as *like, as, compared to,* and so on, check to see if the things being compared are actually the same sort of thing. The two things being compared are *Foodtown's prices* and *Shop Rite,* instead of *Foodtown's prices* and *Shop Rite's prices.* Even though we would assume the speaker was comparing prices to prices if we heard that sentence on television, the comparison has to be made more clearly on the PSAT. Better sentences would read:

> *Larry goes shopping at Foodtown because the prices are better than Shop Rite's prices.*

or even more likely on the PSAT:

> *Larry goes shopping at Foodtown because the prices are better than those at Shop Rite.*

Do You Count?

While we are on the subject of grocery stores, you have probably seen a sign that says *10 items or less* at the checkout counters. Guess what? It is grammatically wrong. When items can be counted, the word *fewer* should be used instead of *less.*

For example:

> If you eat *fewer* French fries, you can use *less* ketchup.

Similar word pairs include *many* (can be counted) versus *much* (cannot be counted)...

> *Many* hands make *much* less work.

...and *number* (can be counted) versus *amount* (cannot be counted).

> The same *number* of people ate different *amounts* of pudding.

Two's Company, Three or More Is...?

Finally, different words must be used when comparing two things versus comparing three or more things. The following examples should jog your memory:

- *More* (two things) versus *most* (three or more things)
  Given vanilla and strawberry as ice cream flavor options, I think vanilla is the *more* appealing option.

In fact, of all the flavors I've tried, I like vanilla the *most*.

- *Less* (two things) versus *least* (three or more things)
  I am *less* likely to be chosen than Judy is.
  I am the *least* likely person to be chosen from the department.
- *Better* (two things) versus *best* (three or more things)
  My math teacher is *better* than the one I had last year.
  My Princeton Review teacher is the *best* teacher I have ever had.
- *Between* (two things) versus *among* (three or more things)
  Between you and me, I never liked her anyway.
  Among all the people here, no one likes her.

Misplaced Modifiers

A modifier is a descriptive word or phrase inserted in a sentence to add dimension to the thing it describes. For example:

As a horse who talked in his sleep, Mr. Ed was unique.

"As a horse who talked in his sleep" is the modifying phrase in this sentence. It describes a characteristic of Mr. Ed. Generally speaking, a modifying phrase should be right next to the thing it modifies. If it is not, the meaning of the sentence may change. For example:

Walking down the road, my mood shifted from bitter to relaxed.

What is walking down the road? According to this sentence, *My mood*, because that is what comes right after the comma. Questions about this mistake can be tricky; we know what the sentence is trying to say and we are likely to give it the benefit of the doubt. But when you see a descriptive phrase in the beginning of a sentence and it is underlined, look closely at the words that come immediately after the comma to see if that is really what the phrase is describing.

Try the following example:

---

17. <u>Perhaps the most beautiful natural vegetation in the world</u>, the west of Ireland explodes each spring with a tremendous variety of wildflowers.

    (A) Perhaps the most beautiful natural vegetation in the world
    (B) In what may be the world's most beautiful natural vegetation
    (C) Home to what may be the most beautiful natural vegetation in the world
    (D) Its vegetation may be the world's most beautiful
    (E) More beautiful in its natural vegetation than anywhere else in the world

How to Crack It

Is the west of Ireland a kind of vegetation? No, so cross off (A). We need an answer that will make the opening phrase modify *the west of Ireland*. Answer choice (B) is still modifying the vegetation, so cross it off. All three other choices fix the problem, but (C) does it the best. (D) separates two complete sentences with a comma, and (E) actually changes the meaning of the sentence by saying that the west of Ireland definitively has the most beautiful vegetation while the original sentence says *perhaps*. ETS's answer is (C).

———————————○———————————

Adjectives/Adverbs

Misplaced modifiers are not the only descriptive errors ETS will test you on. Another way it tries to trip you up is by using adjectives instead of adverbs and vice versa. Remember that an **adjective** modifies a noun, while an **adverb** modifies verbs, adverbs, and adjectives. An adverb usually ends in *–ly*. In the following sentence, circle the adverbs and underline the adjectives:

> The stealthy thief, desperately hoping to evade the persistent police, ran quickly into the dank, dark alley after brazenly stealing the stunningly exquisite jewels.

First, we will list the adjectives along with the nouns they modify: *stealthy* thief, *persistent* police, *dank* alley, *dark* alley, *exquisite* jewels. Now for the adverbs with the words they modify: *desperately* hoping (verb), ran (verb) *quickly*, *brazenly* stealing (verb), *stunningly* exquisite (adjective).

Now try the following Improving Sentences example:

———————————○———————————

15. Movie cameras are no longer particularly costly, but film, development, and editing equipment <u>cause the monetary expense of making a film to add up tremendous</u>.

   (A) cause the monetary expense of making a film to add up tremendous
   (B) add tremendously to the expense of making a film
   (C) much increase the film-making expenses
   (D) add to the tremendous expense of making a film
   (E) tremendously add up to the expense of making a film

How to Crack It

Here we have an adjective/adverb error. What should the last word in the sentence be? Tremendous*ly*. Cross off (A) and also (D), since it doesn't fix the error and changes the meaning of the sentence. (C) is way out there, so cross it off too. In (E), the placement of the *tremendously* is awkward and slightly changes the meaning of the sentence. ETS's answer is (B).

Active/Passive Voice

Last but not least, ETS prefers sentences written in the active voice to sentences written in the passive voice. In the **active voice**, the subject of the sentence is doing something. In the **passive voice**, the main actor becomes the object, and is being acted upon. The word *by* often (but not always) highlights passive voice.

Active:	She took the PSAT.
Passive:	The PSAT was taken *by* her.

Passive voice is not incorrect, but when you see it in a PSAT question, there will generally be a choice that uses the active voice, so if that choice is grammatically correct, pick it.

TECHNIQUE REVIEW

Before we go to Drill 3, we will review some techniques.

For Error ID questions, read the sentence and determine whether you spot an error. If you do spot an error, try to articulate that error to yourself to make sure you are not basing your decision simply on sound. Check the other answers against the grammar rules you have learned, and if you are still sure your original error is the correct answer, pick it.

If you do not spot an error immediately on an Error ID question, check all answer choices against the grammar rules. Eliminate any choices that stand up to scrutiny until you find an error or until only (E) is left.

For Improving Sentences questions, read the sentence and ask the same question—do you spot an error? If you do, try to articulate it to yourself, and if you decide it violates one of the rules we have discussed, eliminate (A) and any answer choice that repeats the error. Compare the remaining answer choices, eliminating errors until you are down to one.

If you do not spot an error immediately on an Improving Sentences question, move straight to comparing answer choices. The differences among the answer choices give you clues to what rules are being tested, and you can eliminate answers based on the rules you have learned. Repeat until only one answer choice is left.

Drill 3

Before we move on to Improving Paragraphs questions, try putting together what you have learned. Do the following Error ID and Improving Sentences questions using your grammar checklist. Remember to trim the fat and use POE. On Improving Sentences questions, do not hesitate to check out the answer choices for a clue to help you spot the error. You may wish to jot down your grammar checklist before you begin. Answers can be found in Part III.

1. When the student council announced its intention to elect a minority representative, <u>neither the principal nor the superintendent were willing to comment on the issue</u>.

   (A) neither the principal nor the superintendent were willing to comment on the issue
   (B) neither the principal or the superintendent were willing to comment on the issue
   (C) neither the principal nor the superintendent was willing to comment on the issue
   (D) neither of the principal nor the superintendent was willing to comment on the issue
   (E) neither the principal or the superintendent was willing to comment on the issue

2. The patient began his difficult postsurgery <u>recovery, but he was</u> able to recover from the psychological effects of the injury.

   (A) recovery, but he was
   (B) recovery, where he was
   (C) recovery only when he was
   (D) recovery only when being
   (E) recovery, also he was

3. <u>It is a more difficult task to learn to type than mastering a simple word-processing program.</u>

   (A) It is a more difficult task to learn to type than mastering a simple word-processing program.
   (B) It is more difficult of a task to learn to type than mastering a simple word-processing program.
   (C) It is a more difficult task to learn to type than to have mastered a simple word-processing program.
   (D) It is a more difficult task to learn to type than simply to master a word-processing program.
   (E) It is a more difficult task to learn to type than to master a simple word-processing program.

4. <u>In 1962, Jackie Robinson gained admission to the National Baseball Hall of Fame, he was the first Black baseball player in the major leagues.</u>

   (A) In 1962, Jackie Robinson gained admission to the National Baseball Hall of Fame, he was the first Black baseball player in the major leagues.
   (B) In 1962, Jackie Robinson, the first Black major-league baseball player, gained admission to the National Baseball Hall of Fame.
   (C) In the National Baseball Hall of Fame in 1962, Jackie Robinson, the first Black baseball player in the major leagues, was admitted to it.
   (D) With admission to the National Baseball Hall of Fame in 1962, he was the first Black major-league player to do it, Jackie Robinson.
   (E) The first Black major-league player was when he was Jackie Robinson, admitted to the national Baseball Hall of Fame in 1962.

5. A well-organized person can go through the day efficiently, <u>wasting little time or they waste none at all</u>.

(A) wasting little time or they waste none at all
(B) wasting little or no time
(C) wasting little time or wasting none at all
(D) wasting either little time or none
(E) either little or no time being wasted

6. When Michelle Shocked recorded her *Arkansas Traveler* album, <u>regional American folk songs were used as inspiration, but it was never copied exactly by her</u>.

(A) regional American folk songs were used as inspiration, but it was never copied exactly by her
(B) regional American folk songs were used as inspiration, but she never copied them exactly
(C) regional American folk songs were used as inspiration by her and not copied exactly
(D) she used regional American folk songs, but they were not exactly copied
(E) she used regional American folk songs as inspiration, but never copied them exactly

7. Educators and parents agree that a daily reading time will not only enhance a child's education <u>but also will encourage the child to read independently</u>.

(A) but also will encourage the child to read independently
(B) but also encouraging the child to read independently
(C) but encourage the child to read independently too
(D) but encourage children to read independently
(E) but also encourage them to read independently

21. Eric's new CD were destroyed when Paula Ann, running
    $\underset{\text{A}}{\underline{\text{were destroyed}}}$

    $\underset{\text{B}}{\underline{\text{quickly}}}$ $\underset{\text{C}}{\underline{\text{through}}}$ the office, stepped on it. $\underset{\text{D}}{\underline{\text{No error}}}$ $\underset{\text{E}}{\underline{}}$

22. Because $\underset{\text{A}}{\underline{\text{their}}}$ $\underset{\text{B}}{\underline{\text{class}}}$ was going on a field trip that day,

    James and Alice $\underset{\text{C}}{\underline{\text{each}}}$ needed a $\underset{\text{D}}{\underline{\text{lunch}}}$ to bring to school.

    $\underset{\text{E}}{\underline{\text{No error}}}$

23. None $\underset{\text{A}}{\underline{\text{of}}}$ the students on the review board is $\underset{\text{B}}{\underline{\text{qualified to}}}$

    ascertain $\underset{\text{C}}{\underline{\text{whether}}}$ the money was $\underset{\text{D}}{\underline{\text{well spent}}}$. $\underset{\text{E}}{\underline{\text{No error}}}$

24. Just $\underset{\text{A}}{\underline{\text{between you and I}}}$, *The Lone Ranger* was the
    $\underset{\text{B}}{\underline{}}$

    dumbest movie I $\underset{\text{C}}{\underline{\text{have}}}$ ever $\underset{\text{D}}{\underline{\text{seen}}}$. $\underset{\text{E}}{\underline{\text{No error}}}$

25. If you $\underset{\text{A}}{\underline{\text{had looked}}}$ at the prices $\underset{\text{B}}{\underline{\text{closely}}}$, you'll see that the

    "economy size" of detergent is $\underset{\text{C}}{\underline{\text{actually}}}$ more expensive

    than the $\underset{\text{D}}{\underline{\text{smaller}}}$ trial sizes. $\underset{\text{E}}{\underline{\text{No error}}}$

26. The $\underset{\text{A}}{\underline{\text{new}}}$ course schedule worked out $\underset{\text{B}}{\underline{\text{splendid}}}$ for all

    of those students who $\underset{\text{C}}{\underline{\text{had been}}}$ $\underset{\text{D}}{\underline{\text{concerned}}}$. $\underset{\text{E}}{\underline{\text{No error}}}$

27. $\underset{\text{A}}{\underline{\text{Many}}}$ young adults find it extremely difficult to $\underset{\text{B}}{\underline{\text{return}}}$

    home from college and $\underset{\text{C}}{\underline{\text{abide with}}}$ the rules $\underset{\text{D}}{\underline{\text{set down}}}$

    by their parents. $\underset{\text{E}}{\underline{\text{No error}}}$

28. I recently heard an $\underset{\text{A}}{\underline{\text{announcement}}}$ $\underset{\text{B}}{\underline{\text{where}}}$ the Rangers

    will be $\underset{\text{C}}{\underline{\text{playing}}}$ a game at home $\underset{\text{D}}{\underline{\text{this weekend}}}$. $\underset{\text{E}}{\underline{\text{No error}}}$

29. Just last month, two weeks after the $\underset{\text{A}}{\underline{\text{announcement}}}$

    of elections in Kazakhstan, 92-year-old Fydor $\underset{\text{C}}{\underline{\text{has cast}}}$ his
    $\underset{\text{B}}{\underline{}}$

    first $\underset{\text{D}}{\underline{\text{vote in}}}$ 70 years. $\underset{\text{E}}{\underline{\text{No error}}}$

Improving Paragraphs

Questions in the Improving Paragraphs section are not just about grammar, but also about the logical flow of the passage and its support of the main idea.

The five Improving Paragraphs questions require you to make corrections to a "first draft" of a student's essay. You will be given a passage composed of approximately three paragraphs. Each paragraph contains numbered sentences. Your job is to "edit" the rough draft to make it better. You are not going to be asked lots of tough questions about the content of the passage, so take about 30 seconds to skim it before going to the questions.

Here is a sample passage for you to skim:

> (1) Conservation and ecology are the hot topics at our school. (2) Students used to just throw everything out in one big garbage pail. (3) Sure, it was easy. (4) It wasn't good for the environment.
>
> (5) I volunteered to head up the conservation team. (6) My friends and I decided to map out our strategies. (7) First we needed to get students to become aware of the problem. (8) Educating was important. (9) A thing to do was implement a recycling program. (10) We checked with the local town government. (11) They would supply the recycling bins. (12) We had to supply the people who'd be willing to recycle. (13) The most important thing students had to learn to do was to separate their garbage. (14) Glass in one container. (15) Plastic in another.
>
> (16) Our final step was to get the teachers and administrators involved. (17) Paper can be recycled too. (18) We ran a poster contest. (19) The winners are hanging in our halls. (20) Reuse, recycle, renew. (21) That's our school's new motto.

Now, before you get out your red pencil and jump in, there are a few more things you need to know. Your passage may consist of 15 or more sentences, each potentially containing some kind of error. However, you will be asked only five questions. Do not spend time fixing errors for which there are no questions. Also, remember that—unlike the other questions in the Writing Skills section—Improving Paragraphs questions do not contain an order of difficulty. So, answer these according to your own POOD and pacing goals.

The Questions

There are three basic types of questions that you will be asked:

- **Revision questions:** These questions ask you to revise sentences or parts of sentences in much the same way as Improving Sentences questions do.

- **Combination questions:** These questions ask you to combine two or more sentences to improve the quality and/or flow of the paragraph.
- **Content questions:** These questions ask you about the passage's content and flow, typically by asking you to insert a sentence before or after a paragraph.

Keep in Mind
On Improving Paragraph questions, choice (A) is usually not the same as the underlined portion.

Revision Questions

As we mentioned, these questions are very similar to Improving Sentences questions. Therefore, you can follow the same basic approach. One warning: There is typically not a "No error" option on Improving Paragraphs questions. Do not assume that (A) is merely a repeat of the given sentence.

Even though the sentence you are revising is provided for you, you may still need to go back to the passage to gain some context when trying to fix a sentence. Before going back, however, use POE. If you have spotted an error in the given sentence, cross off answers that do not fix it. Also, cross off answer choices that contain obvious errors. After doing some POE, go back and read a few sentences before and after the given sentence in the passage. This should be enough context for you to determine the best edit.

Try the following revision question, referring back to the sample passage.

37. In context, what is the best way to revise sentence 9 (reproduced below)?

    A thing to do was implement a recycling program.

    (A) Next, we needed to implement a recycling program.
    (B) Implementing a recycling program was a thing to do.
    (C) A recycling program needed to be implemented.
    (D) Implementing a program for recycling was the step that would be next.
    (E) A program would need to be implemented next for recycling.

How to Crack It

The correct revision will be concise and unambiguous. It will also flow well. We can get rid of choices (B), (D), and (E) before going back to the passage. Choice (B) is as clunky as the given sentence; choices (D) and (E) are awkwardly written.

That leaves (A) and (C). Choice (C) is in the passive voice, which is a reason to be very wary of choosing it. But choice (A) also seems to have a problem: It starts with the word *Next*, and if we do not consider the surrounding context, that looks a little weird. But if we *do* consider the surrounding context, it makes perfect sense. Go back to line 7: "First, we needed to…" Oh, so this is a list! First we did this, and next we did that, and finally we did something else. Answer choice (A) it is.

Combination Questions

Combination questions are revision questions with a twist: You are working with two sentences instead of one. The sentences are almost always reprinted for you underneath the question. As with revision questions, go back to the passage to get context and a sense of flow first.

To combine sentences you will need to work with conjunctions. If the sentences are flowing in the same direction, look for an answer with words like *and, since, as well as*, etc. If the sentences seem to be flowing in opposite directions, look for trigger words in the answer choices such as *however, but, on the contrary*, etc.

Try the following question:

---

38. Which of the following represents the most effective way to combine sentences 20 and 21 (reproduced below)?

    Reuse, recycle, renew. That's our school's new motto.

    (A) Reuse, recycle, renew and you know our school's new motto.
    (B) The new motto of our school is that: "Reuse, recycle, renew."
    (C) "Reuse, recycle, renew" are the new motto of our school now.
    (D) The new motto of our school is reusing, recycling, and renewing.
    (E) "Reuse, recycle, renew" is our school's new motto.

How to Crack It

First, the sentences are moving in the same direction. Your job is to find a clear, concise way to combine them. (A) and (B) are out because they are poorly worded. (C) is a trap: "Reuse, recycle, renew" *is* a motto. Do not be fooled into thinking you need a plural verb simply because there is no "and" in answer choice (C). Choice (D) changes the quoted portion, and therefore the meaning. ETS's answer is (E).

Try another:

---

36. Which of the following represents the best revision of the underlined portions of sentences 7 and 8 (reproduced below)?

First we needed to get students to become aware of the <u>problem. Educating was important</u>.

(A) problem for educating was important
(B) problem of educating. It was important
(C) problem to educate was important
(D) problem: education was important
(E) problem for education was important to us

How to Crack It

Again, we have a same-direction combination here. We need something that flows. (A) and (C) use the wrong prepositions, which slightly change the meaning of the sentence. Cross them off. (B) is as awkward or more awkward than the original sentence. (E) uses the wrong preposition and adds extra awkward stuff. ETS's answer is (D). The colon is a nice, neat way to continue a thought without using two sentences.

Content Questions

ETS will occasionally ask you a question regarding the content and flow of the passage. These questions may ask:

1. Which sentence should immediately follow or precede the passage?
2. Which sentence should be inserted into the passage?
3. What is the best description of the passage as a whole?

If you are asked the third question, you will need to read the whole passage. However, you will more likely be asked one of the first two questions. To answer these, you will need to read the relevant paragraph, but also keep in mind the the main idea and structure of the passage.

Try this example using the sample passage from earlier in this section:

———————○———————

35. Which of the following sentences, if added after sentence 4, would best serve to link the first paragraph to the second paragraph?

(A) Unfortunately, the environment suffered.
(B) Clearly, we had to make a change.
(C) Easy things are often not good for the environment.
(D) However, people can be very lazy.
(E) The school was against any change.

How to Crack It

The question wants us to link the first two paragraphs together, which makes sense only if there is currently a gap between them. So we should look for the gap. The first paragraph is about the wasteful practices that used to be common at this writer's school. Then we begin the second paragraph and all of a sudden we find that the writer has "volunteered to head up the conservation team." What conservation team? There was no mention of a conservation team prior to this sentence. Something is missing! It looks like the link we need to make is between realizing that there are problems and deciding to take action.

If we look at the choices, we find that (A), (C), and (D) all just talk more about the problems with how people at the school dispose of their trash. Those choices do not make the transition to taking action. For that matter, neither does (E), which hints that trying to change the way students throw away their trash will be a futile effort. Only (B) gets us from seeing the problem to doing something about it, so select (B).

———————○———————

Time Is of the Essence

Keep in mind that Improving Paragraphs questions appear at the end of a 30-minute section at the end of a two-hour test. You may not have the time or the energy to complete all of the Improving Paragraphs questions. Therefore, answer the shorter, easier questions first. Then, if you have the time, and still need to answer more questions to hit your pacing goal, do the longer questions. However, always remember your own POOD. If you perform better on Improving Paragraphs questions than you do on Improving Sentences questions and Error IDs, you may want to answer Improving Paragraphs questions first, and then go back to the beginning of the Writing Skills section.

Drill 4

Try the following Improving Paragraphs drill to practice what you have learned. Answers can be found in Part III.

(1) Censorship in the media had been an extremely important issue throughout the twentieth century. (2) In the 1950s television programs and movies had to comply with codes that enforced strict standards of propriety. (3) Couples were shown sleeping in separate beds, and the concept of nudity or verbal profanity was unheard of. (4) In reaction to them, in the 1960s and 1970s the media abandoned the codes in favor of more realistic representations of relationships and everyday life. (5) Filmmakers and songwriters were able to express themselves more honestly and freely. (6) The idea that in the early 1960s the Rolling Stones had to change their lyrics from "let's spend the night together" to "let's spend some time together" seemed almost unlikely by the end of the decade.

(7) Yet in the mid-1980s a period of conservative reaction occurred, turning the cycle around. (8) Explicit song lyrics began to be censored. (9) Warning labels were added to the covers of albums. (10) The labels indicated that some of the language might be "offensive" to the consumer. (11) It is unfortunate that people feel the need to blame the media for societal problems instead of realizing that the media only brings to light the problems that already exist.

(12) Hopefully, our reactions will ultimately break free of all previous patterns. (13) Yet until this happens we must remain content to know that the good parts of the past, as well as the bad, repeat themselves.

35. In context, what is the best version of the underlined portion of sentence 1 (reproduced below)?

Censorship in the media had been an extremely *important issue throughout the twentieth century.*

(A) (as it is now)
(B) was extremely
(C) was an extremely
(D) has been extreme as an
(E) will be an extremely

36. Which of the following would be the best subject for a paragraph immediately preceding this essay?

(A) The types of movies most popular in the 1950s
(B) The changing role of the media over the last 10 years
(C) The ways in which the economy affects society's political views
(D) The role of the media in European countries
(E) The roots of media censorship

37. The author wishes to divide the first paragraph into two shorter paragraphs. The most appropriate place to begin a new paragraph would be

(A) between sentences 1 and 2
(B) between sentences 2 and 3
(C) between sentences 3 and 4
(D) between sentences 4 and 5
(E) between sentences 5 and 6

38. What word could best replace "unlikely" in sentence 6?

(A) strange
(B) conventional
(C) unpopular
(D) inconceivable
(E) unbearable

39. Which would be the best way to revise and combine the underlined portions of sentences 9 and 10 (reproduced below)?

Warning labels were added to the covers of <u>albums. The labels indicated</u> that some of the language might be "offensive" to the consumer.

(A) albums, indicating
(B) albums, which indicated
(C) albums, and they indicated
(D) albums, the indication being
(E) albums, being indicative

Final Words of Wisdom

As with all the sections of the PSAT, do not be afraid to do some POE and make a strategic guess. You will almost always be able to eliminate some answer choices, so you should try to answer the questions you know you can do in your first run through the questions. If you need to answer more questions to reach your pacing goals or if you have started to answer a question but gotten stuck, eliminate whatever you can *quickly*, guess, and move on.

Always remember Pacing, OOD, and POE!

Summary

o About one-fifth of all Improving Sentences and Error ID questions are correct as is—(A) for Improving Sentences and (E) for Error ID.

o Resist using your ear to pick a right or wrong answer. You should always make the decision to keep or eliminate an answer choice based on grammar rules, not by how something sounds.

o Remember to use Plan A or Plan B on all Improving Sentences and Error ID questions, based on whether you spot an error immediately after reading the sentence.

o Verbs have to agree in number, be parallel, and be in the proper tense to be correct.

o Pronouns have to agree, be in the proper case, and not be ambiguous in order to be correct.

o Prepositions are always followed by a noun or pronoun and have to be idiomatically correct, meaning that some words go together just because they do.

o Comparisons must equate two (or more) things that can really be compared, use the correct comparison word based on whether the things being compared can be counted (*less* vs. *fewer*), and use the correct words based on how many things are being compared (*more* vs. *most*).

o Modifiers must be placed directly next to the words they are modifying, so check to see that the placement of a modifier makes sense (and is not "misplaced").

o Adjectives modify only nouns, whereas adverbs modify verbs, adjectives, or other adverbs.

o The test writers prefer active voice over passive voice, so if an answer choice says that something was done by someone, look for a better answer.

Chapter 11
Vocabulary

As you have observed, vocabulary can be an important issue in the Critical Reading sections of the PSAT, particularly in Sentence Completions. This chapter is intended to help you further develop your vocabulary.

HOW TO LEARN VOCABULARY

First, we should discuss how NOT to learn vocabulary. Some people assume that you should open a dictionary and learn each word, one at a time, starting with the letter *A*. This, of course, is not a very well thought-out plan. The kind of vocabulary that appears on the PSAT is actually a fairly narrow range of what is considered by the test writers to be those words that a well-educated college student should know. These are the words that are typically used by good writers of English prose, scholars, and scientists (when they are writing for the public and not in scientific jargon).

To improve your vocabulary, always look up unfamiliar words when you come across them in your reading. A great way to ensure that you do this is to install a free dictionary app on your smartphone. In addition, you should become closely acquainted with The Princeton Review's Hit Parade.

The Hit Parade

The Princeton Review's Hit Parade is a list of vocabulary words that commonly appear on the PSAT and SAT. It starts on page 219 of this book. This list is useful not only because some of these words are likely to appear on your test, but also because it shows you what *kinds* of words are typically tested on the PSAT and SAT. These are the types of words that you should pay particular attention to when you are doing your daily reading. Write them down and learn them!

Flash Cards

Some people like using flash cards as a way to help them learn vocabulary. Flash cards are useful, but be sure to write down not only the word and its definition, but also an example sentence in which you use that word. If you need help, ask a teacher, parent, or friend to help you come up with a sentence. If you have a smart phone or tablet, check out the apps available for building vocabulary, like The Princeton Review's Vocab Challenge.

Some Daily Reading

While you are preparing for these tests, it is important that you get in the habit of reading. This will not only help you on the reading passages, but also help you improve your vocabulary. Make sure to set aside 20–30 minutes *every day* to do some reading.

What should you read? Anything. Everything. Pick your favorite magazine or book. Ideally, read something that is above, but not too much above, your current reading level—but *read something every day*. While you are reading, circle any words that you do not understand, and look them up. Then add them to your list of words to learn. In fact, you should start a vocabulary journal and plan to update and maintain it from now until after you take the SAT.

Fun with Mnemonics
Funny or otherwise memorable sentences can be particularly helpful.

Using These Words

One great way to learn vocabulary is to be annoying. No kidding! Here is how you do it:

Pick a few words each day. Write them down, along with their definitions, on a small note card, which you can refer to if your memory fails you. Now go about your daily business, but use these words every chance you get. Instead of *outgoing*, use the word *gregarious*. Instead of *funny*, use the word *mirthful*. You will really annoy your friends, but you will certainly learn those words.

Mnemonics

Another great technique for learning words is to find a mnemonic device. *Mnemonic* is from the Greek word *mneme*, which means "memory," so a mnemonic device is something that is so foolish or funny that it is unforgettable, and will help remind you of the meaning of a word. (By the way—what other common English word comes from that same Greek root *mneme*? We will tell you in a minute.)

For instance, for the word *excavate*, which means "to make a hole by digging," you can think of the word *cave*. A cave is a hole underground and part of the word ex**cave**ate.

How about another one? Let's try the word *paramount*, which means "of chief importance." You can remember this word because it is like a **mount**ain—it is the biggest and most important thing on the horizon.

Try making mnemonics for each of the following words:

prosaic

flagrant

clandestine

timorous

Once you have made your own mnemonics for the above words, read our examples on the following page.

Prosaic
Rebecca made a prosaic mosaic—it consisted of only one tile.

Flagrant
Burning the flag shows flagrant disrespect for the country.

Clandestine
The clan of spies planned a clandestine maneuver that depended on its secrecy to work.

Timorous
Tiny Tim was timorous; he was afraid that one day a giant would crush him.

And the answer to the earlier question: What other common English word has the same root (*mneme*) as the word *mnemonic*? *Amnesia* (the prefix *a-* means "without"; the word itself means "without memory").

If you would like more help with mnemonics, refer to these other books by The Princeton Review: *Word Smart, More Word Smart, Illustrated Word Smart, More Illustrated Word Smart,* and *How to Remember Everything*. All of these manuals contain some great drills, visuals, or mnemonics to help you memorize more words.

The Hit Parade

Here is a list of the words most commonly found on the PSAT. We have grouped them by topic, so that they will be easier to memorize. Happy studying!

Pronunciation Guide

A is pronounced like the *a* in *hat*

AH is pronounced like the *a* in *father*

AI and AY are pronounced like the *a* in *game*

AW is pronounced like the *aw* in *law*

E is pronounced like the *e* in *hem*

EE is pronounced like the *e* in *me*

I and IH are pronounced like the *i* in *icky*

IE and Y (as a vowel) are pronounced like the *ie* in *lie*

J is pronounced like the *j* in *jam*

O is pronounced like the *o* in *home*

OO is pronounced like the *oo* in *boot*

OR is pronounced like the word *or*

OW is pronounced like the *ow* in *cow*

S is pronounced like the *s* in *sad*

U and UH are pronounced like the *u* in *hum*

ZH is pronounced like the *ge* in *garage*

WEEK 1

Are You Talkin' to Me?

candid (adj)   **KAN did**
completely honest, straightforward

Because Candace was candid about the fact that she was unable to study, the teacher allowed her to take a make-up exam.

conjecture (n)   **kun JEK chur**
inference; guesswork

At this point, Kimaya's hypothesis about single-cell biorhythms is still conjecture; she does not have conclusive evidence.

didactic (adj)   **die DAK tik**
instructive

The tapes were entertaining and didactic; they both amused and instructed children.

euphemism (n)   **YOO fuh miz um**
a mild, indirect, or vague term substituting for a harsh, blunt, or offensive term

"To pass away" is a common euphemism for dying.

extrapolate (v)   **ek STRAP uh layt**
to infer or estimate by extending or projecting known information

Seeing the wrecked bike and his daughter's skinned knees, Heath extrapolated that she had had a biking accident.

incoherent (adj)   **in ko HAIR unt**
lacking cohesion or connection

Maury's sentences were so incoherent that nobody understood a word.

insinuate (v)   **in SIN yoo ayt**
to introduce or communicate stealthily

Sean insinuated that Grace stole the arsenic, but he never came out and said it.

lucid (adj)   **LOO sid**

easily understood; clear

> Our teacher provides lucid explanations of even the most difficult concepts so that we can all understand them.

rhetoric (n)   **RET uh rik**

the art of using language effectively and persuasively

> Since they are expected to make speeches, most politicians and lawyers are well versed in the art of rhetoric.

What's Up, Teach?

acumen (n)   **AK yoo men**

quickness, accuracy, and keenness of judgment or insight

> Judge Ackerman's legal acumen was so well regarded that he was nicknamed the "Solomon of the South."

adroit (adj)   **uh DROYT**

dexterous; deft

> An adroit balloon animal maker, Adrianna became popular at children's parties.

ascertain (v)   **as er TAYN**

to find out, as through investigation or experimentation

> My mother had long suspected my dog; after a week of gathering evidence, we ascertained that Toto had indeed chewed up her favorite pair of shoes.

astute (adj)   **uh STOOT**

shrewd; clever

> Stewart is financially astute; he invests wisely and never falls for scams.

circumspect (adj)   **SER kum spekt**

careful; prudent; discreet

> Ned's circumspect manner makes him a wise appointment to the diplomatic corps.

disseminate (v)   **dis SEM uh nayt**

to scatter widely, as in sowing seed

> The news about Dave's embarrassing moment at the party disseminated quickly through the school; by the end of the day, everyone knew what had happened.

erudition (n)   **er yuh DISH un**

deep, extensive learning

> Professor Rudy's erudition was such that she could answer any question her students put to her.

husbandry (n)   **HUZ bun dree**

the application of scientific principles to agriculture, especially to animal breeding

> After years of practicing animal husbandry, Marsha's husband was able to create a breed of dog that actually walked itself.

pedantic (adj)   **puh DAN tik**

excessively concerned with book learning and formal rules

> Pedro's pedantic tendencies prompted him to remind us constantly of all the grammatical rules we were breaking.

perspicacious (adj)   **per spih KAY shus**

shrewd; clear-sighted

> Persephone's perspicacious mind had solved so many cases that the popular private investagator was able to retire.

pragmatic (adj)   **prag MAT ik**

practical

> Never one for wild and unrealistic schemes, Matt took a pragmatic approach to research.

precocious (adj)   **pre KO shus**

exhibiting unusually early intellectual aptitude or maturity

> Bobby Fischer's precocious intellect made him one of the world's best chess players before he could even drive.

prospectus (n)   **pro SPEK tus**

formal proposal

> Before writing my thesis, I had to submit a detailed prospectus to the department for approval.

rudimentary (adj)   **roo duh MEN tuh ree**

basic; elementary; in the earliest stages of development

> Josh's rudimentary golf skills were easily overpowered by Tiger Woods's amazing performance on the green.

When the Going Gets Tough

abstruse (adj)   **ab STROOS**

difficult to understand

> Abby found her professor's lecture on non-Euclidian geometry abstruse; she doubted anyone else in class understood it either.

callous (adj)   **KAL us**

emotionally hardened; unfeeling

> Callie's callous remark about her friend's cluttered room really hurt his feelings.

convoluted (adj)   **kon vo LOO tid**

intricate; complex

> The directions were so convoluted that we became hopelessly lost.

enigma (n)   **e NIG ma**

a puzzle, mystery, or riddle

> The emu was an enigma; you could never tell what it was thinking.

inscrutable (adj)   **in SKROOT uh bul**

difficult to fathom or understand; impenetrable

> The ancient poet's handwriting was so inscrutable that even the most prominent Latin scholars could not read the manuscript.

reticent (adj)   **RET uh sint**

inclined to keep silent; reserved

Rosanna's reticent behavior caused the interviewer to think her incapable of conversing with other students.

staid (adj)   **STAYD**

unemotional; serious

Mr. Estado was well known for his staid demeanor; he stayed calm even when everyone else celebrated the team's amazing victory.

Cultural Artifacts

arcane (adj)   **ar KAYN**

known or understood by only a few

The dusty archive includes an arcane treasure trove of nautical charts from the Age of Discovery.

assimilate (v)   **uh SIM uh layt**

to absorb or become absorbed; to make or become similar

Keisha assimilated so quickly at her new school that she was named head of the social committee a month after enrolling.

autonomy (n)   **aw TAHN uh mee**

independence; self-determination

Candice gained autonomy upon moving out of her parents' house into her own apartment.

cosmopolitan (adj)   **koz mo PAHL i tun**

worldly; widely sophisticated

Inga was surprisingly cosmopolitan considering that she had never left her tiny hometown in Norway.

derivative (adj)   **duh RIV uh tiv**

something that comes from another source

Special Victims Unit and *Criminal Intent* are derivative spin-offs of the original *Law & Order* drama series.

entourage (n)   AHN ter azh

a group of attendants or associates; a retinue

Top celebrities travel with extensive entourages, which often include security guards, assistants, stylists, managers, publicists, and more.

esoteric (adj)   es oh TAIR ik

intended for or understood by only a small group

Esme's play is extremely esoteric; someone not raised in Estonia would find it difficult to follow.

gaffe (n)   GAF

a clumsy social error; a faux pas

Geoff committed the gaffe of telling his date that he had gone out with her sister the night before.

idiosyncrasy (n)   id ee oh SINK ruh see

characteristic peculiar to an individual or group

She had many idiosyncrasies, one of which was washing her socks in the dishwasher.

insular (adj)   IN suh ler

isolated; narrow or provincial

The family was so insular that no one else could get near them.

orthodox (adj)   OR thuh doks

adhering to the traditional and established, especially in religion

My father held an orthodox view of baseball; he believed that the field should be outside and made of real grass.

potentate (n)   PO tun tayt

one who has the power and position to rule over others; monarch

An omnipotent potentate is a person to be reckoned with; great power in the hands of a great leader is a powerful combination.

Cast Out

castigate (v)   KAS tih gayt
to scold, rebuke, or harshly criticize

Mr. Castile preferred not to castigate student misbehavior publicly; instead, he would quietly send the troublemaker to the principal's office.

censure (v)   SEN shur
to issue official blame

In recent years the FCC has censured networks for the provocative antics of Super Bowl halftime acts; what goes on during the game, however, usually escapes the organization's notice.

denounce (v)   duh NOWNTS
to condemn openly

In many powerful speeches throughout his lifetime, Martin Luther King, Jr. denounced racism as immoral.

reclusive (adj)   ree KLOO siv
seeking or preferring seclusion or isolation

Our neighbors were quite reclusive, hardly ever emerging from behind the closed doors of their home.

relinquish (v)   ree LING kwish
to retire from; give up or abandon

Ricky relinquished his career in order to search for the source of the world's best relish.

renounce (v)   ree NOWNTS
to give up (a title, for example), especially by formal announcement

Nancy renounced her given name and began selling records under the moniker "Boedicia."

vituperative (adj)   vie TOOP ur uh tiv
marked by harshly abusive condemnation

The vituperative speech was so cruel that the members left feeling completely abused.

No Way Around It

circumscribe (v)   SER kum skryb
> *to draw a circle around; to restrict*
>> The archeologist circumscribed the excavation area on the map.

contiguous (adj)   kun TIG yoo us
> *sharing an edge or boundary; touching*
>> The continental United States consists of 48 contiguous states.

WEEK 2

I'll Be the Judge of That!

conciliatory (adj)   kon SIL ee uh tor ee
> *appeasing; soothing; showing willingness to reconcile*
>> After arguing endlessly with them for weeks, Connie switched to a more conciliatory tone with her parents once prom season arrived.

credible (adj)   KRED uh bul
> *capable of being believed; plausible*
>> The shocking but credible report of mice in the kitchen kept Eddie up all night.

exonerate (v)   eg ZON er ayt
> *to free from blame*
>> Xena was exonerated of all criminal charges.

incontrovertible (adj)   in kahn truh VERT uh bul
> *indisputable; not open to question*
>> The videotape of the robbery provided incontrovertible evidence against the suspect—he was obviously guilty.

indict (v)   in DITE
> *to officially charge with wrongdoing or a crime*
>> President Nixon was indicted during the Watergate scandal.

litigious (adj)   **luh TIJ us**

prone to engage in lawsuits

Letitia was a litigious little girl; at one point, she tried to sue her dog.

parity (n)   **PA ruh tee**

equality, as in amount, status, or value (antonym: disparity)

The judges at the Olympics must score each athlete's performance with parity; such impartial treatment is difficult since one always wants to root for one's own country.

partisan (adj)   **PAR tiz un**

devoted to or biased in support of a party, group, or cause

Today's partisan politics are so antagonistic that it is difficult to reach a successful compromise on any issue.

rectitude (n)   **REK ti tood**

moral uprightness; righteousness

Thanks to his unerring sense of fairness and justice, Viktor was a model of moral rectitude; his hometown even erected a statue in his honor.

remiss (adj)   **ree MISS**

lax in attending to duty; negligent

Cassie was remiss in fulfilling her Miss America duties; she did not even come close to ending world hunger.

repudiate (v)   **ree PYOO dee ayt**

to reject the validity or authority of

I repudiated the teacher's arguments about Empress Wu Zetian's reputation by showing him that the reports of her cruelty were from unreliable sources.

sanctimonious (adj)   **sank ti MO nee us**

feigning piety or righteousness

The sanctimonious scholar had actually been plagiarizing other people's work for years.

scrupulous (adj)   SKROO pyoo lus

principled, having a strong sense of right and wrong; conscientious and exacting

Evan's scrupulous behavior began to annoy his friends when he called the cops on them for toilet papering their teacher's house.

solicitous (adj)   so LIS it us

concerned

The parents asked solicitous questions about the college admissions officer's family.

sophistry (n)   SAHF is tree

plausible but misleading or fallacious argument

The professor's sophistry misled the sophomore into incorrect beliefs.

substantiate (v)   sub STAN shee ayt

to support with proof or evidence; verify

The argument was substantiated by clear facts and hard evidence.

veracity (n)   vuh RA si tee

adherence to the truth; truthfulness

Since Vera was known for her veracity, it came as a complete shock when her family found out she had lied on her application.

vindicate (v)   VIN dih kayt

to free from blame

Mrs. Layton was finally vindicated after her husband admitted to the crime.

Flattery Will Get You Nowhere

cajole (v)   kuh JOL

to urge with repeated appeals, teasing, or flattery

The sweet-talking senior cajoled an impressionable junior into seeing *Lord of the Rings* for the tenth time.

chicanery (n) **chik AY ner ee**

trickery

The candidate accused his debate opponent of resorting to cheap chicanery to sway the electorate.

obsequious (adj) **ob SEEK wee us**

fawning and servile

Kevin was so obsequious that even his teachers were embarrassed; as a result, his sucking up rarely led to better grades.

sycophant (n) **SIK uh fant**

insincere, obsequious flatterer

Siggie is such a sycophant; he slyly sucks up to his teachers and reaps the rewards of his behavior.

One Person Can Change the World

altruism (n) **AL troo iz im**

unselfish concern for the welfare of others; selflessness

Alta, a model of altruism, gave her lunch money to a homeless woman who needed it more.

eminent (adj) **EM uh nent**

distinguished; prominent

Emeril Lagasse is one of the most eminent chefs working today; every TV-watcher knows how well known and highly regarded he is.

empathetic (adj) **em puh THET ik**

identification with and understanding of another's situation, feelings, and motives

Emily is one of my most empathetic friends; she can always relate to my emotions.

extol (v) **ek STOL**

to praise highly

Tollivan extolled the virtues of the troll while his teacher looked on amazed.

laudatory (adj)   LAW duh tor ee

full of praise

> The principal's speech was laudatory, congratulating the students on their SAT scores.

magnanimous (adj)   mag NA nuh mus

courageously or generously noble in mind and heart

> The magnanimous prince cared deeply for his country and its people.

philanthropic (adj)   fil un THROP ik

humanitarian; benevolent; relating to monetary generosity

> Phil was a philanthropic soul, always catering to the needy and the underprivileged.

reciprocate (v)   ree SIP ro kayt

to mutually take or give; to respond in kind

> The chef reciprocated his rival's respect; they admired each other so much that they even traded recipes.

Get Rid of It

defunct (adj)   duh FUNKT

no longer existing or functioning

> The theory that the world was flat became defunct when Magellan sailed to the West and did not fall off the earth.

eradicate (v)   er RAD i kayt

to get rid of as if by tearing up by the roots; abolish

> Radcliffe did her best to eradicate the radishes from her farm.

expurgate (v)   EK spur gayt

to remove objectionable content before publication or release

> The Chinese government expurgates nearly all obscene matter from the nation's Internet.

extirpate (v)   EK stir payt

to destroy

> While the family was on vacation, the termites practically extirpated the house.

quell (v)　　　　　　　　　　　　　　　　　**KWEL**

to put down forcibly; suppress

Nell quelled the fight over the quiche by throwing it out the window—she had long given up on reasoning with her sisters.

raze (v)　　　　　　　　　　　　　　　　　**RAYZ**

to level to the ground; demolish

It is difficult to raze a city building without demolishing other structures around it.

squelch (v)　　　　　　　　　　　　　　　　**SKWELCH**

to crush as if by trampling; squash

Sam wanted to keep squash as pets, but Quentin squelched the idea.

stymie (v)　　　　　　　　　　　　　　　　**STY mee**

to thwart or stump

Stan was stymied by the Sudoku puzzle; he just could not solve it.

supplant (v)　　　　　　　　　　　　　　　**suh PLANT**

to usurp the place of, especially through intrigue or underhanded tactics

The ants prepared to supplant the roaches as the dominant insect in the kitchen; their plan was to take the roaches by surprise and drive them out.

If You Can't Say Anything Nice

abase (v)　　　　　　　　　　　　　　　　**uh BAYS**

to lower in rank, prestige, or esteem

Bayard's withering restaurant review was an attempt to abase his former friend, the owner.

deride (v)　　　　　　　　　　　　　　　　**duh RIDE**

to mock contemptuously

Derrick was derided for wearing two different colored socks, but he could not help it—it was laundry day.

derogatory (adj)　　　　　　　　　　　　**duh RAH guh tor ee**

insulting or intended to insult

The unethical politician did not simply attack his opponent's views; he also made derogatory remarks about the other candidate's family and personal hygiene.

disparage (v)　　　　　　　　　　　　**dis PAR uj**

to speak of negatively; to belittle

Wanda disparaged Glen by calling him a cheat and a liar.

effrontery (n)　　　　　　　　　　　　**eh FRON ter ee**

brazen boldness; presumptuousness

The attorney's effrontery in asking such personal questions so shocked Esther that she immediately ran from the office.

ignominy (n)　　　　　　　　　　　　**IG nuh mi nee**

great personal dishonor or humiliation; disgraceful conduct

Ignacio felt great ignominy after the scandal broke.

impugn (v)　　　　　　　　　　　　**im PYOON**

to attack as false or questionable

Instead of taking the high road, the candidate impugned his opponent's character.

mar (v)　　　　　　　　　　　　**MAR**

to damage, especially in a disfiguring way

The perfect day was marred by the arrival of storm clouds.

pejorative (adj)　　　　　　　　　　　　**puh JOR uh tiv**

disparaging, belittling, insulting

Teachers should refrain from using pejorative terms such as *numbskull* and *jackass* to refer to other teachers.

vex (v)　　　　　　　　　　　　**VEKS**

to annoy or bother; to perplex

Bex's mom was vexed when Bex was very vague about her whereabouts for the evening.

vindictive (adj)   vin DIK tiv

   disposed to seek revenge; revengeful; spiteful

   Vincent was very vindictive; when someone hurt him, he responded by
   vigorously plotting revenge.

WEEK 3

Overkill

bombastic (adj)   bom BAS tik

   given to pompous speech or writing

   The principal's bombastic speech bombed in the eyes of the students; it
   only furthered their impression of him as a pompous jerk.

ebullience (n)   eh BUHL yuhns

   intense enthusiasm

   A sense of ebullience swept over the lacrosse fans when their team won
   the game.

embellish (v)   em BELL ish

   to ornament or decorate; to exaggerate

   One can never trust that Anwar's stories are realistic; his details are almost
   always embellished so that his experiences sound more interesting than
   they really are.

exorbitant (adj)   eg ZOR bit int

   exceeding all bounds, as of custom or fairness

   I wanted to buy a Porsche, but the price was exorbitant, so instead I
   purchased a used mail truck.

exuberant (adj)   eg ZOO bur ent

   full of unrestrained enthusiasm or joy

   William was exuberant when he found out that he had gotten into the
   college of his choice.

flagrant (adj)   **FLAY grent**

extremely or deliberately shocking or noticeable

Burning the flag shows flagrant disrespect for the country.

gratuitous (adj)   **gruh TOO uh tus**

given freely; unearned; unnecessary

The film was full of gratuitous sex and violence inessential to the story.

lavish (adj)   **LAV ish**

extravagant

Lavanya's wedding was a lavish affair, with six DJs, two elephants, and a large ice sculpture of the couple.

lugubrious (adj)   **luh GOO bree yus**

mournful, dismal, or gloomy, especially to an exaggerated or ludicrous degree

Lucas's lugubrious eulogy for his pet lobster quickly became ridiculous.

opulent (adj)   **OP yoo lent**

displaying great wealth

The ophthalmologist's opulent home was the envy of his friends; the crystal chandeliers, marble floors, and teak furniture must have cost a fortune.

ornate (adj)   **or NAYT**

elaborately decorated

The wood carvings were so ornate that you could examine them many times and still notice things you had not seen before.

penchant (n)   **PEN chent**

a strong inclination or liking

Penny's penchant for chocolate-covered ants led her to munch on them all day.

redundant (adj)   **ree DUN dint**

needlessly repetitive

The author's speech was terribly redundant, repeating the same phrases, saying the same thing over and over, and constantly reiterating the same point.

ubiquitous (adj)   **yoo BIK wit us**

being or seeming to be everywhere at the same time; omnipresent

Kenny had a ubiquitous little sister; wherever he turned, there she was.

Through Someone Else's Eyes

vicarious (adj)   **vie KA ree us**

felt or undergone as if one were taking part in the experience or feelings of another

Stan, who was never athletic but loved sports, lived vicariously through his brother, a professional basketball player.

vignette (n)   **vin YET**

a short scene or story

The poodle vignette in my new film expresses the true meaning of Valentine's Day.

Lots 'n' Lots

amalgam (n)   **uh MAL gum**

a combination of diverse elements; a mixture

The song was an amalgam of many different styles, from blues to hip hop to folk.

inundate (v)   **IN un dayt**

to overwhelm as if with a flood; to swamp

The day after the ad ran, Martha was inundated with phone calls.

multifarious (adj)   **mul ti FAYR ee us**

diverse; various

The multifarious achievements of Leonardo da Vinci, ranging from architecture and painting to philosophy and science, are unparalleled in our century.

multiplicity (n)   **mul tuh PLI sit ee**

state of being various or manifold; a great number

A multiplicity of views is essential to a healthy multicultural democracy.

Getting Better All the Time

alleviate (v)   **uh LEE vee ayt**

to ease a pain or burden

> Alvin meditated to alleviate the pain from the headache he got after taking the SAT.

ameliorate (v)   **uh MEEL yor ayt**

to make something better; improve

> Winning a silver medal quickly ameliorated Amelia's angst at losing the gold.

beneficial (adj)   **ben uh FISH ul**

producing or promoting a favorable result; helpful

> According to my doctor, tea's beneficial effects may include reducing anxiety.

curative (adj)   **KYUR uh tiv**

able to heal or cure

> The aloe had a curative effect on my sunburn; within hours, the flaking had stopped.

palliative (n)   **PAL lee uh tiv**

relieving or soothing the symptoms of a disease or disorder without effecting a cure

> Watching professional polo on TV became a palliative for the screaming child; it was the only thing that would quiet him.

therapeutic (adj)   **thair uh PYOO tik**

having or exhibiting healing powers

> The therapeutic air of the Mediterranean cured Thomas of his asthma.

Model Behavior

complement (n)   KOM plem ent
something that completes, goes with, or brings to perfection

The lovely computer is the perfect complement to the modern furnishings in Abby's apartment.

epitome (n)   e PIT o mee
a representative or example of a type

She is the epitome of selflessness; no matter how much or little she has, she always gives to others.

felicitous (adj)   fuh LIH sih tus
admirably suited; apt

Jamie Foxx made a felicitous speech when he won his Oscar.

Liar, Liar, Pants on Fire

belie (v)   bee LIE
to misrepresent

He smiled in order to belie his hostility.

debunk (v)   duh BUNK
to expose untruths, shams, or exaggerated claims

The university administration debunked the myth that bunk beds are only for children by installing them in every dorm on campus.

dubious (adj)   DOO bee us
doubtful; of unlikely authenticity

Jerry's dubious claim that he could fly like Superman did not win him any summer job offers.

duplicitous (adj)   doo PLIS uh tus
deliberately deceptive

The duplicitous man duplicated hundred dollar bills and gave the counterfeits to unsuspecting vendors.

fabricate (v)   **FAB ruh kayt**

    to make up in order to deceive

        Fabio fabricated the story that he used to play drums for Metallica; he has never actually held a drumstick in his life.

fallacy (n)   **FAL uh see**

    a false notion

        The idea that there is only one college for you is a fallacy.

mendacious (adj)   **men DAY shus**

    lying; untruthful

        John's mendacious statements on the stand sealed his fate; he was found guilty of lying to the court about his role in the crime.

specious (adj)   **SPEE shus**

    having the ring of truth or plausibility but actually false

        Susie's specious argument seemed to make sense, but when I looked more closely, it was clearly illogical.

On the Fence

ambiguous (adj)   **am BIG yoo us**

    open to more than one interpretation

        Big's eyes were an ambiguous color: In some lights they looked brown, and in others, green.

ambivalent (adj)   **am BIV uh lint**

    simultaneously feeling opposing feelings; uncertain

        Amy felt ambivalent about her dance class: On one hand, she enjoyed the exercise, but on the other, the choice of dances bored her.

apathetic (adj)   **ap uh THET ik**

    feeling or showing little emotion

        The apathetic students did not even bother to vote for class president.

capricious (adj)   **kuh PREE shus**

    impulsive and unpredictable

        The referee's capricious behavior angered the players; he would call a foul for minor contact, but ignore elbowing and kicking.

equivocal (adj)   **e KWIV uh kul**

open to two or more interpretations and often intended to mislead; ambiguous (antonym: unequivocal)

> The politician made so many equivocal statements during the scandal that no one could be sure what, if anything, he had admitted to.

erratic (adj)   **e RAT ik**

markedly inconsistent

> Erroll's erratic behavior made it difficult for his friends to predict what he would do in a given moment.

impetuous (adj)   **im PET choo us**

suddenly and forcefully energetic or emotional; impulsive and passionate

> Mr. Limpet was so impetuous that we never knew what he would do next.

impetus (n)   **IM pit us**

an impelling force or stimulus

> A looming deadline provided Imelda with the impetus she needed to finish her research paper.

sporadic (adj)   **spo RAD ik**

occurring at irregular intervals; having no pattern or order in time

> Storms in Florida are sporadic; it is hard to predict when they are going to occur.

vacillate (v)   **VA sil ayt**

to sway from one side to the other; oscillate

> The cook vacillated between favoring chicken and preferring fish; he just could not decide which to prepare.

whimsical (adj)   **WIM zi kul**

characterized by whim; unpredictable

> Egbert rarely behaved as expected; indeed, he was a whimsical soul whose every decision was anybody's guess.

I Just Can't Take It Anymore

flag (v)   **FLAG**

to decline in vigor or strength; to tire; to droop

After several days climbing mountains in pouring rain, our enthusiasm for the hiking trip began to flag.

jaded (adj)   **JAY did**

worn out; wearied

Jade's experiences had jaded her; she no longer believed that the junk stacked in her garage was going to make her rich.

WEEK 4

She's Crafty

ingenuous (adj)   **in JEN yoo us**

lacking in cunning, guile, or worldliness (antonym: disingenuous)

Janine was so ingenuous that it was too easy for her friends to dupe her.

subterfuge (n)   **SUB ter fyoozh**

a deceptive stratagem or device

The submarine pilots were trained in the art of subterfuge; they were excellent at faking out their enemies.

surreptitious (adj)   **sir up TISH us**

secretive; sneaky

Afraid of failing the test, Sara took a surreptitious glance at her neighbor's test booklet and hoped the teacher did not see her.

Just a Little Bit

dearth (n)   DERTH
scarce supply; lack

There was a dearth of money in my piggybank; it collected dust, not
bills.

modicum (n)   MOD i kuhm
a small, moderate, or token amount

A modicum of effort may result in a small score improvement; in order
to improve significantly, however, you must study as often as possible.

paucity (n)   PAW sit ee
smallness in number; scarcity

The struggling city had a paucity of resources and therefore a high level
of poverty.

squander (v)   SKWAN der
to spend wastefully

Kerri squandered her savings on shoes and was not able to buy her
apartment.

temperate (adj)   TEM per ut
moderate; restrained (antonym: intemperate)

Temperate climates rarely experience extremes in temperature.

tenuous (adj)   TEN yoo us
having little substance or strength; shaky

Her grasp on reality is tenuous at best; she is not even sure what year it is.

I Will Survive

diligent (adj)   **DIL uh jent**

marked by painstaking effort; hard-working

> With diligent effort, they were able to finish the model airplane in record time.

maverick (n)   **MAV rik**

one who is independent and resists adherence to a group

> In the movie *Top Gun*, Tom Cruise played a maverick who often broke rules and did things his own way.

mercenary (n)   **MUR sin air ee**

motivated solely by a desire for money or material gain

> During the war, Mercer was a mercenary; he would fight for whichever side paid him the most for his services.

obstinate (adj)   **OB stin it**

stubbornly attached to an opinion or a course of action

> Despite Jeremy's broken leg, his parents were obstinate; they steadfastly refused to buy him an Xbox.

proliferate (v)   **pro LIF er ayt**

to grow or increase rapidly

> Because cell phones have proliferated in recent years, many new area codes have been created to handle the demand for phone numbers.

tenacity (n)   **te NAS uh tee**

persistence

> With his overwhelming tenacity, Clark was finally able to interview Brad Pitt for the school newspaper.

vigilant (adj)   **VIJ uh lent**

on the alert; watchful

> The participants of the candlelight vigil were vigilant, as they had heard that the fraternity across the street was planning to egg them.

Connect the Dots

extraneous (adj)   **ek STRAY nee us**

irrelevant; inessential

The book, though interesting, had so much extraneous information that it was hard to keep track of the important points.

juxtapose (v)   **JUK stuh pohz**

to place side by side, especially for comparison or contrast

Separately the pictures look identical, but if you juxtapose them, you can see the differences.

superfluous (adj)   **soo PUR floo us**

extra; unnecessary

If there is sugar in your tea, honey would be superfluous.

synergy (n)   **SIN er jee**

combined action or operation

The synergy of hydrogen and oxygen creates water.

tangential (adj)   **tan JEN chul**

merely touching or slightly connected; only superficially relevant

Though Abby's paper was well written, its thesis was so tangential to its proof that her teacher could not give her a good grade.

I Write the Songs

aesthetic (adj)   **es THET ik**

having to do with the appreciation of beauty

Aesthetic considerations determined the arrangement of paintings at the museum; as long as art looked good together, it did not matter who had painted it.

aural (adj)   **AW rul**

of or related to the ear or the sense of hearing

It should come as no surprise that musicians prefer aural to visual learning.

cacophony (n)   **kuh KAH fuh nee**

discordant, unpleasant noise

> Brian had to shield his ears from the awful cacophony produced by the punk band onstage.

dirge (n)   **DERJ**

a funeral hymn or lament

> The dirge was so beautiful that everyone cried, even those who had not known the deceased.

eclectic (adj)   **eh KLEK tik**

made up of a variety of sources or styles

> Lou's taste in music is quite eclectic; he listens to everything from rap to polka.

incongruous (adj)   **in KAHN groo us**

lacking in harmony; incompatible

> My chicken and jello soup experiment failed; the tastes were just too incongruous.

sonorous (adj)   **SAHN ur us**

producing a deep or full sound

> The large and well-rehearsed orchestra combined with the concert hall's excellent acoustics to create a sonorous effect that wowed the audience.

strident (adj)   **STRY dent**

loud, harsh, grating, or shrill

> Bill's strident tone was off-putting to the other attendees at the town council meeting, causing them to discount his arguments.

Dude, This Sucks!

debacle (n)   **duh BAHK ul**

disastrous or ludicrous defeat or failure; fiasco

Jim's interview was a complete debacle; he accidentally locked himself in the bathroom, sneezed on the interviewer multiple times, and knocked over the president of the company.

debilitate (v)   **duh BIL i tayt**

impair the strength of; weaken

Deb ran the New York City marathon without proper training; the experience left her debilitated for weeks.

tumultuous (adj)   **tum UL choo us**

noisy and disorderly

The tumultuous applause was so deafening that the pianist could not hear the singer.

It's All in the Timing

anachronism (n)   **ah nak ruh NIZ um**

the representation of something as existing or happening in the wrong time period

I noticed an anachronism in the museum's ancient Rome display: a digital clock ticking behind a statue of Venus.

archaic (adj)   **ar KAY ik**

characteristic of an earlier time; antiquated; old

"How dost thou?" is an archaic way of saying "How are you?"

dilatory (adj)   **DIL uh tor ee**

habitually late

Always waiting until the last moment to leave home in the morning, Dylan was a dilatory student.

ephemeral (adj)   uh FEM er ul

lasting for only a brief time

> The importance of SAT scores is truly ephemeral; when you are applying, they are crucial, but once you get into college, no one cares how well you did.

redolent (adj)   RED uh lint

fragrant; aromatic; suggestive

> The aroma of apple pie wafted into my room, redolent of weekends spent baking with my grandmother.

temporal (adj)   TEM per ul

of, relating to, or limited by time

> One's enjoyment of a mocha latte is bound by temporal limitations; all too soon, the latte is gone.

Who Can It Be Now?

onerous (adj)   O ner us

troublesome or oppressive; burdensome

> The onerous task was so difficult that Ona thought she would never get through it.

portent (n)   POR tent

indication of something important or calamitous about to occur; omen

> A red morning sky is a terrible portent for all sailors—it means that stormy seas are ahead.

prescience (n)   PRE shens

knowledge of actions or events before they occur; foreknowledge; foresight

> Preetha's prescience was such that people wondered if she was psychic; how else could she know so much about the future?

Boooring

austere (adj)   aw STEER

without decoration; strict

> The gray walls and bare floors of his monastery cell provided an even
> more austere setting than Brother Austen had hoped for.

banal (adj)   buh NAL

drearily commonplace; predictable; trite

> The poet's imagery is so banal that I think she cribbed her work from
> *Poetry for Dummies*.

hackneyed (adj)   HAK need

worn out through overuse; trite

> All Hal could offer in the way of advice were hackneyed old phrases
> that I had heard a hundred times before.

insipid (adj)   in SIP id

uninteresting; unchallenging; lacking taste or savor

> That insipid movie was so predictable that I walked out.

prosaic (adj)   pro ZAY ik

unimaginative; dull (antonym: poetic)

> Rebecca made a prosaic mosaic consisting of identical, undecorated
> tiles.

soporific (adj)   saw puh RIF ik

inducing or tending to induce sleep

> The congressman's speech was so soporific that even his cat was yawning.

vapid (adj)   VAP id

lacking liveliness, animation, or interest; dull

> Valerie's date was so vapid that she thought he was sleeping with his
> eyes open.

WEEK 5

It All Changes So Fast

brevity (n)   **BRE vi tee**
the quality or state of being brief in duration

Brevity = briefness. (You can't get any shorter than that!)

expedient (adj)   **ek SPEE dee ent**
appropriate to a purpose; convenient; speedy

It was more expedient to use FedEx than to use the post office.

transient (adj)   **TRAN zee unt**
passing quickly in time or space

Jack Dawson enjoyed his transient lifestyle; with nothing but the clothes on his back and the air in his lungs, he was free to travel wherever he wanted.

Full On

augment (v)   **awg MENT**
to make greater, as in size, extent, or quantity; to supplement

The model Angele Franju is rumored to have augmented her studies in chemistry with a minor in German literature.

bolster (v)   **BOL ster**
to hearten, support or prop up

The class bolstered Amelia's confidence; she had no idea she already knew so much.

burgeon (v)   **BER jun**
to grow and flourish

The burgeoning Burgess family required a new house because its old one had only one bedroom.

copious (adj)   **KO pee us**
plentiful; having a large quantity

Amy took copious notes during class, using up five large notebooks.

distend (v)   **dis TEND**

to swell out or expand from internal pressure, as when overly full

The balloon distended as it was filled with helium, much like Mike's stomach after Mike ate an entire turkey on Thanksgiving.

grandiose (adj)   **gran dee OHS**

great in scope or intent; grand

The party was a grandiose affair; hundreds of richly dressed guests danced the night away.

prodigious (adj)   **pruh DIJ us**

enormous

Steven Spielberg's prodigious talent has made him the most successful film producer and director of our time.

profundity (n)   **pro FUN di tee**

great depth of intellect, feeling, or meaning

The actor's profundity surprised the director, who had heard that he was a bit of an airhead.

redouble (v)   **ree DUB ul**

to make twice as great; to double

Rita redoubled her efforts to become president of her class by campaigning twice as hard as before.

scintillating (adj)   **SIN til ay ting**

brilliant

The writer's scintillating narrative diverted Izabel's attention away from her other guests.

Don't Make Waves

averse (adj)   **uh VERS**

strongly disinclined

Ava proved so averse to homework that she would break out in hives at the mere mention of it.

conspicuous (adj)   **kun SPIK yoo us**

easy to notice; obvious (antonym: inconspicuous)

The red tuxedo was conspicuous among all the classic black ones. What was he thinking?

demure (adj)   **duh MYUR**

modest and reserved

Muriel was the most demure girl in the class, always sitting quietly in the back of the room and downplaying any compliments she received.

diffident (adj)   **DIF uh dint**

timidity or shyness

Lea's diffident nature often prevented her from speaking out in class.

docile (adj)   **DOS uhl**

submissive to instruction; willing to be taught

The SAT class was so docile that the teacher wondered if she was in the right room.

innocuous (adj)   **in NAHK yoo us**

having no adverse effect; harmless

The plants were as innocuous as they looked; we suffered no ill effects from eating their leaves.

placid (adj)   **PLAS id**

calm or quiet; undisturbed

An ideal place for a quiet summer vacation is a beach house in a placid town.

quiescent (adj)   **kwee ES sint**

quiet, still, or at rest; inactive

Quinn's quiescent behavior made him an ideal roommate.

Do You Agree?

concord (n)   **KON kord**
    agreement (antonym: discord)

        The class was in concord about the decision to perform *Hamlet*, rather
        than *King Lear*, in the spring show.

concur (v)   **kun KUR**
    to agree

        The board concurred that the con artist who had stolen their money
        had to be convicted.

dogmatic (adj)   **dog MAT ik**
    stubbornly attached to insufficiently proven beliefs

        Avik was dogmatic in his belief that the power lines were giving his dog
        headaches.

fastidious (adj)   **fas TID ee us**
    carefully attentive to detail; difficult to please

        Kelly, always so fastidious, dramatically edited our group's report.

intransigent (adj)   **in TRAN zi jent**
    refusal to moderate a position or to compromise

        Jeff was so intransigent in his views that it was impossible to have a
        rational debate with him.

jocular (adj)   **JOK yoo ler**
    characterized by or given to joking

        Yung-Ji's jocular disposition helped him gain popularity.

meticulous (adj)   **muh TIK yoo lus**
    extremely careful and precise

        Since Kelly was so meticulous, we asked her to proofread our group's
        report.

Officer Friendly

affable (adj)   AF uh bul

easy going; friendly

My mom always said that the key to being affable is the ability to make others laugh.

alacrity (n)   uh LAK ruh tee

promptness in response; cheerful readiness; eagerness

I was so happy when I got the acceptance letter from the University of Alaska that I sprinted home with great alacrity to share the good news.

amiable (adj)   AY mee uh bul

friendly; agreeable; good-natured

Mr. Amis was so amiable that he let us call him "Big A."

benign (adj)   be NINE

kind and gentle

Uncle Ben is a benign and friendly man who is always willing to help.

sanguine (adj)   SAN gwin

cheerfully confident; optimistic

Harold's sanguine temperament kept him cheerful, even through somber times.

Nasty Boys

belligerent (adj)   buh LIH jer int

eager to fight; hostile or aggressive

The prosecutor was reprimanded for his belligerent cross-examination of the witness, who had dissolved into tears.

byzantine (adj)   BIZ un teen

extremely complicated or devious

I gave up trying to understand the byzantine tax code and had an accountant file my taxes for me.

cantankerous (adj)   kan TANK er us
ill-tempered and quarrelsome; disagreeable

The dog hid under the tank as a result of the cat's cantankerous disposition.

contentious (adj)   kun TEN shus
quarrelsome

The contentious debate over science class content is increasingly making the news.

deleterious (adj)   dil uh TER ee us
having a harmful effect

It was only once he started his test that Murray realized the deleterious effects of one too many Red Bulls; he could not concentrate, and his hands were shaking so much he could barely write.

exacerbate (v)   eg ZA ser bayt
to increase the severity, violence, or bitterness of; aggravate

Alan's procrastination problems were exacerbated by the monkeys who kept throwing bananas at him while he tried to concentrate.

flippant (adj)   FLIP ent
disrespectfully humorous or casual

Flap's flippant remarks to the teacher got him sent to the principal's office.

insolent (adj)   IN suh lint
insulting in manner or speech

The insolent prime minister stuck her tongue out at the queen.

nefarious (adj)   nuh FAYR ee us
flagrantly wicked; vicious

Dorothy's kindness and bravery triumphed over the nefarious antics of the Wicked Witch of the West.

pernicious (adj)   per NISH us
extremely or irrevocably harmful; deadly

The fertilizer's pernicious effects were not immediately obvious, but researchers became suspicious when all their petunias died.

rancorous (adj)   **RANK er us**

marked by bitter, deep-seated ill will

They had such a rancorous relationship that no one could believe that they had ever gotten along.

repugnant (adj)   **ree PUG nent**

arousing disgust or aversion; offensive or repulsive

The pug's behavior at the dog park was repugnant, causing other dogs to avoid him altogether.

tawdry (adj)   **TAW dree**

gaudy and cheap

Connor's tawdry attire embarrassed his snooty host.

Earth, Wind, and Fire

arboreal (adj)   **ar BOR ee ul**

relating to or resembling a tree or trees

The Rocky Mountain National Forest will celebrate its arboreal splendor with an Arbor Day concert.

invocation (n)   **in vo KAY shun**

a call (usually upon a higher power) for assistance, support, or inspiration

The group invoked the god of war as their protector on the field of battle.

stratify (v)   **STRAT i fy**

to layer or separate into layers

Jonas studied the stratified bedrock and was able to see which time periods went with which layers.

variegated (adj)   **VAR ee ih gay tid**

having streaks, marks, or patches of a different color or colors; varicolored

The wood's markings were so variegated that Mr. Vargas assumed they had been painted on.

verdant (adj)   **VUR dent**

green with vegetation

The garden was verdant after the rain.

Summary

- To learn vocabulary for the PSAT, it is best to take things in small daily doses.

- Flash cards provide a great way to learn vocabulary; customize yours with funny sentences and mnemonics to help you remember words you have trouble with.

- For more help with vocabulary, refer to the *Word Smart* series of books. They are all focused on the words found most often on standardized tests such as the PSAT.

Part III
Drill Answers and
Explanations

CHAPTER 6

Drill 1 Answers

19. C   The *bogus cure is a security blanket* because it convinces people that *things that mankind cannot fix or heal* do not exist. So the bogus cure is (C) *comforting even if it is not effective.* (A), (D), and (E) are not mentioned in the passage, and (B) is mentioned later, unrelated to the security blanket comment.

20. C   The *confidence man* sold fake medicines. The only person in Passage 2 who sells fake medicines is (C) *the herb doctor*, who sells a box *filled with whatever bits of grass and dirt happened to be close by.*

21. B   Both the tonic and the box are supposed to be medicines and are sold as such. (B), *Both were advertised to cure an ailment*, matches this. (C) and (E) are not mentioned in the passage. (A) is mentioned only in Passage 1, and (D) is mentioned only in Passage 2.

22. E   The herb doctor brings up the brawny boxer to say that just because the hunter does not need the medicine does not mean he should badmouth it to the old man. The medicine, after all, will *in mere imagination, if nothing more*, help the old man. So how could the hunter be *so pitiless*? (E), *the hunter should not disparage the old man's belief in the medicine*, basically says this. (B) and (C) are too literal, because the herb doctor mentions the boxer only to make a larger point. (A) and (D) are not mentioned in the passage.

23. D   The author of Passage 1 is against the cure medicines because they can do harm, but he realizes that they can occasionally have some use. So he is (D) *more realistic* than the herb doctor, who is trying his best to lie his way into making a sale.

24. E   We are looking for something mentioned by the author of Passage 1, but not mentioned anywhere in Passage 2. (A) is mentioned in Passage 1 and by the herb doctor near the end of Passage 2, so we can eliminate it. (B) is only sort of mentioned in Passage 2. (C) is mentioned in Passage 1 and shown by the fact that the old man in Passage 2 just bought the medicine. (D) is not mentioned in either passage. This leaves (E), *medicine is generally based on trial and error*, which is mentioned by the author of Passage 1—*we try things, and see if they tend to work*—but nowhere in Passage 2.

CHAPTER 7

Drill 1 Answers

1. **c**   Examples: –7, 0, 1, 8

2. **d**   Examples: .5, 2, 118

3. **g**   Examples: –.5, –2, –118

4. **f**   Examples: –4, 0, 10

5. **b**   Examples: –5, 1, 17

6. **a**   Examples: *Factors* of 12 are 1, 2, 3, 4, 6, and 12. Factors of 10 are 1, 2, 5, and 10.

7. **i**   Examples: *Multiples* of 12 include –24, –12, 0, 12, 24, and so on. Multiples of 10 include 20, –10, 0, 10, 20, 30, and so on.

8. **h**   Examples: 2, 3, 5, 7, 11, and so on. There are no negative *prime numbers*, and 1 is not prime.

9. **e**   Examples: 3 and 4 are *distinct* numbers. –2 and 2 are also distinct.

10. **j**   Examples: In the number 274, 2 is the *digit* in the hundreds place, 7 is the digit in the tens place, and 4 is the digit in the ones place.

11. **o**   Examples: –1, 0, 1, and 2 are *consecutive* numbers. Be careful—sometimes you will be asked for *consecutive even* or *consecutive odd* numbers, in which case you would use just the odds or evens in a consecutive list of numbers.

12. **n**   Examples: 6 is *divisible* by 2 and 3, but not by 4 or 5.

13. **l**   Examples: When you divide 26 by 8, you get 3 with a *remainder* of 2 (2 is left over). When you divide 14 by 5, you get 2 with a remainder of 4 (4 is left over).

14. **k**   Examples: When you add 2 and 3, you get a *sum* of 5. When you add –4 and 1, you get a sum of –3.

15. **r**   Examples: When you multiply 2 and 3, you get a *product* of 6. When you multiply –4 and 1, you get a product of –4.

16. **m**   Examples: When you subtract 2 from 3, you get a *difference* of 1. When you subtract –4 from 1, you get a difference of 5.

17. **q**   Examples: When you divide 2 by 3, you get a quotient of $\frac{2}{3}$. When you divide –4 by 1, you get a quotient of –4.

18. **p**   Examples: The absolute value of –3 is 3. The absolute value of 41 is 41.

Drill 2 Answers

a.   3, 5, 7

b.   1, 2, 5, 10

c.   2, 5

d.   1, 2, 3, 4, 6, 8, 12, 16, 24, 48

e.   2, 3

f.   6, 12, 18, 24, 30, 36, 42

g.   4, 8, 12, 16, 20, 24, 28

h.   42

i.   5 and 6

j.   15 and 2

1.   **C**   51 can be divided evenly by 3 with no remainder.

2.   **E**   The thousandths place is the third to the right of the decimal.

3.   **C**   27 can be divided by 3 and 9.

4.   **C**   The three consecutive integers must be 6, 7, and 8. The least of them is 6.

5.   **B**   If the numbers are 2, 4, 6, 8, and 10, then 8 + 10 = 18 and 2 + 4 = 6. The last two numbers are 12 greater than the first two. (Do not forget that the numbers have to be consecutive and even!)

6.   **A**   While this problem can be solved by listing multiples of 3 and 14, you end up having to list a lot of multiples to get to the answer! When this happens, you can factor instead. 14 can be factored into 2×7, so any number divisible by 3 and 14 must be divisible by 3, 2, and 7. That means it must be divisible by 6 since $2 \times 3 = 6$. Thus, choice (A) is the correct answer.

Drill 3 Answers

a. 3^5

b. 3^1

c. 3^6

d. x^8

e. x^4

f. x^{12}

3.   **A**   If $3^4 = 9^x$, then $81 = 9^x$. Therefore, $x = 2$. You could also rewrite 3^4 as $3 \times 3 \times 3 \times 3 = 9 \times 9$.

5.   **B**   If $(3x)^3 = 3^{15}$, then by the rules of MADSPM, $3x = 15$, and $x = 5$.

11.   **E**   Approach the two equations separately, using the rules of MADSPM. If $x^y \times x^6 = x^{54}$, then $y + 6 = 54$, and $y = 48$. If $(x^3)^z = x^9$, then $3z = 9$, and $z = 3$. Now we know that $y = 48$ and $z = 3$, so $y + z = 51$.

Drill 4 Answers

a.   36

b.   24

c.   20

d. 16π

e. 8π

f. $x = 10, y = 5$

g.   30

h.   22

i.   6

j.   6

k. -1

17. **D** Because this is a square, the two sides are equal. Therefore, $2x + 1 = x + 3$. Solve for x, and you get that x must be 2. Therefore, a side equals $x + 3$ or $2x + 1 = 5$, so the area equals 25.

10. **E** Here are four lines; a and b are parallel, d intersects a and b, and c does not intersect both parallel lines. In statement I, angles 1 and 5 do not have to be equal because a side of angle 1 is line c, which has nothing to do with the parallel lines. Thus, the angles in statement I do not have to be equal, and you can eliminate (B). The angles in statement II have to be equal because angles 2 and 7 are opposite angles (two angles made up of the same two lines) and opposite angles must be equal. Eliminate (A) and (D). The angles in statement III must be equal because angles 3 and 9 are made up of the same line (line d) and one of the parallel lines. In fact, 3, 6, 5, and 9 are all the same "small angle," so eliminate (C). Therefore, statements II and III are true, and the correct answer is (E).

19. **B** This question involves simultaneous equations, so the trick is to stack and combine them. You are being asked for $x + y$, so even getting the same number of x variables as y variables would be useful. Let's see what happens when we add the equations:

$$x + 2y = 12$$

$$2x + y = 9$$

$$3x + 3y = 21$$

Now all we need to do is divide both sides of the equation by 3 to get the expression we are being asked for, $x + y$, and we end up with the answer, 7.

10. **B** When we simplify the fractional exponent, we get $\sqrt{x^5} = 8x$. Squaring both sides gives us $x^5 = 64x^2$. We can divide by x^2 on each side to get $x^3 = 64$ (remember your MADSPM rules!). Finally, taking the cube root of both sides gives us $x = 4$.

Drill 5 Answers

33.　　Because the triangle is isosceles, with $AB = BC$, we know that angles A and C must have the same measure. So angle A must also be 40 degrees. Angles A and C have a combined measure of 80 degrees, and we need 180 total degrees in the triangle. Therefore, x must measure 100.

34.　　If five consecutive integers have a sum of 100, they must be 18, 19, 20, 21, and 22. The next four consecutive integers are 23, 24, 25, and 26. Their sum is 98.

35.　　Because $5x^2 = 125$, we know that $x^2 = 25$ and $x = 5$. Therefore, $5x^3 = 5 \times 125 = 625$.

36.   Remember your prime factor tree? The prime factors of 140 are 2, 2, 5, and 7, but the *distinct* prime factors are 2, 5, and 7. Add them up and you get 14.

CHAPTER 8

Drill 1 Answers

4.   **D**   First, plug in a number for the amount of homework Martha has. Let's say she has 12 pages of work to do. If she does half of this on Tuesday, she does 6 pages, and there are 6 pages left. If, on Wednesday, she does one-third of the remaining 6 pages, that means she does 2 more pages. So she has 4 pages left over from the original 12. What fractional part is left over? $\frac{4}{12}$ or $\frac{1}{3}$.

14.   **D**   Let's plug in numbers for a, b, and c such that $a = \frac{b}{c^2}$. We can pick $4 = \frac{16}{2^2}$. Now the question becomes, what is $\frac{1}{b^2}$ or $\frac{1}{16^2}$? The answer is $\frac{1}{256}$. When you work through all of the answer choices using $a = 4$, $b = 16$, and $c = 2$, which choice says this? Choice (D) does.

12.   **A**   Choose a number to plug in for p. How about 2? Now the problem reads $\frac{\frac{1}{8}}{2(2)} = \frac{1}{32}$. When you plug $p = 2$ into the answers, (A) turns out to be right.

18.   **E**   Variables in the answer choices? Absolutely! So we can plug in our own numbers: For x (Jodi's account), plug in $18 (Does Jodi have to be rich? No! We just need numbers that will make the math easy.). With $18 in her account, $\frac{1}{6}$ for rent is $3 and the car payment is also $3. Subtract that from the $18, and Jodi has $12 left in her account. Now we have to plug in for y (the amount Jodi deposits); we can make that $8, bringing her account balance to $20. Then Jodi purchases a set of knives for $10 ($\frac{1}{2}$ the amount in her account) and has $10 left. Go through all of the answer choices, using $x = 18$ and $y = 8$, and see which one gives you $10. The only one that works is (E).

Drill 2 Answers

8. **C** We should begin by plugging in answer choice (C), 3, for x. Does $3^5 = 243$? Yes. So the answer is (C).

14. **D** If we try plugging in (C), $\frac{1}{4}$, for x, the equation becomes $\frac{6}{4} + 4 = 5$, which is false. If we try plugging in (D), $\frac{1}{2}$, for x, the equation becomes $\frac{12}{4} + 2 = 5$, which is true.

15. **B** This is another great opportunity for Plugging In. Let's plug in a number for a. How about 90, just to make the math easy? If $a = 90$, then the other angle inside the triangle must be equal to 60. Therefore, b must be equal to 120. What choice says 120, remembering that $a = 90$? (B) does.

Drill 3 Answers

a. 90

b. 320

c. 6

d. $x = 8$

e. 120

f. 108

g. 10%

h. $\frac{2,600}{18,600}$ = approximately 14%

i. 40

4.

11. **D** 60% of 80 translates as $\dfrac{60}{100} \times 80$, which is the same as 48. So the problem now reads: 48 is the same as 40% of what number? We can translate this question as $48 = \dfrac{40}{100}x$. Then we solve for x, which equals 120, which is choice (D).

14. **D** 50% of the adults = 15, and 80% of the children = 16, so 31 total people went swimming. 31 out of 50 is 62%.

CHAPTER 9

Drill 1 Answers

5. **B** All we need to do here is plug $x = 3$ into the function, so $f(3) = \dfrac{(5)(3)+9}{(3-1)} = \dfrac{15+9}{2} = \dfrac{24}{2} = 12$. The answer is (B).

10. **B** In this problem, all we need to do is follow the directions given. We replace 6 for a and 8 for b. This gives us $\dfrac{6}{2} + 3(8) - 7$ which equals 20. The answer is choice (B).

12. **B** Since the problem gives us one of the solutions for x, we can plug it into the quadratic to find the value of k. This gives us $(-3)^2 + 8(-3) + k = 0$. The value of k is then 15. If we put k back into the equation, we get $x^2 + 8x + 15 = 0$. We can then factor this quadratic knowing that one of the factors is $(x + 3)$. The other factor must be $(x + 5)$, making the other solution –5. The correct answer is choice (B).

15. **E** The first thing we should do with this problem is factor the quadratics. This turns the equation into $\dfrac{(x+4)(x-2)}{(x-2)(x-5)} = 4$. We can cancel $(x - 2)$ in the numerator and the denominator leaving us with $\dfrac{(x+4)}{(x-5)} = 4$. To solve, we can cross-multiply. This gives us $x + 4 = 4x - 20$. Solving for x gives us a value of 8. You can also plug in the answers. The answer is choice (E).

19. **A** The first thing we need to do here is replace a for x in the function and set this equal to 2, as the second part of the problem states. This gives us $a^2 + 7a + 12 = 2$. Now, in order to be able to solve the quadratic, we need to set the equation equal to zero. By subtracting 2 from both sides, we get $a^2 + 7a + 10 = 0$. Now we can factor the quadratic. This gives us $(a + 5)(a + 2) = 0$. Our solutions for a are then –5 and –2. You can also plug in the answers. The answer choice that contains one of these solutions is (A).

Drill 2 Answers

13. **C** Using the Third Side Rule, we know that the third side of the triangle must be greater than 4, but less than 10. Since the sum of two of the sides is 10, the perimeter must be between 14 and 20. The only choice that is between these values is (C). Alternatively, we could plug in the answers. This could be done by subtracting the sum of the two known sides from the answer choices to find which one has a value between 4 and 10.

8. **C** Since we know that the area of the rectangle is 48, we can figure out the length of the rectangle using the formula $A = l \times w$. Putting in the numbers we have gives us $48 = 6l$. If we divide both sides by 6, the length BC then is 8. In rectangles, all angles are 90 degrees, so we can also use the Pythagorean Theorem to find the hypotenuse. Since we have a 6 and an 8 as the legs of the right triangle, we can identify this as one of the common triples. This gives us a hypotenuse of 10. Since the hypotenuse runs through the center of the circle, we know then that this is the diameter of the circle. If the diameter is 10, the radius is 5. Using the formula for the area of a circle, $A = \pi r^2$, we get $A = \pi(5)^2$, which equals 25π. The answer is choice (C).

14. **C** The problem tells us that the triangle is isosceles and we see there is a right angle present in the figure. This tells us that the base angles are 45 degrees each. Since the length of side AB is 5, that means that the length of side BC is 5 as well. Using the relationships for a 45:45:90 right triangle, we can infer than the length of AC is $5\sqrt{2}$. To find the perimeter, we add all three sides together: $5 + 5 + 5\sqrt{2} = 10 + 5\sqrt{2}$. The correct choice is (C).

16. **E** Angle AOB is 60 degrees, which is $\frac{1}{6}$ of 360 degrees. Since arc AB is 2π, it is $\frac{1}{6}$ of the total circumference. The circumference then is $6 \times 2\pi$, which comes to 12π. The diameter of the circle is 12, making the radius 6. The area of the circle then is 36π, choice (E).

18. **D** Since there is no figure given, we should draw one according to the directions. The figure should look like the following:

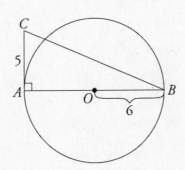

Given that the area of the circle is 36π, the radius is 6. This means that the diameter is 12. The point where a tangent hits the circle makes a 90 degree angle, so angle OAC is 90 degrees. Now that we have a right triangle, we can use the Pythagorean theorem to find that the length of BC is 13. Adding 5 + 12 + 13 gives us 30, choice (D).

CHAPTER 10

Drill 1 Answers

1. *Over* is the preposition, and *the bridge* is the object.

2. *Beyond* is the preposition, and *the green* is the object.

3. *With* is the preposition, and *the other reference books* is the object.

4. The second *to* is the preposition, and *her* is the object. Be careful—*to* also appears in this sentence in front of the verb *return,* but it is not being used as a preposition. *To return* is the whole verb; if *to* were being used as a preposition, it would be followed by a noun. (A verb like *to peel, to writhe,* or *to expire* is said to be in the *infinitive* form.)

Drill 2 Answers

1. to

2. of

3. for

4. of

5. about, for, by

6. by

7. over

8. to

9. from

10. No preposition is used after *considered.*

Drill 3 Answers

1. **C** One thing that splits the answer choices is the *were* versus *was*; this is not easy to see because it appears in the middle of each choice, but it is there. *Neither* follows the same rules as *either* when connecting two subjects: The second subject determines whether we need a singular or plural verb. *The superintendent* is singular, so *was* is correct, and we can eliminate (A) and (B). Of the remaining answer choices, we can eliminate (D) because it adds the word *of* unnecessarily, and we can eliminate (E) because when *neither* is used, it should always be followed by *nor*, not *or*. That leaves (C) as our best answer.

2. **C** The word *but* in the underlined portion indicates a change of direction, but that does not make sense in the sentence. Eliminate (A). (B) can also be eliminated because *where* can only refer to a location. (D) contains the word *being*, which nearly always makes a sentence awkward and wordy. (E) uses a comma incorrectly to connect what should be two separate sentences. (C) contains no errors and has the right meaning, indicating that the physical recovery was contingent upon the psychological one.

3. **E** If you do not spot an error right away, compare the answer choices. One main difference is the form of the word *master*. Answer choices (A), (B), and (C) are not parallel with the verb *to learn,* so we can eliminate those. (D) changes the meaning of the sentence by using *simply* instead of *simple*, so it can be eliminated as well. (E), the best answer, keeps the verbs parallel and does not create any new errors.

4. **B** The original sentence is trying to connect two separate sentences with a comma, so (A) is wrong. (C) is constructed in a very confusing way, leaving an *it* at the end that does not clearly refer to one noun, so it can be eliminated. In choice (D), the phrase between the commas is a complete sentence, so it needs to be marked off with a semicolon or period instead of a comma. Choice (E) says *when he was Jackie Robinson,* which is nonsense (unless the question is about reincarnation). (B) is straightforward and does not introduce new grammatical errors, so it is the best answer.

5. **B** The *they* in the underlined portion does not agree with *A well-organized person*, so (A) is out. (B) does not appear to have any new problems and it fixes the pronoun agreement error, so we can keep it. (C), (D), and (E) fix the pronoun agreement error, but are needlessly wordy, so (B) is correct.

6. **E** The original sentence contains a pronoun agreement problem, because *it* is singular and the *folk songs* it refers to is plural. Get rid of (A). (C) uses the wrong conjunction, as we should have a change in direction, rather than the same direction. (D) changes the intended meaning of the original. (B) and (E) both look all right grammatically, but (B) is passive, so (E) is the right answer because ETS prefers the active voice.

7. **A** The answer choices provide a wealth of information if an error is not immediately apparent. When a sentence uses *not only*, it must be followed with *but also*, so answer choices (C) and (D) are out. One difference in the remaining answer choices is the form of the verb *encourage*. It should be parallel to the verb *enhance,* so (B) can be eliminated. (E) uses *them* to refer to *a child,* which is a pronoun error, leaving (A) as the best answer.

21. **A** The verb *were* is plural, but its subject is *CD*, an abbreviation for the phrase "compact disc," which is singular. Thus, we have a subject-verb agreement error in (A).

22. **E** There is no error in the sentence.

23. **E** There is no error in the sentence. Remember, ETS likes to use *none* as a singular pronoun, so *is* agrees.

24. **B** *You* and *I* are objects of the preposition *between,* so they must be in the object case. *I* is in the subject case, so it is erroneous and (B) is the best answer.

25. **A** The past perfect verb *had looked* does not match the other tenses in the sentence, and we cannot use the past perfect tense since we do not have another action in the past. (A) is the error.

26. **B** *Splendid* is an adjective and it is being used to modify *worked,* a verb. An adverb, such as *splendidly,* would be better. The correct answer is (B).

27. **C** *Abide with* is incorrect; the correct idiom is *abide by.* (C) is the correct answer.

28. **B** *Where* can only be used to describe a location, and an announcement is not a location. *That* would be better, so (B) is the best answer.

29. **C** The present perfect *has cast* is not proper, because there is no continuous action. The correct form is the simple past *cast,* so the correct answer is (C).

Drill 4 Answers

35. **C** Because there is no event in the past that this sentence comes before, the past perfect tense cannot be correct—so eliminate (A). (D) and (E) completely change the meaning of the sentence (and when we get some context from the passage, we can see that this paragraph is a discussion of censorship in the past), so they are gone. (B) leaves out an important word, *an,* which makes the sentence not make sense, so (C) is the best answer.

36. **E** This essay follows a chronological order in its discussion of media censorship, so it would make the most sense to precede it with something that comes before the censorship of the 1950s. Therefore, (E) is the most logical choice.

37. **C**   Sentence 4 changes direction, because it starts talking about a reaction to the standards described in the first three sentences. This change of topic makes (C) the best answer.

38. **D**   This question can be done just like a Vocab-in-Context or Sentence Completion question. Reading sentences 5 and 6 for context, we learn that artists were expressing themselves very freely in reaction to earlier codes of censorship, so we can replace *unlikely* with something like *unthinkable*. (D) is the closest answer.

39. **A**   Remember that there is no "correct as is" unless explicitly stated in the answer choices. (D) and (E) add *being,* which is awkward. (C) includes the pronoun *they,* which is ambiguous because it could refer to either the albums or the warning labels. (B) also does not clearly state whether it was the albums or the labels that indicated something. (A) is the best choice.

Part IV
The Princeton Review Practice Tests and Explanations

Chapter 12
Practice Test 1

SECTION 1
Time — 25 minutes
24 Questions

Directions: For each question in this section, select the best answer from among the choices given and fill in the corresponding circle on the answer sheet.

Each sentence below has one or two blanks, each blank indicating that something has been omitted. Beneath the sentence are five words or sets of words labeled A through E. Choose the word or set of words that, when inserted in the sentence, __best__ fits the meaning of the sentence as a whole.

Example:

Desiring to ------- his taunting friends, Mitch gave them taffy in hopes it would keep their mouths shut.

(A) eliminate   (B) satisfy   (C) overcome
  (D) ridicule   (E) silence

Ⓐ Ⓑ Ⓒ Ⓓ ●

---

1. Though many people are willing to ------- saving the environment when speaking in public, they are often not willing to ------- their lifestyles to help protect the earth.

    (A) promote . . maintain
    (B) condone . . justify
    (C) advocate . . alter
    (D) denounce . . adjust
    (E) champion . . substantiate

2. Due to his ------- personality, Prince Klemens von Metternich dominated the Congress of Vienna after the defeat of Napoleon.

    (A) amiable   (B) pleasant   (C) commanding
      (D) duplicitous   (E) sympathetic

3. The floor of the forest is enlivened by ------- hues whenever the lush canopy is ------- by the strong rays of the sun.

    (A) vibrant . . blemished
    (B) muted . . overwhelmed
    (C) threatening . . enveloped
    (D) mellow . . blanketed
    (E) vivid . . pierced

4. The reclusive nature of the iguana helps to explain the longstanding ------- of fruitful investigations of its behavior in the wild.

    (A) constancy   (B) notoriety   (C) necessity
      (D) paucity   (E) probity

5. The aim of the governor's plan was to make more housing available for middle-income families, but unfortunately she only ------- the problem by making such housing even more scarce.

    (A) repealed   (B) exacerbated   (C) abolished
      (D) hoisted   (E) ingratiated

6. Many people consider Dana ------- because of her friendly and honest manner, but she is actually a ------- negotiator.

    (A) trustworthy . . relaxed
    (B) naive . . shrewd
    (C) taciturn . . decisive
    (D) vigilant . . lenient
    (E) eccentric . . secluded

7. When jazz was first introduced to Europe, many musicians were greatly ------- it and tried to ------- its free-form style.

    (A) drawn to . . emulate
    (B) impressed by . . reject
    (C) attracted to . . originate
    (D) opposed to . . adopt
    (E) afraid of . . accept

8. The senator's aide claimed that even though the United States was established by rebellion, it is now inclined to view ------- in other nations with -------.

    (A) reactionaries . . adoration
    (B) misers . . disdain
    (C) insurgents . . animosity
    (D) autocrats . . malevolence
    (E) revolutionaries . . indifference

GO ON TO THE NEXT PAGE ➡

The passages below are followed by questions based on their content; questions following a pair of related passages may also be based on the relationship between the paired passages. Answer the questions on the basis of what is <u>stated</u> or <u>implied</u> in the passage and in any introductory material that may be provided.

Questions 9-10 are based on the following passage.

The Oulipo, short for *Ouvroir de Littérature Potentielle*, is a literary group that was founded in Paris in 1960. The products of this group are not the novels or short stories that other writing groups churn out. Rather, the business
Line
5   of the Oulipo is to collaboratively produce "constraints" or procedures that must be followed in constructing a text. Following these techniques is not so different from using the centuries-old rules for haikus or sonnets. That poems, novels, and stories are actually created using the Oulipo's methods is
10 almost beside the point. The group considers its product to be the *potential* writing that might be created using its methods.

9. The author brings in the examples of the haiku and the sonnet in order to

(A) create a rhythmic flow in the text of the passage
(B) point out that the Oulipo's methods are completely unoriginal
(C) demonstrate the potential writing produced by Oulipo's "constraints"
(D) connect a new way of writing with long-practiced traditions
(E) indicate the international demographic of the Oulipo

10. The use of the phrase "churn out" in line 4 implies that the author

(A) is unenthusiastic about the work of some literature groups
(B) has little use for the writing methods of the Oulipo
(C) is placing the narrative in a bucolic setting
(D) demands tremendous production from her writing group
(E) is disgusted at the training received at writing schools

Questions 11-12 are based on the following passage.

The Gulf of Tonkin Resolution, passed on August 7, 1964, empowered President Lyndon Johnson to resolve a brewing conflict with the North Vietnamese using whatever means
Line
he deemed necessary. Five days prior to Congress's approval
5   of the resolution, the USS *Maddox*, a naval destroyer, was patrolling the waters in the Gulf of Tonkin near Hon Me, a North Vietnamese island. Three North Vietnamese torpedo boats encountered the *Maddox*, forcing the American vessel to flee. Two days later, the *Maddox* returned to the Gulf of
10 Tonkin accompanied by the USS *Turner Joy*, another naval destroyer. Suspiciously, that evening the *Turner Joy* picked up three high-speed vessels on its radar, but the *Maddox* did not. The *Turner Joy* sought and attacked these ships. Some have hypothesized that President Johnson, who had been quite
15 vocal about the need for an increased military presence in the area, may have manufactured this crisis, but there is no evidence to support such claims.

11. The structure of the passage could best be described as the presentation of a historical event that is

(A) elaborated upon and a possible controversy downplayed
(B) explained, and its repercussions enumerated
(C) cited, and the character of one participant attacked
(D) noted, and its cultural significance elaborated upon
(E) explicated, and its validity questioned

12. The argument that President Johnson did not have any inappropriate involvement with the Gulf of Tonkin incident would be best supported by

(A) a statement from crewmen on the USS *Maddox* stating that they did not see any high-speed vessels the night of August 4th
(B) a report stating that many destroyers at that time had difficulty locating and tracking high-speed vessels
(C) several North Vietnamese soldiers testifying that they were not in the Gulf of Tonkin on the night in question
(D) a report stating that the USS *Maddox* had no mechanical problems with its radar
(E) a poll of Americans stating that the majority believed President Johnson

GO ON TO THE NEXT PAGE

Questions 13-24 are based on the following passages.

The process of changing wild animals into tame ones is known as domestication, an important development in the course of human cultural history. Two reasons for the domestication of animals are explored here.

Passage 1

The geographer Eduard Hahn (1896), in a series of writings at the turn of the century, posed the basic questions involved in the study of the domestication of cattle. These are the questions still raised today, and they are still answered by culture historians substantially in the way he answered them. Hahn pointed to the exceptional position of cattle among animals that have been domesticated. In the case of some animals, domestication may have come about spontaneously. For example, the ancestor of the dog as well as that of the domestic pig probably, as scavengers, sought out man, and gradually man assumed the leadership in the relationship. One may indeed ask, "Who then initially domesticated whom?" Domestication, again, may have been furthered by instincts which make us cherish our own infants and which are aroused by young mammals of somewhat similar bodily proportions. Piglets and dog pups are nursed by women in some primitive societies. But the domestication of wild cattle cannot be explained as an inadvertent process. Wild cattle presumably did not seek human company, and the initiative must have come from man. Furthermore, man must have had a strong motivation since the wild urus was a powerful, intractable animal of whom it is said in Job (Job 39:9-10): "Will the urus be willing to serve thee, or abide by thy crib? Canst thou span him into a plowing harness or will he harrow the valleys after thee?"

Eduard Hahn has postulated that the motive for capturing and maintaining the urus in the captive state was to have available a supply, for sacrificial purposes, of the animal sacred to the lunar mother goddess worshipped over an immense area of the ancient world. The economic uses of the animal would then have been a by-product of a domestication religious in origin. Why the urus was selected as the animal sacred to the deity is uncertain, but this was probably because its gigantic curved horns resembled the lunar crescent. Studies in prehistoric and early historic religion have shown that the bovine was early regarded as an epiphany of the goddess or her consort and was slain in the ritual reenactment of the myth of her death. This myth involves the notion of the death and resurrection in new life of the deity. Of course, if cattle were domesticated because the horns of the urus resembled the moon's crescent, it is possible that other horned animals such as sheep and goats were also domesticated for their horns. For example, it is possible that an unsuccessful attempt to domesticate crescent-horned gazelles was made for this reason.

Passage 2

Man probably entered into a state of beneficial mutualism with certain animal species because, to put it in very general terms, the animals were already socially and psychologically preadapted to being tamed without loss of reproductive abilities. A second factor was that the human culture milieu had evolved to a state of organization such that the animals could be controlled and maintained, generation after generation, in a condition of dependence. At least to some degree these animals had to be protected from predators and provided with food—the latter perhaps only in time of scarcity. The detailed pattern of the process leading to domestication naturally varied with both the particular species and the human culture that were interacting; certainly the domestication of the wolf to the dog by the Maglemosian hunter-collectors of northwestern Europe was different in detail from the domestication of the hoofed food animals by the post-Natufian cultivators. Unfortunately, we know nothing of the details of either process, partly because of our inability to reconstruct the behavior and cultural environment of the people involved and partly because of our ignorance of the psychology of the various wild animals involved.

With the exception of one of the most recently domesticated mammals, the laboratory rat, we know little enough about the behavior patterns of our common domestic animals, but we know much less about the behavior of their wild progenitors. Furthermore, detailed comparative observations of wild and domestic *Rattus norvegicus* emphasize the tremendous behavioral changes undergone by a species during domestication. Thus, psychological studies on domesticates probably cannot yield the total behavior pattern of the wild ancestors. It was, however, these wild ancestors that man first tamed and reared.

The social enzyme that activated the union of man and beast was undoubtedly the human proclivity, not only of children but of women also, to keep pets, although purposeful capture of young animals by men, to serve as hunting decoys, may well have been another avenue toward domestication.

The psychological factor of "imprinting," explored particularly by Lorenz in a notable series of animal experiments, was undoubtedly a major influence in the domestication of birds with precocial young (chickens, ducks, geese, turkeys, and so on). *Imprinting* refers to the tendency, most pronounced in such precocial birds, to recognize and psychologically to attach themselves to the most frequently seen and heard living thing during an early and short "critical period." Typically this would be the mother, and we have thus an instinctive mechanism for recognition of the parent by an active newborn.

GO ON TO THE NEXT PAGE ➡

13. The author's primary purpose in Passage 1 is to

- (A) provide an argument as to why the horns of cattle, sheep, and goats had social significance
- (B) explain a religious motivation for the domestication of cattle and other horned animals
- (C) detail the anatomical differences between wild animals and their domesticated counterparts
- (D) discuss the scavenger nature of wild cattle and how that led them into domestication
- (E) examine the domestication of pigs and dogs based on the similarities of their body proportions to man's

14. The quote in line 12, "Who then . . . whom?" refers to

- (A) the nursing of piglets and puppies by women in some primitive societies
- (B) man's strong motivation to domesticate cattle
- (C) the exceptional position of cattle among animals that have been domesticated
- (D) the theory that pigs and dogs, as scavengers, sought out man
- (E) the controversy inspired by Hahn's cultural history

15. In line 18, "inadvertent" most nearly means

- (A) motivated
- (B) accidental
- (C) sacrificial
- (D) difficult to domesticate
- (E) intractable

16. The myth discussed in lines 34-39 revolves around

- (A) the gigantic curved horns of the urus
- (B) the economic uses of early cattle
- (C) the cow as an incarnation of the moon goddess
- (D) ritual sacrifice of gazelles
- (E) prehistoric reenactments of the creation of the moon

GO ON TO THE NEXT PAGE

17. The author of Passage 2 uses the term "beneficial mutualism" in line 45 to characterize

(A) a harmony of needs between man and some species that leads to the domestication of those species
(B) the domestication experiments with the musk ox
(C) a process opposed to imprinting as a means for offspring to recognize their mother
(D) the reproductive abilities of tamed species
(E) man's protection from predators and provision of food for animals that have been domesticated

18. The author of Passage 2 compares the domestication of the wolf by Maglemosian hunter-collectors to the domestication of hoofed food animals by post-Natufian cultivators in order to

(A) reconstruct the behavior and cultural environment in which domestication occurred
(B) show how ignorant we are of the psychology of wild animals and the peoples who domesticated them
(C) suggest that the process of domestication varied with the species but not with the human culture
(D) support the notion that the process of domestication is dependent upon both the species and the human culture
(E) imply that the process of domestication was a process independent of both the species and the human culture

19. The studies mentioned in Passage 2 with regard to *Rattus norvegicus* revealed

(A) the behavior patterns of wild progenitors of hoofed animals
(B) psychological insights into the laboratory rat
(C) how man first tamed and reared wild animals
(D) that observing a domestic animal can lead to an understanding of its wild counterpart
(E) dramatic differences in behavior between wild and domesticated rats

20. Lorenz's experiments with birds and imprinting are used by the author to support the contention that

(A) imprinting is the method by which young birds recognize and attach themselves to a parent
(B) hunting decoys may have been an avenue of domestication for some species
(C) chickens, ducks, geese, and turkeys are birds that have precocial young
(D) imprinting was a major influence in the domestication of birds
(E) the mother is the parent to which most young attach themselves

GO ON TO THE NEXT PAGE →

21. The authors of the two passages would most likely agree that

(A) the human proclivity to keep pets is the single most important factor in domestication

(B) domestication of some species, such as the wolf-dog, occurred because both man and the species benefited from the arrangement

(C) a combination of imprinting and religious mythology shaped the process by which cattle were domesticated

(D) the purposeful capture of young animals for use in religious ceremonies was a critical stage in the domestication of cattle

(E) women felt sorry for the young animals used as hunting decoys and turned them into pets

22. Which of the following statements best characterizes the main difference between the two passages?

(A) The first focuses on religious motivations for the domestication of cattle, but does not exclude other factors for the domestication of other species, whereas the second covers a variety of motivations for domestication, yet does not rule out religion.

(B) The first presents the hypothesis that religious motivations were responsible for domestication of many species, while the second argues that religious motivations were totally absent in the process of domesticating birds.

(C) The first explores in detail how the scavenger nature of dogs and pigs led to their domestication, and the second argues against that proposition, offering a hypothesis for dog and pig domestication based on a desire for pets and social enzymes.

(D) The first suggests that only horned animals had religious significance, but the second focuses on the use of hoofed animals for food.

(E) The second implicitly criticizes the first for ignoring the importance of psychological insights into wild animal behavior that can be gleaned from studying laboratory rats and birds with precocial young.

23. The authors of both passages would be LEAST likely to agree with which of the following statements?

(A) The bison, a large herbivore with crescent-shaped horns, was probably domesticated initially for religious reasons and then for economic reasons (food and products derived from the animal).

(B) The cat, a scavenger with body proportions similar to humans, probably insinuated itself into human culture, which was able to adapt and accept the animal for the advantages it gave in terms of rodent control.

(C) Reptiles have not been domesticated since they are not scavengers, not a valued food source, lack body proportions similar to humans, and are a species that does not imprint.

(D) The urus is an example of a hoofed and horned food animal that may have been originally domesticated for religious purposes (such as a supply for sacrifice), but whose economic importance led to its continued role and domestication in human society.

(E) *Rattus norvegicus* is an example of a scavenger with body proportions similar to humans, which was probably domesticated through the purposeful capture of the young to use as hunting decoys.

24. The "social enzyme" noted in Passage 2 is most closely associated with which of the following quotations from Passage 1?

(A) "the exceptional position of cattle among animals that have been domesticated" (lines 6-7)

(B) "Will the urus be willing to serve thee, or abide by thy crib?" (lines 22-23)

(C) "Piglets and dog pups are nursed by women in some primitive societies." (16-17)

(D) "the motive for capturing and maintaining the urus . . . was to have available a supply, for sacrificial purposes" (lines 26-28)

(E) "the ancestor of the dog as well as that of the domestic pig probably, as scavengers, sought out man" (lines 9-10)

STOP
If you finish before time is called, you may check your work on this section only.
Do not turn to any other section in the test.

SECTION 2
Time — 25 minutes
20 Questions

Directions: For this section, solve each problem and decide which is the best of the choices given. Fill in the corresponding circle on the answer sheet. You may use any available space for scratchwork.

Notes

1. The use of a calculator is permitted.

2. All numbers used are real numbers.

3. Figures that accompany problems in this test are intended to provide information useful in solving the problems. They are drawn as accurately as possible EXCEPT when it is stated in a specific problem that the figure is not drawn to scale. All figures lie in a plane unless other wise indicated.

4. Unless otherwise specified, the domain of any function f is assumed to be the set of all real numbers x for which $f(x)$ is a real number.

Reference Information

 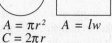 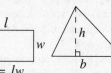

$A = \pi r^2$ $A = lw$ $A = \frac{1}{2}bh$ $V = lwh$ $V = \pi r^2 h$ $c^2 = a^2 + b^2$ Special Right Triangles

$C = 2\pi r$

The number of degrees of arc in a circle is 360.

The sum of the measures in degrees of the angles of a triangle is 180.

---

1. If $12b - 4 = 0$, then $b =$

(A) 4

(B) 3

(C) 0

(D) $\frac{1}{3}$

(E) $\frac{1}{4}$

2. If an oil tank contains 60 gallons of fuel and is $\frac{5}{12}$ full, how many gallons does the tank hold when full?

(A) 72
(B) 84
(C) 128
(D) 144
(E) 720

GO ON TO THE NEXT PAGE

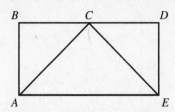

3. If the area of rectangle *ABDE* is 16 square inches, and *C* is the midpoint of $\overline{BD}$, what is the area, in square inches, of $\triangle ACE$?

(A)   2
(B)   4
(C)   6
(D)   8
(E)   16

4. An integer that is a multiple of 32 must also be a multiple of which of the following integers?

(A)   11
(B)   9
(C)   8
(D)   5
(E)   3

5. In $\triangle ABC$ above, what is the value of *x* ?

(A)   18
(B)   23
(C)   32
(D)   38
(E)   42

6. If *x*, *y*, and *z* are consecutive integers and $x < y < z$, what is the sum of *y* and *z* in terms of *x* ?

(A) $2x + 6$
(B) $2x + 4$
(C) $2x + 3$
(D) $2x - 2$
(E) $2x - 1$

GO ON TO THE NEXT PAGE

7. If $(2^a)^b = 64$, then $ab =$

   (A) 2
   (B) 3
   (C) 4
   (D) 5
   (E) 6

---

8. $6\sqrt{18} + 4\sqrt{72} - \left(\sqrt{8} + 10\sqrt{32}\right) =$

   (A) -1
   (B) 0
   (C) 1
   (D) $2\sqrt{2}$
   (E) $6\sqrt{2}$

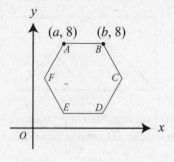

9. In the 6-sided regular polygon above, how many diagonals can be drawn that have negative slope?

   (A) 0
   (B) 1
   (C) 2
   (D) 3
   (E) 4

---

10. If a certain number is 3 more than 7 times itself, what is the number?

   (A) -3

   (B) $-\dfrac{3}{2}$

   (C) $-\dfrac{1}{2}$

   (D) $-\dfrac{3}{8}$

   (E) $\dfrac{1}{2}$

GO ON TO THE NEXT PAGE ⇨

11. Which of the following is equivalent to
    $-12 \le 3b + 3 \le 18$?

    (A) $-5 \le b \le 5$
    (B) $-4 \le b \le 6$
    (C) $-5 \le b \le 6$
    (D) $3 \le b \le 5$
    (E) $5 \le b \le 5$

12. If x is an odd integer divisible by 3, which of the
    following must be divisible by 4 ?

    (A) $x + 1$
    (B) $x + 2$
    (C) $x + 3$
    (D) $2x$
    (E) $2x - 2$

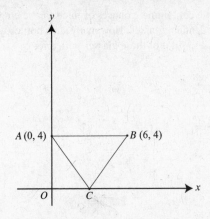

13. If $\overline{AC} \cong \overline{BC}$ in the figure above, what is the perimeter of
    $\triangle ABC$?

    (A) 14
    (B) 15
    (C) 16
    (D) 18
    (E) $10 + 3\sqrt{3}$

$$3, 5, 9, \ldots$$

14. If the nth term in the sequence above is defined by
    $1 + 2^n$, what is the sum of the 5th and 6th terms?

    (A) 33
    (B) 65
    (C) 50
    (D) 98
    (E) 129

GO ON TO THE NEXT PAGE

15. A bottle containing c ounces of juice can be emptied to fill g identical glasses. How many such bottles would be needed to fill n of these glasses with juice?

(A) $\dfrac{gn}{c}$

(B) $\dfrac{cn}{g}$

(C) $\dfrac{g}{n}$

(D) $\dfrac{n}{g}$

(E) $\dfrac{c}{n}$

$$\begin{array}{r} A4B7 \\ -\ A4B \\ \hline 5CA7 \end{array}$$

16. In the subtraction problem of a three-digit number from a four-digit number above, A, B, and C represent three different digits. What digit does C represent?

(A) 0
(B) 2
(C) 4
(D) 7
(E) 8

17. A large cubical block of cheese measures 8 inches on each edge. If a small rectangular solid measuring 4 inches by 2 inches by 2 inches is cut out and thrown away, the volume of the remaining block of cheese is what fraction of its original volume?

(A) $\dfrac{1}{32}$

(B) $\dfrac{3}{4}$

(C) $\dfrac{7}{8}$

(D) $\dfrac{15}{16}$

(E) $\dfrac{31}{32}$

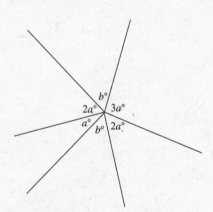

Note: Figure not drawn to scale.

18. In the figure above, what is the value of b in terms of a ?

(A) $90 + 2a$
(B) $180 - 4a$
(C) $180 - 8a$
(D) $360 - 8a$
(E) $360 - 12a$

GO ON TO THE NEXT PAGE

19. If x and y are integers and $y = 4x$, which of the following could be the average (arithmetic mean) of x and y ?

(A) −36
(B) −35
(C) 4
(D) 12
(E) 28

20. If y is directly proportional to the square of x, and $x = 3$ when $y = 18$, then when $y = 2$, $x =$

(A) $\dfrac{1}{3}$

(B) 1

(C) 3

(D) 9

(E) 81

STOP
If you finish before time is called, you may check your work on this section only.
Do not turn to any other section in the test.

SECTION 3
Time — 25 minutes
24 Questions

Directions: For each question in this section, select the best answer from among the choices given and fill in the corresponding circle on the answer sheet.

Each sentence below has one or two blanks, each blank indicating that something has been omitted. Beneath the sentence are five words or sets of words labeled A through E. Choose the word or set of words that, when inserted in the sentence, <u>best</u> fits the meaning of the sentence as a whole.

Example:

Hoping to ------- the dispute, negotiators proposed a compromise that they felt would be ------- to both labor and management.

   (A) enforce . . useful
   (B) end . . divisive
   (C) overcome . . unattractive
   (D) extend . . satisfactory
   (E) resolve . .acceptable

            (A) (B) (C) (D) ●

---

25. While its unique eating habits make the mountain gorilla a fascinating subject for observation, its small population and its shyness serve to ------- many potential studies.

   (A) inspire   (B) release   (C) fortify
     (D) hinder   (E) extenuate

26. Originally designed as work clothes for miners, jeans are now worn by all segments of society, their appeal ------- by their comfort and affordability.

   (A) overwhelmed   (B) corroded   (C) broadened
     (D) lessened   (E) complicated

27. While many consumer electronics are ------- in a very short time by newer technologies, it will be many years before the home computer becomes -------.

   (A) supplanted . . obsolete
   (B) popularized . . uncommon
   (C) noticeable . . forgotten
   (D) discovered . . disparaged
   (E) replaced . . remembered

28. Although many believed that the problems of the community were -------, the members of the governing council refused to give up and devised several ------- solutions.

   (A) insoluble . . ingenious
   (B) intractable . . inconsequential
   (C) exorbitant . . promising
   (D) irrelevant . . lofty
   (E) obscure . . meager

29. So ------- were the voters of Winesburg that, despite the blizzard, 2,500 of the 3,200 residents made their way to the voting sites.

   (A) endemic   (B) relenting   (C) ephemeral
     (D) resolute   (E) erratic

GO ON TO THE NEXT PAGE ⇨

The passages below are followed by questions based on their content; questions following a pair of related passages may also be based on the relationship between the paired passages. Answer the questions on the basis of what is <u>stated</u> or <u>implied</u> in the passage and in any introductory material that may be provided.

Questions 30-33 are based on the following passages.

Passage 1

It is often said that history is written by the winners, and for good reason. Contrary to the revisionist teachings of some "new historicists," history is not by nature an interpretive discipline. Facts are facts are facts, after all. New
5 interpretations of Woodrow Wilson's isolationist policies do not change the fact that the United States entered World War I later than its European counterparts, or that the United States was instrumental in winning that particular war. Trying to rewrite our understanding of U.S. policy does a grave
10 disservice to the facts of history.

Passage 2

History is by nature a discipline of interpretation. The bigger issue is the bias of the interpreter. Much of a historian's job is related to distinguishing relevant information from extraneous material. For too long, the
15 contributions of racial minorities, women, and other groups have been deemed inessential to an understanding of history. Recognizing the vital role of African American soldiers in a segregated military or the factory work of women in World War II will give us a more complete picture of America, both
20 in the past and in the present.

30. On what point would the authors of both passages agree?

(A) History is based on irrefutable facts.
(B) Revisionist history is antithetical to historical analysis.
(C) Historical analysis requires a basis of factual information.
(D) Military victories are the most important part of history.
(E) Interpretation is essential to an understanding of history.

31. Unlike Passage 2, Passage 1 contains

(A) vocabulary specific to the discipline of history
(B) references to historical events
(C) an international perspective
(D) a partisan judgment
(E) a reference to historical bias

32. The conflict between the passages can be most accurately described as that between the importance of

(A) military history and social history
(B) domestic history and international history
(C) objectivity and subjectivity
(D) fact-based analysis and limited interpretation
(E) slander and accuracy

33. The author of Passage 2 is most concerned that

(A) the segregationist policies of the American military were wrong
(B) history cannot be accurately analyzed
(C) historians cannot be trusted
(D) factual analysis is impossible
(E) traditional historical analysis ignores minority groups

GO ON TO THE NEXT PAGE

Questions 34-39 are based on the following passage.

The following excerpt is from an essay by a leading scientist and professor of paleontology. In it he describes how an experience in one field—choral music—led to a revelation about himself.

Thirty years ago, on April 30, 1958, to be exact, I sat with 250 students facing one of the most formidable men of our generation—Peter J. Wilhousky, director of music in the New York City Schools and conductor of the New York All-City High School Chorus. As the warm, and primarily parental, applause receded at the concert's end, Wilhousky returned to the podium of Carnegie Hall, gestured for silence, and raised his baton to conduct the traditional encore, "Madame Jeanette." Halfway through, he turned and, without missing a beat (to invoke a cliché in its appropriate, literal sense), smiled to acknowledge the chorus alumni who stood at their seats or surrounded the podium, singing with their current counterparts. These former members seemed so ancient to me—though none had passed forty, for the chorus itself was by then only twenty years old—and their solidarity moved me to a rare fit of tears at a time when teenage boys did not cry in public.

"Madame Jeanette" is a dangerous little piece, for it ventures so near the edge of cloying sentimentality. It tells the tale, in close four-part a cappella harmony, of a French widow who sits at her door by day and her window by night. There she thinks only of her husband, killed so many years before on the battlefield of St. Pierre, and dreams of the day when they will be reunited at the cemetery of Père Lachaise. With 250 teenagers and sloppy conducting, "Madame Jeanette" becomes a maudlin and embarrassing tearfest. Wilhousky, ever the perfectionist, ever the rationalist, somehow steered to the right side of musicality, and ended each concert with integrity and control.

"Madame Jeanette" was our symbol of continuity. For a very insecure boy, singing second bass on the brink of manhood, "Madame Jeanette" offered another wonderful solace. It ends, for the basses, on a low D-flat, just about as far down the scale as any composer would dare ask a singer to venture. Yes, I knew even then that low did not mean masculine, or capable, or mature, or virile, but that fundament resonated with hope and possibility, even in pianissimo.

We lived, thirty years ago, in an age of readier obedience, but I still marvel at the discipline that Wilhousky could maintain with his mixture of awe (inspired) and terror (promulgated). He forged our group of Blacks from Harlem, Jews from Queens, and Italians from Staten Island into a responsive singing machine. He worked, in part, through intimidation by public ridicule. One day, he stopped the rehearsal and pointed to the tenor section, saying: "You, third row, fourth seat, stand up. You're singing flat. Ten years ago, Julius La Rosa sat in the same seat—and sang flat. And he's still singing flat." (Memory is a curious trickster. La Rosa, in a recent *New Yorker* profile, states that Wilhousky praised him in the same forum for singing so true to pitch. But I know

what I heard. Or is the joke on me?) Each year, he cashiered a member or two for talking and giggling—in public, and with no hope of mercy or reinstatement.

But Peter Wilhousky had another side that inspired us all and conveyed the most important lesson of intellectual life. He was one of the finest choral conductors in America, yet he chose to spend every Saturday morning with high school kids. His only rule, tacit but persuasive, proclaimed: "No compromises." We could sing, with proper training and practice, as well as any group in America; nothing else would be tolerated or even conceptualized. Anything less would not be worth doing at all. I had encountered friendliness, grace, kindness, animation, clarity, and dedication among my teachers, but I had never even considered the notion that unqualified excellence could emerge from anything touched or made by students. The idea, however, is infectious. As I worked with Wilhousky, I slowly personalized the dream that excellence in one activity might be extended to become the pattern, or at least the goal, of an actual life.

34. The author's main purpose in writing the passage is to

(A) urge students to participate in music
(B) worship a gifted individual
(C) analyze a particular piece of music
(D) relate an incident from his childhood
(E) trace the development of a particular attitude

35. The author describes "Madame Jeanette" as a "dangerous little piece" (line 18) because

(A) it can appear trite and melodramatic when performed under less than ideal conditions
(B) it contains seditious material
(C) it has a profoundly moving effect on most audiences
(D) it evokes harrowing images of death and violence
(E) it is a technically difficult piece for most choirs to perform

GO ON TO THE NEXT PAGE

36. It can be inferred from the third paragraph that performing "Madame Jeanette" filled the author with a feeling of

(A) masculinity
(B) insecurity
(C) optimism
(D) melancholy
(E) embarrassment

37. In the context of the passage, the term "readier" (line 38) most nearly means

(A) more prepared
(B) more willing
(C) more complete
(D) more clever
(E) more punctual

38. The author includes the anecdote of the student in the "third row, fourth seat" (lines 45-46) in order to

(A) provide an example of how Wilhousky maintained discipline in the chorus
(B) suggest that Wilhousky had lied about Julius La Rosa
(C) show how cruel and arbitrary Wilhousky could be at times
(D) illustrate how unreliable the human memory can be
(E) imply that Wilhousky liked to trick his students into obeying him

39. The passage suggests that Wilhousky inspired the author to

(A) strive for excellence in all of his endeavors
(B) pursue a career in music
(C) devote himself to helping high school students
(D) attend future performances of the chorus as an alumnus
(E) never resort to compromising with anyone

GO ON TO THE NEXT PAGE ⟶

Questions 40-48 are based on the following passage.

The following passage is adapted from a 2009 novel set in Egypt and the United Kingdom.

Naim loved squash as he did, he thought, because he was never *quite* as good as he wanted to be. Certainly, a large part of it was the competition—no matter how many players you could beat, there were always new ones who could beat you—but if that had been the only hurdle, things might have been easier: after a loss or an unsatisfying win, he spent extra hours at the court, practicing with an almost machine-like consistency, drilling until he couldn't breathe anymore, and hitting hundreds, thousands of shots, trying to store that perfect stroke in his muscle memory. On top of that, his biggest challenge came from his coach, Mr. Shabana, who wanted Naim to play the English style—consistency, endurance, humility—that had never felt right; Naim's own take on the game, more characterized by quick, deceptive movements, odd changes in pace, fancy trick shots, felt much more like the game he was meant to play, much more an expression of himself than the characterless devotion to some sport that existed long before he came along to play it.

But if it wouldn't win his matches or tournaments, or allow him to go pro (his lifelong dream, but one that seemed too hard with a unique, personalized style of play), then why keep playing what Mr. Shabana called this "dead-end" style of squash? Naim couldn't say. He loved to watch the greats from squash history, both the English and the Egyptian champions, and their methodical, uncannily consistent styles of play. Naim himself wanted to be part of this great legion of players. His hope to change the way the game was played and for his name to be known made him think he might be better suited to the bigger stage of tennis: where styles were not so regimented, and the best players were like movie stars.

Naim would not switch to tennis because as he watched a new player on the pro tour, he found the inspiration he had been missing. The player's name was Mohamed El Shorbagy—a young man, not much older than Naim, and also from Naim's home town of Alexandria—but Naim was much more captivated by his style of play. On the same court and against many of the same players that Naim had been watching all these years, El Shorbagy played the traditional game, but he did it with such flair, such incredible confidence and style, that he seemed totally self-taught; he was almost, it seemed, expressing his very soul as he played, the same way one might do in a poem. If Naim watched him carefully—and he did watch him, over and over again—he would occasionally wonder if El Shorbagy's feet were even on the ground. While El Shorbagy would often win, and by wide, convincing margins, he was not a traditional player: to be sure, Mr. Shabana likely would've called his play "savage." But his results spoke for themselves, and he was such a pleasure to watch that the crowds at his matches were always notably large.

Naim himself had been the first to use the word "inspiration" when talking about El Shorbagy's play (and many years after El Shorbagy retired, as Naim told his own students about El Shorbagy's early performances, he would explain his professional career and his subsequent coaching life as impossible without El Shorbagy's influence). Naim took the word from his teachers. If inspiration was the feeling that the sky was the limit, that one could do anything, that one's world had changed in a way that could never be undone—then Naim had experienced that very thing.

40. The first paragraph (lines 1-18) primarily suggests that Naim was

(A) inspired to perfect the English style of play
(B) filled with admiration for his coach
(C) disgusted with his machine-like performance
(D) consumed by his desire to beat every new player
(E) devoted to becoming a better squash player

41. The phrase in lines 5-6 ("but… easier") indicates that Naim was

(A) deliberately trying to make his practice harder
(B) envious of Mr. Shabana's consistency
(C) able to express his individuality through his style of playing
(D) dedicated to improving his game on multiple levels
(E) conflicted about his desire to be a professional squash player

42. In line 8, "drilling" most nearly means

(A) training
(B) penetrating
(C) piercing
(D) teaching
(E) breaking

GO ON TO THE NEXT PAGE

43. Lines 13-18 ("Naim's...it ") suggest which of the following about Naim?

(A) His desire to express himself through his style of play
(B) The emphasis he places on the importance of drills
(C) His belief that squash is the only thing that will ever satisfy him
(D) The fondness he has for the English style
(E) His acceptance of not becoming a pro

44. The second paragraph most directly elaborates on which point made earlier by the narrator?

(A) "he was never *quite* as good as he wanted to be" (line 2)
(B) "things might have been easier" (lines 5-6)
(C) "the English style" (line 12)
(D) "Naim's own take on the game" (lines 13-14)
(E) "some sport that existed long before he came along to play it" (line 18)

45. In line 19, the word "it" refers to which of the following from lines 19-30?

(A) Naim's personal style of play
(B) Naim's love of squash history
(C) The consistent style of English and Egyptian champions
(D) The freer style in tennis
(E) Naim's desire to become a movie star

46. The third paragraph (lines 31-50) primarily serves to

(A) explain an apparent paradox
(B) justify a character's opinion
(C) describe a character's style
(D) recount an important development
(E) contrast differing viewpoints

47. What Naim found most appealing in El Shorbagy's play was its

(A) machine-like consistency
(B) poetic beauty
(C) historical accuracy
(D) expressive power
(E) savage results

48. The parenthetical remarks in lines 52-56 are consistent with which of the following in the passage?

(A) Naim's desire to play in his own style
(B) Naim's love of the greats from squash history
(C) Naim's dedication to Mr. Shabana
(D) Naim's decision to become a tennis player
(E) Naim's many professional victories

STOP

If you finish before time is called, you may check your work on this section only.
Do not turn to any other section in the test.

SECTION 4
Time — 25 minutes
18 Questions

Directions: For this section, solve each problem and decide which is the best of the choices given. Fill in the corresponding circle on the answer sheet. You may use any available space for scratchwork.

Notes

1. The use of a calculator is permitted.

2. All numbers used are real numbers.

3. Figures that accompany problems in this test are intended to provide information useful in solving the problems. They are drawn as accurately as possible EXCEPT when it is stated in a specific problem that the figure is not drawn to scale. All figures lie in a plane unless other wise indicated.

4. Unless otherwise specified, the domain of any function f is assumed to be the set of all real numbers x for which $f(x)$ is a real number.

Reference Information

  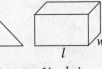 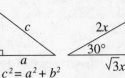

$A = \pi r^2$ $A = lw$
$C = 2\pi r$ $A = \frac{1}{2}bh$ $V = lwh$ $V = \pi r^2 h$ $c^2 = a^2 + b^2$ Special Right Triangles

The number of degrees of arc in a circle is 360.

The sum of the measures in degrees of the angles of a triangle is 180.

---

21. What is the value of z if $3z + 4z + 7z = -42$?

(A) 3

(B) $\frac{1}{3}$

(C) $-\frac{1}{3}$

(D) -3

(E) -588

22. If 10 pecks are equivalent to 2.5 bushels, then 4 bushels are equivalent to how many pecks?

(A) 1
(B) 4
(C) 10
(D) 12.5
(E) 16

GO ON TO THE NEXT PAGE

23. What is the y-intercept of the line with equation $2x + 3y = 12$?

(A) 4

(B) 3

(C) 2

(D) $\dfrac{1}{4}$

(E) $-\dfrac{2}{3}$

24. For $x \neq 0$, $\dfrac{a}{x^2} + \dfrac{7}{x} =$

(A) $\dfrac{a+7x}{x}$

(B) $\dfrac{a+7x}{x^2}$

(C) $\dfrac{a+7}{x^2+x}$

(D) $\dfrac{a+7}{x}$

(E) $\dfrac{a+7}{x^2}$

25. If $y = 6x + 3$ and $y = cx + 3$ are the equations of perpendicular lines, then what is the value of c ?

A) –6

(B) $-\dfrac{1}{6}$

(C) $\dfrac{1}{6}$

(D) $\dfrac{1}{3}$

(E) 6

26. The positive difference between –5 and p is the same as the positive difference between –1 and 2.5. Which of the following could be the value of p ?

(A) –8.5
(B) –6.5
(C) –2.5
(D) 6.5
(E) 8.5

GO ON TO THE NEXT PAGE

27. If $f(x) = x^{-\frac{2}{3}}$, what is the value of $\dfrac{f(8)}{f(3)}$?

(A) $\dfrac{3}{4}$

(B) $\dfrac{4}{\sqrt[3]{9}}$

(C) $\dfrac{8}{3}$

(D) $\sqrt{\dfrac{512}{27}}$

(E) $\dfrac{\sqrt[3]{9}}{4}$

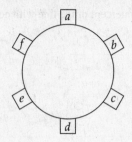

28. The figure above represents a circular amusement park ride with 6 seats, labeled a through f. If two students are to sit next to each other, leaving the other seats empty, how many such arrangements of the two students are possible?

(A)   3
(B)   6
(C)   10
(D)   12
(E)   30

GO ON TO THE NEXT PAGE

Directions for Student-Produced Response Questions

Each of the remaining 10 questions requires you to solve the problem and enter your answer by marking the ovals in the special grid, as shown in the examples below. You may use any available space for scratch work.

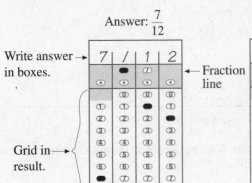

Answer: $\frac{7}{12}$ Answer: 2.5

Write answer → in boxes.   ← Fraction line   ← Decimal point

Grid in → result.

Note: You may start your answers in any column, space permitting. Columns not needed should be left blank.

- Mark no more than one circle in any column.

- Because the answer sheet will be machine-scored, **you will receive credit only if the circles are filled in correctly.**

- Although not required, it is suggested that you write your answer in the boxes at the top of the columns to help you fill in the circles accurately.

- Some problems may have more than one correct answer. In such cases, grid only one answer.

- No question has a negative answer.

- **Mixed numbers** such as $3\frac{1}{2}$ must be gridded as 3.5 or 7/2. (If 3 1 / 2 is gridded, it will be interpreted as $\frac{31}{2}$, not $3\frac{1}{2}$.)

- **Decimal Answers:** If you obtain a decimal answer with more digits than the grid can accommodate, it may be either rounded or truncated, but it must fill the entire grid. For example, if you obtain an answer such as 0.6666..., you should record your result as .666 or .667. **A less accurate value such as .66 or .67 will be scored as incorrect.**

Acceptable ways to grid $\frac{2}{3}$ are:

---

29. What is the value of $\left|-10\right|-\left|3\right|$?

30. If 20 percent of n is 36, what is 0.2 percent of n ?

GO ON TO THE NEXT PAGE

31. In $\triangle RST$, $\overline{RS} \cong \overline{ST}$. If the measure of $\angle S$ is 20°, then what is the degree measure of $\angle T$?

32. If all of the angles in the figure above are right angles, what is its perimeter?

33. If $x - 8 = 5y$ and $x = 23$, then what is the value of $x - y$?

34. What is the product of all the positive integer factors of 20?

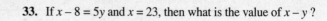

GO ON TO THE NEXT PAGE

35. Marcia can type 18 pages per hour, and David can type 14 pages per hour. If they work together, how many <u>minutes</u> will it take them to type 24 pages?

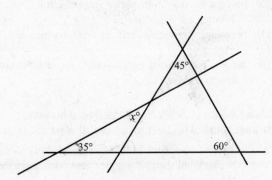

Note: Figure not drawn to scale.

36. What is the value of x in the figure above?

37. If $f(x) = x^2 - x + 4$, a is non-negative, and $f(a) = 10$, then what is the value of a?

38. A box contains only large marbles and small marbles. There are twice as many large marbles as small marbles in the box. The large marbles are all either blue or red, and there are 5 times as many large blue marbles as large red marbles. If one marble is drawn from the box at random, what is the probability that it will be a large blue marble?

STOP
**If you finish before time is called, you may check your work on this section only.
Do not turn to any other section in the test.**

SECTION 5
Time — 30 minutes
39 Questions

Directions: For each question in this section, select the best answer from among the choices given and fill in the corresponding circle on the answer sheet.

The following sentences test correctness and effectiveness of expression. Part of each sentence or the entire sentence is underlined; beneath each sentence are five ways of phrasing the underlined material. Choice A repeats the original phrasing; the other four choices are different. If you think the original phrasing produces a better sentence than any of the alternatives, select choice A; if not, select one of the other choices.

In making your selection, follow the requirements of standard written English; that is, pay attention to grammar, choice of words, sentence construction, and punctuation. Your selection should result in the most effective sentence—clear and precise, without awkwardness or ambiguity.

EXAMPLE:

Bobby Flay baked his first cake <u>and he was thirteen years old then</u>.
(A) and he was thirteen years old then
(B) when he was thirteen
(C) at age thirteen years old
(D) upon the reaching of thirteen years
(E) at the time when he was thirteen

Ⓐ ● Ⓒ Ⓓ Ⓔ

1. After visiting their friends in Paris, my parents told me that <u>in France they sometimes</u> do not wear bathing suits on the beach.

    (A) in France they sometimes
    (B) in France some people
    (C) some people, who are French,
    (D) in France there are some who
    (E) in France, men and women

2. Today's computers <u>are becoming not only more varied and powerful, but also less expensive</u>.

    (A) are becoming not only more varied and powerful, but also less expensive
    (B) not only are becoming more varied and powerful, they cost less
    (C) become not only more varied and powerful, they become less expensive
    (D) becoming more varied and powerful, but also less expensive
    (E) become more varied and powerful, not only, but also less expensive

3. <u>Getting off the chairlift, Neil had adjusted his boot buckles, polished his goggles, and skied down the slope.</u>

    (A) Getting off the chairlift, Neil had adjusted his boot buckles, polished his goggles, and skied down the slope.
    (B) He got off the chairlift, Neil adjusted his boot buckles, polished his goggles, and skied down the slope.
    (C) After getting off the chairlift, Neil adjusted his boot buckles, polished his goggles, and then he went skiing down the slope.
    (D) Neil, after getting off the chairlift, adjusted his boot buckles, polished his goggles, and was skiing down the slope.
    (E) After he got off the chairlift, Neil adjusted his boot buckles, polished his goggles, and skied down the slope.

4. Since they have been told not to do so in their school books, students often hesitate to write in their personal books; yet, circling an unknown word or underlining an important phrase <u>is critically when one wishes to learn something</u>.

    (A) is critically when one wishes to learn something
    (B) is critically being as one might wish to learn something
    (C) is critical when one wishes to learn something
    (D) is critical when you want to learn that something has been
    (E) can only be seen as critical when one wishes to learn something

GO ON TO THE NEXT PAGE

5. One of Humphrey Bogart's earlier movies, Sam Spade is a detective trying to solve the mystery of his partner's death in *The Maltese Falcon.*

(A) One of Humphrey Bogart's earlier movies, Sam Spade is a detective trying to solve the mystery of his partner's death in *The Maltese Falcon.*

(B) One of Humphrey Bogart's earlier movies, *The Maltese Falcon* is a movie in that Sam Spade, detective, tries to solve the mystery of his partner's death.

(C) One of Humphrey Bogart's earlier movies, *The Maltese Falcon* is a mystery where Sam Spade tries to solve his partner's death.

(D) In *The Maltese Falcon*, one of Humphrey Bogart's earlier movies, Sam Spade is a detective trying to solve the mystery of his partner's death.

(E) In *The Maltese Falcon*, one of Humphrey Bogart's roles is that of Sam Spade, a detective trying to solve the mystery of his partner's death, and it was also one of his earlier movies.

6. While Boudin's own paintings have never been held in the highest regard, he is understood to have played a critical role in the education of Impressionist painter Monet.

(A) While Boudin's own paintings have never been held in the highest regard, he is understood to have played a critical role in the education of Impressionist painter Monet.

(B) While Boudin's own paintings were never regarded highly, Monet is seen as having been one of his most educated students.

(C) It is seen that Boudin's critical role in educating the Impressionist painter Monet was held in higher regard than his paintings.

(D) Since Boudin's own paintings have never been held in that high regard, he has been seen as having played a critical role in the education of Impressionist painter Monet.

(E) Since Boudin's own paintings, which were never held in that high regard, were seen as having played a critical role in the education of Impressionist painter Monet.

7. Although everyone was forewarned about the upcoming exam, yet only three students out of the entire class passed it.

(A) yet only three students out of the entire class

(B) only three students out of the entire class

(C) only three students, which was out of the entire class,

(D) yet only three students that were forewarned out of the entire class

(E) but only three students out of the entire class

8. The committee chairpersons agreed to return to their respective committees and they would discuss the proposals made by the executive board.

(A) to return to their respective committees and they would discuss

(B) upon return to their respective committees, thereby discussing

(C) to return to her respective committees to discuss

(D) to return to their respective committees discussing

(E) to return to their respective committees to discuss

9. The clog has come back into fashion recently, yet few people know that originally it was called the sabot, made by hollowing a single piece of wood, and was worn by peasants in Europe.

(A) it was called the sabot, made by hollowing a single piece of wood, and was worn by peasants in Europe

(B) it was called the sabot, making it by hollowing a single piece of wood, and worn by peasants in Europe

(C) it was called the sabot, made by hollowing a single piece of wood, and worn by peasants in Europe

(D) it was called the sabot, making it by hollowing a single piece of wood, and was worn by peasants in Europe

(E) it was called the sabot, and the peasants made it by hollowing a single piece of wood, and wore it in Europe

10. Many say that, after inventing an explosive more powerful than any then known, Alfred Nobel instituted the Nobel Peace Prize to atone for his "accomplishment" and relieve his conscience.

(A) after inventing an explosive more powerful than any then known

(B) after inventing an explosive that was more powerful than any that were then known

(C) after he invented an explosive more powerful than he or any others had then known

(D) after he invented an explosive, it being more powerful than any then known

(E) after inventing an explosive more powerful then any than known

GO ON TO THE NEXT PAGE

11. For many a brilliant actor, <u>being free to interpret their character as they wish</u> is more important than being well paid.

   (A) being free to interpret their character as they wish

   (B) the freedom to interpret his or her character as they wish

   (C) being free to interpret their character as they wishes

   (D) the freedom to interpret his or her character as he or she wishes

   (E) being free to interpret his or her character as he or she wish

12. On Sunday afternoons, Omar and his family enjoy playing Monopoly with the neighbors, <u>and they always win</u>.

   (A) and they always win

   (B) even though they always win

   (C) even though the neighbors always win

   (D) and the neighbors, they always win

   (E) it being that the neighbors always win

13. Known for graduating from college despite being blind and deaf, <u>the fact that Helen Keller spent over six decades fighting for socialist causes is often left out of accounts of her life</u>.

   (A) the fact that Helen Keller spent over six decades fighting for socialist causes is often left out of accounts of her life

   (B) accounts of Helen Keller's life often leave out that she spent over six decades fighting for socialist causes

   (C) many people are unaware that Helen Keller spent over six decades fighting for socialist causes, as this fact is often left out of accounts of her life

   (D) six decades were spent by Helen Keller fighting for socialist causes, though this fact is often left out of accounts of her life

   (E) Helen Keller spent over six decades fighting for socialist causes, a fact often left out of accounts of her life

14. After getting her driver's license, Jenny used her father's car <u>as often as possible, and her father said to put less miles on it</u> by walking to school and work.

   (A) as often as possible, and her father said to put less miles on it

   (B) as often as possible; eventually her father told her to put fewer miles on it

   (C) as often as possible, but then eventually her father told her to be putting fewer miles on it

   (D) as often as possible; eventually her father told her to put less miles on it

   (E) as often as possible, and her father said to be putting less miles on it

15. The French classical composer <u>Maurice Ravel has enlisted as an ambulance driver</u> during World War I.

   (A) Maurice Ravel has enlisted as an ambulance driver

   (B) Maurice Ravel was to be enlisted as an ambulance driver

   (C) Maurice Ravel was enlisting as an ambulance driver

   (D) Maurice Ravel enlisting to be an ambulance driver

   (E) Maurice Ravel enlisted as an ambulance driver

16. <u>The art of carving totem poles with fantastic animal figures were practiced by Pacific Northwest Native American tribes</u>.

   (A) The art of carving totem poles with fantastic animal figures were practiced by Pacific Northwest Native American tribes.

   (B) The art of carving totem poles with fantastic animal figures was practiced by Pacific Northwest Native American tribes.

   (C) The art of carving totem poles with fantastic animal figures were being practiced by Pacific Northwest Native American tribes.

   (D) Pacific Northwest Native American tribes were practicing the art of carving totem poles with fantastic animal figures.

   (E) Pacific Northwest Native American tribes practiced the art of carving totem poles with fantastic animal figures.

GO ON TO THE NEXT PAGE ➔

17. <u>The bristlecone pine, regarded to be one of the varieties of longest living trees, is native to the American West.</u>

(A) The bristlecone pine, regarded to be one of the varieties of longest living trees, is native to the American West.

(B) The bristlecone pine, regarded to be one of the varieties of longest living trees, are native to the American West.

(C) The bristlecone pine, regarded as one of the varieties of longest living trees, are native to the American West.

(D) The bristlecone pine, regarded as one of the longest-lived varieties of trees, is native to the American West.

(E) The bristlecone pine, regarded as being one of the varieties of longest living trees, is native to the American West.

18. Scholars of popular culture have found that <u>the mainstream music of one decade sometimes barely differ with obscure</u> underground music of the previous decade.

(A) the mainstream music of one decade sometimes barely differ with obscure

(B) the mainstream music of one decade sometimes barely differs as compared to obscure

(C) the mainstream music of one decade sometimes barely differs from obscure

(D) the mainstream music of one decade sometimes barely shows any difference in obscure

(E) the mainstream music of one decade sometimes barely differs in obscure

19. <u>P. T. Barnum catered to the taste of the public</u> with such circus acts as Major Tom Thumb and Jumbo the elephant.

(A) P. T. Barnum catered to the taste of the public

(B) P. T. Barnum catering to the taste of the public

(C) P. T. Barnum catering for the taste of the public

(D) P. T. Barnum catered for the taste of the public

(E) P. T. Barnum, having catered to the taste of the public,

20. <u>In the early 1900s, Enrico Caruso was America's finest operatic tenor, more recently opera fans have enjoyed the talents of Plácido Domingo and José Carreras.</u>

(A) In the early 1900s, Enrico Caruso was America's finest operatic tenor, more recently opera fans have enjoyed the talents of Plácido Domingo and José Carreras.

(B) In the early 1900s, Enrico Caruso was America's finest operatic tenor; more recently, opera fans have enjoyed the talents of Plácido Domingo and José Carreras.

(C) In the early 1900s, Enrico Caruso was America's finest operatic tenor; more recently, opera fans were enjoying the talents of Plácido Domingo and José Carreras.

(D) In the early 1900s, Enrico Caruso was America's finest operatic tenor; but more recently, opera fans have enjoyed the talents of Plácido Domingo and José Carreras.

(E) In the early 1900s, Enrico Caruso was America's finest operatic tenor, however, more recently, opera fans have enjoyed the talents of Plácido Domingo and José Carreras.

GO ON TO THE NEXT PAGE

The following sentences test your ability to recognize grammar and usage errors. Each sentence contains either a single error or no error at all. No sentence contains more than one error. The error, if there is one, is underlined and lettered. If the sentence contains an error, select the one underlined part that must be changed to make the sentence correct. If the sentence is correct, select choice E. In choosing answers, follow the requirements of standard written English.

EXAMPLE:

The other players and her significantly improved
   A   B   C

the game plan created by the coaches. No error
            D   E

21. Revered as one of the world's most versatile geniuses,
    A

Leonardo da Vinci excelled in every endeavor
                 B

he attempted and serving as a prototype for the
           C   D

Renaissance man. No error
           E

22. The twins wanted to be a member of the team, but the
              A   B

captain had already made her selections . No error
       C   D   E

23. Of the nominees for the Nobel Prize in Literature
   A   B

this year, few are as qualified as the English novelist
       C   D

Anthony Powell. No error
          E

24. The recent production of Arthur Miller's *A View from*
         A

the Bridge exemplifies the strength of this unsung

masterpiece and demonstrates that the work has been
        B   C

ignored unjust. No error
   D   E

25. Yoga is more than simply a series of stretches and
      A   B

poses; it is a means of centering oneself spiritually

and focus in such a way as to put one's life in order.
    C   D

No error
  E

26. Prior to the Industrial Revolution, children and parents
   A

spend a great deal of time working together to meet the
   B   C

needs of the family . No error
     D   E

27. Neither the president nor the CEO of the three sister
             A

companies was able to determine why the last
      B

quarter's financial reports were so inconsistent with
              C

previous years . No error
    D   E

GO ON TO THE NEXT PAGE →

28. If one is interested <u>in</u> learning more about Jacob
                    <u>A</u>

Lawrence, <u>you should</u> visit the Metropolitan Museum of
       <u>B</u>

Art when next <u>his</u> work <u>is exhibited</u> . <u>No error</u>
            <u>C</u>   <u>D</u>   <u>E</u>

29. <u>Despite</u> the dangerous road conditions
    <u>A</u>

<u>after the blizzard</u> , the company <u>insisted on</u> <u>its</u>
     <u>B</u>   <u>C</u>   <u>D</u>

employees be on time. <u>No error</u>
              <u>E</u>

30. While in training, each member of the team <u>were</u>
                                 <u>A</u>

required to focus exclusively on the tasks associated

<u>with</u> <u>her</u> position, and therefore had little sense of the
<u>B</u>   <u>C</u>

functioning of the team <u>as a whole</u> . <u>No error</u>
                 <u>D</u>   <u>E</u>

31. The gift that Karen and Mary ultimately purchased for

<u>her</u> mother <u>was</u> much <u>less</u> expensive than the gift they
<u>A</u>   <u>B</u>   <u>C</u>

originally intended <u>to purchase</u> . <u>No error</u>
              <u>D</u>   <u>E</u>

32. Deciding to follow his conscience and not <u>give in to</u> the
                                  <u>A</u>

<u>pressure to conform</u> , the local worker was a <u>vocal</u>
     <u>B</u>   <u>C</u>

<u>critic toward</u> the regional vice president. <u>No error</u>
  <u>D</u>   <u>E</u>

33. Many scholars <u>agree</u> that there <u>has been</u> no greater
            <u>A</u>   <u>B</u>

contributor to the advancement <u>of architecture</u> in the
                       <u>C</u>

twentieth century than <u>that of Frank Lloyd Wright.</u>
                     <u>D</u>

<u>No error</u>
 <u>E</u>

34. Constructing a fence <u>ought not to be</u> seen as an
                <u>A</u>

insurmountable task; <u>rather</u> , it should be viewed as a
               <u>B</u>

challenge <u>that</u> can be accomplished by a
       <u>C</u>

<u>combination of</u> perseverance and patience. <u>No error</u>
   <u>D</u>   <u>E</u>

GO ON TO THE NEXT PAGE

Directions: The following passage is an early draft of an essay. Some parts of the passage need to be rewritten.

Read the passage and select the best answers for the questions that follow. Some questions are about particular sentences or parts of sentences and ask you to improve sentence structure or word choice. Other questions ask you to consider organization and development. In choosing answers, follow the requirements of standard written English.

Questions 35-39 are based on the following passage.

(1) Our town needs to make more of an effort to make its museums accessible to children. (2) Raised with frequent exposure to sculpture and paintings, it is much more likely that young people will mature into artists and patrons of the arts.

(3) It is often quite easy to accomplish a great deal simply. (4) Placed slightly lower on the walls, paintings become more visible to children. (5) But extensive programs to encourage children to appreciate art are often not a necessity. (6) Children have a natural enjoyment of art. (7) A museum is an excellent place for a child. (8) We must only understand that these young museum patrons cannot help acting like them. (9) Children should not be asked to be silent, or spend long periods of time in front of any one piece. (10) If necessary, museums should set up special "children's times" during which young people may roam through the building, enjoying the artwork in their own way. (11) A wonderful learning experience! (12) Children can have a great time, and at the same time gain an appreciation of art. (13) Precautions could be taken to make sure that no damage was done.

(14) This is necessary because places like museums must be available for everyone. (15) These changes cannot happen overnight, but if we volunteered and were helping to make these changes in our town's museums, we can realize the goal of making them accessible to people of all ages.

35. Which version of the underlined portion of sentence 8 (reproduced below) provides the most clarity?

We must only understand that these young museum patrons cannot help acting like them.

(A) (as it is now)
(B) like it
(C) as if they were
(D) like what they are
(E) like children

36. After sentence 13, the writer's point would have been strengthened most by the inclusion of

(A) a description of possible damage
(B) an explanation of the precautions to be taken
(C) a historic precedent
(D) an extension of her argument to include other institutions
(E) an explanation of the mission of a museum

37. Which of the following represents the best version of sentence 4 (reproduced below) ?

Placed slightly lower on the walls, paintings become more visible to children.

(A) (As it is now)
(B) Placing them slightly lower on the walls, the paintings become more visible to the children.
(C) For example, paintings placed slightly lower on the walls are more visible to children.
(D) For example, when placed slightly lower on the walls, children can see the paintings better.
(E) Placed paintings that are lower on the walls are more visible to children.

GO ON TO THE NEXT PAGE ➔

38. Which of the following is the best way to combine sentences 10 and 11 (reproduced below)?

If necessary, museums should set up special "children's times." At such times young people may roam through the building, enjoying the artwork in their own way.

(A) To avoid disrupting everyone else, create "children's times" in the museum, during which children could roam throughout the building, enjoying the artwork in their own way.

(B) Museums should set up "children's times," and all children could roam through the museum and enjoy the artwork in their own way.

(C) If necessary, museums should set up "children's times," but only when young people could roam throughout the building, enjoying the artwork in their own way.

(D) To enjoy artwork in their own way, children should be given the freedom to roam throughout the building. And it could be called "children's times."

(E) To avoid disrupting other museum-goers, museums should set up special "children's times," during which children would be allowed to roam throughout the building and enjoy the artwork in their own way.

39. In context, sentence 14 could be made more precise by changing the phrase "This is" to which of the following?

(A) That is

(B) These changes are

(C) The reasons for these changes is that they are

(D) It is

(E) These changes, as mentioned above, are also

STOP

If you finish before time is called, you may check your work on this section only.
Do not turn to any other section in the test.

PRACTICE TEST 1 ANSWERS

Section 1	Section 2	Section 3	Section 4	Section 5	
1. C	1. D	25. D	21. D	1. B	31. A
2. C	2. D	26. C	22. E	2. A	32. D
3. E	3. D	27. A	23. A	3. E	33. D
4. D	4. C	28. A	24. B	4. C	34. E
5. B	5. B	29. D	25. B	5. D	35. E
6. B	6. C	30. C	26. A	6. A	36. B
7. A	7. E	31. A	27. E	7. B	37. C
8. C	8. B	32. C	28. D	8. E	38. E
9. D	9. D	33. E	29. 7	9. C	39. B
10. A	10. C	34. E	30. .36	10. A	
11. A	11. A	35. A	31. 80	11. D	
12. B	12. E	36. C	32. 14	12. C	
13. B	13. C	37. B	33. 20	13. E	
14. D	14. D	38. A	34. 8,000	14. B	
15. B	15. D	39. A	35. 45	15. E	
16. C	16. D	40. E	36. 40	16. E	
17. A	17. E	41. D	37. 3	17. D	
18. D	18. B	42. A	38. $\frac{5}{9}$	18. C	
19. E	19. B	43. A	or	19. A	
20. D	20. B	44. D	.555	20. B	
21. B		45. A	or	21. C	
22. A		46. D	.556	22. A	
23. E		47. D		23. E	
24. C		48. A		24. D	
				25. C	
				26. B	
				27. D	
				28. B	
				29. C	
				30. A	

You will find a detailed explanation for each question beginning on page 314.

SCORING YOUR PRACTICE PSAT

Critical Reading

After you have checked your answers against the answer key, you can calculate your score. For the two Critical Reading sections (Sections 1 and 3), add up the number of correct answers and the number of incorrect answers. Enter these numbers on the worksheet on the next page. Multiply the number of incorrect answers by .25 and subtract this result from the number of correct answers. Then round this to the nearest whole number. This is your Critical Reading "raw score." Next, use the conversion table to convert your raw score to a scaled score.

Math

Calculating your Math score is a bit trickier, because some of the questions have five answer choices (for these, the incorrect answer deduction is .25), and some are Grid-Ins (which have no deduction for wrong answers).

First, check your answers to all of the problem-solving questions on Sections 2 and 4. For Section 2 and questions 21–28 of Section 4, enter the number of correct answers and the number of incorrect answers into the worksheet on the next page. Multiply the number of incorrect answers by .25 and subtract this result from the number of correct answers. For questions 29–38 of Section 4, the Grid-In questions, simply enter the number of correct answers. Now, add up the totals for both types of math questions to give you your total Math raw score. Then you can use the conversion table to find your scaled score.

Writing Skills

The Writing Skills section should be scored just like the Critical Reading sections. Add up the number of correct answers and the number of incorrect answers from Section 5, and enter these numbers on the worksheet on the next page. Multiply the number of incorrect answers by .25 and subtract this result from the number of correct answers. Then round this to the nearest whole number. This is your Writing Skills raw score. Next, use the conversion table to convert your raw scores to scaled scores.

WORKSHEET FOR CALCULATING YOUR SCORE

Critical Reading

	Correct	**Incorrect**

A. Sections 1 and 3   _____ − (.25 × _____) =

A

B. Total rounded Critical Reading raw score

B

Math

	Correct	**Incorrect**

C. Sections 2 and 4—Problem Solving _____ − (.25 × _____) =

C

D. Section 4—Grid-Ins _____ =

D

E. Total unrounded Math raw score (C + D)

E

F. Total rounded Math raw score

F

Writing Skills

	Correct	**Incorrect**

Section 5   _____ − (.25 × _____) =

Total rounded Writing Skills raw score

SCORE CONVERSION TABLE

Math Raw Score	Math Scaled Score	Critical Reading Raw Score	Critical Reading Scaled Score	Writing Skills Raw Score	Writing Skills Scaled Score
0	26	0	25	0	29
1	29	1	27	1	30
2	30	2	29	2	31
3	32	3	30	3	32
4	34	4	32	4	33
5	35	5	33	5	35
6	36	6	34	6	36
7	38	7	36	7	37
8	39	8	37	8	39
9	40	9	38	9	40
10	41	10	39	10	41
11	42	11	40	11	43
12	43	12	41	12	44
13	44	13	42	13	45
14	45	14	43	14	46
15	46	15	44	15	48
16	47	16	45	16	49
17	48	17	46	17	50
18	50	18	47	18	51
19	51	19	48	19	52
20	52	20	49	20	54
21	53	21	50	21	55
22	54	22	51	22	56
23	55	23	52	23	57
24	57	24	53	24	59
25	58	25	54	25	60
26	59	26	54	26	62
27	60	27	55	27	63
28	61	28	56	28	65
29	62	29	57	29	66
30	64	30	58	30	68
31	65	31	59	31	69
32	66	32	60	32	71
33	68	33	61	33	73
34	70	34	62	34	74
35	72	35	62	35	76
36	74	36	63	36	77
37	77	37	64	37	78
38	80	38	66	38	80
		39	67	39	80
		40	68		
		41	69		
		42	71		
		43	72		
		44	74		
		45	76		
		46	78		
		47	80		
		48	80		

SCORE CONVERSION TABLE

Chapter 13
Practice Test 1:
Answers and
Explanations

Section 1

1. **C** It is probably easier to start with the second blank on this question. The clue *protect the earth* indicates that we can fill in the blank with something like *change*. That eliminates answer choices (A), (B), and (E). The trigger *though* tells us that the first part of the sentence goes in a different direction than the second (which tells us that people are not willing to change), so we can write down something like *promote*. That eliminates answer choice (D), so only (C) is left.

2. **C** All we know about Prince Klemens von Metternich is that he *dominated* the Congress of Vienna, so he probably had a *dominating* personality. Only answer choice (C) comes close.

3. **E** The first blank has the clues *enlivened* and *by the strong rays of the sun,* so *lively* would be a good word to write down. (B), (C), and (D), therefore, can go. The second blank is talking about the canopy, which typically covers the forest floor; if the forest floor now has sun shining on it, the canopy must have been *broken through.* (E) is much closer than (A).

4. **D** If the iguana is *reclusive,* then fruitful investigations are probably hard to get. So *rarity* would be a good word to fill in the blank. Answer choice (D) is closest.

5. **B** The governor wanted *more housing,* but she ended up making housing *even more scarce.* That means she *worsened* the problem. The only answer choice that means *worsened* is (B).

6. **B** The clues *friendly and honest manner* tell us we can replace the first blank with *friendly and honest,* so we can eliminate (C), (D), and (E). We have a trigger, *but,* which tells us the second part of the sentence goes in the opposite direction, so we can write down *not friendly and honest* for the second blank. The closest answer is (B).

7. **A** Because we do not have clues for each blank here, we should go by the relationship between the blanks. The blanks have a relationship of similarity; either the musicians loved it and wanted to promote it, or they hated it and wanted to get rid of it. So we would write down *same.* (A) has a relationship of similarity, so we can keep it. (B), (D), and (E) are going in opposite directions, and (C) has no relationship, so we can eliminate those.

8. **C** The first blank can be replaced with something like *rebellion,* based on the clue *rebellion* in the sentence. That eliminates (B) and (D). We can see now in the answer choices that the first words in each pair are actually people, but that does not matter—following the technique, we are still right on track. The triggers *even though* and *now* tell us that the second blank is going to have a negative word in it; the United States now views rebels as *bad.* That eliminates (A), which has a positive word, and (E), which has a neutral word, leaving only (C).

9. **D** Answer choice (D) is correct because the passage states that the *centuries-old rules* are *not so different* from Oulipo techniques. (B) is extreme, (C) can be eliminated as the group has been meeting only since 1960, and neither (A) nor (E) is supported by evidence from the passage.

10. **A**   Answer choice (A) is correct because *churn out* indicates quantity instead of quality. (B) is incorrect because the phrase is not a reference to Oulipo. There is no evidence for (C) or (D) in the passage, and (E) is extreme—ETS isn't going to include a passage by an author who is "disgusted."

11. **A**   Answer choice (E) is too ambitious, as no historical event can be explicated in a short passage. Cultural significance is not mentioned, so we can eliminate answer choice (D). There is no explanation to support (B), and President Johnson's character is not attacked, as (C) says. As for (A), there is in fact a possible controversy downplayed: The contention that President Johnson manufactured the Gulf of Tonkin crisis is waved away in the last sentence. So (A) is a good fit.

12. **B**   The argument would be strengthened by a report explaining the discrepancy between the two destroyers. Which answer choice says this? (C) and (E) are not relevant to the scope of the passage. (A) and (D) do not resolve the discrepancies between the two destroyers, so they actually weaken the argument. But (B) makes the argument stronger by explaining how it could be that the USS *Maddox* did not pick up the other ships on its radar. Be careful when dealing with weaken/strengthen questions, as the opposite answer to what you are looking for will generally be in the answer choices.

13. **B**   This is a primary purpose question, so we want an answer choice that describes what the author was trying to accomplish in Passage 1. (C) is clearly outside the scope of the passage. (D) confuses cattle with pigs and dogs as to which species are scavengers. (A) and (E) are too narrow. (B) is a nice summary of the argument at the end of the passage, so it is the best choice.

14. **D**   Here we have a line reference question, so go back to the quote and read above and below it. The quote refers to the interactive nature of the domestication of species such as pigs and dogs. Thus, (B), (C), and (E) are not correct. (A) refers to the same general notion, but it is too narrow, leaving us with answer choice (D).

15. **B**   This is a Vocab-in-Context question. We want to come up with our own word based on the context of the passage. We might come up with something like *unplanned*. (A), (C), (D), and (E) are all distracters based on the language of the passage. (B) is closest to our word.

16. **C**   Here is another line reference question, so go back to the passage and read five lines above and five lines below. The myth is described as the life and death of the moon goddess. (A) misses the focus, so it can be eliminated. (B) is out of context. Gazelles are mentioned later, as an afterthought, so (D) is incorrect. (E) is a distracter that garbles the words of the paragraph. (C) is the best option.

17. **A**   The passage indicates that the animals were susceptible to domestication, and the human culture was evolved enough to control the animal. The correct answer needs to reflect both elements. (D) and (E) focus on one side or the other. (B) is out of context. (C) is not even in the ballpark. Knowing the vocabulary helps a lot: We are looking for an answer choice that reflects a *mutually beneficial* relationship. (A), with its mention of "harmony," fits the bill.

18.   **D**   This is a lead word question. Look for the word *Maglemosian* and you will find it in line 63. Then read five lines up and five lines down to find the answer. The author is emphasizing that we do not really know what happened, but domestication clearly differed with respect to both species and human culture. Since the author gives no details, (A) is clearly not the answer. While (B) is probably true, it is not the answer to the question. (C) is out, as the point of mentioning both cultures was to indicate that culture is important. (E) is gone for basically the same reason; culture and species are important. Only (D) says this.

19.   **E**   This is a Lead Word question. Find where the passage talks about *Rattus norvegicus* and see what the studies revealed. The passage states that "the tremendous behavioral changes undergone by a species during domestication…cannot yield the total behavior pattern of the wild ancestors." Only (E) reflects that statement. (A) is a distracter based on confusion about what *Rattus norvegicus* is. (B) is a distracter based on the language of the passage, but the passage does not say that psychological insights were learned. (C) and (D) are the direct opposites of the implication of the paragraph.

20.   **D**   This is another Lead Word question, so search for where the passage talks about Lorenz's imprinting experiments. The fourth paragraph tells us that imprinting helped domesticate birds. (A), (B), (C), and (E) are all true, but none answer the question. The question is, "What is the author saying about the role of imprinting in domestication?" (D) answers that question.

21.   **B**   Here we need to select an answer that is consistent with the views of both authors. (A) has extreme language: *the single most important factor*, so cross it out. Imprinting applies mainly to birds and not to mammals, so (C) is incorrect. (D) is wrong because capturing animals for ceremonies is a possible stage, not a critical stage. (E) presents what we perhaps would like to think, but it is neither stated nor implied in the passage. (B) answers the question.

22.   **A**   The difference in the two passages is really one of emphasis, based in part on the species discussed. The two are closest in terms of dogs and pigs, but neither rules out what the other describes about the domestication of various species. (B) is incorrect since Passage 1 deals mainly with the religious significance of cattle, not other species. (C) is incorrect since Passage 1 treats dogs and pigs in passing; cattle are the focus of Passage 1. (D) is too narrow a construction of both passages. (E) is incorrect because Passage 1 doesn't deal with studying lab rats and birds. (A) is our best choice.

23.   **E**   Here we need an answer choice that shows a difference between the authors' views or something that states an idea they both reject. (A), (B), (C), and (D) combine ideas from each passage that the authors would agree on. (E) garbles the hypotheses: Lab rats were not used as hunting decoys!

24.   **C**   The "social enzyme" has to do with the "proclivity…to keep pets." Neither passage notes the roles of cattle as "pets," so (A), (B), and (D) are incorrect. The scavenger behavior has to do with dogs and pigs seeking out man, not man keeping them as pets, so (E) is incorrect. (C) is our answer.

Section 2

1. **D**   To solve for b, our first step should be to move the 4 to the other side of the equation by adding 4 to both sides. This will give us $12b = 4$. Now we divide each side by 12, and get $b = \dfrac{1}{3}$.

2. **D**   Before doing any math on this problem, we should ballpark and eliminate answers we know are wrong. The question tells us that 60 gallons represents $\dfrac{5}{12}$ of the full tank—or a little less than half. So the full tank will need to be a little more than twice 60 gallons, or something a little larger than 120. This makes choices (A), (B), and (E) unreasonable, so we can eliminate those choices. The answer has to be either (C) or (D). To figure out which, we can try plugging in the answer choices. Is $\dfrac{5}{12}$ of 128 equal to 60? No, that equals 10.67. So we will try choice (D). Is $\dfrac{5}{12}$ of 144 equal to 60? Yes, so (D) is the answer.

3. **D**   To make this problem easier, we can plug in some numbers for the sides of this rectangle. We can pick whichever numbers we want, as long as they make the area equal to 16. So let's assume that the rectangle has dimensions 8 and 2. This makes the base of the triangle 8 and the height 2, so the area of the triangle will be $\dfrac{1}{2} \times 8 \times 2$ or 8. (Even if we made the dimensions of the rectangle 16 and 1, we would still get the same answer!) You may also know the rule that a triangle inscribed in a rectangle will have exactly half the area of that rectangle; but even without knowing the rule, by plugging in some values we can figure it out.

4. **C**   The first multiple of 32 is 32, so the correct choice must divide evenly into 32. In other words, 32 must be a multiple of the correct choice. Is 32 a multiple of 11? No; nor is it a multiple of 9, 5, or 3. So we can eliminate (A), (B), (D), and (E). (C) is our answer.

5. **B**   This looks like a good opportunity to Plug In The Answers. If we plug in (C), 32, we find that angle A is 32, angle B is 94, and angle C is 90—which adds to way more than 180, the number of degrees in any triangle. This eliminates (C), (D), and (E). When we try (B), 23, we get a triangle whose angles measure 23, 67, and 90. Perfect!

6. **C**   Since we have variables in the answer choices, we should plug in. We can plug in whatever consecutive numbers we want for x, y, and z, provided that we obey the rule that $x < y < z$. Let's choose 2 for x, 3 for y, and 4 for z, since those are easy numbers. The question then asks: What is the sum of y and z? Using our numbers, the answer will be $3 + 4$, which makes 7. Now the question is: Which of the answer choices gives 7, using our value of 2 for x? Answer choice (C) gives $2(2) + 3$, which equals 7.

7. **E**   This question looks nasty, but if we remember our MADSPM rules, it becomes much easier. Whenever we raise an exponent to another exponent, it is the same as multiplying the exponents together. So $(2^a)^b$ is the same thing as $2^{a \times b}$. Using a calculator we can figure out that $64 = 2^6$, so $a \times b$ must be equal to 6.

8. **B**   To answer this question, we must remember our rules for adding and subtracting roots: We can only add or subtract if the number under the radical sign is the same. So first, we have to simplify the expressions. $6\sqrt{18}$ can be rewritten as $6\sqrt{9 \times 2}$. Since we have a perfect square under the radical sign, we can square root it and pull it out, giving us $6 \times 3\sqrt{2}$, or $18\sqrt{2}$.

$4\sqrt{72}$ equals $4\sqrt{36 \times 2}$, which becomes $4 \times 6\sqrt{2}$ or $24\sqrt{2}$.

$\sqrt{8}$ equals $\sqrt{4 \times 2}$, which equals $2\sqrt{2}$.

$10\sqrt{32}$ equals $10\sqrt{16 \times 2}$, which equals $10 \times 4\sqrt{2}$, which becomes $40\sqrt{2}$.

So finally we have $18\sqrt{2} + 24\sqrt{2} - (2\sqrt{2} + 40\sqrt{2})$. Now all of our roots have been simplified to something $\sqrt{2}$, so we can add and subtract normally. Starting inside the parentheses, $2\sqrt{2} + 40\sqrt{2} = 42\sqrt{2}$. $18\sqrt{2} + 24\sqrt{2} - 42\sqrt{2} = 0$. Of course, you can also do this problem on your calculator.

9. **D**   A line with negative slope is one that you can draw going down and to the right from any starting point. Lines $\overline{AE}$ and $\overline{BD}$ will not count, since they have no slope. The only ones we can draw are $\overline{AC}$, $\overline{FD}$, and $\overline{AD}$.

Do not be thrown off by the coordinates given for points A and B—they are just there to assure you that segments AB and DE actually are parallel to the x-axis.

10. **C**   You can Plug In The Answers here, but in this case translation is a little bit easier: Once we have $x = 3 + 7x$, we can subtract $7x$ from both sides to leave us with $-6x = 3$. Divide both sides by -6 and we find that x is equal to 3 divided by -6, which equates to choice (C).

11. **A**   Like many problems on the PSAT, this question will be difficult if we try to do it all at once. Instead, let's break it down into bite-sized pieces. We will start with just part of the inequality, $-12 \le 3b + 3$. Remember that we can solve inequalities just like equations—provided that if we multiply or divide by a negative value, we swap the direction of the inequality sign. To solve this part of the inequality, though, we just need to subtract 3 from each side (giving us $-15 \le 3b$) and then divide each side by 3, which leaves us with $-5 \le b$. Now we can eliminate several choices that we know will not work: (B), (D), and (E) do not have -5 in them. Now we will work on the other part of the inequality: $-3b + 3 \le 18$. If we subtract 3 from each side and then divide by 3, we get $b \le 5$. Now we can cross off (C), and we are left with (A).

12. **E**   Let's start by plugging in a number for x. We need an odd integer divisible by 3, so we can choose $x = 9$. The question asks us which of the following must be divisible by 4. (A) says $x + 1$, or 10, which is not divisible by 4. (B) says $x + 2$, or 11, which is also not divisible by 4. This allows us to

eliminate (A) and (B). (C) says $x + 3$, or 12, which is divisible by 4, so we should leave (C) in. (D) says 18, which is not divisible by 4, so we can eliminate this choice too. (E) says 16, which can be divided by 4, so we should leave it in. Now we are down to (C) and (E). Let's pick another number for x and keep working. How about $x = 15$? In this case, (C) gives us 18, which is not divisible by 4. This eliminates (C), so the answer is (E).

13. **C** To find the perimeter, we need to find the lengths of each of the sides of this triangle. Side AB is fairly easy, since we can just count the points: from (0, 4) to (6, 4) is a length of 6. However, finding sides $\overline{AC}$ and $\overline{BC}$ is a little more difficult. The problem tells us that $\overline{AC} \cong \overline{BC}$, so we know that point C must be on the x-axis right in between points A and B—which places it at coordinate (3, 0).

Now, to find the length of $\overline{AC}$, we can look at the triangle formed by A, C, and the origin. This triangle has a base of 3, since point C is at (3, 0), and a height of 4, since point A is at (0, 4). This makes a right triangle with sides 3 and 4, so side $\overline{AC}$ must be equal to 5. We can do the same thing to solve for side $\overline{BC}$. So we know that the sides of this triangle are 6, 5, and 5 for a total perimeter of 16.

14. **D** Let's plug 5 and 6 in for n to find the 5th and 6th terms. The 5th term is $1 + 2^5 = 1 + 32 = 33$. The 6th term is $1 + 2^6 = 1 + 64 = 65$. The sum of the 5th and 6th terms is $33 + 65 = 98$, choice (D).

15. **D** Since we have variables in the answer choices, we should plug in on this problem. To make the math work easily, we can pick 5 for c, 10 for g, and 20 for n. If 1 bottle containing 5 ounces will fill 10 glasses, then how many bottles will be needed to fill 20 glasses? Two bottles. So now 2 is our target answer. Using 5 for c, 10 for g, and 20 for n, (A) equals 40, which is too large. (B) gives 10, which is also too large. (C) gives .5, which is too small. (D) gives 2, which is our target, but we must remember to do POE completely and check the remaining answer choice. (E) gives .25, which is too small.

16. **D** Note that the letters are standing in for one-digit numbers, not variables. If $7 - B = 7$, B must represent 0. Now the problem is $A407 - A40 = 5CA7$. If we carry a one from the 4 to the 0, we get $10 - 4 = A$, which means A is equal to 6. Now we have $6407 - 640 = 5C67$. Once we calculate from here, we get $C = 7$, answer choice (D).

17. **E** This question is testing volume. The volume of the original block of cheese is $8 \times 8 \times 8$, or 512. The piece that we cut out measures $4 \times 2 \times 2$, so its volume is 16. If we subtract 16 from 512, we get 496. The fractional part that remains will be $\dfrac{496}{512}$, or $\dfrac{31}{32}$—choice (E).

18. **B** This figure is not drawn to scale, so we cannot trust our eyes on this question. We can, however, still plug in, since we have variables in the answer choices. Let's plug in 30 for a and see what happens. If we make $a = 30$, then we will have values for four of our angles: angle a (30), angle $2a$ (60), angle $3a$ (90), and the other angle that measures $2a$ (60). This makes a total of 240 degrees out of 360. This means that the other angles, b and b, must add up to 120. So b must be equal to 60. The question asks us for the measure of b, so 60 is our answer. Now we must see which choice (remembering that $a = 30$) gives 60. This shows us that (B) is the answer.

19. **B** If we are averaging two numbers x and y, then this average will always be half of the sum of these numbers. Let's try some values for x and y and see what kind of numbers we get. Since $y = 4x$, if $x = 5$ then $y = 20$, and their sum is 25. If $x = 6$ then $y = 24$, and their sum is 30. If $x = 7$ then $y = 28$, and their sum is 35. It looks like the sum of x and y will always be a multiple of 5. Now we can look at the choices we have, starting with (C). If the average of x and y is 4, then their sum will be 8. But we know that the sum of x and y will always be a multiple of 5, so (C) cannot be right. Likewise for answer choices (D) and (E): If the average is 12, the sum of x and y will be 24; if their average is 28, their sum would have to be 56. So neither of these could be right. The only answer choice that would give us a sum of x and y as a multiple of 5 is choice (B).

20. **B** To solve direct proportion questions, just set up a proportion. In this case, $\dfrac{y_1}{\left(x_1\right)^2} = \dfrac{y_2}{\left(x_2\right)^2}$ becomes $\dfrac{18}{\left(3\right)^2} = \dfrac{2}{\left(x_2\right)^2}$. Cross-multiplying and solving gives you $x_2 = 1$, choice (B).

Section 3

25. **D** The sentence mentions *small population* and *shyness,* which are both factors that would *hurt* studies, so *hurt* is a good word to fill in the blank. Only (D) comes close to the same definition.

26. **C** *All segments of society* provides a good clue to tell us that something like *increased* or *made popular* would be a good replacement for the blank, making (C) the best answer choice.

27. **A** It looks like we can start with the first blank easily enough: What happens to old technology when new technology comes along? It gets *replaced*, which allows us to eliminate (B), (C), and (D). A trigger helps us nail down the second blank: *While many* consumer electronics are replaced, apparently the home computer is an exception, and it will be many years before it becomes…*useless*, maybe? That allows us to eliminate (E). (A) still works, so pick (A).

28. **A** Let's work on the first blank. We have the clue *refused to give up* and the trigger word *although*, which means that a good word for the first blank would be something like *insurmountable*. That eliminates (C), (D), and (E). For the second blank, we know that we are looking for something positive, perhaps *good* or *clever*. That eliminates (B), so (A) is correct.

29. **D** If 2,500 out of 3,200 residents made their way through a blizzard to vote, they must have been pretty *determined*. (D) has the closest definition.

30. **C** Answer choice (C) is correct; both passages mention the importance of facts or relevant information. (A) and (B) are incorrect; only Passage 1 supports those answers. (D) is extreme. (E) is wrong because only the author of Passage 2 would agree with the answer.

31. **A** Answer choice (A) is correct; Passage 1 mentions *new historicist*, revisionism. (B) is wrong because both passages mention historical events. (C) is incorrect because both passages are focused on U.S. history, and both mention one of the world wars. (D) is wrong because both passages are partisan—one toward conservative historical analysis, one toward revisionist history. (E) is never mentioned.

32. **C** Answer choice (C) is correct; Passage 1 claims that *facts are facts*, while Passage 2 admits the possibility of bias. (A) is wrong because both passages mention military history. (B) is wrong because both deal with U.S. history. (D) is wrong because Passage 2 deals with bias, not limited interpretation. (E) is too extreme.

33. **E** Answer choice (E) is correct; the second passage is concerned that historians overlook the contributions of minority groups. (A) is too narrow. (B) and (D) are extreme. (C) is extreme and offensive.

34. **E** The author's main purpose in writing the passage, as can be seen in the last paragraph, is to show how his experiences with the choir affected his approach to other areas of his life. While (C) and (D) occur in the passage, neither adequately summarizes the entire passage. In (B), *worship* is too strong. (A) is never mentioned in the passage. Therefore, (E) is the best answer.

35. **A** This is a line reference question, so we must go to the passage and read enough to get the context. In describing "Madame Jeanette," the author uses terms such as *cloying sentimentality*, and states that, when performed by teenagers under the guidance of *sloppy conducting*, it becomes *maudlin* and an *embarrassing tearfest*. (B) and (D) are never mentioned in the passage. (C) is incorrect because the piece becomes compelling and poignant only under the guidance of a director of Wilhousky's caliber. While (E) might look tempting, the reader is never told that the piece is technically difficult for most choirs, and we are never told that this is a reason for it to be considered "dangerous." Therefore, (A) is the best answer.

36. **C** In lines 32–33, the author states that performing the piece was a *wonderful solace* for an insecure boy of his age, and later in the paragraph he refers to its ability to fill him with a sense of *hope and possibility*. This makes (C) the best answer.

37. **B** This is a Vocab-in-Context question, so we should come up with our own word. The author states in line 42 that he *still marvels* at the level of obedience Wilhousky was able to command, which implies that children at that time were quite obedient to begin with. So perhaps *more common* will work. While (A), (C), (D), and (E) could be considered plausible definitions of the word *ready*, only (B) is close to our word. Thus, it is the best answer.

38. **A** This question asks us why the author included a particular detail. The author introduces the anecdote of the boy in the third row immediately after discussing how Wilhousky instilled discipline "through intimidation by public ridicule," and the boy's story serves as an example of this. (B) is incorrect because the author himself confesses that he is uncertain about what was really said, so we cannot be sure that Wilhousky was really lying. This also eliminates (E), since we cannot be sure that he is really trying to *trick* his students. (D) is incorrect because while the author does mention the human memory, this is not the purpose of the anecdote. While the author suggests that Wilhousky was a disciplinarian, it is hard to find evidence in the passage that the author would go so far as to call him *cruel*, which eliminates (C). Therefore, (A) is the best answer.

39. **A** In the last paragraph, the author states that, as a result of working with Wilhousky, the author "slowly personalized the dream that excellence in one activity might be extended to become the pattern, or at least the goal, of an actual life." (B), (C), (D), and (E) are never mentioned. Therefore, (A) is the best answer.

40. **E** The first paragraph says that *Naim loved squash,* and describes how *he spent extra hours at the court, practicing with an almost machine-like consistency, drilling until he couldn't breathe anymore, and hitting hundreds, thousands of shots, trying to store that perfect stroke in his muscle memory,* which is all evidence that he was *devoted to becoming a better squash player* as choice (E) states. The other choices use words from the passage but are not supported by evidence from the passage.

41. **D** The phrase in questions, *but if that had been the only hurdle, things might have been easier,* suggests that there is more than one aspect to Naim's problem of not being *as good as he wanted to be.* Only choice (D) addresses *multiple levels.* While the sentence goes on to describe the time and effort Naim put into improving his game, choice (A) is only partially correct, because it doesn't address the other part of Naim's problem, which is described later in the paragraph, *his biggest challenge came from his coach.*

42. **A** This sentence describes Naim *practicing,* so look for a word that means something similar. Choice (A) is the only one that fits. The other choices give other meanings of the work *drilling,* but do not work in this context.

43. **A** Be careful about the word *suggest* in the question. The correct answer will still have direct support in the passage, so pay attention to what the line in question say: *Naim's own take on the game, more characterized by quick, deceptive movements, odd changes in pace, fancy trick shots, felt much more like the game he was meant to play, much more an expression of himself than the characterless devotion to some sport that existed long before he came along to play it.* These lines are essentially saying that Naim preferred his own, personal style of playing squash, as choice (A) says.

44. **D** The first sentence of this paragraph poses a question: *if it wouldn't win his matches or tournaments, or allow him to go pro..., then why keep playing what Mr. Shabana called this "dead-end" style of squash?,* which refers to Naim's own personal style of playing as described at the end of the

first paragraph. The rest of the paragraph goes on to explain that *Naim couldn't say* why he kept playing his own way, and that *His hope to change the way the game was played… made him think he might be better suited to the bigger stage of tennis.* In other words, he was so dedicated to his style that he was considering changing sports. Only choice (D) refers to Naim's personal style.

45.   A   *It* keeps Naim from winning or going pro, and is the same as the *"dead-end" style of squash* referred to at the end of the sentence. The *"dead-end" style* is Mr. Shabana's term for what he doesn't like about Naim's playing. The first paragraph states that Mr. Shabana *wanted Naim to play the English style*, but that Naim wanted to play his own way. Therefore, *it* must refer to Naim's *personal style* as in choice (A). Choice (B), (C), and (D) all appear in the second paragraph, but none of them are what keeps Naim from winning.

46.   D   Just as Naim is considering switching to a different sport, he discovers *a new player on the pro tour* who is to become *the inspiration he had been missing.* The third paragraph describes this change of heart and Naim's renewal of interest in squash, which is an *important development* as in choice (D). While it does *describe* El Shorbagy's *style* as in choice (C), that is only part of the paragraph.

47.   D   El Shorbagy's style is described as playing with *such flair, such incredible confidence and style, that he seemed totally self-taught; he was almost, it seemed, expressing his very soul as he played, the same way one might do in a poem.* Naim is therefore moved by El Shorbagy's ability to express himself, as choice (D) states. A poem is mentioned as a similar mode of expression; El Shorbagy's play is not actually described as *poetic*, thus eliminating choice (B).

48.   A   The parentheses come in a sentence explaining how Naim was inspired by El Shorbagy, and the words inside describe Naim's *professional career and his subsequent coaching life as impossible without El Shorbagy's influence.* The third paragraph states that Naim did not switch to playing tennis *because as he watched a new player on the pro tour, he found the inspiration he had been missing. The player's name was Mohamed El Shorbagy.* In other words, El Shorbagy's influence inspired Naim to keep playing squash, which he had been considering giving up because he wanted to play in his own style. Choice (A) most effectively captures this idea. While Naim's professional career is mentioned, the passage does not say he had many professional victories, thus eliminating choice (E).

Section 4

21.   D   We can add the like terms to find $14z = -42$. Divide by 14 to find $z = -3$.

22.   E   This question is asking us to compare pecks and bushels, so we can set up a proportion: $\dfrac{10 \text{ pecks}}{2.5 \text{ bushels}} = \dfrac{x \text{ pecks}}{4 \text{ bushels}}$. Then we can cross-multiply and solve for x, which results in $x = 16$.

23. **A** The slope-intercept form of the equation of a line is $y = mx + b$, where m is the slope, and b is the y-intercept. So we would manipulate this equation to solve for y. Subtracting $2x$ from both sides of the equation and then dividing both sides by 3 gives us $y = -\dfrac{2}{3}x + 4$, so the y-intercept is 4.

24. **B** We have variables in the answer choices, so we should plug in. Try $a = 3$ and $x = 2$. The expression turns into $\dfrac{3}{4} + \dfrac{7}{2}$, which equals $\dfrac{17}{4}$, our target number. Now we can replace a with 3 and x with 2 in the answers to see which hits our target. Only (B) does.

25. **B** The slope-intercept form of the equation of a line is $y = mx + b$, where m is the slope and b is the y-intercept. So the slope of the line given by the first equation is 6. To find the slope of a perpendicular line, we would take the negative reciprocal. So $c = -\dfrac{1}{6}$.

26. **A** Positive difference just means the absolute value of the difference. So for $|-1 - 2.5|$, the difference is 3.5. Plug in the answer choices to find the one with the difference of 3.5: $|(-5) - (-8.5)| = 3.5$.

27. **E** Negative exponents mean to take the reciprocal of the positive exponent. For example, $y^{-2} = \dfrac{1}{y^2}$, and $2^{-3} = \dfrac{1}{2^3}$. For fractional exponents, the denominator tells us what root of the number to take and the numerator acts as a normal exponent. So, $f(x)$ is $\dfrac{1}{\sqrt[3]{x^2}}$. First, let's find $f(8)$: $\dfrac{1}{\sqrt[3]{8^2}} = \dfrac{1}{\sqrt[3]{64}} = \dfrac{1}{4}$. Next, let's find $f(3)$: $\dfrac{1}{\sqrt[3]{3^2}} = \dfrac{1}{\sqrt[3]{9}}$. Put these values in for $\dfrac{f(8)}{f(3)}$. So, $\dfrac{\frac{1}{4}}{\frac{1}{\sqrt[3]{9}}} = \dfrac{1}{4} \div \dfrac{1}{\sqrt[3]{9}} = \dfrac{1}{4} \times \sqrt[3]{9} = \dfrac{\sqrt[3]{9}}{4}$. Remember to look at the answer choices so you do not keep trying to simplify when there is no need to.

28. **D** The first student has 6 choices of where to sit. For each place the first student sits, the second student has 2 choices of where to sit—only on either side of the first student. (So, if the first student sits in seat b, the second student can sit in seat a or seat c.) Thus, the total number of possible arrangements is $6 \times 2 = 12$.

29. **7** The vertical bars around a number mean absolute value, which tells us to find the distance on the number line between that number and zero. To find the absolute value of a negative number, simply remove the negative sign. The absolute value of $|-10|$ is 10, and the absolute value of $|3|$ is 3. So, $10 - 3 = 7$.

30. **.36**   Start with the first part of the question. Twenty percent of n is 36. If we translate this into math, it becomes $\frac{20}{100}n = 36$. Now we can solve for n by reducing $\frac{20}{100}$ to $\frac{1}{5}$ and by multiplying each side by 5. $\frac{1}{5}n = 36$, so $n = 36 \times 5$. This gives us $n = 180$. Now we translate the other part and plug in 180 for n. What is .2 percent of 180 becomes: $x = \frac{.2}{100} \times 180$. Now we solve for x, and get $x = .36$.

31. **80**   When we draw it, we see that triangle RST is isosceles, with angle R equal to angle T. Since there are 180 degrees in a triangle, and we are told that angle S is 20 degrees, angles R and T must add up to 160 degrees. Since R has the same measure as T, each is 80 degrees.

32. **14**   While we do not know the exact lengths of the bottom or right side of the figure, we do not need to know them. We know that the unknown horizontal edges must have a total length of 3, and the unknown vertical edges must have a total length of 4.

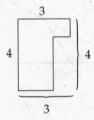

Therefore, we know that the total perimeter of the object is $4 + 3 + 4 + 3 = 14$. You can also plug in values for the missing side lengths, so long as the horizontal ones add up to 3 and the vertical ones add up to 4.

33. **20**   Since the problem tells us the value of x, which is 23, we can put this into the equation and solve for y. $23 - 8 = 5y$, so we know that $15 = 5y$ and $3 = y$. Now we know the value of y. However, on this problem, we must remember that we are not just solving for y; we are solving for $x - y$. So the correct answer is $23 - 3$, or 20.

34. **8,000**   We can start by finding all of the positive integer factors of 20. We can factor 20 into 1×20, 2×10, and 4×5. The question asks for the product of these numbers, which will be $1 \times 20 \times 2 \times 10 \times 4 \times 5$, or 8,000.

35. **45**   If Marcia types 18 pages per hour, and David can type 14 pages per hour, then together they will be able to type $18 + 14$, or 32 pages per hour. To see what fraction of an hour it will take them to type 24 pages, we can set up a proportion:

$$\frac{32 \; pages}{1 \; hour} = \frac{24 \; pages}{x \; hours}$$

If we solve for *x*, we can see that they can type 24 pages in .75 of an hour. But that is not our answer! The question asks for the answer in minutes. Three-quarters of an hour is equal to 45 minutes, so the answer is 45.

36. **40** When it is difficult to tell where to start on a geometry question, it is best to begin filling in what you know. Since we know that the angles in a triangle always add up to 180, we can figure out the third angle of the triangle with angles 45 and 60. The sum of these angles is 105, so the third angle must measure 75. This means that the angle next to it on the line must also measure 105. Now in the triangle on the left, we have angles 105 and 35. Together these angles make 140, so we know that the third angle (marked with an *x*) is equal to 40.

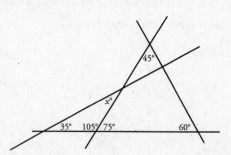

37. **3** Since the problem tells us that $f(a) = 10$, and that $f(x) = x^2 - x + 4$, we can plug *a* into the function for *x* so $f(a) = a^2 - a + 4$, and $10 = a^2 - a + 4$. Now we need to factor to solve for *a*. If we subtract 10 from both sides of the equation, we get $a^2 - a - 6 = 0$, which we can factor as $(a - 3)(a + 2) = 0$. The value of *a* could be 3 or –2, but since the question tells us that *a* is non-negative, the value of *x* must be 3.

38. $\frac{5}{9}$ **or .555 or .556**

When the problem asks for relationships between numbers (read: fractions, percents, ratios, probabilities) but does not give any actual numbers, we can plug in! Let's start with the large blue and large red marbles and work our way out: Say there are 2 large red marbles and 10 large blue marbles. That means there are 12 large marbles, so there must be 6 small marbles, giving us a total of 18 marbles. Therefore, the probability of picking a large blue marble out of the whole box is $\frac{10}{18}$. That will not fit in the grid, so we can reduce it to $\frac{5}{9}$ or divide it out to get .555 or .556.

Section 5

1. **B** *They* is an ambiguous pronoun—does it refer to the French, the friends, or the parents? (B) is the only answer that fixes the pronoun problem without changing the meaning of the sentence.

2. **A** The sentence is correct as written. It is a little awkward, but none of the answers improves the sentence.

3. **E** The *had* form of the verb suggests that Neil did these things before getting on the ski lift, so (A) is wrong. (B) contains a comma splice. (C) and (D) introduce parallelism errors. (E) is the correct choice.

4. **C** *Critically* is an adverb, but the sentence needs an adjective to modify *circling* and *underlining*. (Yes, they look like verbs, but they are the subjects of the second part of the sentence, so we treat them like nouns.) (A) and (B) are gone, then, and (E) adds way too many redundant words, so we can eliminate it, too. The first difference between (C) and (D) is *one* versus *you. One* stays in the same voice as the other subjects in the sentence, and *you* does not. (D) also has some extra words on the end, so it does not work anyway, and (C) is correct.

5. **D** The sentence has a misplaced modifier; Sam Spade is not a movie. (You do not have to be a film buff to know that—the sentence says that Sam Spade is a detective and the movie is *The Maltese Falcon*.) So (A) can be eliminated, and so can (E), which does not fix the misplaced modifier. (B) mentions that *The Maltese Falcon* is a movie twice, so it is redundant, and also the phrase "Sam Spade, detective" is awkward. (C) uses *where* to describe a thing, not a place. (D) fixes the misplaced modifier problem without adding new errors, so it is the best answer.

6. **A** The sentence is correct as written.

7. **B** The sentence has a redundant conjunction; *yet* is unnecessary because there is already an *although* at the beginning. So we can eliminate (A), as well as (D) and (E), which do not solve the problem. (B) and (C) say the same thing, but (B) is short and sweet while (C) is awkward and wordy, so (B) is correct.

8. **E** The pronoun *they* in the underlined portion is ambiguous—we do not know whether it refers to the chairpersons or the committees—so (A) is gone. (B) unnecessarily introduces *thereby*, and both (B) and (D) change the verb form, so we can eliminate them. (C) replaces *their* with *her*, which does not agree with the subject, *chairpersons*. Only (E) fixes the error without creating new ones.

9. **C** The verbs in the underlined portion are not parallel, so (A) can be eliminated. (B) and (D) do not fix the parallelism problem. (E) changes the meaning slightly, so (C) is our best answer.

10. **A** The sentence is correct as written.

11. **D** The word *actor* is singular, so *their character* is wrong; *his or her character* is correct. Eliminate (A) and (C). For the same reason, *as they wish* is wrong, so eliminate (B), and *as he or she wish* has an agreement error that you can spot without even referring back to the rest of the sentence, so eliminate (E). That leaves (D).

12. **C** *They* is an ambiguous pronoun; we do not know whether it refers to *Omar and his family* or *neighbors*. (B) repeats the problem. (D) fixes the ambiguity but is redundant, and (E) adds awkwardness by adding *being* unnecessarily.

13. **E** This one is easier than it might look. Who was known for graduating from college despite being blind and deaf? Helen Keller was: not *the fact*, not *accounts*, not *many people*, and not *six decades*. Eliminate (A), (B), (C), and (D). Only (E) fixes the error.

14. **B** Miles can be counted, so the comparison word *less* is incorrect; therefore, we can eliminate (A), (D), and (E). The *to be putting* in (C) is awkward, which typically happens when an *–ing* verb is added, so (B) is the best answer.

15. **E** The verb *has enlisted* is in present perfect tense, but the action happened in the past and does not continue to the present. Only (E) has the correct verb tense.

16. **E** (A) and (C) both have the verb *were*, which does not agree with the subject, *art*. (B) is passive, and (D) has the progressive tense *were practicing*, which changes the meaning. (E) is in active voice with no grammatical errors.

17. **D** There is a clear split between the answer choices, so we can use that to determine the first thing being tested. (A) and (B) have *regarded to be*, and (C), (D), and (E) have *regarded as*. Which idiom is correct? *Regarded as* is correct, so we can eliminate (A) and (B). Now we must look for differences in the remaining answer choices. (C) has the plural verb *are*, while (D) and (E) have the singular verb *is*. Since the subject is *the bristlecone pine*, *is* is correct, and we can eliminate (C). (E) adds an unnecessary *being*, making the answer choice awkward and wordy, so (D) is the best answer.

18. **C** The correct idiom here is *differs from*. The only choice with the correct form is (C).

19. **A** The sentence is correct as written.

20. **B** The sentence uses a comma to connect two independent clauses. We need a period, a semicolon, or a conjunction here, so we can eliminate (A). (C) improperly changes the tense. (D) is incorrect because we do not want a semicolon *and* a conjunction. (E) adds a *however*, but a semicolon is still needed. Only (B) joins the independent clauses correctly, with a semicolon.

21. **C** The verb *serving* is not parallel to *attempted*. *Served* would be correct.

22. **A** *A member* does not agree with *twins*. *Members* would be correct.

23. **E** The sentence is correct as written.

24. **D** *Unjust* is an adjective, yet it is modifying the verb *ignored*. The adverb *unjustly* would be correct.

25. **C** The verb *focus* is not parallel to *centering*. *Focusing* would be correct.

26. **B** The verb *spend* is in the wrong tense in the context of the sentence. *Spent,* which is in past tense, would be correct.

27. D   *Previous years* is being compared to *last quarter's financial reports*, creating an incorrect comparison. *Previous years' reports* or *those of previous years* would be correct.

28. B   The pronoun *you* is being used to replace *one*, which is in a different form. *One* would be correct.

29. C   *Insisted on* is an incorrect idiom. *Insisted that* would be correct.

30. A   *Were* is paired up with the singular pronoun *each*, but a singular verb is needed. *Was* would be correct.

31. A   The possessive pronoun *her* does not agree with the subject that it is replacing, *Karen and Mary*. *Their* would be correct.

32. D   *Critic toward* is an incorrect idiom. *Critic of* would be correct.

33. D   *That of* is being compared to *contributor*, which is an apples-and-oranges comparison. Leaving out *that of* entirely would be correct.

34. E   The sentence is correct as written.

35. E   The answer choice that provides the most clarity would be the one that identifies who *them* is. (E) is the only answer choice that does that.

36. B   (B) is the answer choice that is most relevant to the passage; all the other answer choices are too far out of scope.

37. C   (C) and (D) provide the best transition from sentence 3 with the addition of *for example,* but (D) and (A) have misplaced modifiers—are the children going to be placed on the walls? (E) is passive and (B) is very awkward. Therefore, (C) is the best answer.

38. E   Though most of (A) flows well with no errors, the answer choice has a missing verb at the end that makes it incorrect. (B) and (C) contain awkward transitions. (D) has the ambiguous pronoun *if.* Only (E) retains the meaning, has a good flow, and does not introduce new errors.

39. B   A good replacement for *This is* would agree with (and make clear) what is being referred to. (A), (C), and (D) do not do that. (E) introduces the redundant *as mentioned above,* so (B) is the best answer.

Chapter 14
Practice Test 2

SECTION 1
Time — 25 minutes
24 Questions

Directions: For each question in this section, select the best answer from among the choices given and fill in the corresponding circle on the answer sheet.

Each sentence below has one or two blanks, each blank indicating that something has been omitted. Beneath the sentence are five words or sets of words labeled A through E. Choose the word or set of words that, when inserted in the sentence, best fits the meaning of the sentence as a whole.

Example:

Desiring to ------- his taunting friends, Mitch gave them taffy in hopes it would keep their mouths shut.

(A) eliminate   (B) satisfy   (C) overcome
   (D) ridicule   (E) silence

1. Unlike her award-winning first book, Roberta's new volume can only be considered a ------- effort.

   (A) significant   (B) mediocre   (C) whimsical
       (D) feasible   (E) laudable

2. Most animals respond to ------- with excessive violence; in contrast, some remain ------- when facing serious physical danger.

   (A) kindness . . calm
   (B) peril . . aggressive
   (C) sympathy . . impassive
   (D) neutrality . . belligerent
   (E) threats . . placid

3. Unfortunately, many of Aristotle's works are ------ to us, since they were ------- along with the ancient library at Alexandria.

   (A) unknown . . promoted
   (B) lost . . destroyed
   (C) meaningless . . investigated
   (D) important . . chastised
   (E) clear . . suppressed

4. Engineers attribute the building's ------- during the earthquake, which destroyed more rigid structures, to the surprising ------- of its steel girders.

   (A) obliteration . . strength
   (B) damage . . weakness
   (C) survival . . inadequacy
   (D) endurance . . suppleness
   (E) devastation . . inflexibility

5. Prior to the discovery of one intact ancient burial site in Central America, it had been thought that all of the Mayan tombs had been ------- by thieves.

   (A) levitated   (B) exacerbated   (C) inculpated
       (D) delayed   (E) desecrated

6. Although the first viewers of *Waiting for Godot* jeered and called the play -------, later audiences came to recognize the ------- of the piece, and it soon became one of the classics of world theater.

   (A) abominable . . impenetrability
   (B) complicated . . fickleness
   (C) lenient . . unpleasantness
   (D) melancholy . . triteness
   (E) preposterous . . subtlety

7. In his later works, Langston Hughes's discussions of ethnic issues in America became increasingly -------, as he relied less on veiled criticism and more on direct confrontation.

   (A) concrete   (B) coherent   (C) forthright
       (D) confused   (E) delineated

8. Few would call the company president ------- ; in fact, he would often ------- the ideas of his subordinates, alleging that they were his own.

   (A) xenophobic . . exemplify
   (B) original . . expropriate
   (C) innovative . . inculcate
   (D) duplicitous . . arrogate
   (E) egregious . . steal

GO ON TO THE NEXT PAGE

The passages below are followed by questions based on their content; questions following a pair of related passages may also be based on the relationship between the paired passages. Answer the questions on the basis of what is <u>stated</u> or <u>implied</u> in the passage and in any introductory material that may be provided.

Questions 9-12 are based on the following passages.

Passage 1

Medicine as a discipline is focused on the concept of "complete benevolence": that is, the purpose of medicine is to heal patients. This idea has been espoused by doctors and other medical professionals since time immemorial. The
line
5   Hippocratic Oath—conceived by doctors in ancient Greece and still used today—reinforces this idea: according to the oath, the first job of a medical worker is to "do no harm" to the patient. Complete benevolence is the highest moral standard of science and should be the focus of every doctor's
10 practice and decision-making ability.

Passage 2

Patient care is a large part of medicine; this fact cannot be denied. However, medicine is a science, and as such its primary goal is a quest for knowledge. Without the use of human subjects in laboratory experiments, doctors would still
15 be using leeches to cure their patients. The use of humans as well as lab animals to further science has led to the development of vaccines, cures for common aliments, and the introduction of revolutionary drug therapies. Doctors are healers, but care for their patients should never interfere with
20 the process of scientific discovery.

9. The difference between the two passages' views on the purposes of medicine can best be described as the difference between an emphasis on

   (A) research on human subjects and research on animal subjects
   (B) subjective care and objective care
   (C) sympathy and practicality
   (D) patients' rights and doctors' rights
   (E) patient care and science

10. Which of the following would the author of Passage 1 most likely claim in response to the author of Passage 2's assertion that scientific discovery is paramount in medicine?

   (A) Scientific discovery is impossible without practical tests.
   (B) The Hippocratic Oath reveals medicine's value system.
   (C) More patients die under the care of surgeons than under family doctors.
   (D) Humans use scientific discovery to destroy life as well as preserve it.
   (E) Preliminary research often reaches inaccurate conclusions.

11. The author of Passage 1 refers to the Hippocratic Oath in order to

   (A) support the claim that patient care has been a primary concern of doctors for millennia
   (B) highlight changes in ancient Greek medicine and modern medicine
   (C) disprove the usefulness of modern laboratory experiments
   (D) allude to a higher standard of medicine than the one currently used
   (E) differentiate between medicine and research

12. On which of the following points would the authors of both passages most likely agree?

   (A) Patient care and scientific discovery are sometimes incompatible.
   (B) Patients are essential to the practice of medicine.
   (C) Patient care and research can coexist for the good of the patient.
   (D) Medicine is a science of discovery.
   (E) Medicine has always valued patients over everything else.

GO ON TO THE NEXT PAGE →

Questions 13-24 are based on the following passages.

The following passages both concern ecological conservation. Passage 1 discusses the Serengeti, one of the last remaining African nature preserves, while Passage 2 discusses a specific conservation study there.

Passage 1

There is no other plain in the world comparable to the Serengeti. Wild animals still graze in obscure corners of the African continent from Cape Town to Chad, but as civilization moves in, the animals are quickly crowded out; in Botswana, for example, the northwest corner was said to hold abundant game up until 1973, but now the diamond industry is preparing to drill wells for its mines and the Okavango Basin, which sustained the game, may be drained out. Every major civilization has eventually destroyed its wildlife, and civilization is fast overtaking Africa.

The Serengeti remains the great anachronism, its survival maintained through an odd, almost mystical series of countervailing conditions that have thus far managed to tip a fragile balance slightly to the side of the animals: population increases vs. drought and famine; cattle proliferation vs. pestilence and disease; land pressure for cultivation vs. tourist income; scientific research vs. the vagaries of nature.

The Serengeti's agonies are local and for the most part unrealized by the rest of the world; its importance as a cultural resource for the world community, however, is unchallenged. Scientists see it as a sort of an ecological paradise regained, however briefly, and not only for its importance as the last gathering place for the rich diversity of African wildlife but as well for the light it may shed on the larger question of man's survival.

"The Serengeti is basic to the concerns of conservation," says William Conway, director of the Bronx Zoo. "If animals can live there, so can man; if not, man cannot. It is the case of what is often referred to as the canary simile—the miners in Wales took canaries into the pits to serve as an early-warning system; when the foul air killed the canaries, the miners knew it was time to get out. There are practical aspects to all this. The production of the Salk vaccine required the destruction of 600,000 wild monkeys over a three-year period. Between the United States and Japan, science is currently using them up at the rate of 100,000 a year." Peter Jackson, director of information at the World Wildlife Fund, says, "All our domestic crops and animals have been bred from wild stock, and especially among plants it is the genetic resources available in the wild which have helped to produce new wild yields." Conway asks, "Do we save animals for themselves or for ourselves? Will man set aside for tomorrow something he can use today? It hasn't happened yet. Does man truly want wildlife on Earth, and is he willing to make the sacrifices necessary to keep it here?"

Passage 2

Of all his projects, John Owen's decision to establish a scientific observation in the midst of the Serengeti Plain was his most inspired. In 1961, the wildebeest appeared to be overgrazing the grasslands of the Serengeti. Owen felt he ought to find out if this was so; and if it was, what should be done about it. Soon, in characteristic fashion, he virtually backed the new government into the establishment of an observatory station.

In order to answer Owen's early question of whether the wildebeest were overgrazing the Serengeti, the scientists first had to establish the relationship of the wildebeest to their food supply. In 1958, the Michael Grzimek Laboratory had counted 99,000 wildebeest. In 1963, Lee and Martha Talbot counted 240,000. By 1969, there would be more than half a million. It appeared that, in fact, the wildebeest were not overgrazing the Serengeti; by the mid-1960s some of the reason for this would become clear. There was a severe drought in 1960-1961 that had since ended. However, although the grasses feeding the wildebeest within the park had become thick and healthy, the land surrounding the Serengeti, which fed cattle, was overgrazed. Inexplicably, as the cattle outside the park were starving, the wildebeest inside were flourishing.

The fact that the wildebeest population was increasing is significant. More important, however, is the fact that a principal regulating mechanism tended to keep their numbers below levels that would have damaged their habitat. In other words, even though the high rainfall throughout the 1960s produced more food for more animals, there were never too many animals for the grass that was there. Thus, the wildebeest population was regulated by a symmetrical relationship between the wildebeests' birth and death rates, the number of animals adjusted by the death rate—starvation as a form of control even in a time of abundance.

What had now become apparent to the scientists of the Research Institute was that the grasslands of the Serengeti formed a self-sustaining ecological system. Everything, they found, was interdependent—fire, rain, soil, grass, the host of animals. Each living thing depended on the other, each flourished because of the other. The Serengeti, with its extraordinary residents, was at a stage, still undisturbed, of an evolutionary process that had been going on for hundreds of thousands of years.

GO ON TO THE NEXT PAGE

13. Passage 1 implies which one of the following about the northwest corner of Botswana?

   (A) All of its wildlife will be destroyed through increasing encroachment by civilization.
   (B) After 1973, it was no longer home to as much wildlife as it had previously been.
   (C) Its problems are local concerns and have no effect on the world ecology.
   (D) The world must study its ecological destruction in order to prevent similar tragedies.
   (E) The Okavango Basin was drained to make room for diamond mines.

14. The author of Passage 1 believes that we should study the problems of the Serengeti plain because

   (A) many other regions of the world share similar concerns
   (B) of the disappearance of certain types of wildlife
   (C) the natural balance may be now tipping toward mankind
   (D) the results of this study may assist humanity in its quest for survival
   (E) of increasing development in the region

15. The author of Passage 1 quotes Conway (lines 26-36) in order to

   (A) point out the distinction between survival and conservation drawn in the previous paragraph
   (B) show why current conservation methods have failed to achieve the desired results
   (C) provide further support for the claim that conservation assists humans as well as animals
   (D) discuss conservation methods from earlier centuries
   (E) support the position that the Serengeti is no longer an interesting subject of study

16. The word "yields" (line 41) most nearly means

   (A) reservations
   (B) claims
   (C) output
   (D) traffic
   (E) difficulties

GO ON TO THE NEXT PAGE

17. The examples of the miners in Wales and the Salk vaccine (lines 29-34) provide support for which one of the following claims?

   (A) Animals may in some cases be able to help humans live longer and happier lives.
   (B) Wherever people can live, animals can live there also.
   (C) The natural competition between animals and humans in the wild is detrimental to humans.
   (D) Animals that cannot be tamed are of no use to humans.
   (E) Advances in medical science will be impossible without the continued use of animals for scientific experimentation.

18. The author of Passage 2 mentions that prior to John Owen

   (A) there had been no attempt made to study the Serengeti
   (B) the national government was reluctant to support any scientific research
   (C) there had been some investigation of the wildlife on the Serengeti
   (D) the Serengeti was a natural habitat virtually unknown to humans
   (E) other scientists had unsuccessfully attempted to enlist governmental support for their studies

19. The author of Passage 2 discusses the three studies that counted the number of wildebeest (lines 57-60) in order to

   (A) show that many scientists were working on the same problem of wildebeest populations
   (B) support the claim that the Serengeti was not being overgrazed
   (C) discuss the effects of a severe drought on animal populations
   (D) demonstrate the importance of cattle in the Serengeti ecosystem
   (E) show the dramatic climatic changes that occurred during the 1960s

20. The phrase "principal regulating mechanism" in line 71 refers to

   (A) the natural limit placed on population growth by the food supply
   (B) the way in which the wildebeest were harmful to the environment
   (C) the difference between wildlife on the Serengeti and wildlife just outside the Serengeti
   (D) the effect of humanity's attempts to control disease in wildlife
   (E) the interaction of different types of wildlife in the Serengeti

GO ON TO THE NEXT PAGE

21. According to the author of Passage 2, the primary conclusion of the Research Institute was that

(A) the wildebeest was an isolated and unique case of wildlife population growth

(B) humans were in danger of disturbing the ecological balance on the Serengeti

(C) the Serengeti was a good example of a breakdown in a natural food chain

(D) the Serengeti was a complex ecosystem with each member closely linked to the rest of the structure

(E) the evolution of life on the Serengeti was coming to an end

22. For which of the following claims made in Passage 1 does Passage 2 provide the strongest evidence?

(A) "Between the United States and Japan, science is currently using them [wild monkeys] up at the rate of 100,000 a year." (lines 35-36)

(B) "Scientists see it as sort of an ecological paradise regained . . . for the light it may shed on the larger question of man's survival." (lines 21-25)

(C) "Every major civilization has eventually destroyed its wildlife, and civilization is fast overtaking Africa." (lines 8-10)

(D) "'All our domestic crops and animals have been bred from wild stock . . .'" (lines 37-39)

(E) "The Serengeti remains the great anachronism, its survival maintained through an odd, almost mystical series of countervailing conditions that have thus far managed to tip a fragile balance slightly to the side of the animals." (lines 11-14)

23. The author of Passage 2 would most likely argue that if the Serengeti continues to develop according to recent trends, it will probably

(A) eventually no longer be able to support wildlife

(B) remain relatively stable for the foreseeable future

(C) push back against the encroachment of civilization and regain lost territory

(D) rapidly evolve new species of plants and animals that are better adapted to coexisting with civilization

(E) be destroyed by researchers

24. Both authors would agree that the success of the Serengeti in maintaining its ecosystem is due in part to

(A) a variety of different counterbalancing elements

(B) humanity's lack of interest in the development of the plain

(C) conservation efforts focusing on maintaining the fragile ecosystem

(D) the fear of animals that keeps most people away from the Serengeti

(E) the success of certain species in fully utilizing the abundant natural resources

STOP

**If you finish before time is called, you may check your work on this section only.
Do not turn to any other section in the test.**

SECTION 2
Time — 25 minutes
20 Questions

Directions: For this section, solve each problem and decide which is the best of the choices given. Fill in the corresponding circle on the answer sheet. You may use any available space for scratchwork.

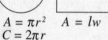

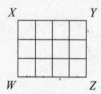

1. If each of the 12 small squares in the figure above has a side of length 2, what is the perimeter of rectangle *WXYZ* ?

(A) 28
(B) 32
(C) 36
(D) 46
(E) 56

2. If z is an even integer, which of the following must be an odd integer?

(A) $3z$
(B) $3z - 1$
(C) $2z$
(D) $2z - 2$
(E) $z + 2$

GO ON TO THE NEXT PAGE

3. If 16 feet of a 96-foot-tall tree are below ground, approximately what percent of the tree is above ground?

(A) 16.6%
(B) 20%
(C) 25%
(D) 33.3%
(E) 83.3%

4. The number of holiday cookies sold at a certain bakery in the month of December varies directly with the day of the month. If 24 holiday cookies are sold on the 4th day of December, how many holiday cookies are sold on the 20th day of December?

(A) 72
(B) 108
(C) 120
(D) 144
(E) 176

5. If $x = \dfrac{5n}{20}$, what is the value of n in terms of x ?

(A) $\dfrac{x}{40}$

(B) $4x$

(C) $40x$

(D) $100x$

(E) $200x$

6. If $f(x) = 4x^2 + 3x + 8$, then $f(x) - 4 =$

(A) $x^2 + 3x - 4$
(B) $x^2 - x - 8$
(C) $2x^2 + x + 8$
(D) $4x^2 - x + 4$
(E) $4x^2 + 3x + 4$

GO ON TO THE NEXT PAGE

7. Eighty students went on a class trip. If there were 14 more boys than girls on the trip, how many girls went on the trip?

   (A) 66
   (B) 47
   (C) 40
   (D) 33
   (E) 26

8. If the area of one face of a cube is 36, what is the volume of the cube?

   (A) 18
   (B) 36
   (C) 64
   (D) 72
   (E) 216

Bake Sale Results	
Item	**Number Sold**
Cupcakes	33
Cookies	68
Small cakes	w
Large cakes	z
Doughnuts	24

9. At a bake sale, a total of 260 items were sold, as shown in the table above. If four times as many small cakes as large cakes were sold, what is the value of z ?

   (A) 22
   (B) 27
   (C) 32
   (D) 39
   (E) 135

10. For which of the following lists is the average (arithmetic mean) less than the median?

   (A) 1, 2, 6, 7, 8
   (B) 2, 4, 6, 8, 11
   (C) 4, 4, 6, 8, 8
   (D) 4, 5, 6, 7, 8
   (E) 4, 5, 6, 11, 12

GO ON TO THE NEXT PAGE

11. During a sale, for every three shirts purchased at regular price, a customer can buy a fourth at 50% off. If the regular price of a shirt is $4.50, and a customer spent $31.50 on shirts, how many shirts did the customer purchase?

   (A) 5
   (B) 6
   (C) 7
   (D) 8
   (E) 9

12. If $\dfrac{x^2 - x - 12}{2x^2 - 10x + 8} = \dfrac{5}{2}$, what is the value of x ?

   (A) $\dfrac{1}{2}$

   (B) 2

   (C) $\dfrac{5}{2}$

   (D) 3

   (E) 5

13. If the value of x is at most 10 less than twice the amount by which z is greater than y, which of the following expresses x in terms of y and z ?

   (A) $x \le 2(z - y - 10)$
   (B) $x \le 2(z - y) - 10$
   (C) $x \le 10 - 2(z - y)$
   (D) $x \ge 10 - 2(z - y)$
   (E) $x \ge 2(z - y) - 10$

14. Which of the following is the product of two consecutive multiples of 3 ?

   (A) 240
   (B) 255
   (C) 270
   (D) 285
   (E) 300

GO ON TO THE NEXT PAGE

15. What are the coordinates of the midpoint of the line segment with endpoints (6, –3) and (6, 9) ?

(A) (3, 3)
(B) (3, 6)
(C) (6, 1)
(D) (6, 3)
(E) (6, 6)

16. The ratio of *a* to *b* is 4 : 7 and the ratio of *c* to *d* is 2 : 5. Which of the following is equivalent to the ratio of *bc* to *ad* ?

(A) $\dfrac{8}{35}$

(B) $\dfrac{7}{10}$

(C) $\dfrac{1}{2}$

(D) 2

(E) $4\dfrac{3}{8}$

17. A student took five tests. He scored an average (arithmetic mean) of 80 on the first three tests and an average of 90 on the other two. Which of the following must be true?

I. The student scored more than 85 on at least one test.
II. The average (arithmetic mean) score for all five tests is less than 85.
III. The student scored less than 80 on at least two tests.

(A) I only
(B) II only
(C) I and II
(D) II and III
(E) I and III

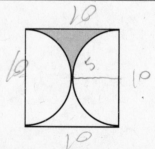

18. The figure above shows two semicircles inscribed in a square. If the square has a side of length 10, what is the area of the shaded region?

(A) $50 - 75\pi$

(B) $50 - 25\pi$

(C) $100 - 25\pi$

(D) $\dfrac{100 - 25\pi}{2}$

(E) $\dfrac{100 - 75\pi}{2}$

GO ON TO THE NEXT PAGE

19. If x is a positive integer such that $\dfrac{x}{4}$ is an odd integer and $\dfrac{x}{3}$ is an even integer, which of the following statements must be true?

    I. $\dfrac{x}{4} - \dfrac{x}{3}$ is odd.

    II. x is odd.

    III. $\left(\dfrac{x}{3}\right)^2$ is even.

(A) I only
(B) II only
(C) I and II
(D) I and III
(E) I, II, and III

20. A circle and a triangle have equal areas. If one base of the triangle has length 9, and the altitude to that base has length 8, what is the radius of the circle?

(A) 6

(B) 6π

(C) $\dfrac{6}{\sqrt{\pi}}$

(D) $\sqrt{72\pi}$

(E) 72

STOP

If you finish before time is called, you may check your work on this section only.
Do not turn to any other section in the test.

SECTION 3
Time — 25 minutes
24 Questions

Directions: For each question in this section, select the best answer from among the choices given and fill in the corresponding circle on the answer sheet.

Each sentence below has one or two blanks, each blank indicating that something has been omitted. Beneath the sentence are five words or sets of words labeled A through E. Choose the word or set of words that, when inserted in the sentence, best fits the meaning of the sentence as a whole.

Example:

Desiring to ------- his taunting friends, Mitch gave them taffy in hopes it would keep their mouths shut.

(A) eliminate   (B) satisfy   (C) overcome
   (D) ridicule   (E) silence

---

25. Though he is usually very ------- at such occasions, John was surprisingly quiet at his engagement party.

    (A) reserved   (B) outgoing   (C) successful
       (D) irreverent   (E) vague

26. Although a few critics loved Isabel's new play, it never achieved the ------- success necessary for a long run in the theaters.

    (A) intellectual   (B) eccentric   (C) persuasive
       (D) dignified   (E) popular

27. Despite their very ------- cultural and religious backgrounds, the leaders of the civil rights march were able to put their differences behind them and fight for a ------- goal.

    (A) diverse . . common
    (B) different . . poetic
    (C) similar . . joint
    (D) indifferent . . unified
    (E) incompatible . . remote

28. The ------- water made it extremely difficult for the divers to search for the sunken treasure, as they could see no more than a few feet in front of their faces.

    (A) transparent   (B) murky   (C) malodorous
       (D) turgid   (E) noxious

29. She was a very ------- student; she checked every reference in her papers and always used the correct form in her footnotes.

    (A) prodigious   (B) supercilious   (C) punctilious
       (D) acute   (E) inspirational

GO ON TO THE NEXT PAGE

The passages below are followed by questions based on their content; questions following a pair of related passages may also be based on the relationship between the paired passages. Answer the questions on the basis of what is <u>stated</u> or <u>implied</u> in the passage and in any introductory material that may be provided.

Questions 30-31 are based on the following passage.

Elizabeth Cady Stanton, along with her more famous colleague Susan B. Anthony, was one of the architects of the Women's Suffrage Movement. An avid diarist, she frequently recorded events in her journal. Of her historic first meeting with Miss Anthony in May 1851, she wrote these words: "How well I remember the day! . . . There she stood, with her good earnest face and genial smile, dressed in gray delaine, hat and all the same color, relieved with pale blue ribbons, the perfection of neatness and sobriety. I liked her thoroughly, and why I did not at once invite her home with me to dinner I do not know . . ."

30. Stanton writes "How well I remember the day!" primarily to emphasize

(A) the vividness with which she can recall this significant meeting
(B) the beauty of the fall afternoon in her small town
(C) the fact that Susan B. Anthony later claimed to have no recollection of their first meeting
(D) the excitement she felt in meeting a famous person like Susan B. Anthony
(E) the paramount importance this meeting had in furthering the suffrage movement

31. The author uses the word "relieved" in line 8 to mean

(A) pleased
(B) calmed
(C) contrasted
(D) replaced
(E) reassured

Questions 32-33 are based on the following passage.

Studies have shown that male scientists tend to formulate their most influential theories while they are still fairly young. Albert Einstein, for instance, published his breakthrough work on relativity at the tender age of 26. One recent theory explains this phenomenon by contending that young male scientists, like young criminals, are subconsciously motivated by the desire to attract a mate. Most male criminals commit crimes in their late twenties and early thirties; most male scientists make the greatest impact in their respective fields during the same period in their lives. After these scientists have found mates, according to this theory, their predilection for pursuing momentous scientific discoveries declines. In a similar vein, the severity and frequency of illegal activity among male criminals generally diminishes after they marry. Both types of men have already attained the ultimate goal: a spouse.

32. In line 11, "predilection" most nearly means

(A) natural curiosity
(B) strong dislike
(C) intellectual ability
(D) financial compensation
(E) underlying preference

33. The primary argument of the "recent theory" in line 4 is that

(A) young male scientists are essentially criminals
(B) the main goal of momentous scientific discoveries is for the scientist to attract a mate
(C) criminals commit crimes in their late twenties in order to attract a mate
(D) people should make great discoveries if they seek a mate
(E) the actions of one group of individuals are analogous to those of another in that the unconscious purpose of each is the same

GO ON TO THE NEXT PAGE

Questions 34-39 are based on the following passage.

The passage below is a short story written in 1982 that focuses on the reliability of an individual's perceptions of the outside world. The author investigates the psychology of several characters as they respond to a situation in their town.

One night a terrible screaming sounded through the city. It sounded so loudly and piercingly that there was not a soul who did not hear it. Yet when people turned to one another in
Line fear and were about to remark "Did you hear it, that terrible
5 screaming?" they changed their minds, thinking: "Perhaps it was my imagination, perhaps I have been working too hard or letting my thoughts get the upper hand" (one must never work too hard or be dominated by one's thoughts); "perhaps if I confess that I heard this terrible screaming others will label
10 me insane, I shall be hidden behind locked doors and sit for the remaining years of my life in a small corner, gazing at the senseless writing on the wall."

Therefore no one confessed to having heard the screaming. Work and play, love and death, continued as
15 usual. Yet the screaming persisted. It sounded day and night in the ears of the people of the city, yet all remained silent concerning it, and talked of other things. Until one day a stranger arrived from a foreign shore. As soon as he arrived in the city he gave a start of horror and exclaimed to the
20 Head of the Welcoming Committee, "What was that? Why, it has not yet ceased! What is it, that terrible screaming? How can you possibly live with it? Does it continue night and day? Oh, what sympathy I have for you in this otherwise fair untroubled city!"
25 The Head of the Welcoming Committee was at a loss. On the one hand the stranger was a Distinguished person whom it would be impolite to contradict; on the other hand, it would be equally unwise for the Head of the Welcoming Committee to acknowledge the terrible screaming. He decided to risk
30 being thought impolite.

"I hear nothing unusual," he said lightly, trying to suggest that perhaps his thoughts had been elsewhere, and at the same time trying to convey his undivided attention to the concern of the Distinguished Stranger. His task was difficult. The
35 packaging of words with varied intentions is like writing a letter to someone in a foreign land and addressing it to oneself; it never reaches its destination.

The Distinguished Stranger looked confused. "You hear no terrible screaming?"
40 The Head of the Welcoming Committee turned to his assistant. "Do you perhaps hear some unusual sound?"

The Assistant who had been disturbed by the screaming and had decided that very day to speak out, to refuse to ignore it, now became afraid that perhaps he would lose his job if he
45 mentioned it. He shook his head.

"I hear nothing unusual," he replied firmly.

The Distinguished Stranger looked embarrassed. "Perhaps it is my imagination," he said apologetically. "It is just as well that I have come for a holiday to your beautiful city. I have
50 been working very hard lately."

Then aware once again of the terrible screaming he covered his ears with his hands.

"I fear I am unwell," he said. "I apologize if I am unable to attend the banquet, in honor of my arrival."
55 "We understand completely," said the Head of the Welcoming Committee.

So there was no banquet. The Distinguished Stranger consulted a specialist who admitted him to a private rest home where he could recover from his disturbed state of mind
60 and the persistence in his ears of the terrible screaming.

The specialist finished examining the Distinguished Stranger. He washed his hands with a slab of hard soap, took off his white coat, and was preparing to go home to his wife when he thought suddenly, "Suppose the screaming does
65 exist?"

He dismissed the thought. The Rest Home was full, and the fees were high. He enjoyed the comforts of civilization. Yet supposing, just supposing, that all the patients united against him, that all the people of the city began to
70 acknowledge the terrible screaming? What would be the result? Would there be a complete panic? Was there really safety in numbers where ideas were concerned?

He stopped thinking about the terrible screaming. He climbed into his Jaguar and drove home.
75 The Head of the Welcoming Committee, disappointed because he could not attend another banquet, yet relieved because he would not be forced to justify another item of public expenditure, also went home to his wife. They dined on a boiled egg, bread and butter and a cup of tea, for they
80 both approved of simple living.

Then they went to the bedroom, switched out the light and enjoyed the illusion of uncomplicated dreams.

And outside in the city the terrible screaming continued its separate existence, unacknowledged. For you see its name
85 was silence. Silence had found its voice.

34. What is the purpose of the parenthetical statement in lines 7-8 ?

(A) It signals that the narrator disapproves of the informal tone of the people's thoughts.

(B) It offers advice directly to the reader of the story.

(C) It suggests that people tend to rationalize decisions that might be questionable.

(D) It indicates that the people in the story are suffering from schizophrenia.

(E) It emphasizes how surprising the people found the scream.

GO ON TO THE NEXT PAGE ⟶

35. With which of the following statements would the author most likely agree?

(A) Trust the perceptions of those around you rather than obsessing about your own ideas.

(B) It is important to fall in with the beliefs of others.

(C) Insanity always spreads most quickly at night.

(D) People should never agree with the sensory perceptions of those surrounding them.

(E) Sometimes people fear speaking out about even terrible events.

36. In line 19, "start" most nearly means

(A) sympathetic stare

(B) quick beginning

(C) sudden jump

(D) pleased surprise

(E) endless scream

37. It can be inferred from the passage that the author believes that the "packaging of words with varied intentions" (line 35)

(A) guarantees the reception of those words

(B) needs to be translated for those from other countries

(C) always conveys several different meanings according to the listener

(D) should be used by dignitaries dealing with foreign visitors

(E) is inherently unlikely to convey the ideas behind the words, regardless of what those ideas are

38. According to the passage, one reason the Rest Home specialist dismisses the thought that the screaming might exist is that

(A) the status quo affords him a lifestyle replete with material possessions

(B) acknowledging the screaming would certainly lead to complete panic

(C) if the screaming were real, the Rest Home would have to begin admitting more patients

(D) such a conclusion would go against his professional training

(E) he cannot accept that a foreigner such as the Distinguished Stranger might be right

39. This story can best be described as

(A) a fable about how fears of job security lead to cowardice

(B) an allegory that illustrates the pernicious effects of fear

(C) a metaphor for insanity

(D) a trivialization of the crippling effects of silence

(E) a symbol of the benefits of modernity

GO ON TO THE NEXT PAGE →

Questions 40-48 are based on the following passage.

Though slang may appear on the surface to be unworthy of serious study, Mario Pei in his 1954 book All About Language *offers an astute examination of the history of slang and its significance in modern society.*

Dialects are a matter of geography. Slang is nationwide. There are some who think that only poorer and less educated people use slang. This is not necessarily true. A little bit of
Line slang, in fact, is used by practically everybody. Slang is a
5 departure from standard, accepted language, but it may easily turn into standard language if it meets with enough favor. Or it may die out and leave little or no trace.

English is a language very rich in slang, but the mortality among slang words is very high. People who make up our
10 dictionaries usually admit slang expressions on probation. They are either placed in a separate section of the dictionary, or marked "colloquial" or "vulgar" or "slang." If they survive a certain number of years, the label is removed, and they are admitted on a basis of equality with other words. If they
15 disappear from use, they vanish also from the dictionaries.

In a many good cases, slang words and uses can be traced to one individual. Dizzy Dean, of baseball fame, is responsible for "goodasterous" as the opposite of "disastrous," and "slud" as the past of "slide." Walter Winchell started
20 the expression "making whoopee," and Shakespeare himself was the first to use, at least in writing, "beat it" and "not so hot." But far more often the creator of the slang expression is unknown.

Slang as we said before is nationwide. The expressions
25 we see would be understood pretty much anywhere in America. Dialect is local, as where sections of the Midwest use "mango" in the sense of "green pepper." Two other items that call for discussion are cant and jargon. Jargon is a form of speech current in a given class or profession and
30 hardly understood on the outside. Cant, the language of the underworld, is a variety of jargon. A French poet of the fifteenth century, François Villon, used in many of his poems a type of Paris underworld cant that cannot be understood today. American and British cant has been mysterious in the
35 past, but today large segments of it are known, having been spread by detective stories, and many of its expressions have become general slang and even regular language. "Sawbuck" for "$10" and "grand" for "$1,000" are generally understood and even used, though they are not the best language in the
40 world. Other cant expressions that have acquired a measure of respectability are "take the rap," "take for a ride," "throw the book at," "blow one's top," "frisk," and "gat." But there are many others not so well known, like "quizmaster" for "District Attorney."
45 There are jargons of the various professions and trades, even jargons of the sexes and age-levels. Bankers, lawyers, and doctors will talk among themselves in specialized languages that people on the outside have difficulty following. So do scientists, technicians, teachers, and scholars in every
50 field. But it is not only the intellectual professions that have

jargons; it is also the manual trades and occupations. From them, too, many words have come into the general language. Shipboard terminology is very extensive and complicated, as
55 you know if you have read stories about ships, particularly the old sailing vessels. When you speak of "knowing the ropes," "keeping on an even keel," "keeping a weather eye open," "giving plenty of leeway," you are using sailors' expressions that have become general. But there are many more such
60 expressions that have not entered the general language and that you have to look up in the dictionary if you want to understand all the details of a sea story.

There is a jargon for the military, railroad workers, rodeo people, truck drivers, and soda fountain attendants. In short,
65 there is no occupation that doesn't have its own special terminology that baffles outsiders. Though linguists might condemn the investigation of slang as unworthy of legitimate study, there is certainly the possibility that its widespread use might cause some of it to become part of the standard language sooner than they think.

40. In line 1, the phrase "Slang is nationwide" refers to the view that

(A) the use of slang is not restricted to a particular group of people
(B) slang is considered equivalent to standard English
(C) dictionary writers often accept slang on a trial basis
(D) the controversy over slang's popularity is not just a local problem, but also a national concern
(E) jargon is something that both professional and nonprofessional people have in common

41. In line 8, "rich" most nearly means

(A) wealthy
(B) abundant
(C) entertaining
(D) seasoned
(E) productive

GO ON TO THE NEXT PAGE →

42. In the third paragraph, the author refers to Dizzy Dean and Shakespeare in order to

   (A) present the reader with some of the more amusing examples of slang

   (B) show how slang became popular both in sports and literature

   (C) illustrate how both men shared similar phrases in their everyday speech

   (D) explain that slang can usually be traced back to a single person

   (E) offer examples of single individuals who were responsible for certain expressions

43. It can be inferred that "cant," as mentioned in line 30, was most popularly used by

   (A) criminals

   (B) French aristocracy

   (C) Midwestern farmers

   (D) bankers and doctors

   (E) the military

44. It can be inferred from the passage that François Villon provides an example of

   (A) how slang adds a unique quality to any piece of literature

   (B) why certain slang expressions seem to enter into standard, accepted language

   (C) how some expressions pass out of use over time

   (D) how slang can make the difference in a writer's career

   (E) why the French underworld during the fifteenth century was able to thrive for so long

45. The author describes certain examples of cant as "not the best language in the world" in lines 39-40 so as to

   (A) convey his opposition to the popular belief that cant has become one of the most accepted dialects

   (B) describe the overwhelming popularity that cant seems to possess

   (C) find a reason that cant is generally understood and even used

   (D) communicate that such speech is not universally regarded as proper

   (E) imply his distaste for the use of cant in society

46. In line 40, "measure" most nearly means

   (A) rhythm

   (B) meter

   (C) degree

   (D) melody

   (E) regulation

47. The author mentions "shipboard terminology" in line 53 in order to illustrate

   (A) that slang evolved within manual trades as well as intellectual fields

   (B) the intellectual background that inspired such general terms as "keeping on an even keel"

   (C) the complications that often followed sailors who worked on old sailing vessels

   (D) the distinction between complicated nautical terms and more general terms like "knowing the ropes"

   (E) the importance of understanding phrases like "keeping a weather eye open" in order to become an accomplished sailor

48. The author is primarily concerned with

   (A) defining the importance of jargon in intellectual professions

   (B) explaining the origins of slang and its different variations

   (C) tracing the history of slang

   (D) discussing how certain professions have been affected by the popularity of cant

   (E) describing the effect that a single individual can have on slang

STOP

If you finish before time is called, you may check your work on this section only.
Do not turn to any other section in the test.

SECTION 4
Time — 25 minutes
18 Questions

Directions: For this section, solve each problem and decide which is the best of the choices given. Fill in the corresponding circle on the answer sheet. You may use any available space for scratchwork.

Notes

1. The use of a calculator is permitted.

2. All numbers used are real numbers.

3. Figures that accompany problems in this test are intended to provide information useful in solving the problems. They are drawn as accurately as possible EXCEPT when it is stated in a specific problem that the figure is not drawn to scale. All figures lie in a plane unless other wise indicated.

4. Unless otherwise specified, the domain of any function f is assumed to be the set of all real numbers x for which $f(x)$ is a real number.

Reference Information

       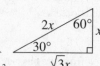

$A = \pi r^2$ $A = lw$ $A = \frac{1}{2}bh$ $V = lwh$ $V = \pi r^2 h$ $c^2 = a^2 + b^2$ Special Right Triangles

$C = 2\pi r$

The number of degrees of arc in a circle is 360.

The sum of the measures in degrees of the angles of a triangle is 180.

---

21. A certain computer downloads 4 files of equal size per second. How many files of the same size will it download in 2 <u>minutes</u>?

(A)   6
(B)   8
(C) 120
(D) 240
(E) 480

22. In $\triangle ABC$, $AB = BC = CA$. If $\triangle ABC$ is congruent to $\triangle DEF$ then what is the measure of $\angle D$?

(A) 180°
(B) 150°
(C) 120°
(D)   90°
(E)   60°

GO ON TO THE NEXT PAGE ⇒

23. Three roommates share their monthly rent payment in a ratio of $7 : 8 : 10$. If the monthly rent is $1,200, then what is the amount of the <u>greatest</u> share?

(A) $336
(B) $360
(C) $384
(D) $400
(E) $480

24. If $qs \neq 0$, then $\dfrac{2p}{q} - \dfrac{r}{2s} =$

(A) $\dfrac{4ps - qr}{2qs}$

(B) $\dfrac{2p - r}{2qs}$

(C) $-\dfrac{pr}{qs}$

(D) $\dfrac{2p - r}{q + 2s}$

(E) $\dfrac{2p - r}{q - 2s}$

25. If $abcd \neq 0$, $c = ab^{-2}$ and $d = a^{-1}b^4$, what is the value of cd in terms of a and b ?

(A) $\dfrac{1}{ab^8}$

(B) $a\sqrt[8]{b}$

(C) b^2

(D) $\left(\sqrt{a}\right)\left(\sqrt[5]{b}\right)$

(E) $\dfrac{a}{b}$

26. If $a = 9x^2 + 4$ and $b = 3x + 2$, what is a in terms of b ?

(A) $b^2 - 4b + 8$
(B) $b^2 - 4b + 4$
(C) b^2
(D) $9b^2 - 36b + 72$
(E) $9b^2 + 36b + 72$

GO ON TO THE NEXT PAGE

27. In a group of 15 integers, the probability of randomly

selecting an even number is $\frac{1}{3}$. Based on this information,

which of the following can be determined?

   I. The probability of selecting
      an odd number

  II. The probability of selecting
      a number that is not the
      mode

 III. The average (arithmetic
      mean) of the greatest and
      least numbers in the group

(A) None
(B) I only
(C) II only
(D) III only
(E) I and II only

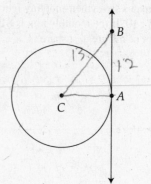

Note: Figure not drawn to scale.

28. In the figure above, the circle with center C is tangent
to $\overline{AB}$ at point A. If $AB = 12$ and the length of segment
$\overline{BC}$ (not drawn) is 13, what is the area of the circle with
center C ?

(A) 10π
(B) 25π
(C) 144π
(D) 169π
(E) 313π

GO ON TO THE NEXT PAGE

Directions for Student-Produced Response Questions

Each of the remaining 10 questions requires you to solve the problem and enter your answer by marking the ovals in the special grid, as shown in the examples below. You may use any available space for scratch work.

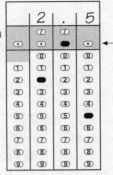

Answer: $\frac{7}{12}$

Write answer → in boxes.

← Fraction line

Grid in → result.

Answer: 2.5

← Decimal point

Note: You may start your answers in any column, space permitting. Columns not needed should be left blank.

- Mark no more than one circle in any column.

- Because the answer sheet will be machine-scored, **you will receive credit only if the circles are filled in correctly.**

- Although not required, it is suggested that you write your answer in the boxes at the top of the columns to help you fill in the circles accurately.

- Some problems may have more than one correct answer. In such cases, grid only one answer.

- No question has a negative answer.

- **Mixed numbers** such as $3\frac{1}{2}$ must be gridded as 3.5 or 7/2. (If [3 1 / 2] is gridded, it will be interpreted as $\frac{31}{2}$, not $3\frac{1}{2}$.)

- **Decimal Answers:** If you obtain a decimal answer with more digits than the grid can accommodate, it may be either rounded or truncated, but it must fill the entire grid. For example, if you obtain an answer such as 0.6666..., you should record your result as .666 or .667. **A less accurate value such as .66 or .67 will be scored as incorrect.**

Acceptable ways to grid $\frac{2}{3}$ are:

29. In the figure above, what is the value of $x + y$?

ℓ_1 — $y°$ $x°$

ℓ_2 — $41°$

$|| \ell_2$

30. If x is a negative integer and $|x| < 3$, what is one possible value of $|x|$?

GO ON TO THE NEXT PAGE ➡

31. Two numbers have the property that their sum is equal to their product. If one of these numbers is 4, what is the other number?

32. If $\frac{1}{2}a$, $\frac{1}{2}a$, and a are the degree measures of a triangle, what is the value of a ?

6, 8, 12, . . .

33. In the sequence above, the nth term can be expressed as $4 + 2^n$. What is the value of the 6th term?

34. What is the greatest of 4 consecutive integers whose sum is 414 ?

GO ON TO THE NEXT PAGE →

35. What is the area of a square with a diagonal of length $3\sqrt{2}$?

36. If n is a prime number greater than 3, then $6n$ has exactly how many positive integer divisors?

37. If $x + y = 5$ and $x^2 - y^2 = 16$, what is the value of $x - y$?

38. Sally, Abdul, and Juanita have volunteered to stuff a certain number of envelopes for a local charity. Working by herself, Sally could stuff all the envelopes in exactly 3 hours. Working by himself, Abdul could stuff all the envelopes in exactly 4 hours. Working by herself, Juanita could stuff all the envelopes in exactly 6 hours. If Sally, Abdul, and Juanita work together at these rates to stuff all the envelopes, what fraction of the envelopes will be stuffed by Juanita?

STOP
If you finish before time is called, you may check your work on this section only.
Do not turn to any other section in the test.

SECTION 5
Time — 30 minutes
39 Questions

Directions: For each question in this section, select the best answer from among the choices given and fill in the corresponding circle on the answer sheet.

The following sentences test correctness and effectiveness of expression. Part of each sentence or the entire sentence is underlined; beneath each sentence are five ways of phrasing the underlined material. Choice A repeats the original phrasing; the other four choices are different. If you think the original phrasing produces a better sentence than any of the alternatives, select choice A; if not, select one of the other choices.

In making your selection, follow the requirements of standard written English; that is, pay attention to grammar, choice of words, sentence construction, and punctuation. Your selection should result in the most effective sentence—clear and precise, without awkwardness or ambiguity.

EXAMPLE:

Bobby Flay baked his first cake <u>and he was thirteen years old then</u>.
(A) and he was thirteen years old then
(B) when he was thirteen
(C) at age thirteen years old
(D) upon the reaching of thirteen years
(E) at the time when he was thirteen

1. A large predatory snake, <u>the muscular body of a boa constrictor</u> can reach over 10 feet in length.

   (A) the muscular body of a boa constrictor
   (B) a boa constrictor whose muscular body
   (C) a boa constrictor's muscular body
   (D) the boa constrictor has a muscular body that
   (E) as well as having a muscular body, the boa constrictor

2. The audience's response was better than Martin could possibly have <u>expected, having received</u> a standing ovation and great cheers from the crowd.

   (A) expected, having received
   (B) expected; and so he was receiving
   (C) expected; he received
   (D) expected: including the reception of
   (E) expected, he was receiving

3. Watering your plant too often is as unhealthy <u>than if you do not water it</u> often enough.

   (A) than if you do not water it
   (B) as not watering it
   (C) as if one were not to water it
   (D) than not watering
   (E) as for not watering it

4. Not only did the ancient Egyptians know about the North Pole, <u>but they also knew in precisely which direction it lay</u>.

   (A) but they also knew in precisely which direction it lay
   (B) but they had also known in precisely which direction it lay
   (C) also knowing its precise direction
   (D) also precisely knowing its direction
   (E) but knowing its precise direction as well

5. <u>The Luna space probes were the first to enter solar orbit and photograph the far side of the moon, in 1959 they were launched.</u>

   (A) The Luna space probes were the first to enter solar orbit and photograph the far side of the moon, in 1959 they were launched.
   (B) Launched in 1959, the Luna space probes were the first to enter solar orbit and photograph the far side of the moon.
   (C) In 1959, the first solar orbit and photograph of the far side of the moon was taking place when the Luna space probes were launched.
   (D) The launching of the Luna space probes was in 1959, the solar orbit was entered and the far side of the moon was photographed.
   (E) The first solar orbit was when the Luna space probes were launched in 1959, and the first photograph of the far side of the moon was taken as well.

GO ON TO THE NEXT PAGE

6. Perhaps the best-known of all southern American writers, <u>William Faulkner's famous books include</u> *The Sound and the Fury* and *As I Lay Dying*.

   (A) William Faulkner's famous books include
   (B) William Faulkner's books are famous for including
   (C) William Faulkner has included among his famous books
   (D) William Faulkner is famous for such books as
   (E) William Faulkner is famous for including such books as

7. When the coach of the basketball team spoke, <u>new uniforms for all the players were implied, but it was not promised by him</u>.

   (A) new uniforms for all the players were implied, but it was not promised by him
   (B) new uniforms for all the players were implied, but he did not actually promise it
   (C) new uniforms for all the players were implied by him and not actually promised
   (D) he implied new uniforms for all the players, but they were not actually promised by him
   (E) he implied, but did not actually promise, that he would get new uniforms for all the players

8. When Michelle was younger, she was hired by a local furniture store to watch the store in the mornings <u>as well as cleaning the windows</u>.

   (A) as well as cleaning the windows
   (B) and she also cleaned the windows
   (C) as well as to clean the windows
   (D) the cleaning of windows also being done by her
   (E) together with cleaning the windows

9. Jason was nervous about the race he had to run, <u>this</u> nervousness gave him the energy to run even faster than he had expected.

   (A) this
   (B) furthermore
   (C) but this
   (D) for which
   (E) that

10. <u>The earliest design for a helicopter drawn by Leonardo da Vinci</u>, the Italian artist and inventor, more than four hundred years ago.

    (A) The earliest design for a helicopter drawn by Leonardo da Vinci
    (B) Among the earliest designs for a helicopter by Leonardo da Vinci
    (C) Leonardo da Vinci drew the earliest design for a helicopter
    (D) Leonardo da Vinci, creator of one of the earliest design for a helicopter
    (E) The earliest design for a helicopter was drawn by Leonardo da Vinci

GO ON TO THE NEXT PAGE

11. After reading Mary Shelley's masterpiece *Frankenstein*, I couldn't hardly believe that she was only nineteen when she wrote it.

(A) I couldn't hardly believe
(B) I could hardly not believe
(C) I could not hardly believe
(D) I could hardly believe
(E) I could hardly be believing

12. Both Caleb and Joy seem like they are intending to become doctors.

(A) like they are intending to become doctors
(B) like they are intending to become a doctor
(C) to be intending to become doctors
(D) to be intending on becoming doctors
(E) like their intent is of becoming a doctor

13. Hydrogen in combination with oxygen forms the molecule we call water.

(A) in combination with oxygen
(B) in its combining with oxygen
(C) in the combination of it and oxygen
(D) having combined itself with oxygen
(E) with oxygen in combination

14. Neither a broken leg nor an upset stomach has prevented Jason to play the flute in this year's concert.

(A) has prevented Jason to play
(B) have stopped Jason playing
(C) have prevented Jason from playing
(D) has prevented Jason from playing
(E) have stopped Jason in his playing

15. Zora Neale Hurston, author of *Their Eyes Were Watching God*, is considered as one of the finest writers in the Harlem Renaissance.

(A) is considered as one of the finest writers in
(B) is considered one of the finest writers of
(C) is considered to be one of the finest writers among
(D) considered as one of the finest writers of
(E) is the consideration of one of the finest writers of

GO ON TO THE NEXT PAGE

16. Since Jonas Salk and Albert Sabin created protective vaccines, <u>Americans are no longer concerned with the spread of polio</u>.

    (A) Americans are no longer concerned with the spread of polio
    (B) Americans are no longer concerned with spreading polio
    (C) Americans have no longer been concerned about the spread of polio
    (D) Americans are no longer concerned about the spreading polio
    (E) Americans are no longer concerned in the spreading of polio

17. The Brothers Grimm collected, <u>wrote, and published a book of fairy tales, they also wrote the first comprehensive German dictionary</u>.

    (A) wrote, and published a book of fairy tales, they also wrote the first comprehensive German dictionary
    (B) wrote, and published a book of fairy tales; but were also writing the first comprehensive German dictionary
    (C) wrote, and published both a book of fairy tales and the first comprehensive German dictionary
    (D) wrote and published a book of fairy tales; and the first comprehensive German dictionary
    (E) wrote and published a book of fairy tales, they were also writing the first comprehensive German dictionary

18. The age-old practice of <u>extracting syrup from maple trees provides a natural source of sugar that has been done for many years</u>.

    (A) extracting syrup from maple trees provides a natural source of sugar that has been done for many years
    (B) extracting syrup from maple trees provides a natural source of sugar, and it has been done for many years throughout history
    (C) extracting syrup from maple trees provides a natural source of sugar
    (D) extracting syrup from maple trees, providing a natural source of sugar
    (E) extracting syrup from maple trees providing a natural source of sugar has been done over time for many years

19. <u>If all citizens would take a more proactive stance on environmental issues,</u> Americans could look forward to a future of cleaner air and water.

    (A) If all citizens would take a more proactive stance on environmental issues,
    (B) Were all citizens to take a more proactive stance on environmental issues,
    (C) Were all citizens taking a more proactive stance on environmental issues,
    (D) If all citizens would be taking a more proactive stance on environmental issues,
    (E) If all citizens would have taken a more proactive stance on environmental issues,

20. Children attending Camp Northwoods need to <u>bring a stamp for the letters they will write home to their parents</u>.

    (A) bring a stamp for the letters they will write home to their parents
    (B) bring a stamp for the letters he or she will write home to their parents
    (C) bring stamps for the letters he or she will write home to their parents
    (D) bring stamps for the letter they will write home to their parents
    (E) bring stamps for the letters they will write home to their parents

GO ON TO THE NEXT PAGE

The following sentences test your ability to recognize grammar and usage errors. Each sentence contains either a single error or no error at all. No sentence contains more than one error. The error, if there is one, is underlined and lettered. If the sentence contains an error, select the one underlined part that must be changed to make the sentence correct. If the sentence is correct, select choice E. In choosing answers, follow the requirements of standard written English.

EXAMPLE:

The other players and her significantly improved
    A   B   C

the game plan created by the coaches. No error
            D   E

Ⓐ ● Ⓒ Ⓓ Ⓔ

21. The actors were exhausted , but each was able to
          A   B

remember all the complicated lines on opening night .
       C   D

No error
  E

22. Mary Anne was indebted with her mother for all the
                     A   B

hard work her mother had done in preparation for the
          C   D

party. No error
       E

23. One way to determine the accuracy of reference books
         A

is to check the credentials of its editorial board .
B C   D

No error
  E

24. It is more convenient to reply to email at one's own
       A   B   C

convenience than answering the phone every time it
              D

rings. No error
       E

25. The works of Stephen King are similar to Peter Straub ,
                   A   B

a fact that is not surprising since the two men are friends
                  C

and have even collaborated on two novels. No error
    D   E

26. In flight, a flock of geese encounters scarcely no wind
                 A   B

resistance because of the "v" formation it employs.
       C   D

No error
  E

27. Vital to any analysis of the causes of the Russian
              A

Revolution are an understanding of the many alliances
        B   C

between political parties in the early 1900s. No error
      D   E

GO ON TO THE NEXT PAGE →

28. Many of the players were professionals who , in prior
      A   B   C

    years, had received gold medals. No error
                  D   E

29. A recent conducted poll shows that people are littering
         A   B

    less frequently, a development that reflects a great
                                          C

    change in the public's attitude toward the environment.
                                         D

    No error
      E

30. Neither the giant alligator   or the tiny lizard
                     A   B

    is the cause of Joey's nightmares. No error
          C   D   E

31. Marjorie, the newest of the two violinists who
                      A

    have recently joined the symphony, has excellent tone
          B   C

    and a marvelous command of her instrument. No error
                                D   E

32. The more you read the early works of Michel Tournier,
        A   B

    the more the books begin to provoke an emotional
       C   D

    reaction. No error
                  E

33. Although they are widely used, standardized test scores
                A

    are not a reliant indicator of a student's academic
     B   C   D

    potential. No error
                   E

34. Since 1960, less than three graduates from our school
                   A   B

    have won the Rhodes Scholarship. No error
     C   D   E

GO ON TO THE NEXT PAGE →

Directions: The following passage is an early draft of an essay. Some parts of the passage need to be rewritten.

Read the passage and select the best answers for the questions that follow. Some questions are about particular sentences or parts of sentences and ask you to improve sentence structure or word choice. Other questions ask you to consider organization and development. In choosing answers, follow the requirements of standard written English.

Questions 35-39 are based on the following passage.

(1) I used to have an irrational fear of bees. (2) Anytime I heard a buzzing sound, my heart would start to beat faster and faster. (3) Sometimes breathing was hard.

(4) I've always loved working in my garden. (5) But once spring came around, all the bees came out. (6) I was terrified of going outside. (7) My garden began to wither away. (8) Finally, I decided to do something about it. (9) I called up my friend Anne. (10) Her uncle happens to be a beekeeper. (11) I wanted to ask if I could meet him. (12) Anne's uncle agreed to take me to his hives the next day. (13) From the second I woke up that day, I was petrified, but luckily, Anne's uncle was very understanding. (14) He suited me up in beekeeping gear so that I couldn't get stung, and then he showed me his bee hives.

(15) To my surprise, I found myself fascinated by them. (16) Anne's uncle described how they are organized in castes, how they act as pollinators, and how they make honey. (17) I was so interested by what he said that I went to the library that very night and researched bees for hours. (18) And now—now I can't keep away from bees. (19) Each morning, I have visited Anne's uncle, helping out with the hives, while in the afternoon, I devote my time to my garden surrounded by bees.

35. Which of the following sentences, if added after sentence 3, would best link the first paragraph with the rest of the essay?

(A) It seems that I have had this fear of bees for an eternity.
(B) There were even times that I couldn't move my body, so intense was my fear of bees.
(C) Unfortunately, I couldn't ignore my fear of bees, because I have a garden.
(D) Usually, gardening is a pleasurable experience.
(E) I try not to be afraid of bees, but in my garden it's impossible.

36. Which of the following is the best way to revise and combine sentences 6 and 7 (reproduced below)?

I was terrified of going outside. My garden began to wither away.

(A) Being terrified of going outside, my garden began to wither away.
(B) Though going outside terrified me, my garden began to wither away.
(C) Since going outside did terrify me, it was then my garden began to wither away.
(D) Going outside terrified me, so my garden began to wither away.
(E) My garden, withering away, as I was terrified of going outside.

37. The phrase "to do something about it" in sentence 8 can best be made more specific by being rewritten as which of the following?

(A) to make my garden grow again
(B) to learn more about bees
(C) to get in touch with a beekeeper
(D) to combat my fear of bees
(E) to reconsider my feelings

38. Which of the following versions of sentence 15 (reproduced below) is most effective?

To my surprise, I found myself fascinated by them.

(A) (As it is now)
(B) To my surprise, I found myself fascinated by it.
(C) To my surprise, they have been very fascinating to me.
(D) To my surprise, I found myself fascinated by the bees.
(E) Fascination was surprisingly found by me in them.

39. In the context of the third paragraph, which of the following is the best version of the underlined portion of sentence 19 (reproduced below)?

Each morning, I have visited Anne's uncle helping out with the hives, while in the afternoon, I devote my time to my garden surrounded by bees.

(A) (as it is now)
(B) I visit Anne's uncle to help out
(C) having visited Anne's uncle and helping out
(D) visiting Anne's uncle to help out
(E) visiting Anne's uncle has helped out

STOP
If you finish before time is called, you may check your work on this section only.
Do not turn to any other section in the test.

NO TEST MATERIAL ON THIS PAGE.

PRACTICE TEST 2 ANSWERS

Section 1	Section 2	Section 3	Section 4	Section 5	
1. B	1. A	25. B	21. E	1. D	31. A
2. E	2. B	26. E	22. E	2. C	32. E
3. B	3. E	27. A	23. E	3. B	33. C
4. D	4. C	28. B	24. A	4. A	34. A
5. E	5. B	29. C	25. C	5. B	35. C
6. E	6. E	30. A	26. A	6. D	36. D
7. C	7. D	31. C	27. B	7. E	37. D
8. B	8. E	32. E	28. B	8. C	38. D
9. E	9. B	33. E	29. 139	9. C	39. B
10. B	10. A	34. C	30. 1 or 2	10. E	
11. A	11. D	35. E	31. $\frac{4}{3}$ or 1.33	11. D	
12. B	12. B	36. C		12. C	
13. B	13. B	37. E	32. 90	13. A	
14. D	14. C	38. A	33. 68	14. D	
15. C	15. D	39. B	34. 105	15. B	
16. C	16. B	40. A	35. 9	16. C	
17. A	17. C	41. B	36. 8	17. C	
18. C	18. D	42. E	37. $\frac{16}{5}$ or 3.2	18. C	
19. B	19. D	43. A		19. B	
20. A	20. C	44. C	38. $\frac{2}{9}$ or .222	20. E	
21. D		45. D		21. E	
22. E		46. C		22. A	
23. B		47. A		23. D	
24. A		48. B		24. D	
				25. B	
				26. B	
				27. B	
				28. E	
				29. A	
				30. B	

You will find a detailed explanation for each question beginning on page 375.

SCORING YOUR PRACTICE PSAT

Critical Reading

After you have checked your answers against the answer key, you can calculate your score. For the two Critical Reading sections (Sections 1 and 3), add up the number of correct answers and the number of incorrect answers. Enter these numbers on the worksheet on the next page. Multiply the number of incorrect answers by .25, and subtract this result from the number of correct answers. Then round this to the nearest whole number to get your Critical Reading "raw score." Next, use the conversion table to convert your raw score to a scaled score.

Math

Calculating your Math score is a bit trickier, because some of the questions have five answer choices (for these, the incorrect answer deduction is .25), and some are Grid-Ins (which have no deduction for incorrect answers).

First, check your answers to all of the problem-solving questions on Sections 2 and 4. For Section 2 and questions 21–28 of Section 4, enter the number of correct answers and the number of incorrect answers into the worksheet on the next page. Multiply the number of incorrect answers by .25, and subtract this result from the number of correct answers. For questions 29–38 of Section 4, the Grid-In questions, simply enter the number of correct answers. Now, add up the totals for both types of math questions to give you your total Math raw score. Then you can use the conversion table to find your scaled score.

Writing Skills

The Writing Skills section should be scored just like the Critical Reading sections. Add up the number of correct answers and the number of incorrect answers from Section 5, and enter these numbers on the worksheet on the next page. Multiply the number of incorrect answers by .25 and subtract this result from the number of correct answers. Then round this to the nearest whole number. This is your Writing raw score. Next, use the conversion table to convert your raw scores to scaled scores.

WORKSHEET FOR CALCULATING YOUR SCORE

Critical Reading

	Correct	Incorrect

A. Sections 1 and 3 _____ – (.25 × _____) =

[A]

B. Total rounded Critical Reading raw score

[B]

Math

	Correct	Incorrect

C. Sections 2 and 4—Problem Solving _____ – (.25 × _____) =

[C]

D. Section 4—Grid-Ins _____ =

[D]

E. Total unrounded Math raw score (C + D)

[E]

F. Total rounded Math raw score

[F]

Writing Skills

	Correct	Incorrect

Section 5 _____ – (.25 × _____) =

Total rounded Writing Skills raw score

SCORE CONVERSION TABLE

Math Raw Score	Math Scaled Score	Critical Reading Raw Score	Critical Reading Scaled Score	Writing Skills Raw Score	Writing Skills Scaled Score
0	26	0	25	0	29
1	29	1	27	1	30
2	30	2	29	2	31
3	32	3	30	3	32
4	34	4	32	4	33
5	35	5	33	5	35
6	36	6	34	6	36
7	38	7	36	7	37
8	39	8	37	8	39
9	40	9	38	9	40
10	41	10	39	10	41
11	42	11	40	11	43
12	43	12	41	12	44
13	44	13	42	13	45
14	45	14	43	14	46
15	46	15	44	15	48
16	47	16	45	16	49
17	48	17	46	17	50
18	50	18	47	18	51
19	51	19	48	19	52
20	52	20	49	20	54
21	53	21	50	21	55
22	54	22	51	22	56
23	55	23	52	23	57
24	57	24	53	24	59
25	58	25	54	25	60
26	59	26	54	26	62
27	60	27	55	27	63
28	61	28	56	28	65
29	62	29	57	29	66
30	64	30	58	30	68
31	65	31	59	31	69
32	66	32	60	32	71
33	68	33	61	33	73
34	70	34	62	34	74
35	72	35	62	35	76
36	74	36	63	36	77
37	77	37	64	37	78
38	80	38	66	38	80
		39	67	39	80
		40	68		
		41	69		
		42	71		
		43	72		
		44	74		
		45	76		
		46	78		
		47	80		
		48	80		

Chapter 15
Practice Test 2:
Answers and
Explanations

Section 1

1. **B** Since Roberta's first book was award-winning but her second is unlike it, we could fill in the blank with a word that means not award-winning. Only (B) comes close.

2. **E** If we do the second blank first, the trigger *in contrast* tells us the blank will be opposite from our clue, *excessive violence*. So, *not violent* would be a good word to write down for the blank, and we can eliminate (B) and (D). Our clue for the first blank is *serious physical danger*, because that is what the animals we are comparing here are responding to. So a good word for the first blank would be *danger*. Out of (A), (C), and (E), the only one that fits is (E). Remember, do not waste your time checking the first word in (B) or (D) because we have already eliminated them!

3. **B** We do not have very specific clues for the individual blanks, so we can work on the relationship between the blanks. The word *since* tells us there is a cause-effect relationship between the first and second blanks, which will be a relationship of similarity. (We also know that the words will probably be negative because of the clue *unfortunately*, but we may not even need that information.) Only (B) has a relationship of similarity.

4. **D** We know that other structures were destroyed during the earthquake, so *survival* might be a good word for the first blank. That lets us eliminate (A), (B), and (E). Remember, even if we see our exact word in the answer choices, we still need to finish the process because our word could be paired with a word that does not fit in the other blank. If more rigid buildings were destroyed and the girders had a surprising quality, it is probably *flexibility*, the opposite of *rigidity*. That allows us to eliminate (C), and only (D) fits.

5. **E** The clue *intact* and the time trigger *prior* tell us to fill in the blank with an opposite word, such as *destroyed*. Only (E) means the same thing as *destroyed*. Remember, if you do not know what a word in the answer choices means, leave it! It could be correct.

6. **E** The clue *jeered* tells us that the first viewers did not like the play, so we could write down something like *terrible* for the first blank. That gets rid of (B), (C), and (D). The trigger word *although* tells us the sentence is going to change directions, and the clue *classics of world theater* also tells us that the second blank is going to be a positive word, so perhaps we could write down *quality* for the second blank. *Impenetrability* does not come close, so the correct answer is (E).

7. **C** The clue *relied more on direct confrontation* tells us that *confrontational* is a good replacement for the blank. (C) is the closest fit.

8. **B** Let's do the second blank first, since we have better clues for it. *Alleging that they were his own* tells us that a word like *steals* would be a good replacement for the blank. That gets rid of (A) and (C). Now we can look at the first blank. Because he steals ideas, few people would call the company president ethical or creative or anything positive. That eliminates (D) and (E), leaving us with (B).

9. **E** The first passage puts patients first; the second puts the quest for knowledge first. (E) is closest to that idea. (A) is incorrect because only Passage 2 deals with both animal and human lab subjects. (B) is wrong because subjective care is never mentioned. (C) is wrong because we are never told which approach is more practical. (D) is wrong because the conflict is between care and knowledge, not doctors and patients.

10. **B** The author of Passage 1 points to the Hippocratic Oath as a cornerstone of medical treatment. The other answers are not discussed in Passage 1.

11. **A** The author draws parallels between ancient and modern medicine to emphasize the importance of patient care in medicine. (B) and (D) are incorrect because the author does not mention a change in priorities or make a value judgment about modern medicine. (C) is never indicated by the passage and is extreme. (E) is not mentioned in the passage, so (A) is the only supported answer.

12. **B** Both passages mention the importance of patients in the practice of medicine. (A) is wrong because scientific discovery is not mentioned in Passage 1. (C) is out of scope. (D) is only the opinion of Passage 2. (E) is wrong because Passage 2 does not indicate the primacy of patient care.

13. **B** Here we are being asked to infer something about the northwestern corner of Botswana. The passage tells us in lines 5–6 that "the northwest corner was said to hold abundant game up until 1973." The author would not have added "until 1973" unless something had changed in 1973! This makes (B) the best choice. (A) is too extreme ("All of its wildlife will be destroyed"). (C) is also too extreme ("no effect") and wrong as well. (D) argues that the world "must" do something, which is almost never right. (E) says the basin "was drained" when the passage says only that it "may be drained" (lines 8–9).

14. **D** Why does the author of the first passage believe that we should study the Serengeti? The Serengeti is, according to the third paragraph, important because of the "light it may shed on... man's survival." (A), (B), and (E) are not supported by the passage, and (C) is the opposite of information stated in the passage. (D) is a nice paraphrase of the passage, making it the correct answer.

15. **C** This question is asking for the purpose of a quote. The quote shows how the animals' survival is linked to man's survival. (C) is the answer closest to this. (A), (B), (D), and (E) are not mentioned in the passage.

16. **C** This is a Vocab-in-Context question. The clue *produce* tells us we can replace yields with something like products, making (C) the best answer.

17. **A** Go back to lines 31–37 and read for context. The canaries are used to help save human lives, as are the wild monkeys used to create the Salk vaccine. (B) is reversing information stated in the passage. (C) and (D) are not supported by the passage, and (E) is extreme.

18. **C** Here we have a Lead Word question. We should find where the passage mentions John Owen and read before that. The author mentions that the wildebeest had appeared to be overgrazing and that they had been counted in 1958; therefore, there had been some prior study of them. That is what (C) says. (A) and (B) are extreme. (D) and (E) are unsupported by the passage.

19. **B** This is a line reference question. Go back to lines 57–60, read above and below, and think why the author discusses the three studies. The studies show that the wildebeest were not overgrazing, as their population was increasing. This is what (B) says. (A), (C), (D), and (E) are not supported by the passage.

20. **A** The "principal regulating mechanism" was the way in which the wildebeest population was naturally controlled through starvation, birth, and death. (B) is not supported by the passage, and (C), (D), and (E) are not even mentioned in the passage.

21. **D** What did the Research Institute conclude? According to the last paragraph, the Serengeti consists of a system of interdependent relationships. (D) is an excellent paraphrase of this. (A), (C), and (E) are not supported by the passage. (B), while it is a logical conclusion to make with outside information, is not mentioned in the passage.

22. **E** Passage 2 shows how the animals in the Serengeti have maintained their survival, supporting the claim made in (E). (A), (B), (C), and (D) are not affected by the information presented in Passage 2.

23. **B** The author of Passage 1 says that the Serengeti is self-regulating through a complex ecosystem. (A) is the opposite of this claim. (C), (D), and (E) are not supported by the passage. (B) is the best answer.

24. **A** Both authors recognize the system of interdependencies present in the Serengeti. (B), (C), (D), and (E) are not supported by both passages. (A) is.

Section 2

1. **A** We can see that the perimeter of this rectangle is made up of 14 segments—four sides each on top and bottom, and three each on the left and right sides. Each of these segments has length 2, so the whole perimeter will be 14 times 2, or 28.

2. **B** Let's try plugging in a number for z to solve this problem. What if we try making $z = 2$? (Remember that we have to obey the rule in the question, which says that z must be an even integer.) If $z = 2$, then (A) becomes 6, (B) becomes 5, (C) becomes 4, (D) becomes 2, and (E) becomes 4. Since the question asks which of the following must be an odd integer, we can eliminate any of the choices that are not odd integers. This means we get to eliminate (A), (C), (D), and (E). This leaves us only with (B), which must be our answer.

3. **E** If 16 feet of the tree are below ground, then the other 80 feet of the tree must be above ground. Thus, the fraction of the tree that is above ground is $\frac{80}{96}$. Now we can divide on the calculator to get .883 or 83.3 percent.

4. **C**   To solve a direct variation problem, set up a proportion. If 24 cookies are sold on the 4th of the month, finding the number sold on the 20th sets up as $\dfrac{\text{Day }4}{24 \text{ cookies}} = \dfrac{\text{Day }20}{x \text{ cookies}}$; cross-multiplying the proportion gives 120 cookies.

5. **B**   This question has the words "in terms of" and variables in the answer choices in it, so we know this is a good Plugging In problem. Let's try plugging in a nice easy number for n. If we make $n = 2$, then we can solve so that x must be equal to $\dfrac{1}{2}$. The question then asks for the value of n. According to the numbers we picked, $n = 2$. So we will write that number down and circle it—that is our target. Now whichever answer choice equals 2 (remembering that $x = \dfrac{1}{2}$) will be our answer. (A) is equal to $\dfrac{\frac{1}{2}}{40}$, which does not equal 2. (B) is equal to $4 \times \dfrac{1}{2}$, which *does* equal 2. We must check the other choices to be sure; (C) equals 20, (D) equals 50, and (E) equals 100, so (B) is correct.

6. **E**   This is a tricky question, designed more to test our ability to read and pay attention. The "minus 4" given here is outside the notation $f(x)$, indicating that the function $4x^2 + 3x + 8$ should simply have 4 subtracted from it, leaving $4x^2 + 3x + 4$. (This is very different from asking what $f(x - 4)$ would equal, which is an easy mistake to make if we are not reading carefully.)

7. **D**   This is a great Plugging In The Answers problem, but we can do some Ballparking first to narrow down the answer choices we have to work with. Since there are 80 students on the trip and there were more boys than girls, the number of girls has to be less than 40. That immediately eliminates (A), (B), and (C)! Now we can start with either of the remaining answer choices and PITA. Let's start with (D): If there are 33 girls, we can add 14 for a total of 47 boys. Does $33 + 47$ equal 80? Yes, so (D) is the correct answer.

8. **E**   This question is testing whether we understand how to calculate the volume of a cube. Remember that the volume of any object is equal to the base times the height times the depth. Since each of these is the same on a cube, we can just take any one side and cube it (or multiply it by itself, and then by itself again) to get the volume. But first we need to figure out the length of the sides. Since the area of a square face is 36, and the area of a square is equal to one side squared, we know that each side must measure 6. Therefore, the volume of the cube will be $6 \times 6 \times 6$, or 216.

9. **B**   Because this problem gives us actual amounts (no ratios, variables, etc.) in the answer choices, and it is structured to tempt us to write an equation, it is a great Plugging In The Answers problem. We will start with (C) and say that z equals 32. Then w would equal 4 times that, or 128. Add those numbers to the 125 items already in the chart (33 cupcakes + 68 cookies + 24 doughnuts), and we get 285. The problem said our total was 260, so (C) is too large—which means we can also eliminate (D) and (E). Moving on to (B), we get z equals 27, so w equals 108. Add 27 and 108 to the 125 items already in the chart, and we get 260—answer choice (B).

10. **A** For this problem, you must know the meaning of "median," which is the middle number in any group of numbers when they have been put in order. In this case, you will notice that the median of each group of numbers is 6. So the question is: Which group has an average that is less than 6? Of course, one way to solve this is to find the average of each group using your calculator. With a little test-taking logic, though, we can narrow down the choices. Choices (C) and (D) have numbers that are evenly spaced around the middle number (6), so you can probably tell at a glance that their averages will both be 6. Choices (B) and (E) have numbers to the right of 6 that are farther from 6 than the numbers on the left, so their averages will be greater than 6. Verify your work by finding the average of the numbers in choice (A)—it is the only one with an average less than 6.

11. **D** This is another great question for PITA—Plugging In The Answers. Let's start with (C). If a customer buys 7 shirts, then the total bill will be:

shirt 1	4.50
shirt 2	4.50
shirt 3	4.50
shirt 4 (50% off)	2.25
shirt 5	4.50
shirt 6	4.50
shirt 7	4.50
Total:	$29.25

This is a bit less than the $31.50 that we know the customer spent, so (C), (B), and (A) can be eliminated and we should try a larger number. Moving on to (D), for 8 shirts, the total would be:

shirt 1	4.50
shirt 2	4.50
shirt 3	4.50
shirt 4 (50% off)	2.25
shirt 5	4.50
shirt 6	4.50
shirt 7	4.50
shirt 8 (50% off)	2.25
Total:	$31.50

Our total is $31.50, so (D) is correct.

12. **B** We can factor the top and bottom of the expression to try to find something to cancel out. Starting with the top: $x^2 - x - 12 = (x - 4)(x + 3)$. Next, we factor the bottom: $2x^2 - 10x + 8 = 2(x^2 - 5x + 4) = 2(x - 4)(x - 1)$. So, the equation is now $\dfrac{(x-4)(x+3)}{2(x-4)(x-1)} = \dfrac{5}{2}$. The $(x - 4)$ cancels out of the top and

bottom. So, $\dfrac{(x+3)}{2(x-1)} = \dfrac{5}{2}$. Multiply both sides by 2, to get $\dfrac{(x+3)}{(x-1)} = 5$. Multiply both sides by $(x-1)$

to get $x + 3 = 5x - 5$. Subtract x from both sides and add 5 to both sides to get $8 = 4x$. Divide by 4 to

get $x = 2$.

13. **B** This could be done with Plugging In because there are variables in the answer choices, but translating English to Math is also a great way to go—do whatever works better for you. Let's try translating: *Is at most* means *the greatest value x could be*, which in math terms means ≤. So $x ≤$ something. Already, we can get rid of (D) and (E). *10 less* means we have to subtract 10. (A) and (B) look promising because they both have –10 in them. *The amount by which z is greater than y* means $z - y$, and twice that is $2(z - y)$. The –10 should be outside the parentheses, so the only answer that completely matches is (B).

14. **C** Instead of figuring out all the factors of each of the answer choices and looking for consecutive multiples of three, we can simply take consecutive multiples of 3 and multiply them until we get in the ballpark of the answer choices. 3 and 6 have a product of 18, which is way too small, so let's move up a bit. 12 and 15 have a product of 180, so that is closer, but still too small. 15 and 18 have a product of 270, which is answer choice (C).

15. **D** If the line segment is defined by points (6, –3) and (6, 9), we know that the *x*-coordinate (6) does not change. The line, therefore, goes from –3 to 9 vertically through 6 on the *x*-axis. This is a distance of 12 units, so halfway will be 6 units from each end. This places the midpoint at 3 on the vertical line. So, the final coordinates of the midpoint will be (6, 3). (We could also have made a quick sketch to help us visualize the problem.)

16. **B** If the ratio of *a* to *b* is 4 : 7 and the ratio of *c* to *d* is 2 : 5 then we can simply plug in the numbers 4 for *a*, 7 for *b*, 2 for *c*, and 5 for *d*. This makes the ratio of *bc* to *ad* equal to (7)(2) to (4)(5), which is a ratio of 14 : 20. This reduces to 7 : 10, which is answer choice (B).

17. **C** Notice the word *must* in the question? Let's plug in so that we can work with real numbers, and because the word *must* is in the problem, we can expect to plug in more than once. Because we want to use numbers that are easy to work with, let's use 78, 80, and 82 for the first three tests and 88 and 92 for the last two. That makes I true, II true, and III false. Since the question asks for what must be true, and we have seen an example in which III is false, we can eliminate any answer choice that contains III, such as (D) and (E).

18. **D** First, let's do some Ballparking. Since the square has a side of length 10, the area of the square is 100. The shaded region is pretty small in comparison—maybe about 10 or 12. Only (D) comes close to that approximation; (A), (B), and (E) are negative! (Remember, π is approximately 3.)

If we want to check our Ballparking with math, we would again start with 100 as the area of the square. Next, we will remove the area of the circle to get the size of the remaining area (which includes the shaded region, and the identically shaped area just below it). Since these are each semi-circles, together they will make one complete circle, with a radius of 5. (We know the radius is 5 because it is half of one side of the square.) This means that the area of the circle will be 25π. So once we remove the area of the circle, what is left is $100 - 25\pi$. Now the shaded region is only half of this, so we need to divide by 2, and the area of the shaded region will be $\dfrac{100 - 25\pi}{2}$.

19. **D**   We know from the *must* in this problem that we should be prepared to plug in more than once. The value of x has to be divisible by both 3 and 4, because $\dfrac{x}{4}$ and $\dfrac{x}{3}$ are both integers. So we can try 12 for x; 12 gives us an odd integer for $\dfrac{x}{4}$ and an even integer for $\dfrac{x}{3}$. Now we can look at the Roman numerals.

Roman numeral I is true, because $3 - 4$ is odd. In fact, since the problem tells us directly that $\dfrac{x}{4}$ is odd and $\dfrac{x}{3}$ is even, and an odd number minus an even number will always be odd, we can eliminate any answer choice that does not have I in it, namely (B).

Roman numeral II is not true this time, because 12 is not odd. So we can eliminate any remaining answer choices that have II in them: (C) and (E).

Now we just have to figure out if III *must* be true. It is true with the first number we plugged in, because $\left(\dfrac{12}{3}\right)^2 = 16$, which is even. In fact, since we know from the problem that $\dfrac{x}{3}$ is always even, the square of $\dfrac{x}{3}$ will always be even, so III is correct. That leaves us with only answer choice (D).

20. **C**   Let's start by finding the area of the triangle. We know that the triangle has a base of 9 and a height of 8, so its area will be $\dfrac{1}{2} \times 9 \times 8$, or 36. Now, we know that the triangle and the circle have equal areas, so the circle must also have area 36. To solve for the radius of the circle, remember the formula for the area of a circle, which is $a = \pi r^2$. We know the area is 36, so we know that $36 = \pi r^2$.

To solve for the radius r we first need to divide each side by π, which gives us $\dfrac{36}{\pi} = r^2$.

Now we take the square root of each side:

$$\sqrt{\dfrac{36}{\pi}} = r, \text{ so}$$

$$\dfrac{6}{\sqrt{\pi}} = r$$

This is answer choice (C).

Section 3

25. **B** The clue *quiet* and triggers *though* and *surprisingly* tell us that we need to fill in the blank with an opposite word of *quiet*, such as *talkative*. Answer choice (B) comes closest.

26. **E** The trigger *although* and clue *a few critics* indicate that Isabel needed something more than a few critics' support, so *broad* would be a good replacement for the blank. Only (E) fits that definition.

27. **A** The clue *differences* tells us that *different* would be a good word for the first blank, allowing us to eliminate (C) and (D). We need something opposite for the second blank, since they put their differences *behind them*, so *same* is a good word to write down for the second blank. That eliminates (B) and (E), so only (A) is left.

28. **B** Since the divers *could see no more than a few feet in front of their faces,* the water was *opaque* or even *not see-through.* (B) comes closest to our word.

29. **C** The clues are *checked every reference* and *always used the correct form,* so *careful* or *thorough* are good words for the blank. That allows us to eliminate all answer choices except (C).

30. **A** The quote emphasizes what a strong impression meeting Susan B. Anthony had on the author, and is supported by the author's ability to recollect the event in detail. (B), (C), and (E) are not even mentioned in the passage, and (D) is not supported.

31. **C** The pale blue ribbons would *stand out* against the gray clothes, making (C) the best answer.

32. **E** *Predilection* can be replaced with a word such as *tendency,* based on the context of the passage. The closest answer choice is (E).

33. **E** The theory says that both scientists and criminals are driven to achieve in their own fields by the prospect of attracting mates, which is best described by answer choice (E). (A) and (D) are not supported by the passage, and (B) and (C) state the theory incompletely. Furthermore, (B) is too strong in suggesting that finding a mate is the *main* goal of scientific discoveries.

34. **C** This question asks what role the parenthetical statement plays in the story. This means we have to read a few lines back and a few lines ahead to get a sense of the context. When we do this, we find that people are worried about the sudden screaming, but do not have the courage to be the first to bring it up. The parenthetical statement offers a scientific-sounding excuse for their inaction—otherwise known as a *rationalization*—and that makes (C) correct. (A) suggests that the narrator believes that everyone should think in the third person, which goes against common sense. (B) makes it sound as if the author actually believes the parenthetical statement is important advice, when the opposite is true: The quoted thoughts are actually being mocked here. (D) pulls a psychiatric diagnosis pretty much out of nowhere, and (E) is wrong because the passage did not say anything about the people being surprised.

35. **E** This question asks with which of five statements the author would agree. Of course, you cannot read the author's mind; the only thing you have to go by is the passage. Although there is no line reference, we are still early in the passage. In this case, we have a tale of a city that is haunted by a mysterious screaming that everyone is afraid to talk about. That makes the answer (E).

36. **C** This is a Vocab-in-Context question. It asks about the moment that the foreign visitor arrives in the city and hears the screaming for the first time. He gives a ------- of horror: a squeal? a jump? Something like that. (C) looks good. (B) does not mean squeal or jump and (D) does not fit, because he certainly was not pleased. (A) is too calm to be the stranger's reaction: a sympathetic stare of horror? And (E) is based on a misreading: The stranger is startled by the endless scream, not producing it.

37. **E** The line being asked about reads, "The packaging of words with varied intentions is like writing a letter to someone in a foreign land and addressing it to oneself; it never reaches its destination." That is, the message does not get through. That is what (E) says. (A) and (C) say exactly the opposite of the author's intended meaning. (B) is too literal; the stranger does not really need a translation, because he speaks the same language as the head of the welcoming committee. (D) can be tempting, because there is a foreign visitor in town, but the author does not mention dignitaries and is not advocating the "packing of words with varied intentions" either.

38. **A** Lines 66–67 answer this question for us: "He dismissed the thought. The Rest Home was full, and the fees were high. He enjoyed the comforts of civilization." If the Rest Home is full, and fees are high, then the specialist is making a lot of money. This is confirmed by the next sentence: The "comforts of civilization" are material luxuries—a nice house, a nice car, fine food, that sort of thing. (In line 74 we learn that he drives a Jaguar.) So (A) is clearly the answer, so long as we know that "replete with" means "full of." (B) is too strong, since line 71 indicates that panic is only a possibility. (C) would benefit the specialist, so that is no reason to dismiss the thought. (D) does not have any support in the passage, while (E) attributes to him a xenophobia, or fear of foreigners, which also has no support in the text.

39. **B** This question asks us to sum up the purpose of the whole passage. We have read enough of the passage to know that this is a story in which one night a city is suddenly filled with the sound of an endless, disembodied screaming. This is surreal enough that we can probably conclude that the screaming is symbolic. What does it symbolize? Whatever it stands for, knowing that the screaming is a metaphor for something means that we can eliminate (D), which is too literal and which also wrongly calls the story a "trivialization." We can also eliminate (C) and (E), since the story may *contain* many metaphors and symbols, but is not itself a metaphor for or symbol of anything. (A) is not completely right; while job security is mentioned (the assistant fears he will be fired), it is not the main theme. This leaves us with (B), which seems right: An allegory is a story based around an extended metaphor, as this one is.

40. **A** If we go back and read the lines immediately following the idea that slang is nationwide, we find what Pei means by this: "There are some who think that only poorer and less educated people use slang. This is not necessarily true. A little bit of slang, in fact, is used by practically everybody." That is, slang is used by everyone, both educated people and less educated people. Now we need to find a choice that is a close paraphrase of this idea, which is choice (A). Choice (E) is tempting, but the notion of jargon is not addressed until the fourth paragraph, so it cannot be the correct answer to a question about the first paragraph.

41. **B** To solve this Vocab-in-Context question, read the sentence and figure out what the meaning of the word should be from the context. In this case, we would probably put in a phrase like *has a lot*. The choice that comes closest to this in meaning is (B).

42. **E** This question not only gives us the lead words Dizzy Dean and Shakespeare, but also tells us where the answer will be found: in the third paragraph. So we should go back to that part of the passage and see what it says. The first line states that, "In a many good cases, slang words and uses can be traced to one individual." Shakespeare and Dizzy Dean are given as examples, so our answer should be a paraphrase of this line. Thus, (A), (B), and (C) can be eliminated. Be careful about (D), which has deceptive wording. Though the passage does say that slang can be traced to one person "in many good cases," the world "usually" is too strong. (E) is best.

43. **A** According to lines 30–31, the word *cant* was the "language of the underworld." This has to be our answer; now we need to find the choice that best paraphrases *underworld*, which is choice (A).

44. **C** We can use the lead words *François Villon* to find the place in the passage where the answer to this question will be found. François Villon is mentioned in the fourth paragraph, around lines 32–35. The passage states at that point that he "used in many of his poems a type of Paris underworld cant that cannot be understood today." Evidently, the passage cites him in order to show that some kinds of speech can no longer be understood in modern times. Now we must look for a choice that paraphrases this idea. Choice (C) says exactly this: that some kinds of speech are no longer current usage. None of the other choices have evidence to support them from this part of the passage.

45. **D** Let's go back to the lines in question and read what the author says at that point in the passage. He says that some examples of cant "are generally understood and even used, though they are not the best language in the world." So even if the expressions are not always appropriate, they are almost always understood. Now we need a paraphrase of that. (A), (B), and (C) find no support in the passage. (E) is too broad and a little too negative. (D) is a good paraphrase.

46. **C** Here is another Vocab-in-Context question. If we cover up the word *measure* and use context to put our own word in the blank, we would probably choose something like *a certain amount*. Choice (C) comes closest to this in meaning.

47.   **A**   We can go back to the passage, around the middle of the fifth paragraph, where these lines appear. The passage states, "But it is not only the intellectual professions that have jargons; it is also the manual trades and occupations," and then goes on to cite the example of shipboard terminology. This means that shipboard terminology is cited as an example of how jargon has evolved in manual trades and occupations, as well as in other places. Now we must find a choice that paraphrases this idea, which is what choice (A) does.

48.   **B**   According to the blurb, this passage is about the history and significance of slang. Already this should make (B) and (C) look like good choices, but let's see why the others can be eliminated. Choices (D) and (E) are too narrow—cant and important individuals are mentioned only in one paragraph each, so they could not be the main idea. Likewise, jargon is only discussed in one paragraph, so choice (A) can be eliminated. Now we are down to (B) and (C). This is a tough choice, but (C) is a little too broad—it is very difficult to do a complete history of slang in only a few paragraphs. But to discuss some of the origins and variations is more feasible, and this what the passage tries to do.

Section 4

21.   **E**   First we can convert minutes to seconds by setting up a proportion: $\dfrac{1\,\text{min}}{60\,\text{sec}}=\dfrac{2\,\text{min}}{x\,\text{sec}}$. Cross-multiply to find that 2 minutes is 120 seconds. Next, we can set up another proportion to find the number of files: $\dfrac{4\,\text{files}}{1\,\text{sec}}=\dfrac{z\,\text{files}}{120\,\text{sec}}$. Cross-multiply to find $z=480$.

22.   **E**   Draw triangle *ABC* with equal sides. If it is equilateral, that means all the angles are equal, too. Remember, congruent figures have the same shape and size, so draw triangle *DEF* to look the same as triangle *ABC*. Since all three angles in triangle *ABC* are equal and add up to 180 degrees, they must each be 60 degrees, as are all of the angles in triangle *DEF*.

23.   **E**   Make a ratio box. The sum of 7, 8, and 10 is 25, and $\dfrac{1{,}200}{25}=48$, so the multiplier is 48. The largest share is 10, and $10 \times 48 = 480$.

24.   **A**   Plugging in $p = 5$, $q = 2$, $r = 6$, and $s = 3$ turns the expression into $\dfrac{\cancel{2}(5)}{\cancel{2}}-\dfrac{6}{2(3)}=5-1=4$, our target number. Now we can plug in the same numbers for the variables in the answer choices, to see which equals 4. (A) equals 4, but we have to go through all of the answer choices to make sure only one of them equals our target. (B) equals $\dfrac{1}{3}$, so we can eliminate it. (C) is going to be negative, so we can eliminate it with Ballparking. (D) equals $\dfrac{1}{2}$, and (E) equals -1, so only (A) is equal to our target.

25. **C** Because we have variables in the answer choices, this is a Plugging In problem. The easiest variables to start with are a and b, because they are being used repeatedly and having so many things done to them. Let's plug in $a = 3$ and $b = 2$. Therefore, $c = 3 \times \dfrac{1}{4} = \dfrac{3}{4}$ (remember, negative exponents mean to take the reciprocal of the number being raised to an exponent) and $d = \dfrac{1}{3} \times 2^4 = \dfrac{16}{3}$. So $cd = \dfrac{3}{4} \times \dfrac{16}{3}$, or 4. Our target is 4, so now we need to go through all the answer choices and eliminate anything that does not equal 4. We can ballpark out (A), because it is going to be a fraction less than 1. (B) would also be way too small. (C) works, because $2^2 = 4$, but remember we have to keep going until the end. (D) is going to be way too small, and (E) is $\dfrac{3}{2}$, so only (C) equals our target. Alternatively, you can just say that $c = \dfrac{a}{b^2}$ and $d = \dfrac{b^4}{a}$, so $cd = \dfrac{a}{b^2} \times \dfrac{b^4}{a}$. Cross-cancel and you are left with b^2.

26. **A** Let's plug in our own numbers, starting with x. If $x = 2$, then $a = 9(2^2) + 4 = 40$ and $b = 3(2) + 2 = 8$. The question asks for the value of a, so 40 is our target. (A) equals 40, so we can keep it and work through the rest of the answer choices. We can ballpark (B) out because it is going to be 4 less than (A). (C) equals 64, so it is too large. (D) equals 360 and (E) is even larger, so (A) is the only answer that works.

27. **B** From the information provided we know that $\dfrac{1}{3}$ of the 15 integers are even. That means $\dfrac{2}{3}$ of the 15 integers are odd. To find a probability we need the relationship of number of things that meet the requirement to the total number of things. Therefore, Roman numeral I can be determined because the probability of selecting an odd number is $\dfrac{2}{3}$. Roman numeral II cannot be determined; we have no idea how many numbers in the group are not the mode. Roman numeral III cannot be determined because we do not know what the greatest and least numbers in the group are.

28. **B** First, we should draw in $\overline{BC}$ and $\overline{AC}$. A line tangent to a circle is perpendicular to the radius at the point of contact. So, $\overline{AB}$ is perpendicular to $\overline{AC}$, and ABC is a right triangle. If you do not recognize it as a 5-12-13 triangle, you could have used the Pythagorean theorem to find the third side: $AC^2 + 12^2 = 13^2$. So, $AC = 5$. That means the radius of the circle is 5. Plug that into Area $= \pi r^2 = \pi(5)^2 = 25\pi$.

29. **139** We do not actually have to know the individual values of x and y to solve this problem. We know that we have two parallel lines in this diagram, so we know that the angle opposite the angle measuring 41 degrees must also measure 41 degrees.

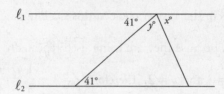

Therefore we have an angle of 41 degrees plus the angles marked x and y on the same line—which tells us that their sum must be 180. So we know that $41 + x + y = 180$ and that $x + y$ therefore must equal 139.

30.   **1 or 2**

x is a negative integer but $|x|$ is less than 3. So what values of x could satisfy that inequality? If $x = -1$, then $|x| = 1$ and that would work. If $x = -2$, then $|x| = 2$ and that would work. If $x = -3$ then $|x| = 3$ and that is not less than 3. Other negative values for x will have the same problem, so the only values of x that satisfy the inequlity are -1 and -2. However, we are looking for the value of $|x|$, and thus the answer is 1 or 2.

31. $\dfrac{4}{3}$ **or 1.33**

If the sum of 4 and some number (we can call it x) is equal to $4 + x = 4x$. Now we can solve for x:

$$4 + x = 4x$$

By subtracting x from each side we get:

$$4 = 3x$$
$$\text{so,} \quad \frac{4}{3} = x$$

That makes our answer $\dfrac{4}{3}$ or 1.33.

32. **90** We know that the angles in a triangle always add up to 180, so we know that $\dfrac{1}{2}a + \dfrac{1}{2}a + a = 180$. Now we can solve for a. If we add $\dfrac{1}{2}a + \dfrac{1}{2}a + a$, we get $2a$, so we know that $2a = 180$ and that $a = 90$.

33. **68** The question is really saying that the first term is $4 + 2^1 = 6$, the second term is $4 + 2^2 = 8$, etc. So, the 6th term is $4 + 2^6$. Let's apply PEMDAS and work with the exponent first: $4 + 2^6 = 4 + 64$. Then, we can add to get 68.

34. **105** The best way to try to find four consecutive integers whose sum is 414 is to start by finding the average: Each number is somewhere in the neighborhood of 103. So we can just start trying these numbers: 103 + 104 + 105 + 106 equals 418, which is too large. So let's try 102 + 103 + 104 + 105. That makes 414, so these are our four consecutive integers. The question asks for the greatest of them, so the answer is 105.

35. **9** Remember that an isosceles right triangle (which is the same as half of a square) with a side of x will have a hypotenuse of $x\sqrt{2}$. So to get a diagonal of $3\sqrt{2}$, the sides of the triangle (and therefore of the square) must be equal to 3. If the sides of the square are equal to 3, then its area will be equal to 3 times 3, or 9.

36. **8** We should be Plugging In on this problem. We need to choose a value for n that is a prime number greater then 3, so let's try using 5. The question then reads: How many divisors of 30 are there? The divisors of 30 are 1 and 30, 2 and 15, 3 and 10, 5 and 6, for a total of 8 divisors. For whichever values of n we try, we will always get the same answer.

37. $\dfrac{16}{5}$ **or 3.2**

   We know that $x^2 - y^2 = 16$, and since $x^2 - y^2$ can be written as $(x + y)(x - y)$, we know that $(x + y)(x - y) = 16$. The question also tells us that $(x + y) = 5(x - y) = 16$. The question then asks us for $(x - y)$, which we can now solve for: $\dfrac{16}{5}$, or 3.2.

38. $\dfrac{2}{9}$ **or .222**

   Since we do not know how many total envelopes there are to stuff, and therefore the question is asking for fractions of an unknown, this is a great Plugging In problem. Let's say there are 120 envelopes to stuff. (120 is a good number because 120 is divisible by 3, 4, and 6.) If Sally could stuff all the envelopes in 3 hours, she works at a rate of 40 envelopes per hour. Abdul can stuff all the envelopes in 4 hours, so he works at a rate of 30 envelopes per hour. Juanita would take 6 hours to stuff all the envelopes, so she works at a rate of 20 envelopes per hour. Therefore, the group can stuff envelopes at a rate of 90 per hour (40 + 30 + 20), since they do the whole job together. Juanita will stuff 20 of every 90 envelopes, or $\dfrac{2}{9}$. We can grid that in as is, or divide on a calculator to get .222.

Section 5

1. **D** Remember to watch out for misplaced modifiers when there is a phrase followed by a comma at the beginning of the sentence. In this case, *A large predatory snake* modifies *the muscular body*, which is incorrect. Only (B) and (D) put *boa constrictor* in front of the underlined portion, where it belongs, so we can eliminate the other answer choices. (B) does not make a complete sentence, though, so (D) is the best answer.

2. **C** Be very careful of verbs that end in *-ing* on the PSAT. They often indicate awkward constructions that should be avoided. "Having received" in this case is a good example of this type of problem. In addition to being awkward, it is also passive, so you can cross off (A). (B) and (D) add in a lot of unnecessary words. Remember, on Improving Sentences questions, you want simple, concise answers when possible. (E) simply splices two sentences together with a comma. (C) is concise and correctly uses a semicolon to separate the two clauses.

3. **B** The split between the answer choices shows that we need to make a decision between *than* and *as*. The correct idiom is *as...as* (e.g., "dancing is *as* fun *as* singing"), so we can eliminate (A) and (D). (C) changes the pronoun *you*, used in the underlined portion, to *one*, so it can be eliminated. (B) and (D) say the same thing, but (B) says it without adding redundant words, so it is the best choice.

4. **A** The sentence is correct as written.

5. **B** (A) and (D) try to splice two sentences together with a comma, so we can eliminate them. (C) has all the events of the sentence happening at the same time. Furthermore, it is passive, as is answer choice (E). (B) is the only answer choice that fixes the problem without adding new ones.

6. **D** As is typical when a sentence starts with a phrase followed by a comma, this sentence has a misplaced modifier. William Faulkner's books were not famous writers—William Faulkner was. So (A) and (B) are incorrect. (C) and (E) use the word *including* to make it sound like Faulkner was doing something, when in fact he was simply known for certain books. Only (D) is short and direct, so it is the best answer.

7. **E** The sentence is passive in two places: *were implied* and *not promised by him*. Only (E) fixes both errors.

8. **C** *Cleaning* is not parallel to the other verb in the sentence, *to watch*. Only (C) makes the verbs parallel.

9. **C** Here again we have two sentences spliced together with a comma, so the underlined portion needs a conjunction that better connects the two parts of the sentence. Since the second part goes in a different direction than the first part, the conjunction *but* is the best option, and (C) is correct.

10. **E** The underlined portion is missing a verb, and only (C) and (E) correct the problem. However, (C) puts *helicopter* before the modifying phrase, *the Italian artist and inventor*, which creates a misplaced modifier. (E) does not create a misplaced modifier, so it is the best choice.

11. **D** *Couldn't hardly* is a double negative, and only (D) and (E) correct the error. (D) is shorter and more direct, so it is the best answer.

12. **C** *Seem...to be* is the correct idiom, so we can eliminate (A), (B), and (E). *Intending to* is another idiom, so (C) is correct.

13. **A** The sentence is correct as written.

14. **D** *Prevented...to* is an incorrect idiom, so we can eliminate (A). The proper idiom is *prevented...from*. The remaining answer choices are split between *have* and *has,* so we need to decide whether a singular or plural verb is necessary. Subjects joined by *neither...nor* follow the same rule as subjects followed by *either...or;* if they are both singular, the subject is singular. So we need a singular verb, and only (D) fits the bill.

15. **B** *Considered* does not require either *as* or *to be* after it, so (A), (C), and (D) can be eliminated. (E) changes the meaning of the sentence, suggesting that Hurston herself was a consideration of some kind, so we can eliminate it. That leaves only (B).

16. **C** *Concerned about* is the correct idiom, so we can eliminate (A), (B), and (E). Choice (D) changes the meaning of the sentence, so (C) is correct.

17. **C** Here we have two sentences spliced together with a comma, so we can eliminate (A) and also (E), which repeats the error. (B) and (D) are incorrect because a semicolon must connect two independent clauses, which leaves only (C).

18. **C** The *natural source of sugar* is not something that can be done, as the sentence states. (A), (B), and (E) all have that error. (A), (B), and (E) are also redundant because the sentence already says that this is an age-old practice, making it unnecessary to also say that it has been done for many years. (D) creates a sentence fragment. (C) fixes the error without creating new ones.

19. **B** The word *would* does not belong in the "if" part of a sentence; if-clauses should use the word *were.* For example, "If I *were* rich, I would buy an expensive car," or "*Were* I to exercise more often, I could probably lose weight." So we can eliminate (A), (D), and (E). (C) is out because *taking* is not right. We are not talking about something that is happening right now. (B) is the best choice.

20. **E** As written, the sentence says that all the *children* are sharing one big *stamp.* This seems unlikely. They really ought to bring *stamps,* plural. That narrows it down to (D) and (E). (D) says that the children are writing one single letter. That needs to be *letters,* so (E) is the answer.

21. **E** The sentence is correct as written.

22. **A** The preposition *with* is not idiomatically correct when paired with *indebted. Indebted to* would be correct.

23. **D** The possessive pronoun *its* does not agree with the subject, *reference books. Their* would be correct.

24. **D** The verb *answering* is not parallel to the verb *to reply*. The correct form would be *to answer*.

25. **B** *Peter Straub* is being compared to *the works of Stephen King,* which creates an improper comparison. *To the works of Peter Straub, those of Peter Straub,* or *to Peter Straub's* would be correct.

26. **B** *Scarcely no* is a double negative. *Scarcely any* would be correct.

27. **B** The verb *are* is plural and is paired with a singular subject, *understanding. Is* would be correct. Be careful—sometimes a subject can come after the verb.

28. **E** The sentence is correct as written.

29. **A** The adjective *recent* is being used to modify the verb *conducted,* but an adverb should be used instead. *Recently* would be correct.

30. **B** *Or* is not correct when paired with *neither. Nor* would be correct.

31. **A** The adjective *newest* should only be used when comparing three or more things, and the sentence says that there are two violinists. *Newer* would be correct.

32. **E** The sentence is correct as written.

33. **C** *Reliant* is a diction error, as it means dependent. *Reliable* would be correct.

34. **A** The comparison *less* should only be used when the things being compared cannot be counted. Since Rhodes scholars can be counted, *fewer* would be correct.

35. **C** The first paragraph needs a sentence that connects the author's narrative about being afraid of bees to the fact that the author has a garden (that happens to be a good attractor of bees). (A) and (B) do not mention the garden. (D) does not mention the bees. (E) mentions both, but does not flow well into the second paragraph. (C) flows well from the first paragraph to the second.

36. **D** (A) creates a misplaced modifier, as it says the garden is terrified of going outside. (B) creates a change of direction between the two parts of the sentence, which is incorrect because the first sentence is the cause of the second sentence. (C) combines the sentences in a way that shows the causal relationship, but it is awkward. (E) is missing a verb and is constructed awkwardly. Only (D) is combined well.

37. **D** (D) best describes what the author does about the garden withering away, as is described in the rest of the passage.

38. **D** The pronoun *them* is ambiguous; it is not clear what it replaces. (B), (C), and (E) also contain ambiguous pronouns. Only (D) clearly states what the pronoun is replacing: the bees.

39. **B** Because the last part of the paragraph is set in the present, which is made clear in sentence 18, the clearest replacement for the underlined portion should be set in the present tense. Therefore, (B) is the best answer.

The Princeton Review

PSAT

UR NAME: _____
(Print)　　　Last　　　　　First　　　　M.I.

GNATURE: _____ DATE: ___/___/___

ME ADDRESS: _____
(rint)　　　　　　　Number and Street

City　　　State　　　Zip

E-MAIL: _____

ONE NO.: _____ SCHOOL: _____ CLASS OF: _____
(rint)

IMPORTANT: Please fill in these boxes exactly as shown on the back cover of your text book.

SCANTRON F-17982-PRP　P3　2803 628 5 4 3 2 1

© The Princeton Review, Inc.

5. YOUR NAME

First 4 letters of last name				FIRST INIT	MID INIT
Ⓐ	Ⓐ	Ⓐ	Ⓐ	Ⓐ	Ⓐ
Ⓑ	Ⓑ	Ⓑ	Ⓑ	Ⓑ	Ⓑ
Ⓒ	Ⓒ	Ⓒ	Ⓒ	Ⓒ	Ⓒ
Ⓓ	Ⓓ	Ⓓ	Ⓓ	Ⓓ	Ⓓ
Ⓔ	Ⓔ	Ⓔ	Ⓔ	Ⓔ	Ⓔ
Ⓕ	Ⓕ	Ⓕ	Ⓕ	Ⓕ	Ⓕ
Ⓖ	Ⓖ	Ⓖ	Ⓖ	Ⓖ	Ⓖ
Ⓗ	Ⓗ	Ⓗ	Ⓗ	Ⓗ	Ⓗ
Ⓘ	Ⓘ	Ⓘ	Ⓘ	Ⓘ	Ⓘ
Ⓙ	Ⓙ	Ⓙ	Ⓙ	Ⓙ	Ⓙ
Ⓚ	Ⓚ	Ⓚ	Ⓚ	Ⓚ	Ⓚ
Ⓛ	Ⓛ	Ⓛ	Ⓛ	Ⓛ	Ⓛ
Ⓜ	Ⓜ	Ⓜ	Ⓜ	Ⓜ	Ⓜ
Ⓝ	Ⓝ	Ⓝ	Ⓝ	Ⓝ	Ⓝ
Ⓞ	Ⓞ	Ⓞ	Ⓞ	Ⓞ	Ⓞ
Ⓟ	Ⓟ	Ⓟ	Ⓟ	Ⓟ	Ⓟ
Ⓠ	Ⓠ	Ⓠ	Ⓠ	Ⓠ	Ⓠ
Ⓡ	Ⓡ	Ⓡ	Ⓡ	Ⓡ	Ⓡ
Ⓢ	Ⓢ	Ⓢ	Ⓢ	Ⓢ	Ⓢ
Ⓣ	Ⓣ	Ⓣ	Ⓣ	Ⓣ	Ⓣ
Ⓤ	Ⓤ	Ⓤ	Ⓤ	Ⓤ	Ⓤ
Ⓥ	Ⓥ	Ⓥ	Ⓥ	Ⓥ	Ⓥ
Ⓦ	Ⓦ	Ⓦ	Ⓦ	Ⓦ	Ⓦ
Ⓧ	Ⓧ	Ⓧ	Ⓧ	Ⓧ	Ⓧ
Ⓨ	Ⓨ	Ⓨ	Ⓨ	Ⓨ	Ⓨ
Ⓩ	Ⓩ	Ⓩ	Ⓩ	Ⓩ	Ⓩ

TEST FORM

_____

DATE OF BIRTH

MONTH	DAY		YEAR	
○ JAN				
○ FEB				
○ MAR	⓪	⓪	⓪	⓪
○ APR	①	①	①	①
○ MAY	②	②	②	②
○ JUN	③	③	③	③
○ JUL		④	④	④
○ AUG		⑤	⑤	⑤
○ SEP		⑥	⑥	⑥
○ OCT		⑦	⑦	⑦
○ NOV		⑧	⑧	⑧
○ DEC		⑨	⑨	⑨

3. TEST CODE / 4. PHONE NUMBER

(bubble columns 0–9 for each digit)

7. SEX

○ MALE
○ FEMALE

8. OTHER

1 Ⓐ Ⓑ Ⓒ Ⓓ Ⓔ
2 Ⓐ Ⓑ Ⓒ Ⓓ Ⓔ
3 Ⓐ Ⓑ Ⓒ Ⓓ Ⓔ

1 READING

1 Ⓐ Ⓑ Ⓒ Ⓓ Ⓔ	8 Ⓐ Ⓑ Ⓒ Ⓓ Ⓔ	15 Ⓐ Ⓑ Ⓒ Ⓓ Ⓔ	22 Ⓐ Ⓑ Ⓒ Ⓓ Ⓔ
2 Ⓐ Ⓑ Ⓒ Ⓓ Ⓔ	9 Ⓐ Ⓑ Ⓒ Ⓓ Ⓔ	16 Ⓐ Ⓑ Ⓒ Ⓓ Ⓔ	23 Ⓐ Ⓑ Ⓒ Ⓓ Ⓔ
3 Ⓐ Ⓑ Ⓒ Ⓓ Ⓔ	10 Ⓐ Ⓑ Ⓒ Ⓓ Ⓔ	17 Ⓐ Ⓑ Ⓒ Ⓓ Ⓔ	24 Ⓐ Ⓑ Ⓒ Ⓓ Ⓔ
4 Ⓐ Ⓑ Ⓒ Ⓓ Ⓔ	11 Ⓐ Ⓑ Ⓒ Ⓓ Ⓔ	18 Ⓐ Ⓑ Ⓒ Ⓓ Ⓔ	
5 Ⓐ Ⓑ Ⓒ Ⓓ Ⓔ	12 Ⓐ Ⓑ Ⓒ Ⓓ Ⓔ	19 Ⓐ Ⓑ Ⓒ Ⓓ Ⓔ	
6 Ⓐ Ⓑ Ⓒ Ⓓ Ⓔ	13 Ⓐ Ⓑ Ⓒ Ⓓ Ⓔ	20 Ⓐ Ⓑ Ⓒ Ⓓ Ⓔ	
7 Ⓐ Ⓑ Ⓒ Ⓓ Ⓔ	14 Ⓐ Ⓑ Ⓒ Ⓓ Ⓔ	21 Ⓐ Ⓑ Ⓒ Ⓓ Ⓔ	

2 MATHEMATICS

1 Ⓐ Ⓑ Ⓒ Ⓓ Ⓔ	8 Ⓐ Ⓑ Ⓒ Ⓓ Ⓔ	15 Ⓐ Ⓑ Ⓒ Ⓓ Ⓔ
2 Ⓐ Ⓑ Ⓒ Ⓓ Ⓔ	9 Ⓐ Ⓑ Ⓒ Ⓓ Ⓔ	16 Ⓐ Ⓑ Ⓒ Ⓓ Ⓔ
3 Ⓐ Ⓑ Ⓒ Ⓓ Ⓔ	10 Ⓐ Ⓑ Ⓒ Ⓓ Ⓔ	17 Ⓐ Ⓑ Ⓒ Ⓓ Ⓔ
4 Ⓐ Ⓑ Ⓒ Ⓓ Ⓔ	11 Ⓐ Ⓑ Ⓒ Ⓓ Ⓔ	18 Ⓐ Ⓑ Ⓒ Ⓓ Ⓔ
5 Ⓐ Ⓑ Ⓒ Ⓓ Ⓔ	12 Ⓐ Ⓑ Ⓒ Ⓓ Ⓔ	19 Ⓐ Ⓑ Ⓒ Ⓓ Ⓔ
6 Ⓐ Ⓑ Ⓒ Ⓓ Ⓔ	13 Ⓐ Ⓑ Ⓒ Ⓓ Ⓔ	20 Ⓐ Ⓑ Ⓒ Ⓓ Ⓔ
7 Ⓐ Ⓑ Ⓒ Ⓓ Ⓔ	14 Ⓐ Ⓑ Ⓒ Ⓓ Ⓔ	

3 READING

25 Ⓐ Ⓑ Ⓒ Ⓓ Ⓔ	33 Ⓐ Ⓑ Ⓒ Ⓓ Ⓔ	41 Ⓐ Ⓑ Ⓒ Ⓓ Ⓔ
26 Ⓐ Ⓑ Ⓒ Ⓓ Ⓔ	34 Ⓐ Ⓑ Ⓒ Ⓓ Ⓔ	42 Ⓐ Ⓑ Ⓒ Ⓓ Ⓔ
27 Ⓐ Ⓑ Ⓒ Ⓓ Ⓔ	35 Ⓐ Ⓑ Ⓒ Ⓓ Ⓔ	43 Ⓐ Ⓑ Ⓒ Ⓓ Ⓔ
28 Ⓐ Ⓑ Ⓒ Ⓓ Ⓔ	36 Ⓐ Ⓑ Ⓒ Ⓓ Ⓔ	44 Ⓐ Ⓑ Ⓒ Ⓓ Ⓔ
29 Ⓐ Ⓑ Ⓒ Ⓓ Ⓔ	37 Ⓐ Ⓑ Ⓒ Ⓓ Ⓔ	45 Ⓐ Ⓑ Ⓒ Ⓓ Ⓔ
30 Ⓐ Ⓑ Ⓒ Ⓓ Ⓔ	38 Ⓐ Ⓑ Ⓒ Ⓓ Ⓔ	46 Ⓐ Ⓑ Ⓒ Ⓓ Ⓔ
31 Ⓐ Ⓑ Ⓒ Ⓓ Ⓔ	39 Ⓐ Ⓑ Ⓒ Ⓓ Ⓔ	47 Ⓐ Ⓑ Ⓒ Ⓓ Ⓔ
32 Ⓐ Ⓑ Ⓒ Ⓓ Ⓔ	40 Ⓐ Ⓑ Ⓒ Ⓓ Ⓔ	48 Ⓐ Ⓑ Ⓒ Ⓓ Ⓔ

The Princeton Review
PSAT

4 MATHEMATICS

21 Ⓐ Ⓑ Ⓒ Ⓓ Ⓔ
22 Ⓐ Ⓑ Ⓒ Ⓓ Ⓔ
23 Ⓐ Ⓑ Ⓒ Ⓓ Ⓔ
24 Ⓐ Ⓑ Ⓒ Ⓓ Ⓔ

25 Ⓐ Ⓑ Ⓒ Ⓓ Ⓔ
26 Ⓐ Ⓑ Ⓒ Ⓓ Ⓔ
27 Ⓐ Ⓑ Ⓒ Ⓓ Ⓔ
28 Ⓐ Ⓑ Ⓒ Ⓓ Ⓔ

ONLY ANSWERS ENTERED IN THE OVALS IN EACH GRID AREA WILL BE SCORED. YOU WILL NOT RECEIVE CREDIT FOR ANYTHING WRITTEN IN THE BOXES ABOVE THE OVALS.

29 | 30 | 31 | 32 | 33

(grid-in answer bubbles, digits 0–9 for each of the four columns)

34 | 35 | 36 | 37 | 38

(grid-in answer bubbles, digits 0–9 for each of the four columns)

5 WRITING SKILLS

1 Ⓐ Ⓑ Ⓒ Ⓓ Ⓔ
2 Ⓐ Ⓑ Ⓒ Ⓓ Ⓔ
3 Ⓐ Ⓑ Ⓒ Ⓓ Ⓔ
4 Ⓐ Ⓑ Ⓒ Ⓓ Ⓔ
5 Ⓐ Ⓑ Ⓒ Ⓓ Ⓔ
6 Ⓐ Ⓑ Ⓒ Ⓓ Ⓔ
7 Ⓐ Ⓑ Ⓒ Ⓓ Ⓔ
8 Ⓐ Ⓑ Ⓒ Ⓓ Ⓔ
9 Ⓐ Ⓑ Ⓒ Ⓓ Ⓔ
10 Ⓐ Ⓑ Ⓒ Ⓓ Ⓔ
11 Ⓐ Ⓑ Ⓒ Ⓓ Ⓔ
12 Ⓐ Ⓑ Ⓒ Ⓓ Ⓔ
13 Ⓐ Ⓑ Ⓒ Ⓓ Ⓔ

14 Ⓐ Ⓑ Ⓒ Ⓓ Ⓔ
15 Ⓐ Ⓑ Ⓒ Ⓓ Ⓔ
16 Ⓐ Ⓑ Ⓒ Ⓓ Ⓔ
17 Ⓐ Ⓑ Ⓒ Ⓓ Ⓔ
18 Ⓐ Ⓑ Ⓒ Ⓓ Ⓔ
19 Ⓐ Ⓑ Ⓒ Ⓓ Ⓔ
20 Ⓐ Ⓑ Ⓒ Ⓓ Ⓔ
21 Ⓐ Ⓑ Ⓒ Ⓓ Ⓔ
22 Ⓐ Ⓑ Ⓒ Ⓓ Ⓔ
23 Ⓐ Ⓑ Ⓒ Ⓓ Ⓔ
24 Ⓐ Ⓑ Ⓒ Ⓓ Ⓔ
25 Ⓐ Ⓑ Ⓒ Ⓓ Ⓔ
26 Ⓐ Ⓑ Ⓒ Ⓓ Ⓔ

27 Ⓐ Ⓑ Ⓒ Ⓓ Ⓔ
28 Ⓐ Ⓑ Ⓒ Ⓓ Ⓔ
29 Ⓐ Ⓑ Ⓒ Ⓓ Ⓔ
30 Ⓐ Ⓑ Ⓒ Ⓓ Ⓔ
31 Ⓐ Ⓑ Ⓒ Ⓓ Ⓔ
32 Ⓐ Ⓑ Ⓒ Ⓓ Ⓔ
33 Ⓐ Ⓑ Ⓒ Ⓓ Ⓔ
34 Ⓐ Ⓑ Ⓒ Ⓓ Ⓔ
35 Ⓐ Ⓑ Ⓒ Ⓓ Ⓔ
36 Ⓐ Ⓑ Ⓒ Ⓓ Ⓔ
37 Ⓐ Ⓑ Ⓒ Ⓓ Ⓔ
38 Ⓐ Ⓑ Ⓒ Ⓓ Ⓔ
39 Ⓐ Ⓑ Ⓒ Ⓓ Ⓔ

The Princeton Review®

PSAT

R NAME: _____
(nt) Last   First   M.I.

NATURE: _____ DATE: _____ / _____ / _____

ME ADDRESS: _____
(nt)   Number and Street

_____ E-MAIL: _____
ity   State   Zip

NE NO.: _____ SCHOOL: _____ CLASS OF: _____
(nt)

IMPORTANT: Please fill in these boxes exactly as shown on the back cover of your text book.

SCANTRON F-17982-PRP   P3 2803 628 5 4 3 2 1
© The Princeton Review, Inc.

5. YOUR NAME

First 4 letters of last name				FIRST INIT	MID INIT
Ⓐ	Ⓐ	Ⓐ	Ⓐ	Ⓐ	Ⓐ
Ⓑ	Ⓑ	Ⓑ	Ⓑ	Ⓑ	Ⓑ
Ⓒ	Ⓒ	Ⓒ	Ⓒ	Ⓒ	Ⓒ
Ⓓ	Ⓓ	Ⓓ	Ⓓ	Ⓓ	Ⓓ
Ⓔ	Ⓔ	Ⓔ	Ⓔ	Ⓔ	Ⓔ
Ⓕ	Ⓕ	Ⓕ	Ⓕ	Ⓕ	Ⓕ
Ⓖ	Ⓖ	Ⓖ	Ⓖ	Ⓖ	Ⓖ
Ⓗ	Ⓗ	Ⓗ	Ⓗ	Ⓗ	Ⓗ
Ⓘ	Ⓘ	Ⓘ	Ⓘ	Ⓘ	Ⓘ
Ⓙ	Ⓙ	Ⓙ	Ⓙ	Ⓙ	Ⓙ
Ⓚ	Ⓚ	Ⓚ	Ⓚ	Ⓚ	Ⓚ
Ⓛ	Ⓛ	Ⓛ	Ⓛ	Ⓛ	Ⓛ
Ⓜ	Ⓜ	Ⓜ	Ⓜ	Ⓜ	Ⓜ
Ⓝ	Ⓝ	Ⓝ	Ⓝ	Ⓝ	Ⓝ
Ⓞ	Ⓞ	Ⓞ	Ⓞ	Ⓞ	Ⓞ
Ⓟ	Ⓟ	Ⓟ	Ⓟ	Ⓟ	Ⓟ
Ⓠ	Ⓠ	Ⓠ	Ⓠ	Ⓠ	Ⓠ
Ⓡ	Ⓡ	Ⓡ	Ⓡ	Ⓡ	Ⓡ
Ⓢ	Ⓢ	Ⓢ	Ⓢ	Ⓢ	Ⓢ
Ⓣ	Ⓣ	Ⓣ	Ⓣ	Ⓣ	Ⓣ
Ⓤ	Ⓤ	Ⓤ	Ⓤ	Ⓤ	Ⓤ
Ⓥ	Ⓥ	Ⓥ	Ⓥ	Ⓥ	Ⓥ
Ⓦ	Ⓦ	Ⓦ	Ⓦ	Ⓦ	Ⓦ
Ⓧ	Ⓧ	Ⓧ	Ⓧ	Ⓧ	Ⓧ
Ⓨ	Ⓨ	Ⓨ	Ⓨ	Ⓨ	Ⓨ
Ⓩ	Ⓩ	Ⓩ	Ⓩ	Ⓩ	Ⓩ

TEST FORM

_____

DATE OF BIRTH

3. TEST CODE

⓪	⓪	⓪	⓪
①	①	①	①
②	②	②	②
③	③	③	③
④	④	④	④
⑤	⑤	⑤	⑤
⑥	⑥	⑥	⑥
⑦	⑦	⑦	⑦
⑧	⑧	⑧	⑧
⑨	⑨	⑨	⑨

4. PHONE NUMBER

⓪	⓪	⓪	⓪	⓪	⓪	⓪
①	①	①	①	①	①	①
②	②	②	②	②	②	②
③	③	③	③	③	③	③
④	④	④	④	④	④	④
⑤	⑤	⑤	⑤	⑤	⑤	⑤
⑥	⑥	⑥	⑥	⑥	⑥	⑥
⑦	⑦	⑦	⑦	⑦	⑦	⑦
⑧	⑧	⑧	⑧	⑧	⑧	⑧
⑨	⑨	⑨	⑨	⑨	⑨	⑨

DATE OF BIRTH

MONTH	DAY		YEAR	
⭘ JAN				
⭘ FEB				
⭘ MAR	⓪	⓪	⓪	⓪
⭘ APR	①	①	①	①
⭘ MAY	②	②	②	②
⭘ JUN	③	③	③	③
⭘ JUL		④	④	④
⭘ AUG		⑤	⑤	⑤
⭘ SEP		⑥	⑥	⑥
⭘ OCT		⑦	⑦	⑦
⭘ NOV		⑧	⑧	⑧
⭘ DEC		⑨	⑨	⑨

7. SEX

⭘ MALE
⭘ FEMALE

8. OTHER

1 Ⓐ Ⓑ Ⓒ Ⓓ Ⓔ
2 Ⓐ Ⓑ Ⓒ Ⓓ Ⓔ
3 Ⓐ Ⓑ Ⓒ Ⓓ Ⓔ

1 — READING

1 Ⓐ Ⓑ Ⓒ Ⓓ Ⓔ   8 Ⓐ Ⓑ Ⓒ Ⓓ Ⓔ   15 Ⓐ Ⓑ Ⓒ Ⓓ Ⓔ   22 Ⓐ Ⓑ Ⓒ Ⓓ Ⓔ
2 Ⓐ Ⓑ Ⓒ Ⓓ Ⓔ   9 Ⓐ Ⓑ Ⓒ Ⓓ Ⓔ   16 Ⓐ Ⓑ Ⓒ Ⓓ Ⓔ   23 Ⓐ Ⓑ Ⓒ Ⓓ Ⓔ
3 Ⓐ Ⓑ Ⓒ Ⓓ Ⓔ   10 Ⓐ Ⓑ Ⓒ Ⓓ Ⓔ   17 Ⓐ Ⓑ Ⓒ Ⓓ Ⓔ   24 Ⓐ Ⓑ Ⓒ Ⓓ Ⓔ
4 Ⓐ Ⓑ Ⓒ Ⓓ Ⓔ   11 Ⓐ Ⓑ Ⓒ Ⓓ Ⓔ   18 Ⓐ Ⓑ Ⓒ Ⓓ Ⓔ
5 Ⓐ Ⓑ Ⓒ Ⓓ Ⓔ   12 Ⓐ Ⓑ Ⓒ Ⓓ Ⓔ   19 Ⓐ Ⓑ Ⓒ Ⓓ Ⓔ
6 Ⓐ Ⓑ Ⓒ Ⓓ Ⓔ   13 Ⓐ Ⓑ Ⓒ Ⓓ Ⓔ   20 Ⓐ Ⓑ Ⓒ Ⓓ Ⓔ
7 Ⓐ Ⓑ Ⓒ Ⓓ Ⓔ   14 Ⓐ Ⓑ Ⓒ Ⓓ Ⓔ   21 Ⓐ Ⓑ Ⓒ Ⓓ Ⓔ

2 — MATHEMATICS

1 Ⓐ Ⓑ Ⓒ Ⓓ Ⓔ   8 Ⓐ Ⓑ Ⓒ Ⓓ Ⓔ   15 Ⓐ Ⓑ Ⓒ Ⓓ Ⓔ
2 Ⓐ Ⓑ Ⓒ Ⓓ Ⓔ   9 Ⓐ Ⓑ Ⓒ Ⓓ Ⓔ   16 Ⓐ Ⓑ Ⓒ Ⓓ Ⓔ
3 Ⓐ Ⓑ Ⓒ Ⓓ Ⓔ   10 Ⓐ Ⓑ Ⓒ Ⓓ Ⓔ   17 Ⓐ Ⓑ Ⓒ Ⓓ Ⓔ
4 Ⓐ Ⓑ Ⓒ Ⓓ Ⓔ   11 Ⓐ Ⓑ Ⓒ Ⓓ Ⓔ   18 Ⓐ Ⓑ Ⓒ Ⓓ Ⓔ
5 Ⓐ Ⓑ Ⓒ Ⓓ Ⓔ   12 Ⓐ Ⓑ Ⓒ Ⓓ Ⓔ   19 Ⓐ Ⓑ Ⓒ Ⓓ Ⓔ
6 Ⓐ Ⓑ Ⓒ Ⓓ Ⓔ   13 Ⓐ Ⓑ Ⓒ Ⓓ Ⓔ   20 Ⓐ Ⓑ Ⓒ Ⓓ Ⓔ
7 Ⓐ Ⓑ Ⓒ Ⓓ Ⓔ   14 Ⓐ Ⓑ Ⓒ Ⓓ Ⓔ

3 — READING

25 Ⓐ Ⓑ Ⓒ Ⓓ Ⓔ   33 Ⓐ Ⓑ Ⓒ Ⓓ Ⓔ   41 Ⓐ Ⓑ Ⓒ Ⓓ Ⓔ
26 Ⓐ Ⓑ Ⓒ Ⓓ Ⓔ   34 Ⓐ Ⓑ Ⓒ Ⓓ Ⓔ   42 Ⓐ Ⓑ Ⓒ Ⓓ Ⓔ
27 Ⓐ Ⓑ Ⓒ Ⓓ Ⓔ   35 Ⓐ Ⓑ Ⓒ Ⓓ Ⓔ   43 Ⓐ Ⓑ Ⓒ Ⓓ Ⓔ
28 Ⓐ Ⓑ Ⓒ Ⓓ Ⓔ   36 Ⓐ Ⓑ Ⓒ Ⓓ Ⓔ   44 Ⓐ Ⓑ Ⓒ Ⓓ Ⓔ
29 Ⓐ Ⓑ Ⓒ Ⓓ Ⓔ   37 Ⓐ Ⓑ Ⓒ Ⓓ Ⓔ   45 Ⓐ Ⓑ Ⓒ Ⓓ Ⓔ
30 Ⓐ Ⓑ Ⓒ Ⓓ Ⓔ   38 Ⓐ Ⓑ Ⓒ Ⓓ Ⓔ   46 Ⓐ Ⓑ Ⓒ Ⓓ Ⓔ
31 Ⓐ Ⓑ Ⓒ Ⓓ Ⓔ   39 Ⓐ Ⓑ Ⓒ Ⓓ Ⓔ   47 Ⓐ Ⓑ Ⓒ Ⓓ Ⓔ
32 Ⓐ Ⓑ Ⓒ Ⓓ Ⓔ   40 Ⓐ Ⓑ Ⓒ Ⓓ Ⓔ   48 Ⓐ Ⓑ Ⓒ Ⓓ Ⓔ

The Princeton Review
PSAT

4
MATHEMATICS

21 Ⓐ Ⓑ Ⓒ Ⓓ Ⓔ
22 Ⓐ Ⓑ Ⓒ Ⓓ Ⓔ
23 Ⓐ Ⓑ Ⓒ Ⓓ Ⓔ
24 Ⓐ Ⓑ Ⓒ Ⓓ Ⓔ

25 Ⓐ Ⓑ Ⓒ Ⓓ Ⓔ
26 Ⓐ Ⓑ Ⓒ Ⓓ Ⓔ
27 Ⓐ Ⓑ Ⓒ Ⓓ Ⓔ
28 Ⓐ Ⓑ Ⓒ Ⓓ Ⓔ

ONLY ANSWERS ENTERED IN THE OVALS IN EACH GRID AREA WILL BE SCORED. YOU WILL NOT RECEIVE CREDIT FOR ANYTHING WRITTEN IN THE BOXES ABOVE THE OVALS.

29 · · · ·
30 · · · ·
31 · · · ·
32 · · · ·
33 · · · ·

34 · · · ·
35 · · · ·
36 · · · ·
37 · · · ·
38 · · · ·

5
WRITING SKILLS

1 Ⓐ Ⓑ Ⓒ Ⓓ Ⓔ
2 Ⓐ Ⓑ Ⓒ Ⓓ Ⓔ
3 Ⓐ Ⓑ Ⓒ Ⓓ Ⓔ
4 Ⓐ Ⓑ Ⓒ Ⓓ Ⓔ
5 Ⓐ Ⓑ Ⓒ Ⓓ Ⓔ
6 Ⓐ Ⓑ Ⓒ Ⓓ Ⓔ
7 Ⓐ Ⓑ Ⓒ Ⓓ Ⓔ
8 Ⓐ Ⓑ Ⓒ Ⓓ Ⓔ
9 Ⓐ Ⓑ Ⓒ Ⓓ Ⓔ
10 Ⓐ Ⓑ Ⓒ Ⓓ Ⓔ
11 Ⓐ Ⓑ Ⓒ Ⓓ Ⓔ
12 Ⓐ Ⓑ Ⓒ Ⓓ Ⓔ
13 Ⓐ Ⓑ Ⓒ Ⓓ Ⓔ

14 Ⓐ Ⓑ Ⓒ Ⓓ Ⓔ
15 Ⓐ Ⓑ Ⓒ Ⓓ Ⓔ
16 Ⓐ Ⓑ Ⓒ Ⓓ Ⓔ
17 Ⓐ Ⓑ Ⓒ Ⓓ Ⓔ
18 Ⓐ Ⓑ Ⓒ Ⓓ Ⓔ
19 Ⓐ Ⓑ Ⓒ Ⓓ Ⓔ
20 Ⓐ Ⓑ Ⓒ Ⓓ Ⓔ
21 Ⓐ Ⓑ Ⓒ Ⓓ Ⓔ
22 Ⓐ Ⓑ Ⓒ Ⓓ Ⓔ
23 Ⓐ Ⓑ Ⓒ Ⓓ Ⓔ
24 Ⓐ Ⓑ Ⓒ Ⓓ Ⓔ
25 Ⓐ Ⓑ Ⓒ Ⓓ Ⓔ
26 Ⓐ Ⓑ Ⓒ Ⓓ Ⓔ

27 Ⓐ Ⓑ Ⓒ Ⓓ Ⓔ
28 Ⓐ Ⓑ Ⓒ Ⓓ Ⓔ
29 Ⓐ Ⓑ Ⓒ Ⓓ Ⓔ
30 Ⓐ Ⓑ Ⓒ Ⓓ Ⓔ
31 Ⓐ Ⓑ Ⓒ Ⓓ Ⓔ
32 Ⓐ Ⓑ Ⓒ Ⓓ Ⓔ
33 Ⓐ Ⓑ Ⓒ Ⓓ Ⓔ
34 Ⓐ Ⓑ Ⓒ Ⓓ Ⓔ
35 Ⓐ Ⓑ Ⓒ Ⓓ Ⓔ
36 Ⓐ Ⓑ Ⓒ Ⓓ Ⓔ
37 Ⓐ Ⓑ Ⓒ Ⓓ Ⓔ
38 Ⓐ Ⓑ Ⓒ Ⓓ Ⓔ
39 Ⓐ Ⓑ Ⓒ Ⓓ Ⓔ

Acknowledgments

Thanks to Jonathan Chiu and Leah Murnane for their thorough review. Thanks also to Mary Beth Garrick, Kristen O'Toole, Deborah Silvestrini, and Jim Melloan, and the staff and students of The Princeton Review.

Special thanks to Adam Robinson, who conceived of and perfected the Joe Bloggs approach to standardized tests, and many other techniques in this book.

NOTES